樋口大輔

I realize it's already the second
anniversary of the series!
Thank you.
I wonder if I've also grown a little.
Shô is finally facing the second turning
point in his soccer life. The first turning
point was when he transferred schools to
Josui. Jumping into a new place is scary
and requires courage, but let's believe in
ourselves and take that first step!

– Daisuke Higuchi

Daisuke Higuchi's manga career began in 1992 when the
artist was honored with third prize in the 43rd Osamu
Tezuka Award. In that same year, Higuchi debuted as
creator of a romantic action story titled *Itaru*. In 1998,
Weekly Shonen Jump began serializing *Whistle!*
Higuchi's realistic soccer manga became an instant hit
with readers and eventually inspired an anime series,
debuting on Japanese TV in May of 2002.

WHISTLE!
VOL. 13: DANCE WITH THE FEAR

The SHONEN JUMP Manga Edition

STORY AND ART BY
DAISUKE HIGUCHI

English Adaptation/Drew Williams
Translation/Naomi Kokubo
Touch-up Art & Lettering/Jim Keefe
Cover, Graphics & Layout/Sean Lee
Editor/Jonathan Tarbox

Managing Editor/Frances E. Wall
Editorial Director/Elizabeth Kawasaki
VP & Editor in Chief/Yumi Hoashi
Sr. Director of Acquisitions/Rika Inouye
Sr. VP of Marketing/Liza Coppola
Exec. VP of Sales & Marketing/John Easum
Publisher/Hyoe Narita

Printed in the U.S.A.

Published by VIZ Media, LLC
P.O. Box 77010
San Francisco, CA 94107

SHONEN JUMP Manga Edition
10 9 8 7 6 5 4 3 2 1
First printing, September 2006

Story and Art by
Daisuke Higuchi

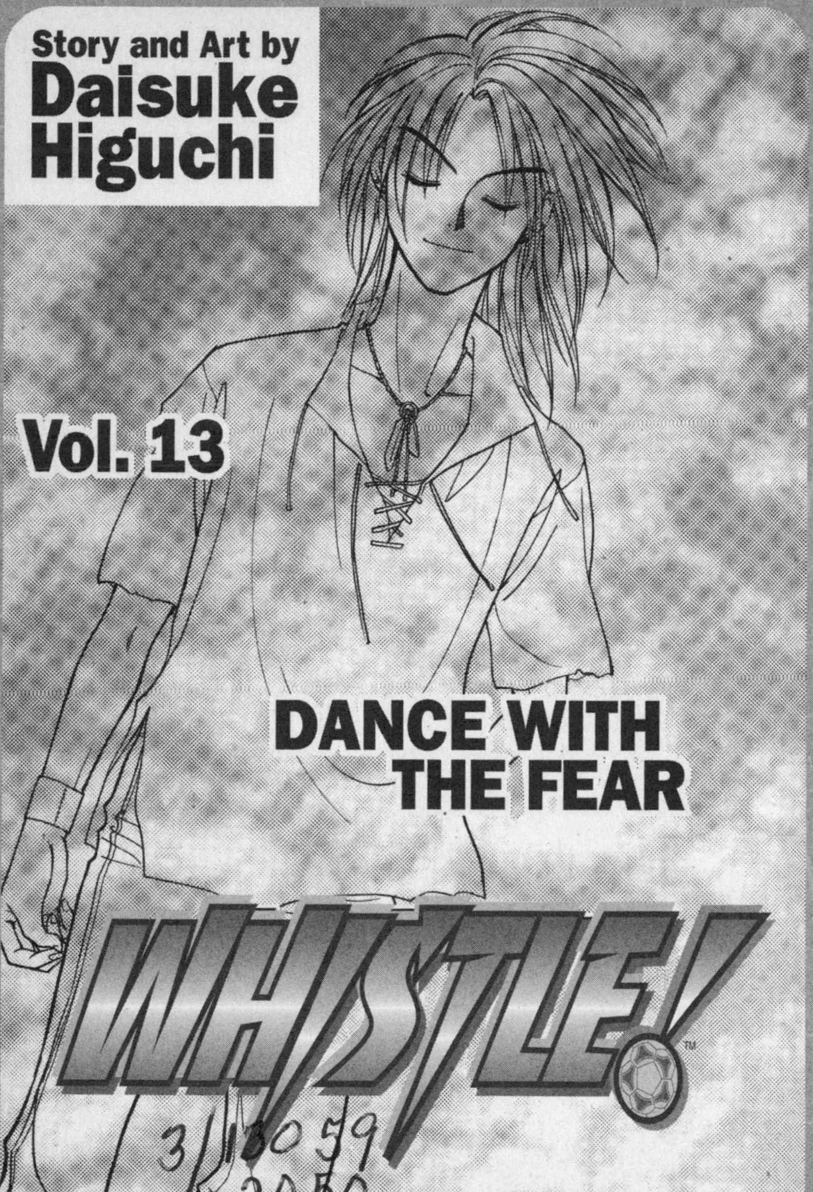

Vol. 13

DANCE WITH THE FEAR

WHISTLE!™

SHŌ KAZAMATSURI

- JOSUI JUNIOR
  SOCCER TEAM
  FORWARD

jGRAPHIC
NOVEL

AKIRA SAIONJI

TSUBASA SHIINA

TATSUYA MIZUNO

- JOSUI JUNIOR HIGH
  SOCCER TEAM
  MIDFIELDER

TAKASHI NARUMI

MEISEI JUNIOR HIGH

FORWARD

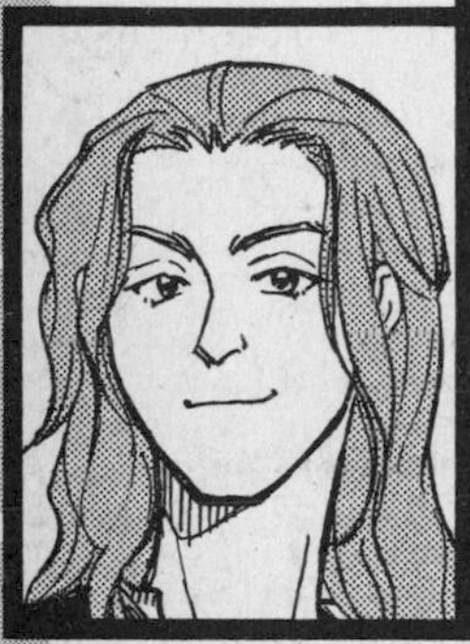

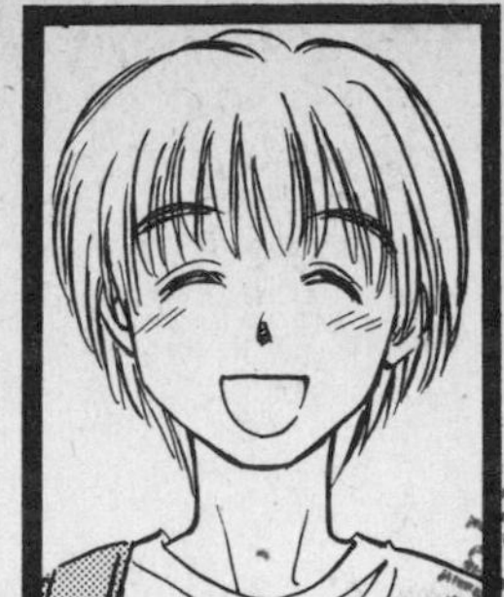

TAKI SUGIHARA

TAKANAWA JUNIOR HIGH

MIDFIELDER

DAICHI FUWA

JOSUI JUNIOR HIGH SOCCER TEAM

GOAL KEEPER

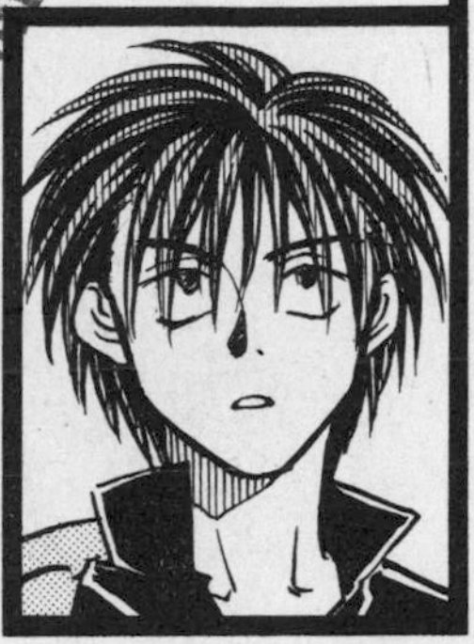

STORY

TO REALIZE HIS DREAM, SHŌ KAZAMATSURI, A BENCH WARMER AT SOCCER POWERHOUSE MUSASHINOMORI, TRANSFERRED TO JOSUI JUNIOR HIGH SO HE COULD PLAY THE GAME HE LOVES.

JOSUI'S SOCCER TEAM WAS A JOKE UNTIL SOUJŪ MATSUSHITA, A FORMER JAPAN LEAGUE PLAYER, TOOK ON THE COACHING DUTIES. UNDER MATSUSHITA'S GUIDANCE, THE TEAM HAS BECOME A FORCE TO BE RECKONED WITH. THEY BLASTED THROUGH THE DISTRICT PRIMARY TOURNAMENT, DEFEATING RAKUYŌ JUNIOR HIGH BEFORE HOLDING OFF HIBA JUNIOR HIGH TO WIN THE TOURNAMENT FINALS.

MEANWHILE, PLANS TO FORM A TOKYO SELECT TEAM--AN ELITE SQUAD CREATED TO FACE INTERNATIONAL COMPETITION--WERE WELL UNDER WAY. FROM JOSUI, SHŌ, TATSUYA MIZUNO AND DAICHI FUWA WERE INVITED TO JOIN THE TEAM'S TRAINING CAMP.

HOW WILL SHŌ FARE AGAINST THE BEST JUNIOR PLAYERS IN TOKYO?

WHISTLE!

**Vol. 13
DANCE WITH
THE FEAR**

STAGE.108 Mini Game

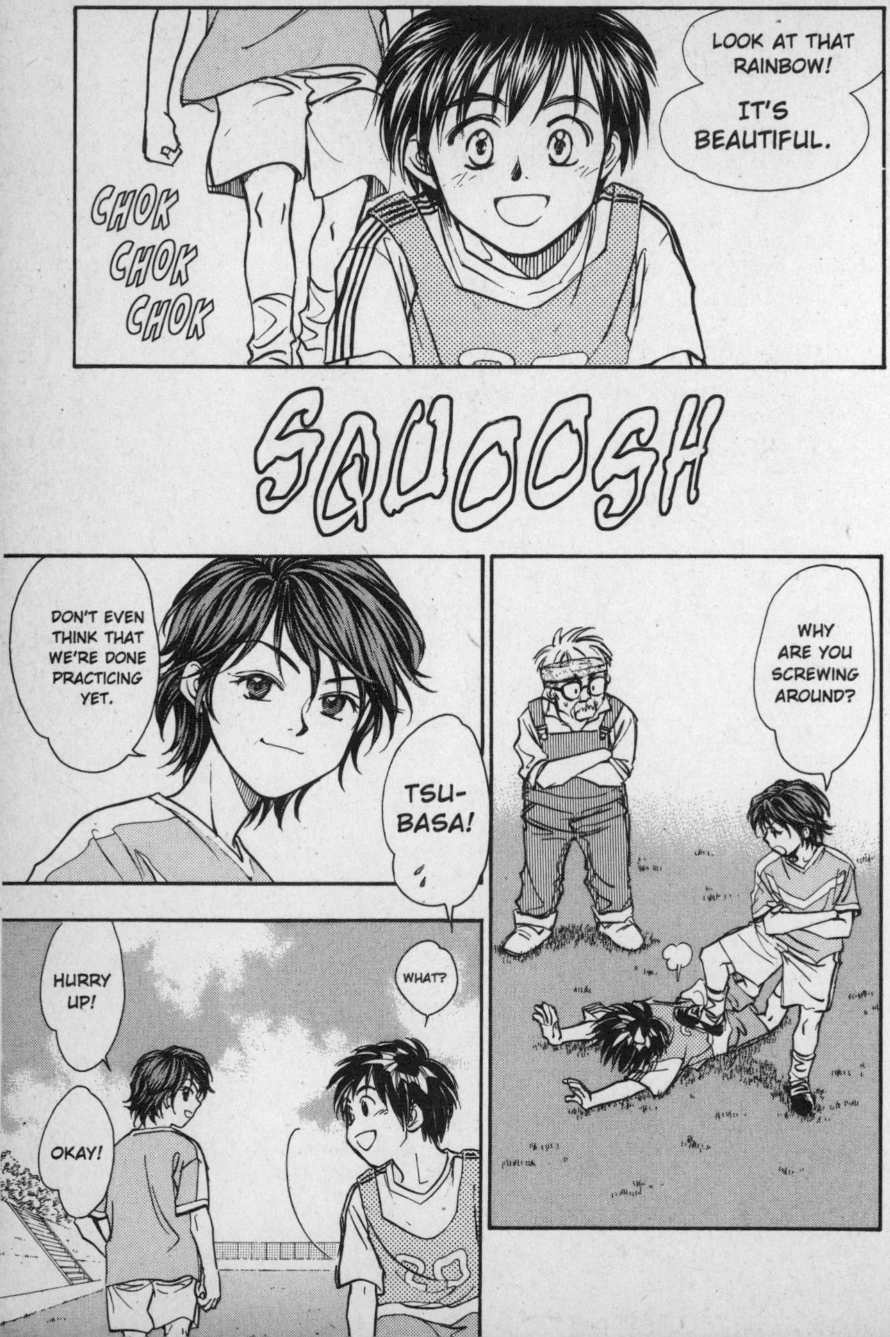
LOOK AT THAT RAINBOW!
IT'S BEAUTIFUL.
CHOK CHOK CHOK
SQUOOSH
WHY ARE YOU SCREWING AROUND?
DON'T EVEN THINK THAT WE'RE DONE PRACTICING YET.
TSU-BASA!
WHAT?
HURRY UP!
OKAY!

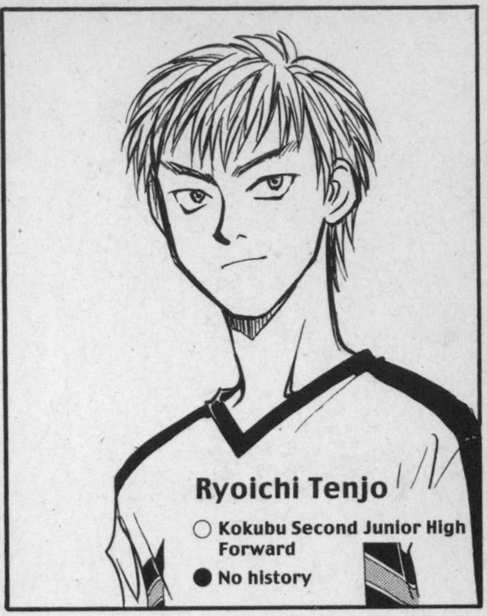
Ryoichi Tenjo
○ Kokubu Second Junior High
Forward
● No history

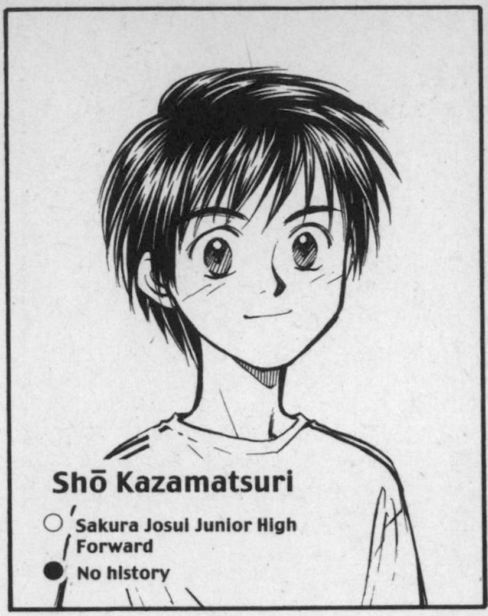
Shō Kazamatsuri
○ Sakura Josui Junior High
Forward
● No history

STAGE.108 Mini Game

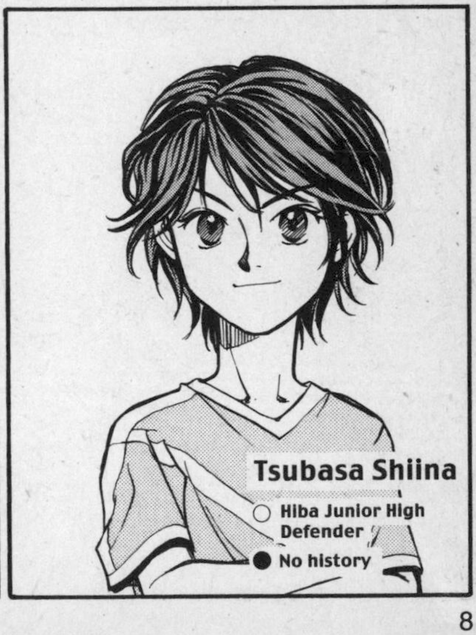
Tsubasa Shiina
○ Hiba Junior High
Defender
● No history

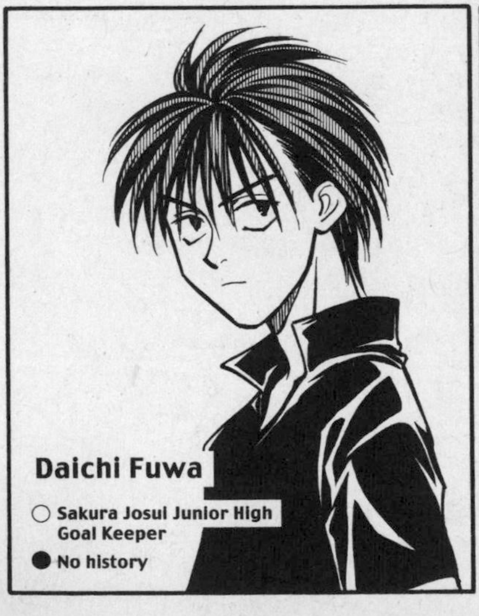
Daichi Fuwa
○ Sakura Josui Junior High
Goal Keeper
● No history

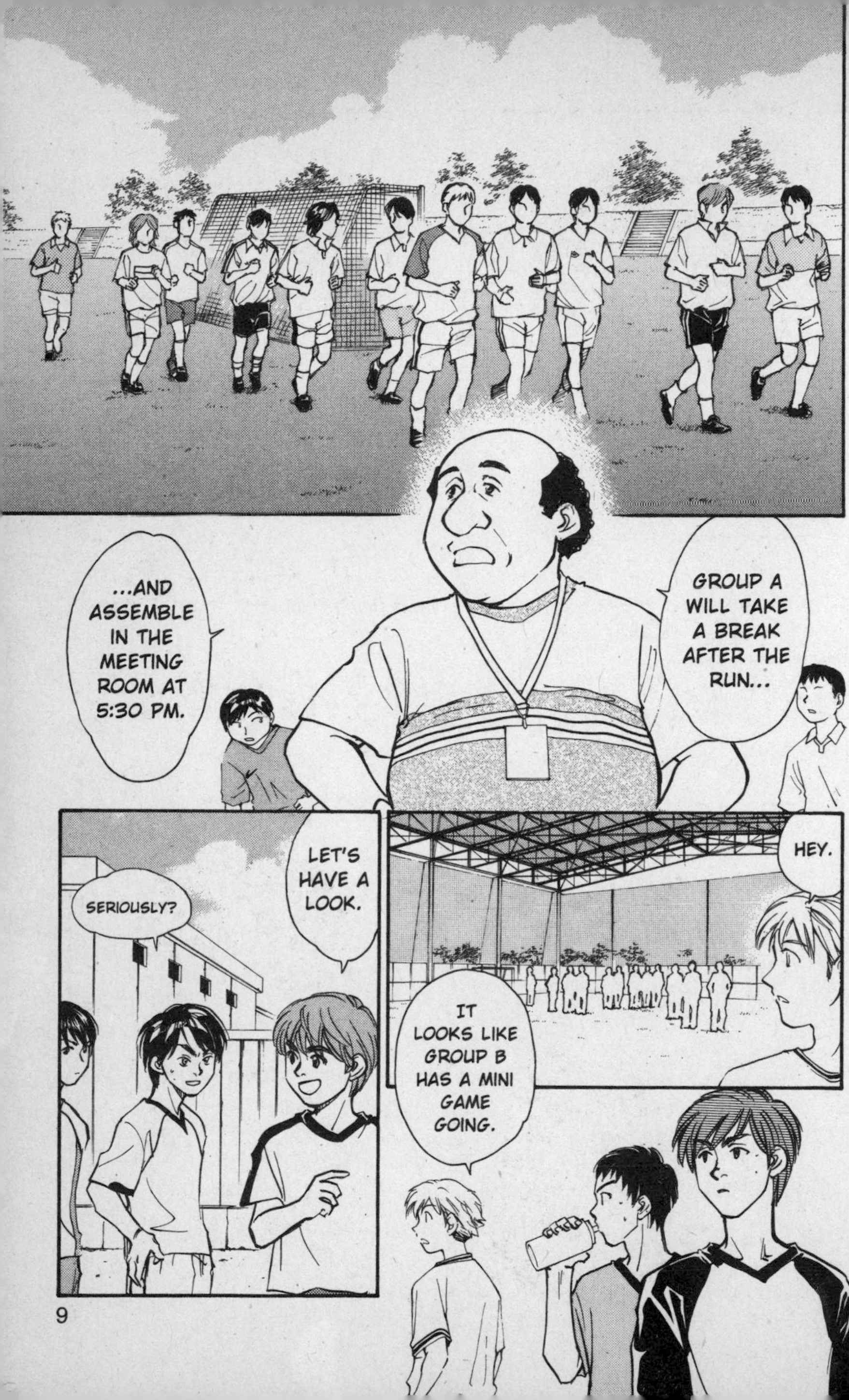
GROUP A WILL TAKE A BREAK AFTER THE RUN...
...AND ASSEMBLE IN THE MEETING ROOM AT 5:30 PM.
HEY.
IT LOOKS LIKE GROUP B HAS A MINI GAME GOING.
LET'S HAVE A LOOK.
SERIOUSLY?

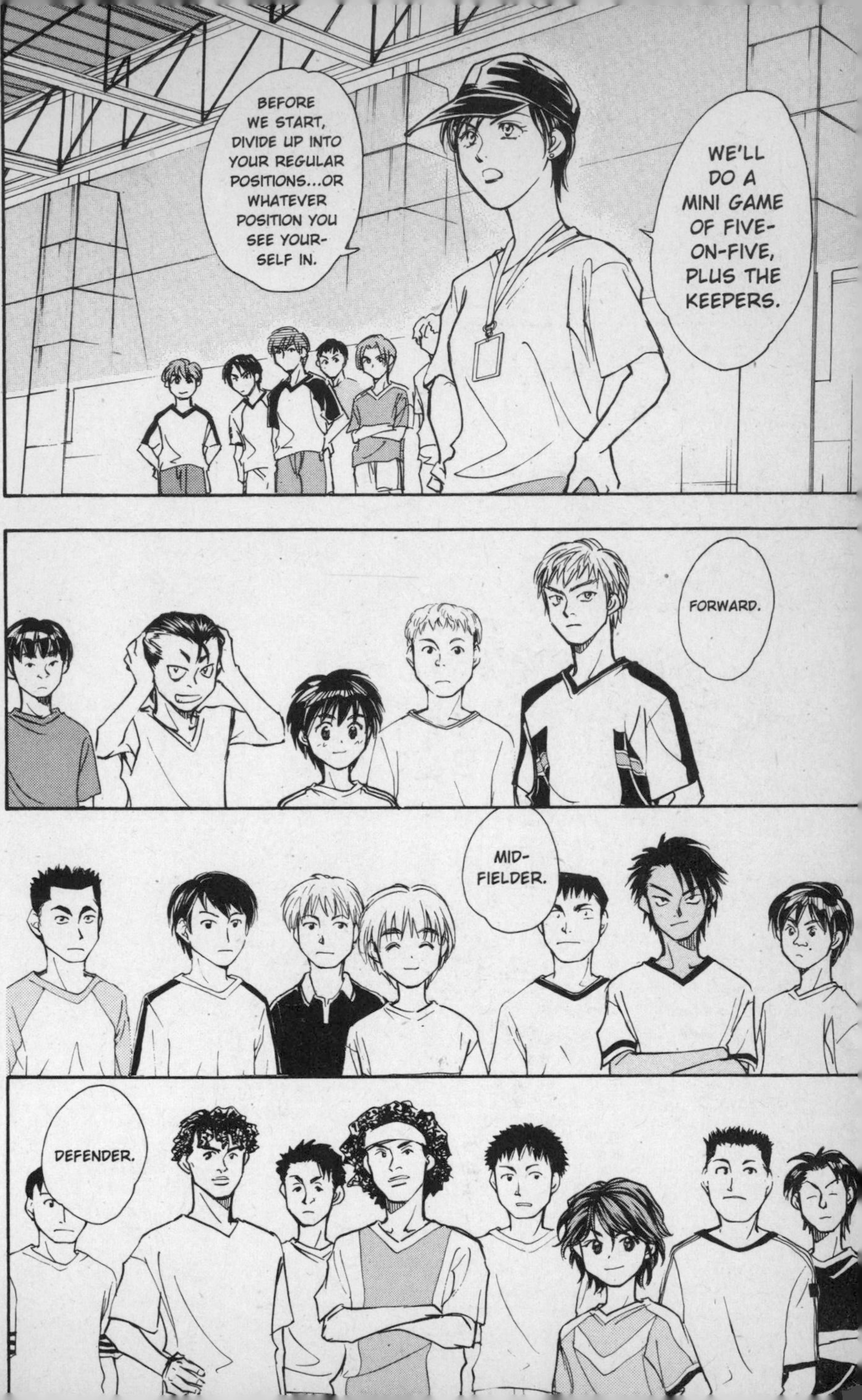
WE'LL DO A MINI GAME OF FIVE-ON-FIVE, PLUS THE KEEPERS.
BEFORE WE START, DIVIDE UP INTO YOUR REGULAR POSITIONS...OR WHATEVER POSITION YOU SEE YOUR-SELF IN.
FORWARD.
MID-FIELDER.
DEFENDER.

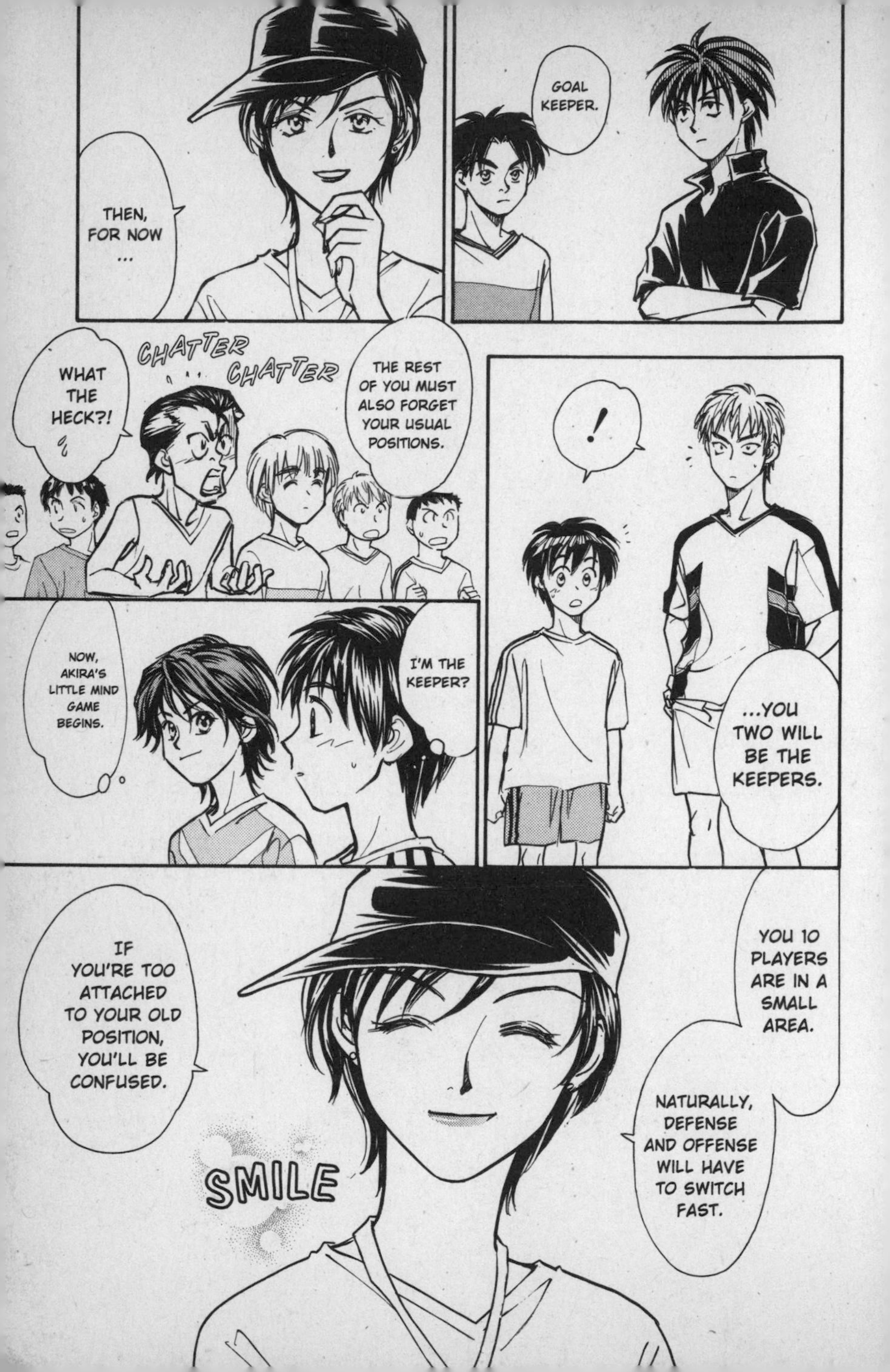
GOAL KEEPER.
THEN, FOR NOW ...
!
...YOU TWO WILL BE THE KEEPERS.
THE REST OF YOU MUST ALSO FORGET YOUR USUAL POSITIONS.
CHATTER CHATTER
WHAT THE HECK?!
I'M THE KEEPER?
NOW, AKIRA'S LITTLE MIND GAME BEGINS.
YOU 10 PLAYERS ARE IN A SMALL AREA.
NATURALLY, DEFENSE AND OFFENSE WILL HAVE TO SWITCH FAST.
IF YOU'RE TOO ATTACHED TO YOUR OLD POSITION, YOU'LL BE CONFUSED.
SMILE

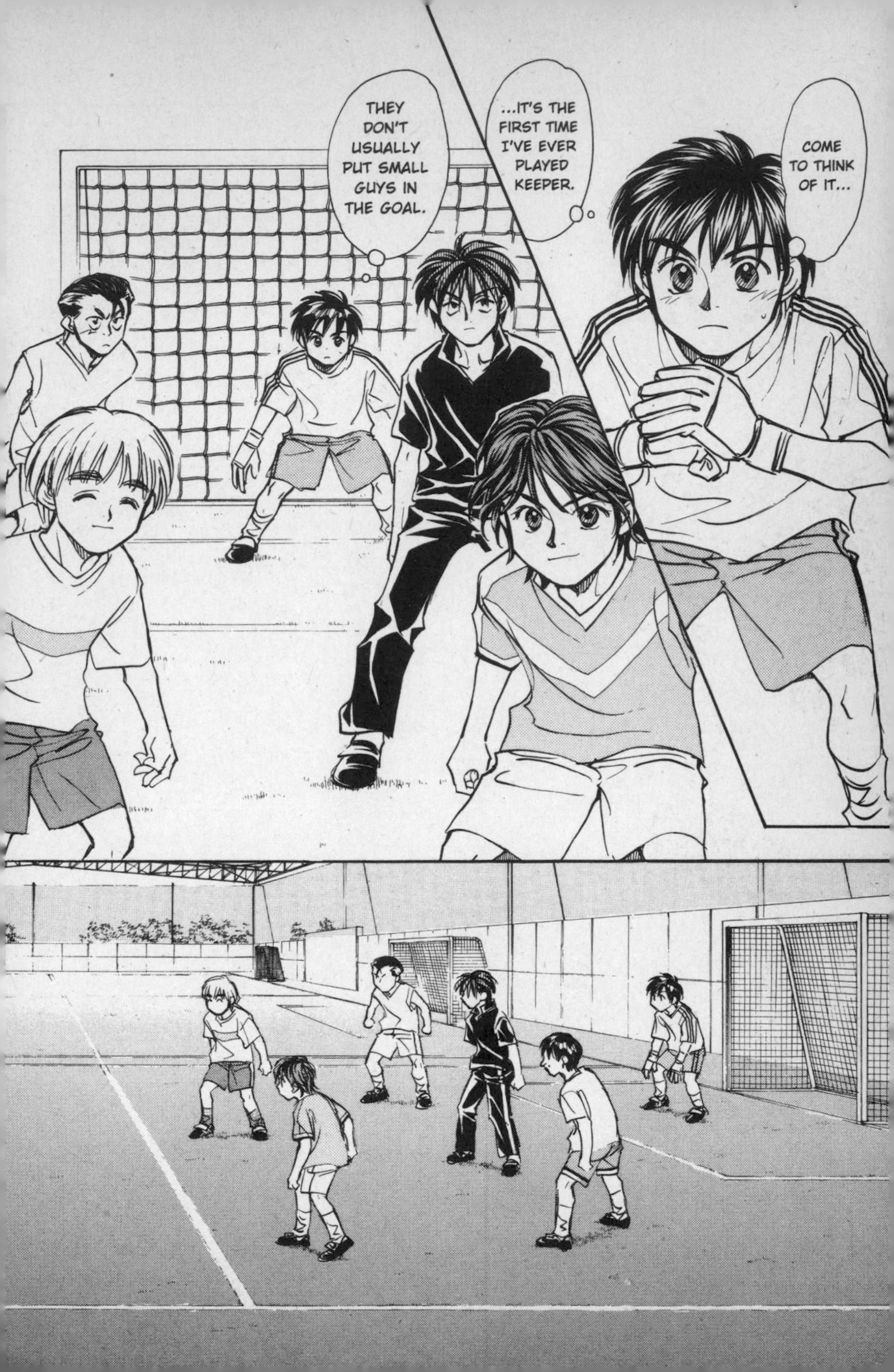
COME TO THINK OF IT...
...IT'S THE FIRST TIME I'VE EVER PLAYED KEEPER.
THEY DON'T USUALLY PUT SMALL GUYS IN THE GOAL.

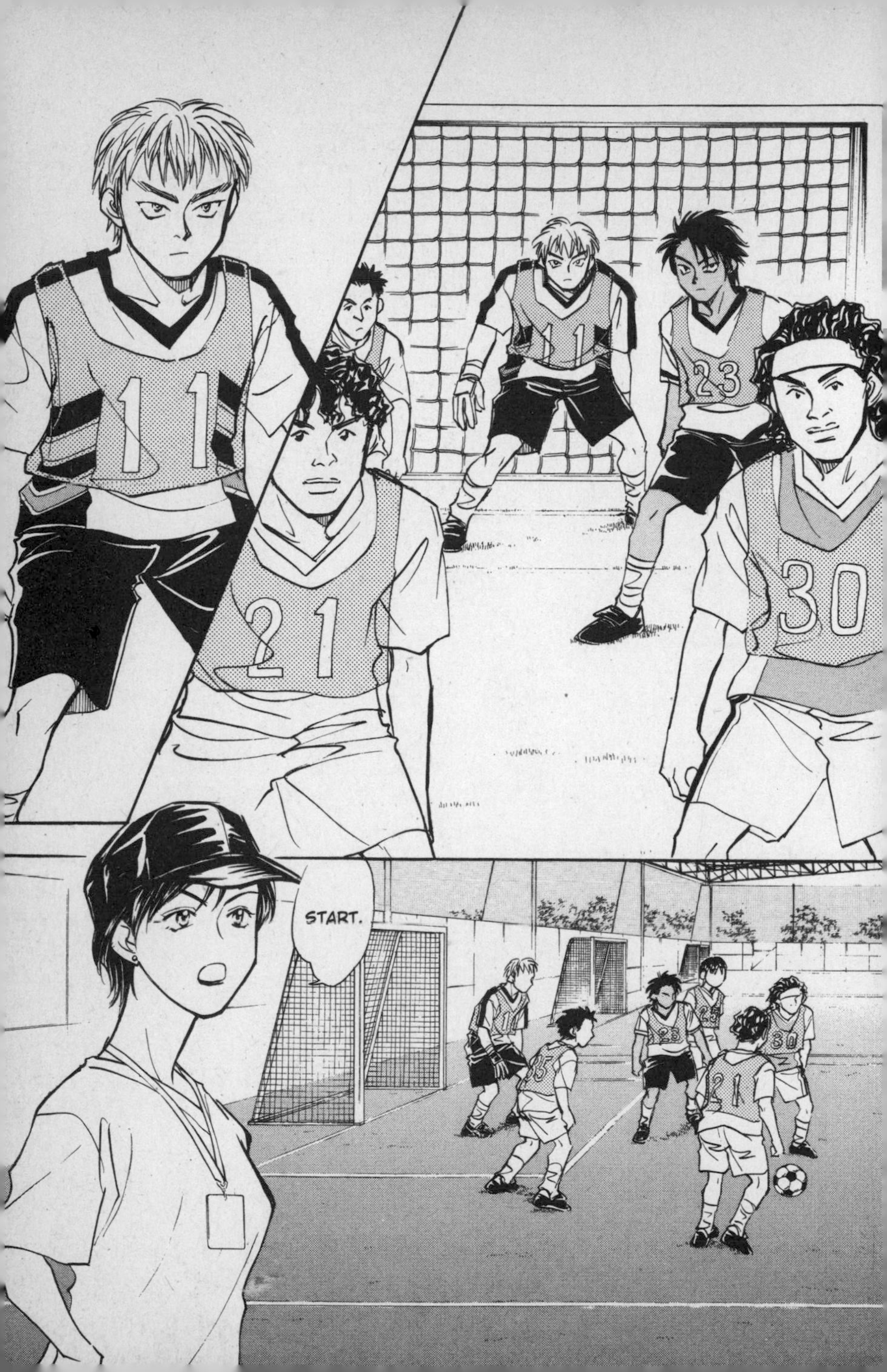
START.

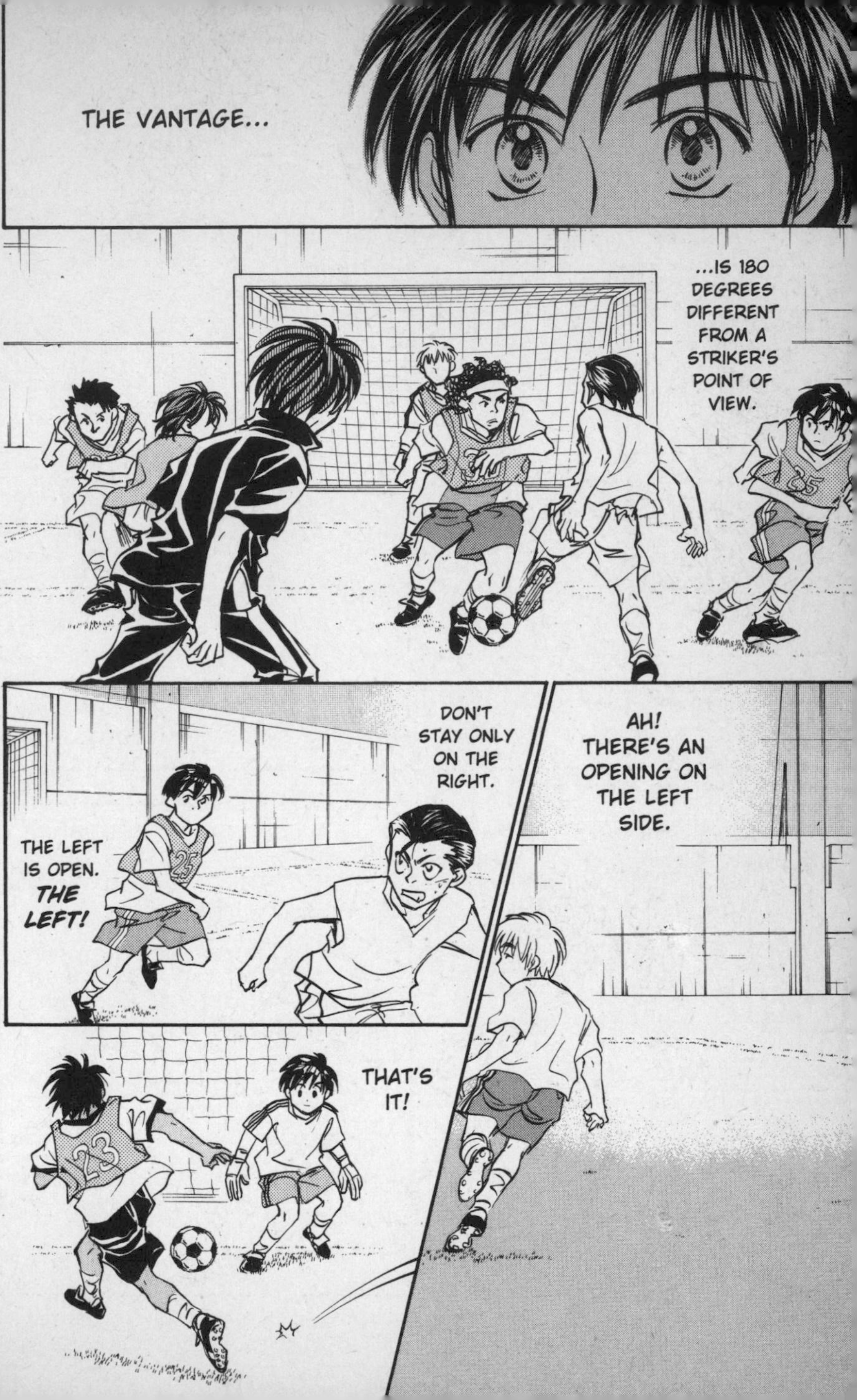
THE VANTAGE...
...IS 180 DEGREES DIFFERENT FROM A STRIKER'S POINT OF VIEW.
AH! THERE'S AN OPENING ON THE LEFT SIDE.
DON'T STAY ONLY ON THE RIGHT.
THE LEFT IS OPEN. *THE LEFT!*
THAT'S IT!

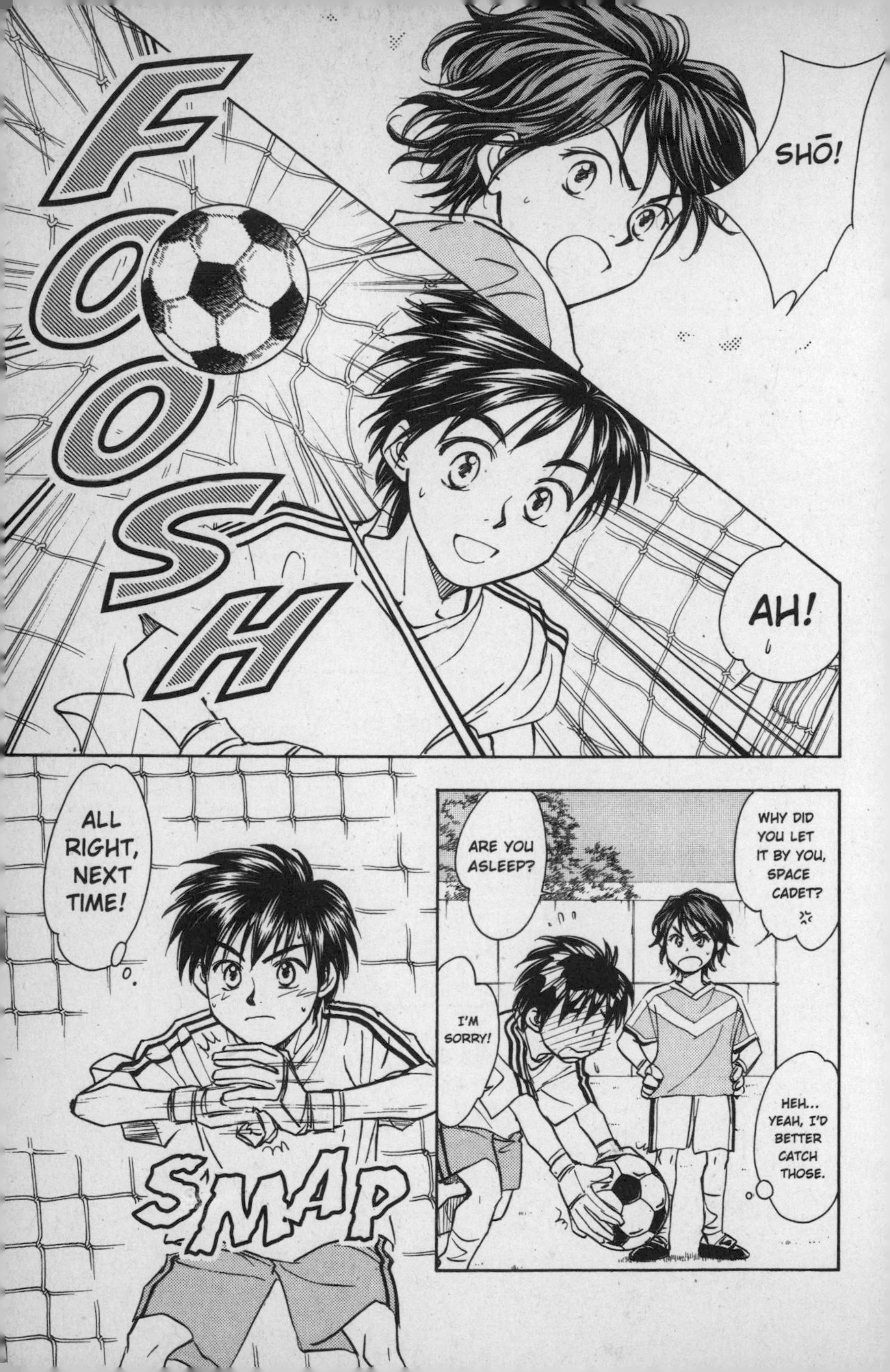
SHŌ!
FOOSH
AH!
WHY DID YOU LET IT BY YOU, SPACE CADET?
ARE YOU ASLEEP?
I'M SORRY!
HEH... YEAH, I'D BETTER CATCH THOSE.
ALL RIGHT, NEXT TIME!
SMAP

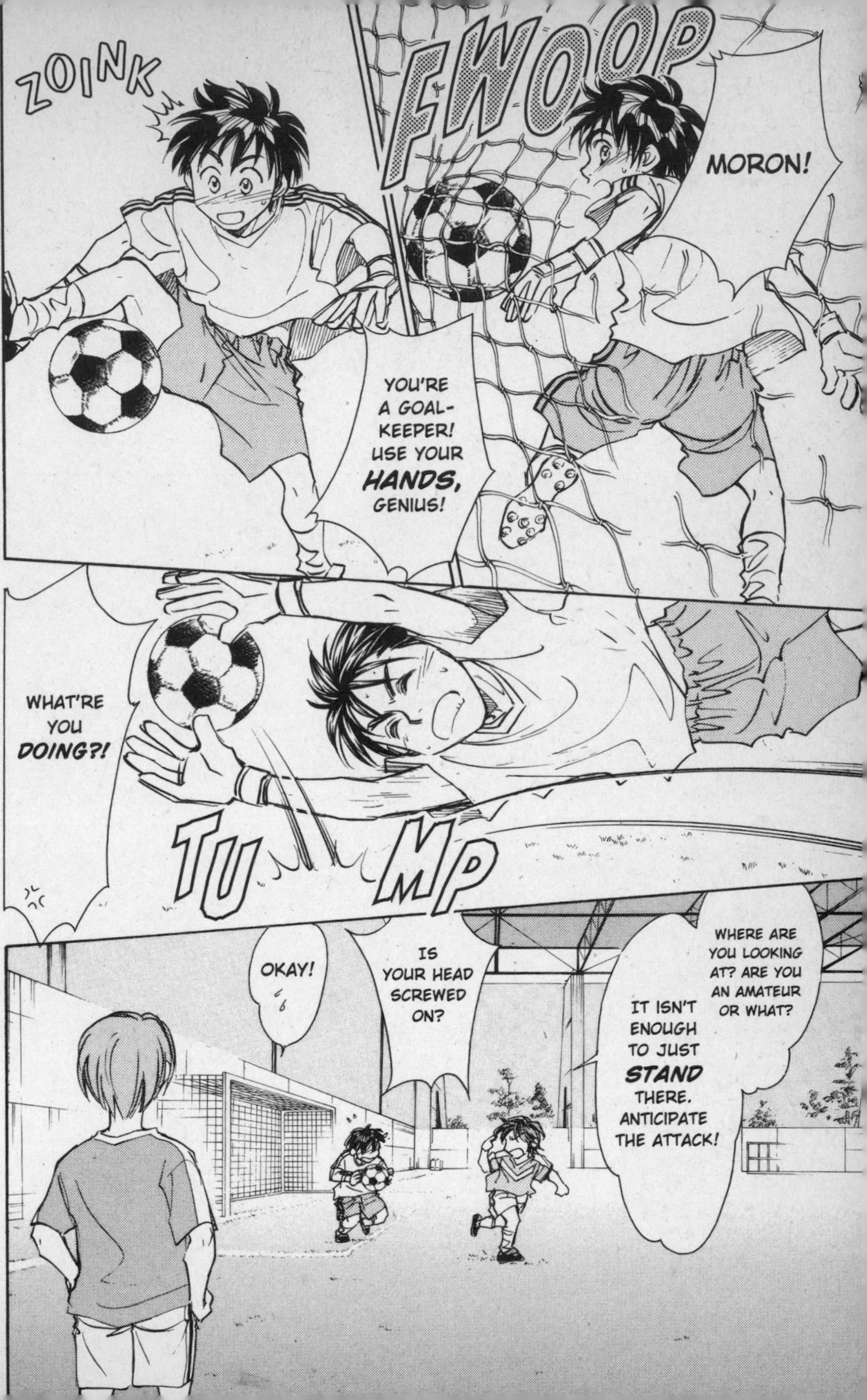
MORON!
FWOOP
ZOINK
YOU'RE A GOAL-KEEPER! USE YOUR **HANDS,** GENIUS!
WHAT'RE YOU ***DOING?!***
TUMP
WHERE ARE YOU LOOKING AT? ARE YOU AN AMATEUR OR WHAT?
IT ISN'T ENOUGH TO JUST ***STAND*** THERE. ANTICIPATE THE ATTACK!
IS YOUR HEAD SCREWED ON?
OKAY!

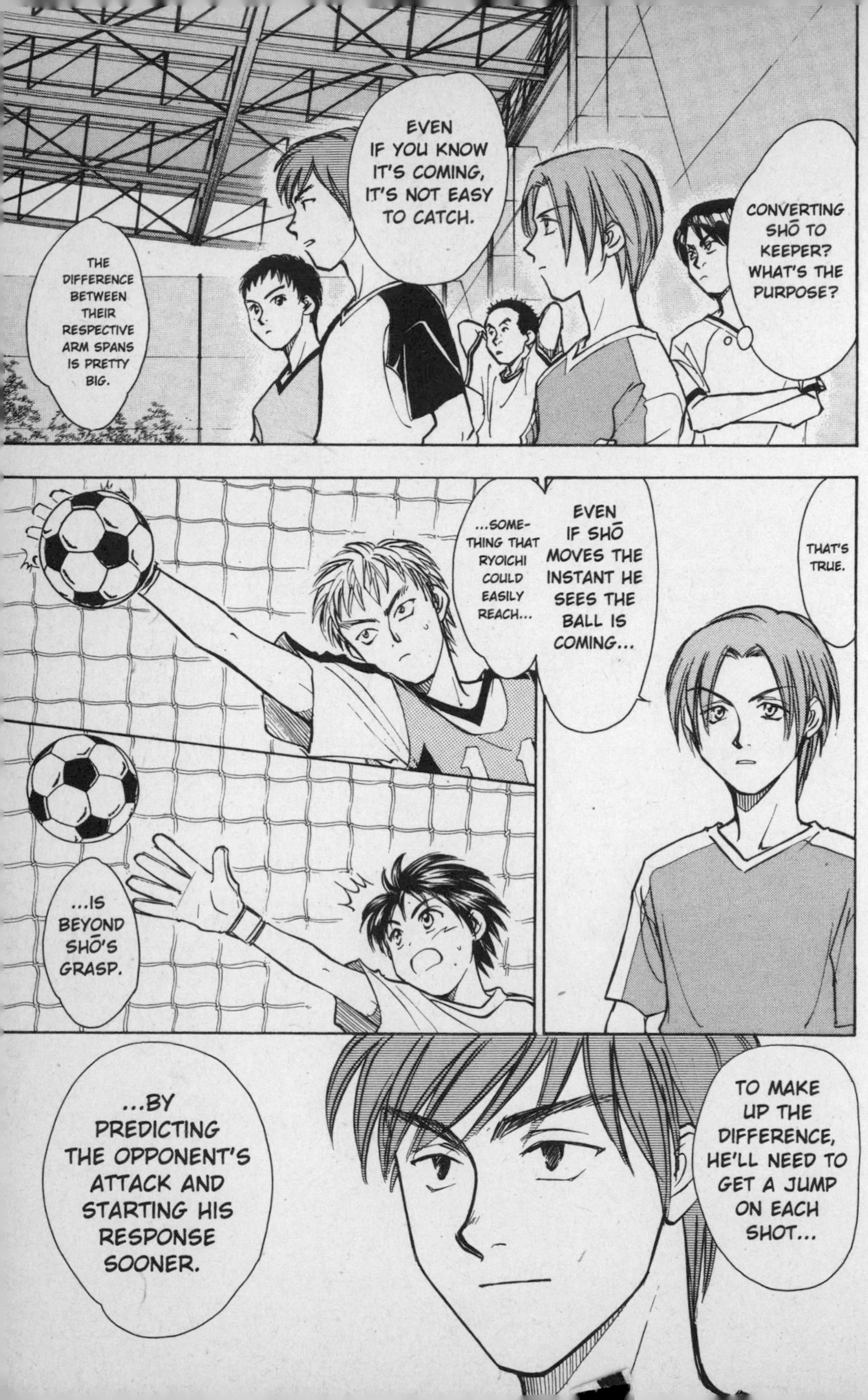
CONVERTING SHŌ TO KEEPER? WHAT'S THE PURPOSE?
EVEN IF YOU KNOW IT'S COMING, IT'S NOT EASY TO CATCH.
THE DIFFERENCE BETWEEN THEIR RESPECTIVE ARM SPANS IS PRETTY BIG.
THAT'S TRUE.
EVEN IF SHŌ MOVES THE INSTANT HE SEES THE BALL IS COMING...
...SOMETHING THAT RYOICHI COULD EASILY REACH...
...IS BEYOND SHŌ'S GRASP.
TO MAKE UP THE DIFFERENCE, HE'LL NEED TO GET A JUMP ON EACH SHOT...
...BY PREDICTING THE OPPONENT'S ATTACK AND STARTING HIS RESPONSE SOONER.

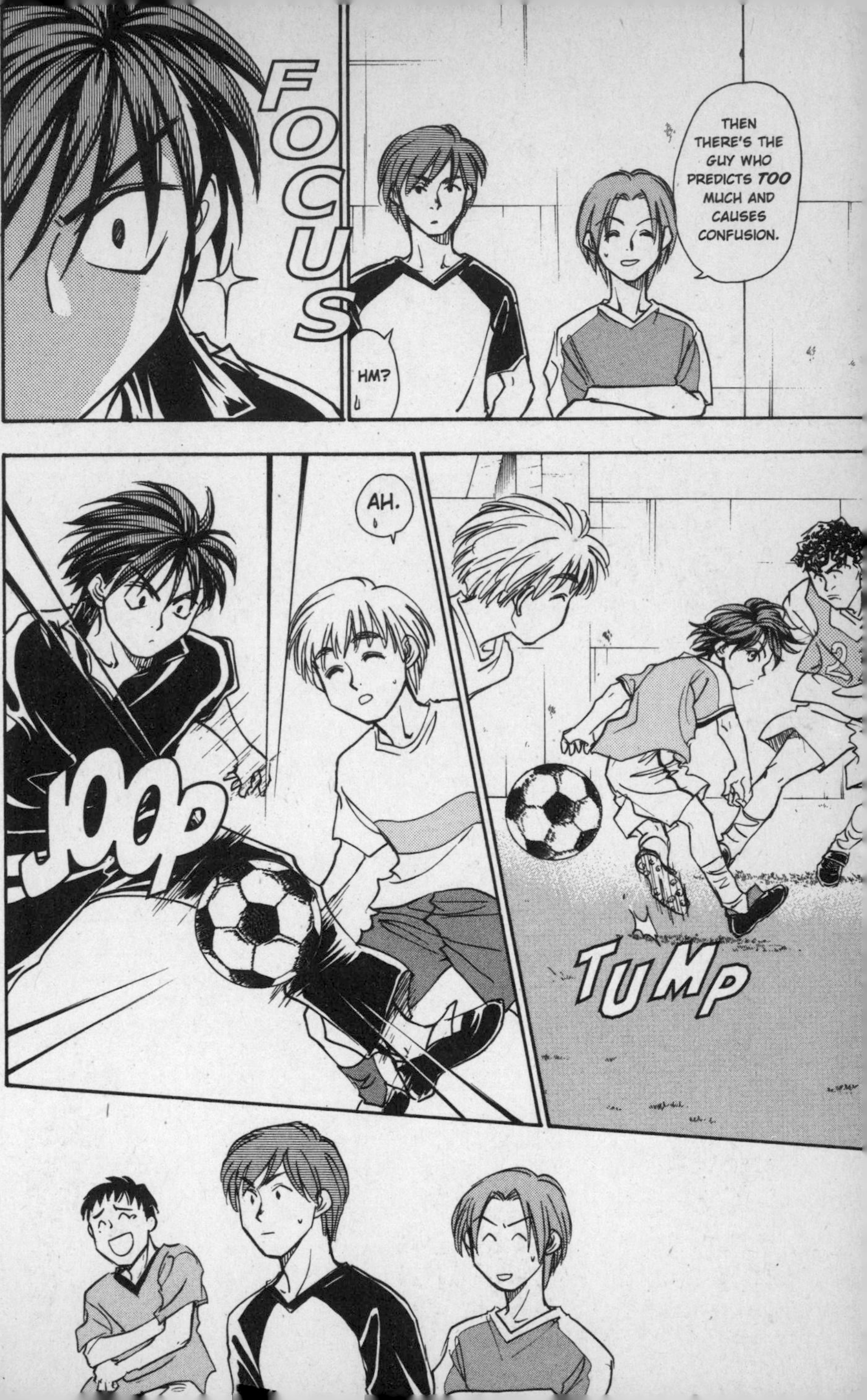
THEN THERE'S THE GUY WHO PREDICTS *TOO* MUCH AND CAUSES CONFUSION.
HM?
FOCUS
TUMP
AH.
JOOP

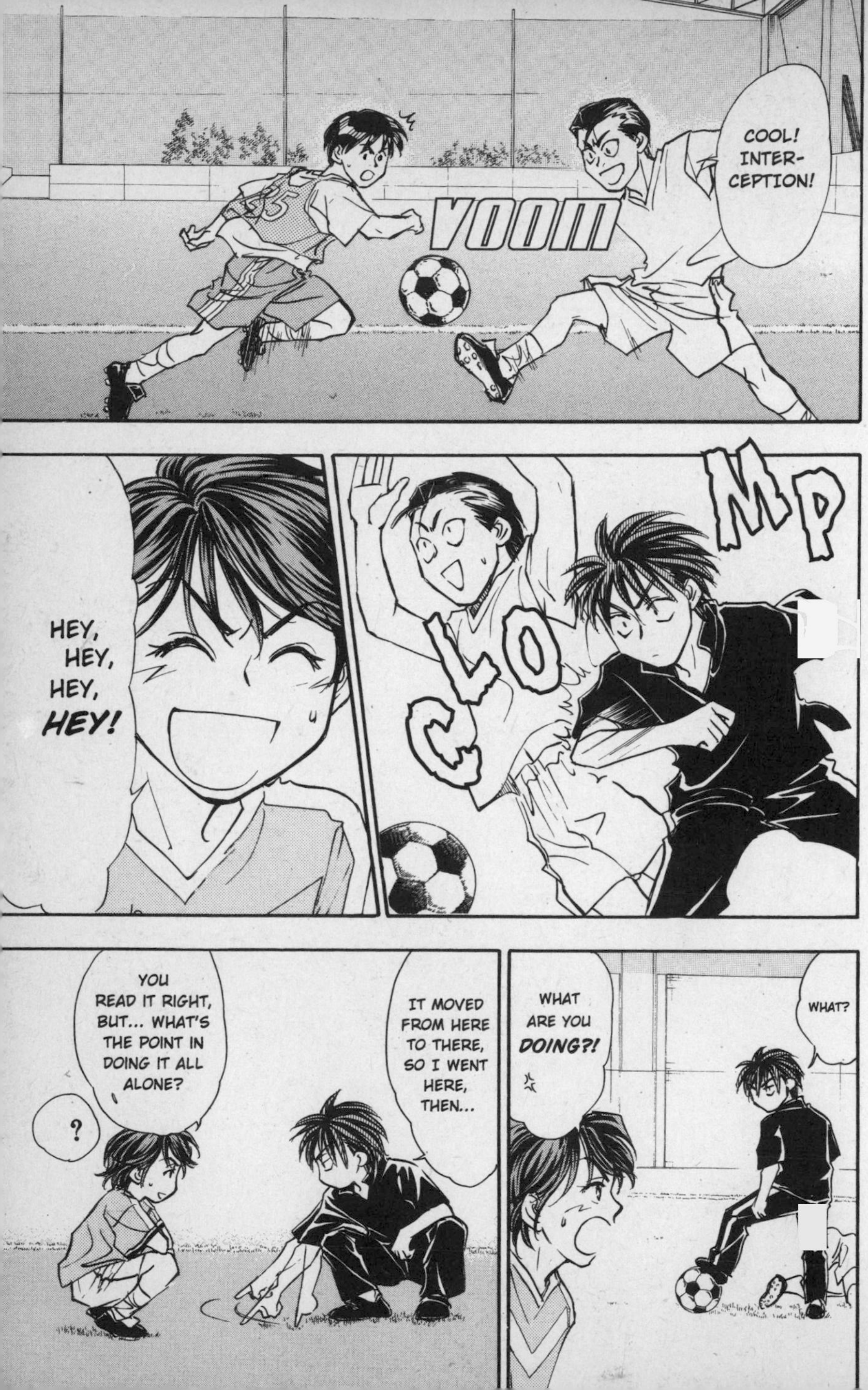
COOL! INTER-CEPTION!
VOOM
CLOMP
HEY, HEY, HEY, HEY!
WHAT?
WHAT ARE YOU DOING?!
IT MOVED FROM HERE TO THERE, SO I WENT HERE, THEN...
YOU READ IT RIGHT, BUT... WHAT'S THE POINT IN DOING IT ALL ALONE?
?

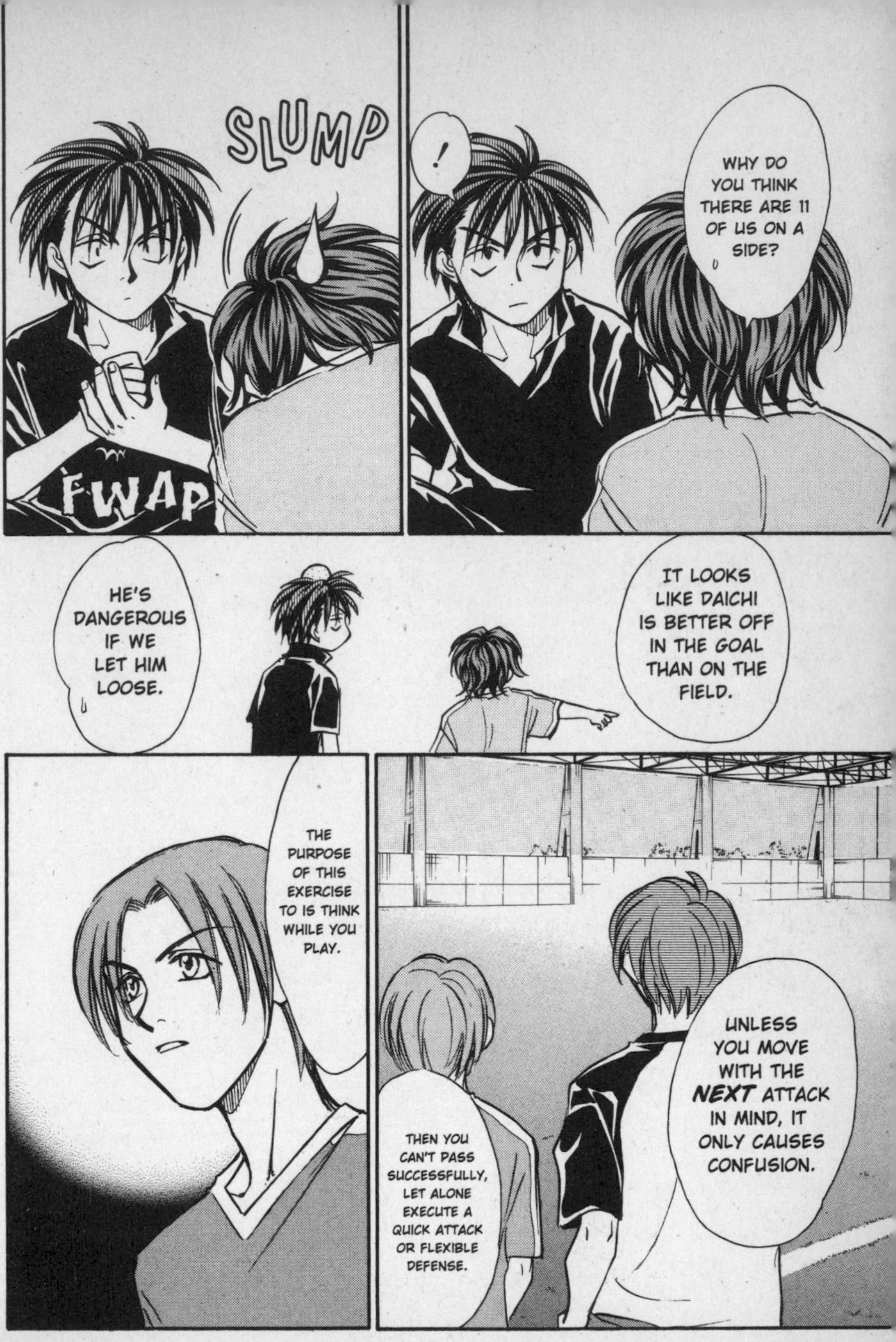
!
WHY DO YOU THINK THERE ARE 11 OF US ON A SIDE?
SLUMP
FWAP
IT LOOKS LIKE DAICHI IS BETTER OFF IN THE GOAL THAN ON THE FIELD.
HE'S DANGEROUS IF WE LET HIM LOOSE.
UNLESS YOU MOVE WITH THE NEXT ATTACK IN MIND, IT ONLY CAUSES CONFUSION.
THEN YOU CAN'T PASS SUCCESSFULLY, LET ALONE EXECUTE A QUICK ATTACK OR FLEXIBLE DEFENSE.
THE PURPOSE OF THIS EXERCISE TO IS THINK WHILE YOU PLAY.

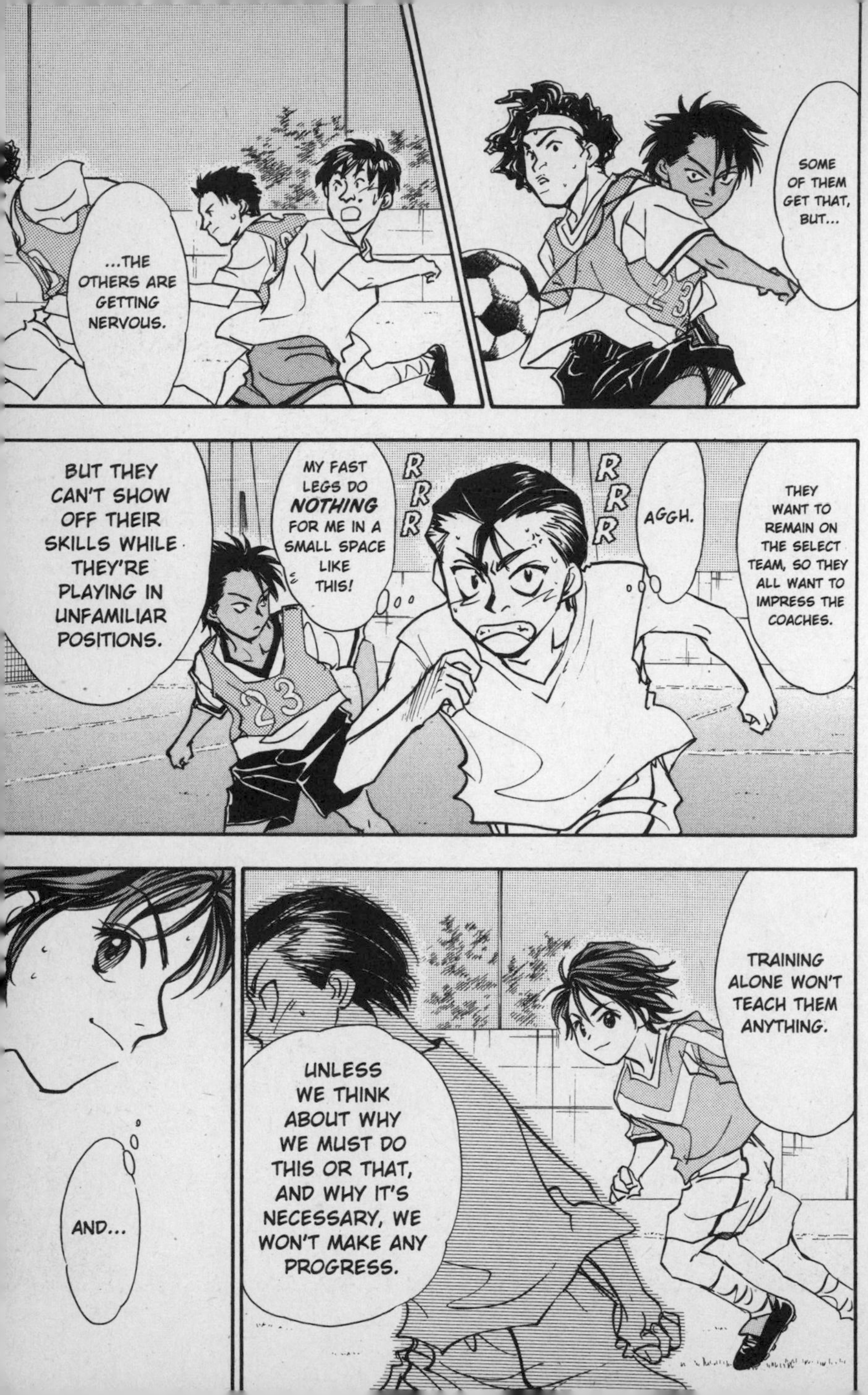
SOME OF THEM GET THAT, BUT...
...THE OTHERS ARE GETTING NERVOUS.
THEY WANT TO REMAIN ON THE SELECT TEAM, SO THEY ALL WANT TO IMPRESS THE COACHES.
AGGH.
RRR
MY FAST LEGS DO **NOTHING** FOR ME IN A SMALL SPACE LIKE THIS!
RRR
BUT THEY CAN'T SHOW OFF THEIR SKILLS WHILE THEY'RE PLAYING IN UNFAMILIAR POSITIONS.
TRAINING ALONE WON'T TEACH THEM ANYTHING.
UNLESS WE THINK ABOUT WHY WE MUST DO THIS OR THAT, AND WHY IT'S NECESSARY, WE WON'T MAKE ANY PROGRESS.
AND...

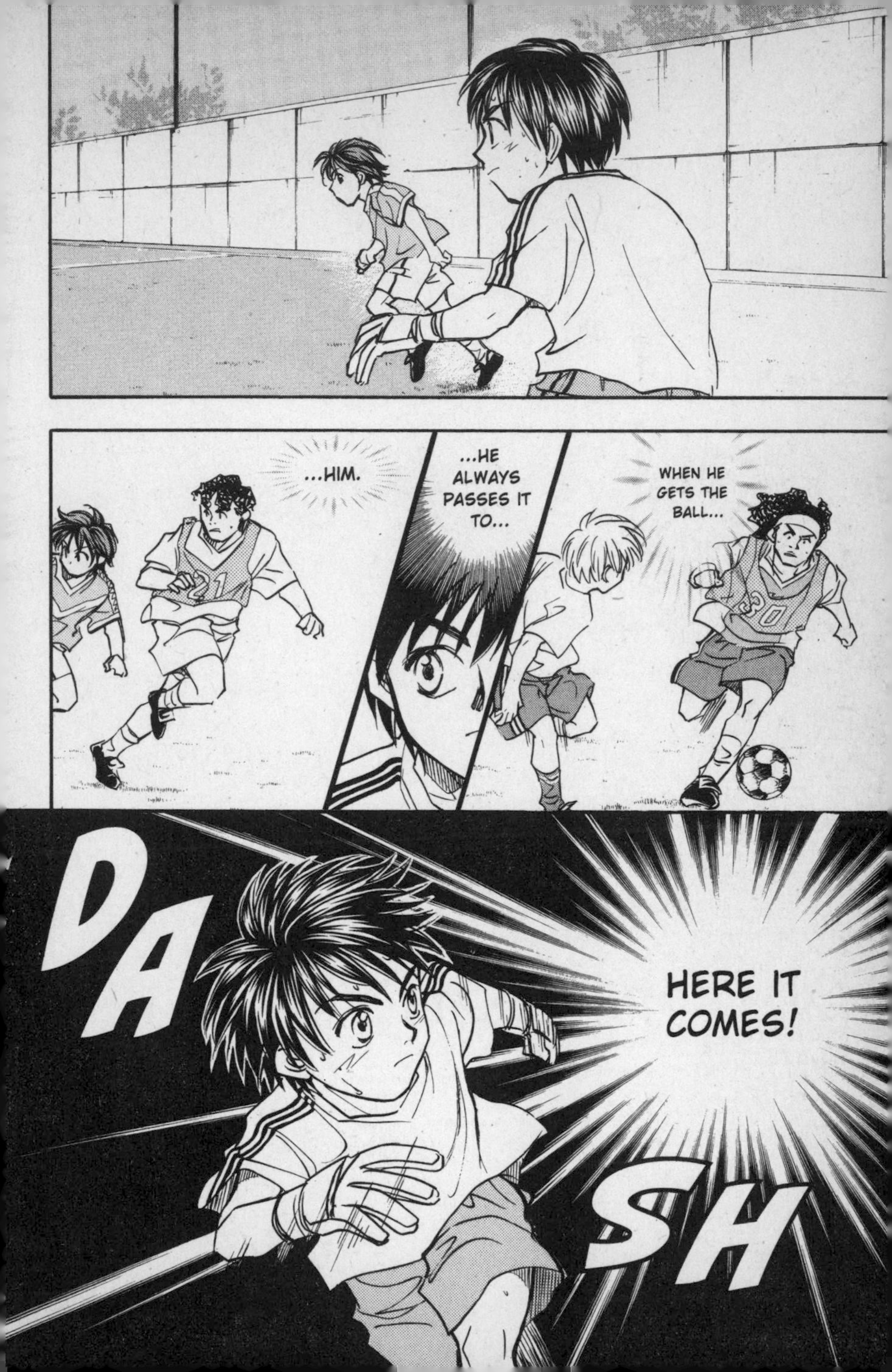
WHEN HE GETS THE BALL...
...HE ALWAYS PASSES IT TO...
...HIM.
HERE IT COMES!
DASH

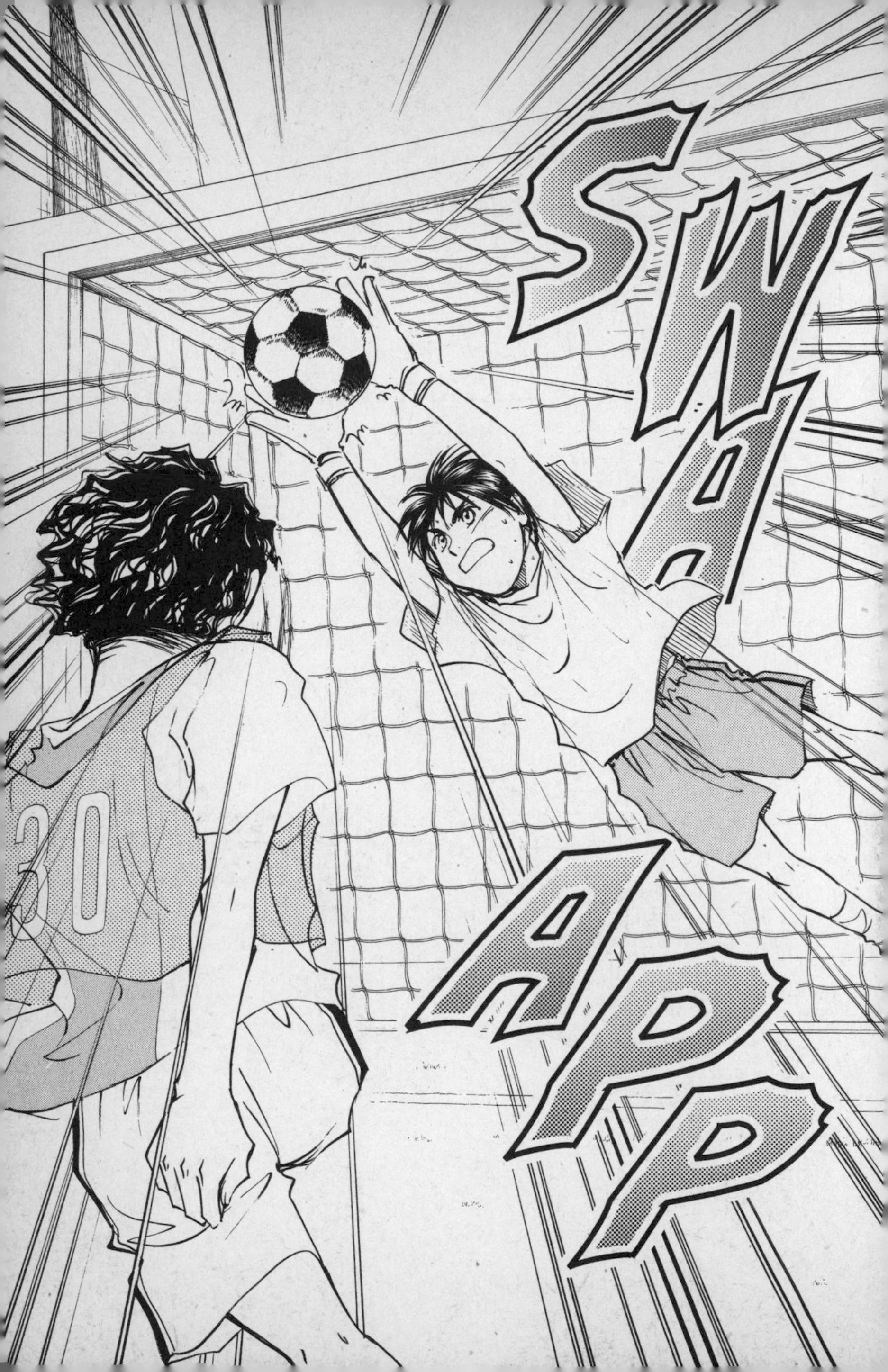
SWAAPP

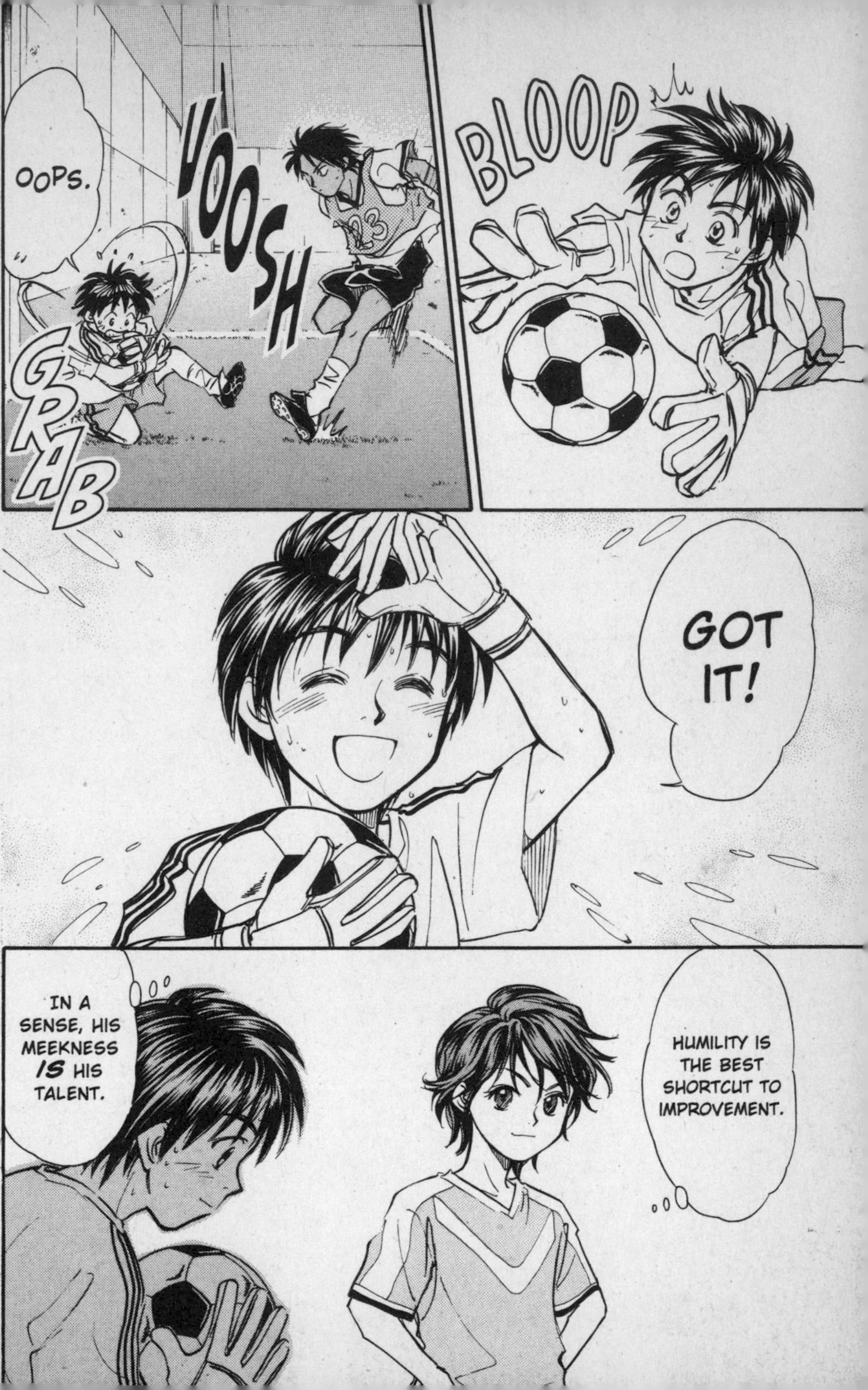
BLOOP
VOOSH
OOPS.
GRAB
GOT IT!
HUMILITY IS THE BEST SHORTCUT TO IMPROVEMENT.
IN A SENSE, HIS MEEKNESS *IS* HIS TALENT.

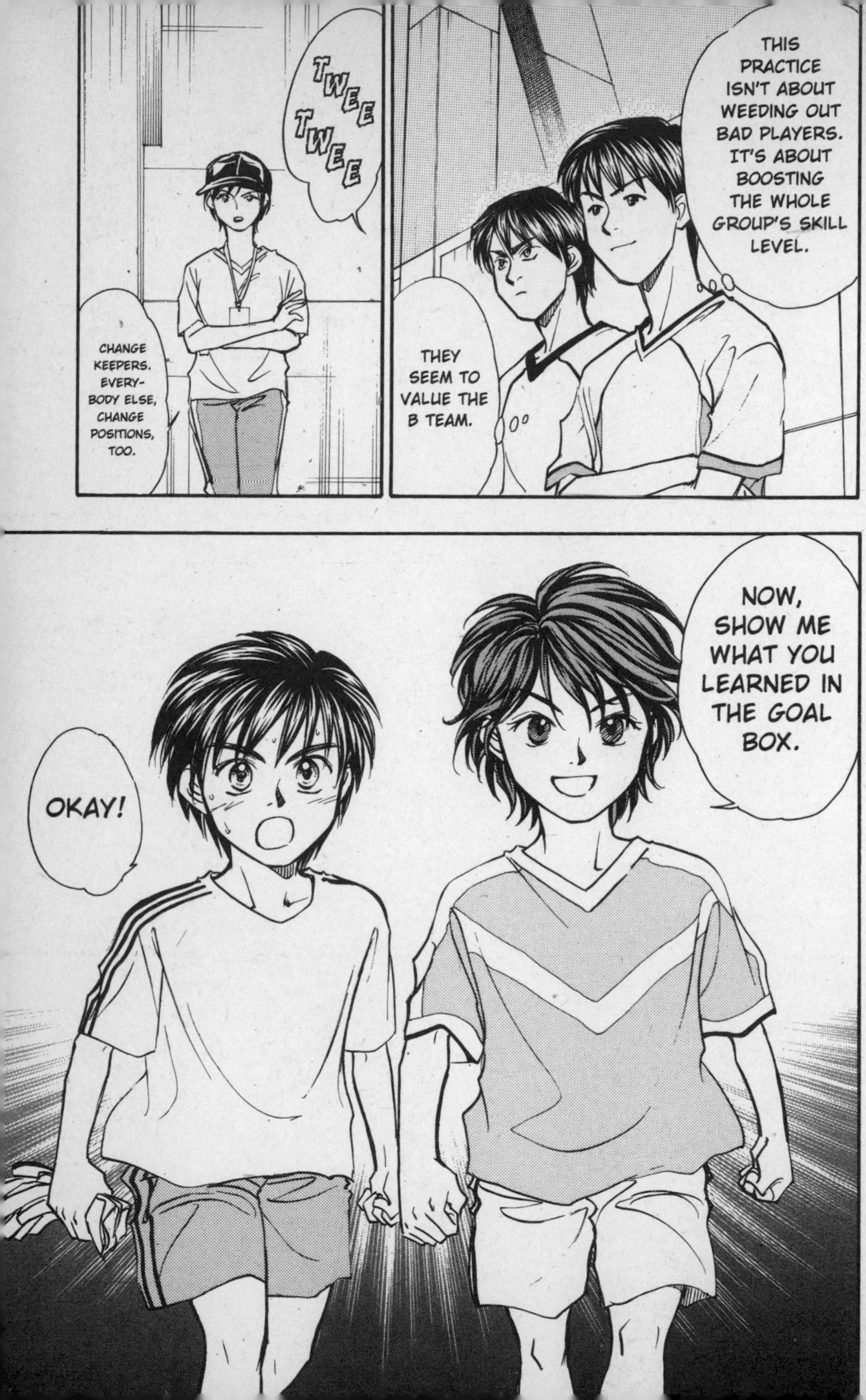
THIS PRACTICE ISN'T ABOUT WEEDING OUT BAD PLAYERS. IT'S ABOUT BOOSTING THE WHOLE GROUP'S SKILL LEVEL.
THEY SEEM TO VALUE THE B TEAM.
TWEE TWEE
CHANGE KEEPERS. EVERY-BODY ELSE, CHANGE POSITIONS, TOO.
NOW, SHOW ME WHAT YOU LEARNED IN THE GOAL BOX.
OKAY!

WHISTLE!™

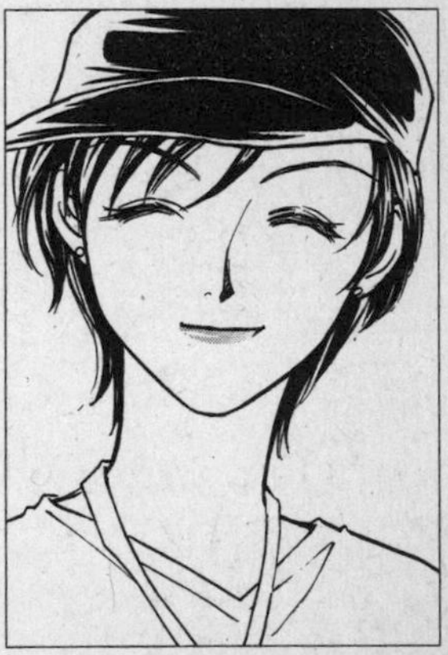

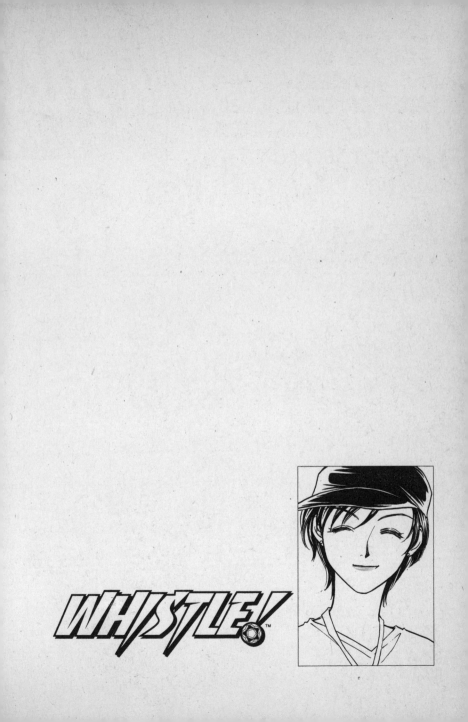

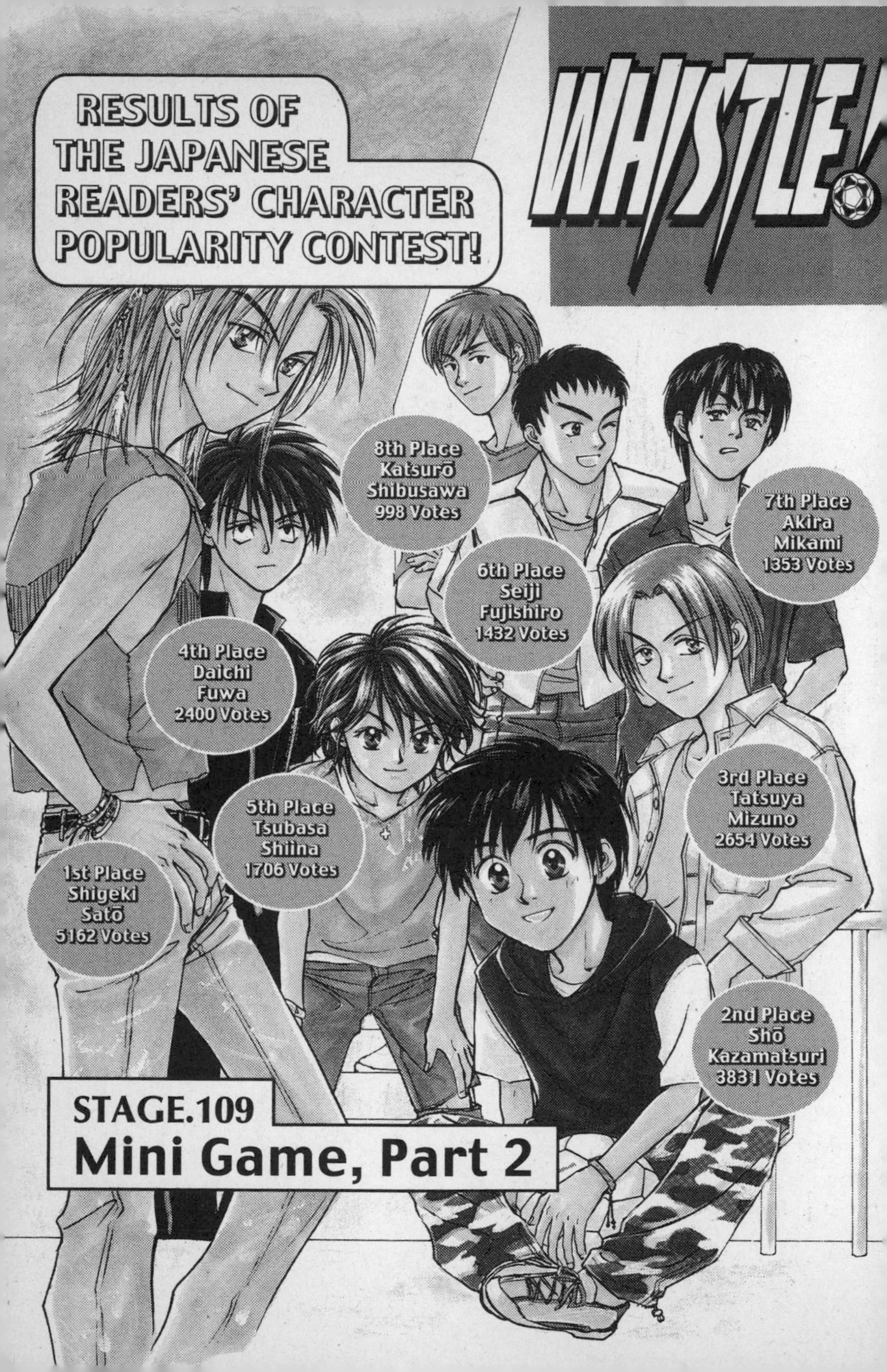

WHISTLE!
RESULTS OF THE JAPANESE READERS' CHARACTER POPULARITY CONTEST!
7th Place Akira Mikami 1353 Votes
8th Place Katsurō Shibusawa 998 Votes
6th Place Seiji Fujishiro 1432 Votes
4th Place Daichi Fuwa 2400 Votes
3rd Place Tatsuya Mizuno 2654 Votes
5th Place Tsubasa Shiina 1706 Votes
1st Place Shigeki Satō 5162 Votes
2nd Place Shō Kazamatsuri 3831 Votes
STAGE.109
Mini Game, Part 2

Results Of The Japanese Readers' Character Popularity Contest!

9th place and the rest turned out this way!

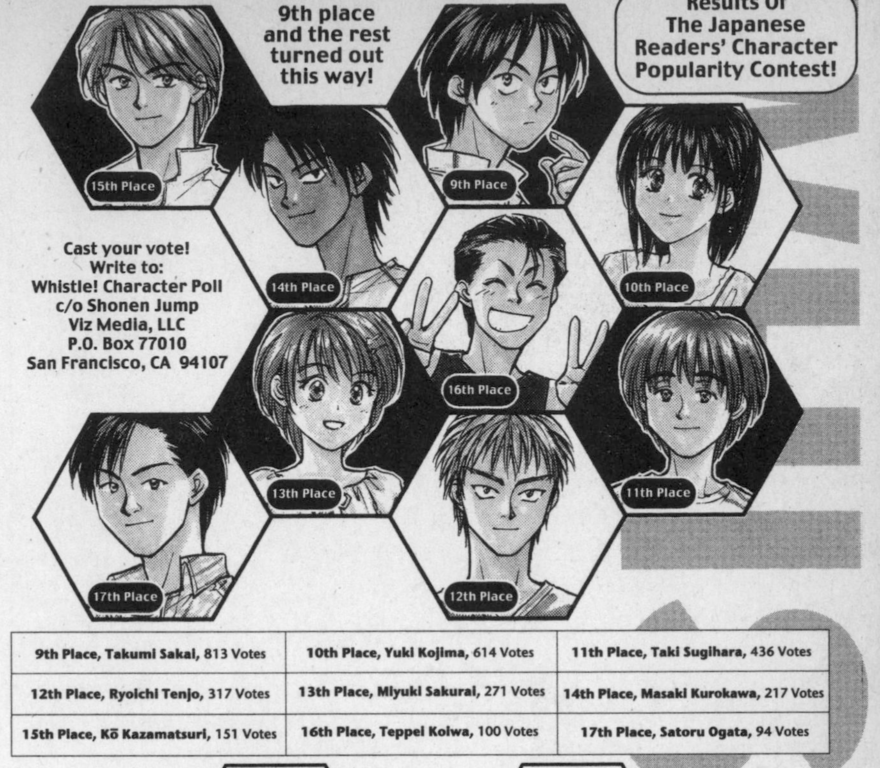
15th Place
9th Place
14th Place
10th Place
16th Place
13th Place
11th Place
17th Place
12th Place

Cast your vote!
Write to:
Whistle! Character Poll
c/o Shonen Jump
Viz Media, LLC
P.O. Box 77010
San Francisco, CA 94107

9th Place, Takumi Sakai, 813 Votes	**10th Place, Yuki Kojima,** 614 Votes	**11th Place, Taki Sugihara,** 436 Votes
12th Place, Ryoichi Tenjo, 317 Votes	**13th Place, Miyuki Sakurai,** 271 Votes	**14th Place, Masaki Kurokawa,** 217 Votes
15th Place, Kō Kazamatsuri, 151 Votes	**16th Place, Teppei Koiwa,** 100 Votes	**17th Place, Satoru Ogata,** 94 Votes

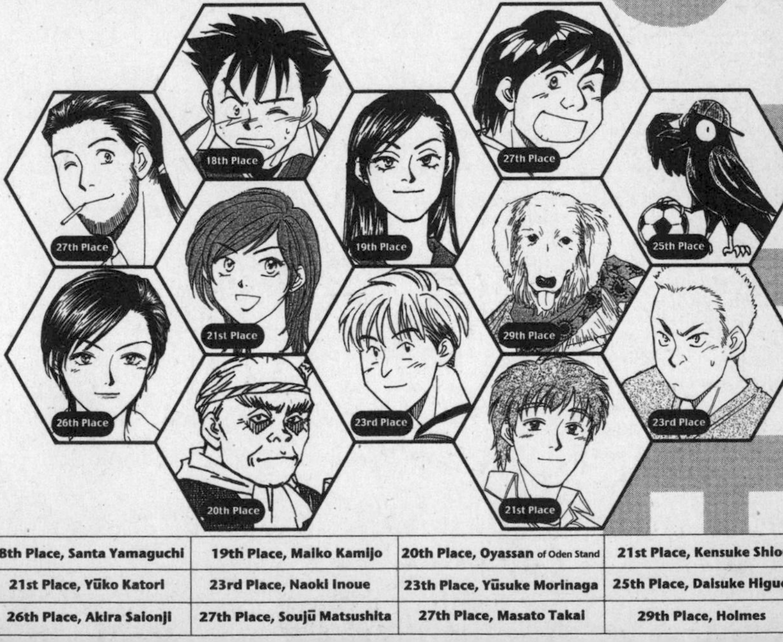
18th Place
27th Place
27th Place
19th Place
25th Place
21st Place
29th Place
26th Place
23rd Place
23rd Place
20th Place
21st Place

18th Place, Santa Yamaguchi	**19th Place, Maiko Kamijo**	**20th Place, Oyassan** of Oden Stand	**21st Place, Kensuke Shiomi**
21st Place, Yūko Katori	**23rd Place, Naoki Inoue**	**23th Place, Yūsuke Morinaga**	**25th Place, Daisuke Higuchi**
26th Place, Akira Saionji	**27th Place, Soujū Matsushita**	**27th Place, Masato Takai**	**29th Place, Holmes**

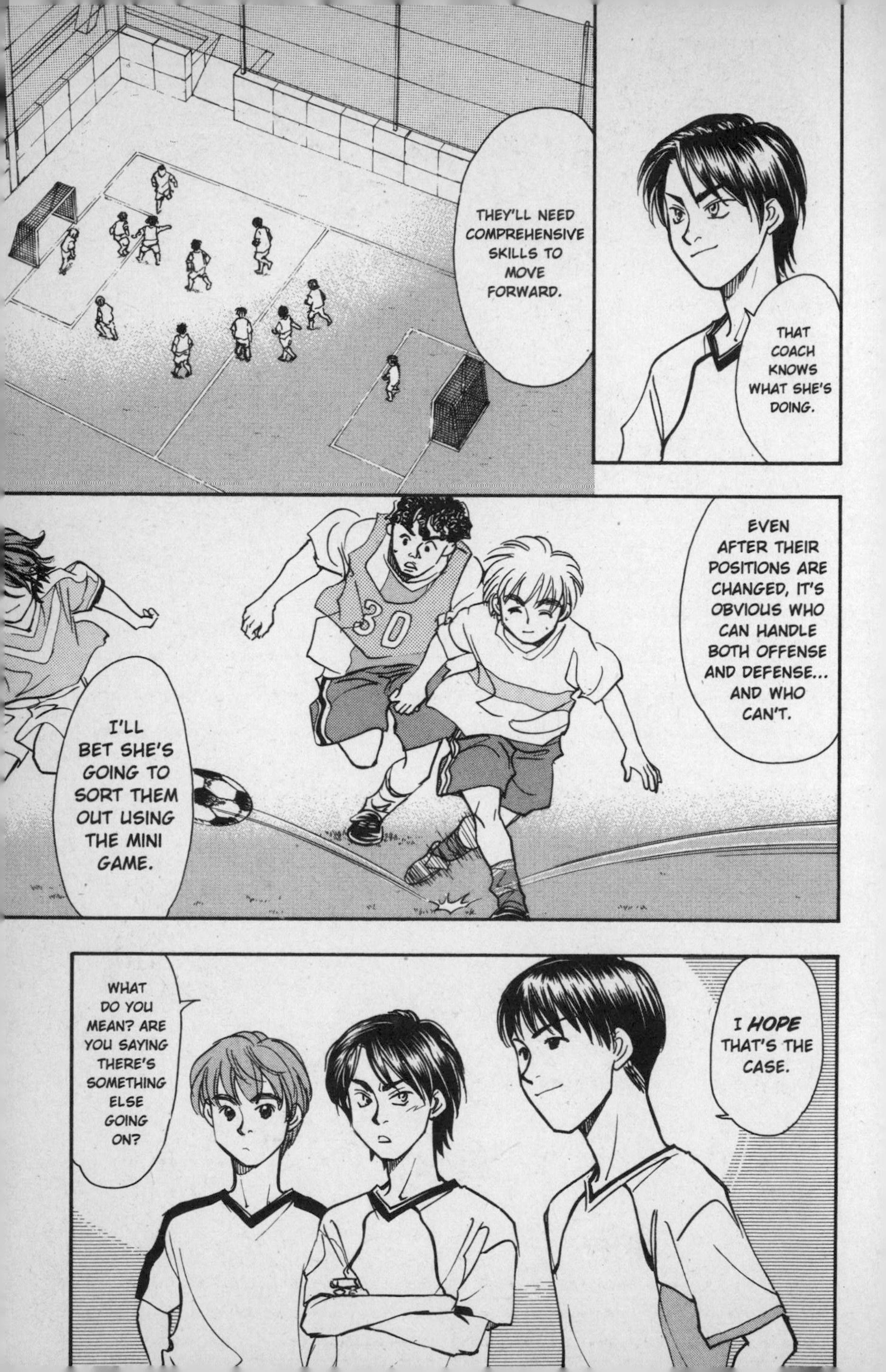
THAT COACH KNOWS WHAT SHE'S DOING.
THEY'LL NEED COMPREHENSIVE SKILLS TO MOVE FORWARD.
EVEN AFTER THEIR POSITIONS ARE CHANGED, IT'S OBVIOUS WHO CAN HANDLE BOTH OFFENSE AND DEFENSE... AND WHO CAN'T.
I'LL BET SHE'S GOING TO SORT THEM OUT USING THE MINI GAME.
I *HOPE* THAT'S THE CASE.
WHAT DO YOU MEAN? ARE YOU SAYING THERE'S SOMETHING ELSE GOING ON?

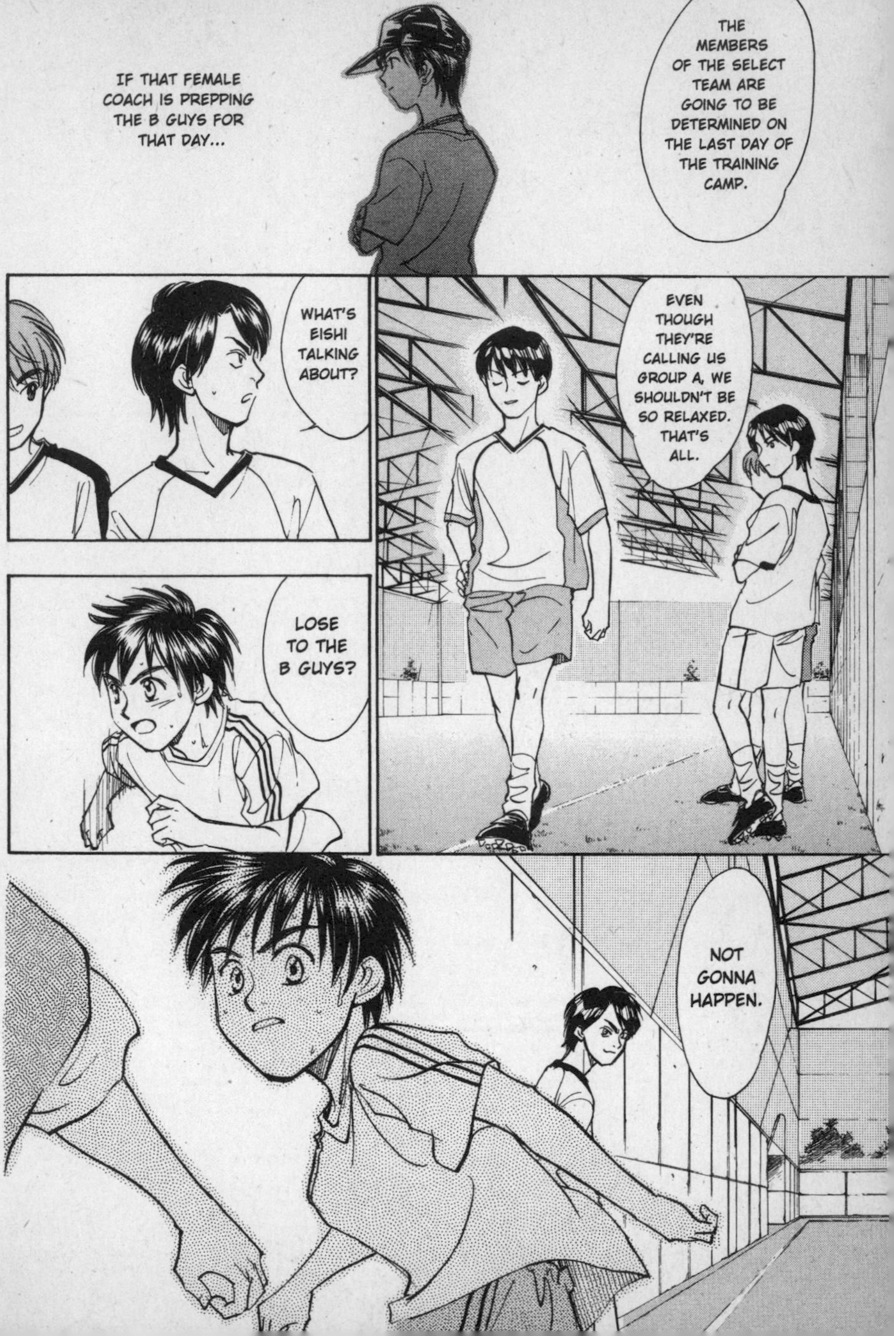
THE MEMBERS OF THE SELECT TEAM ARE GOING TO BE DETERMINED ON THE LAST DAY OF THE TRAINING CAMP.
IF THAT FEMALE COACH IS PREPPING THE B GUYS FOR THAT DAY...
EVEN THOUGH THEY'RE CALLING US GROUP A, WE SHOULDN'T BE SO RELAXED. THAT'S ALL.
WHAT'S EISHI TALKING ABOUT?
LOSE TO THE B GUYS?
NOT GONNA HAPPEN.

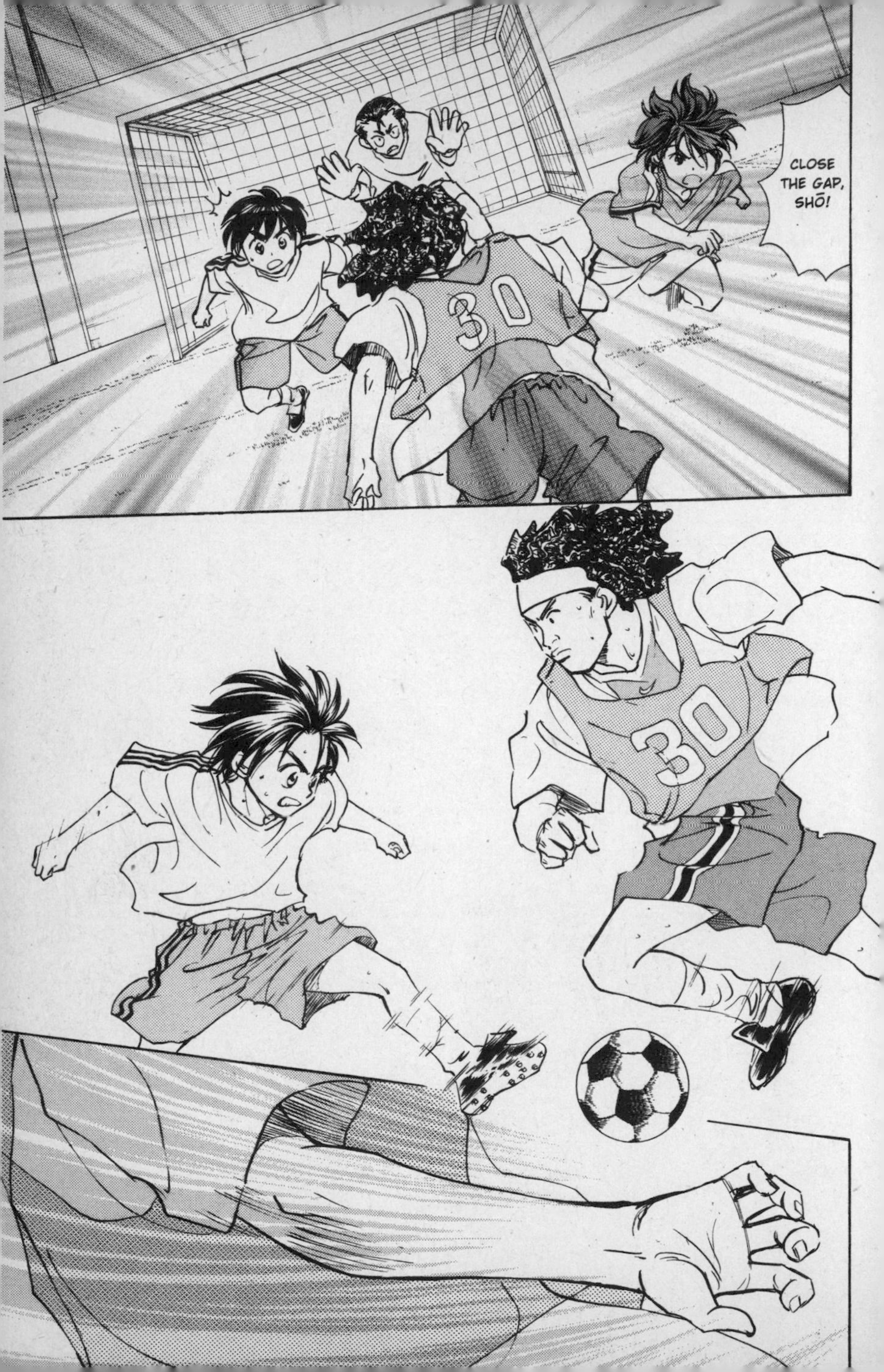
CLOSE THE GAP, SHŌ!

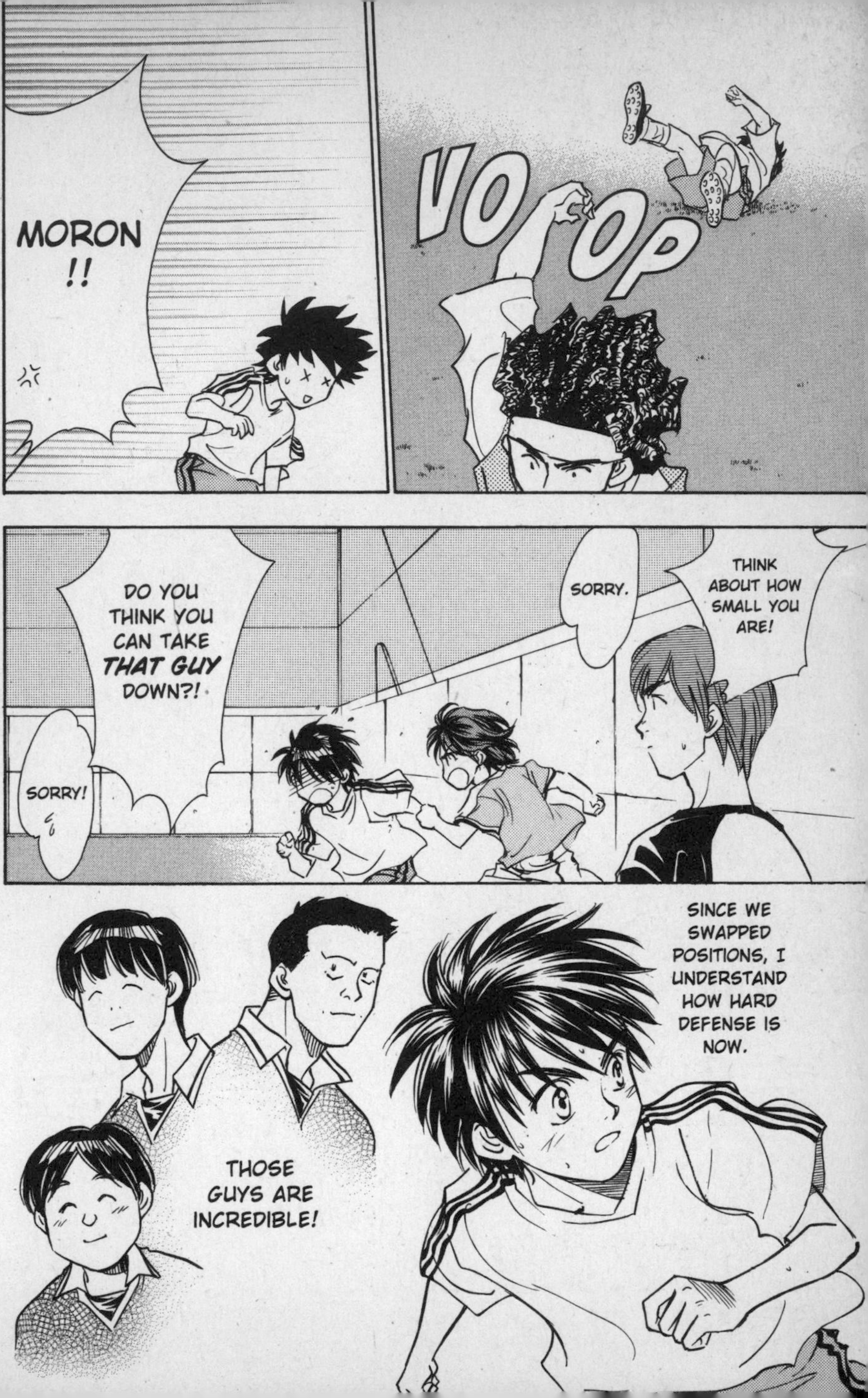
VOOP
MORON !!
THINK ABOUT HOW SMALL YOU ARE!
SORRY.
DO YOU THINK YOU CAN TAKE *THAT GUY* DOWN?!
SORRY!
SINCE WE SWAPPED POSITIONS, I UNDERSTAND HOW HARD DEFENSE IS NOW.
THOSE GUYS ARE INCREDIBLE!

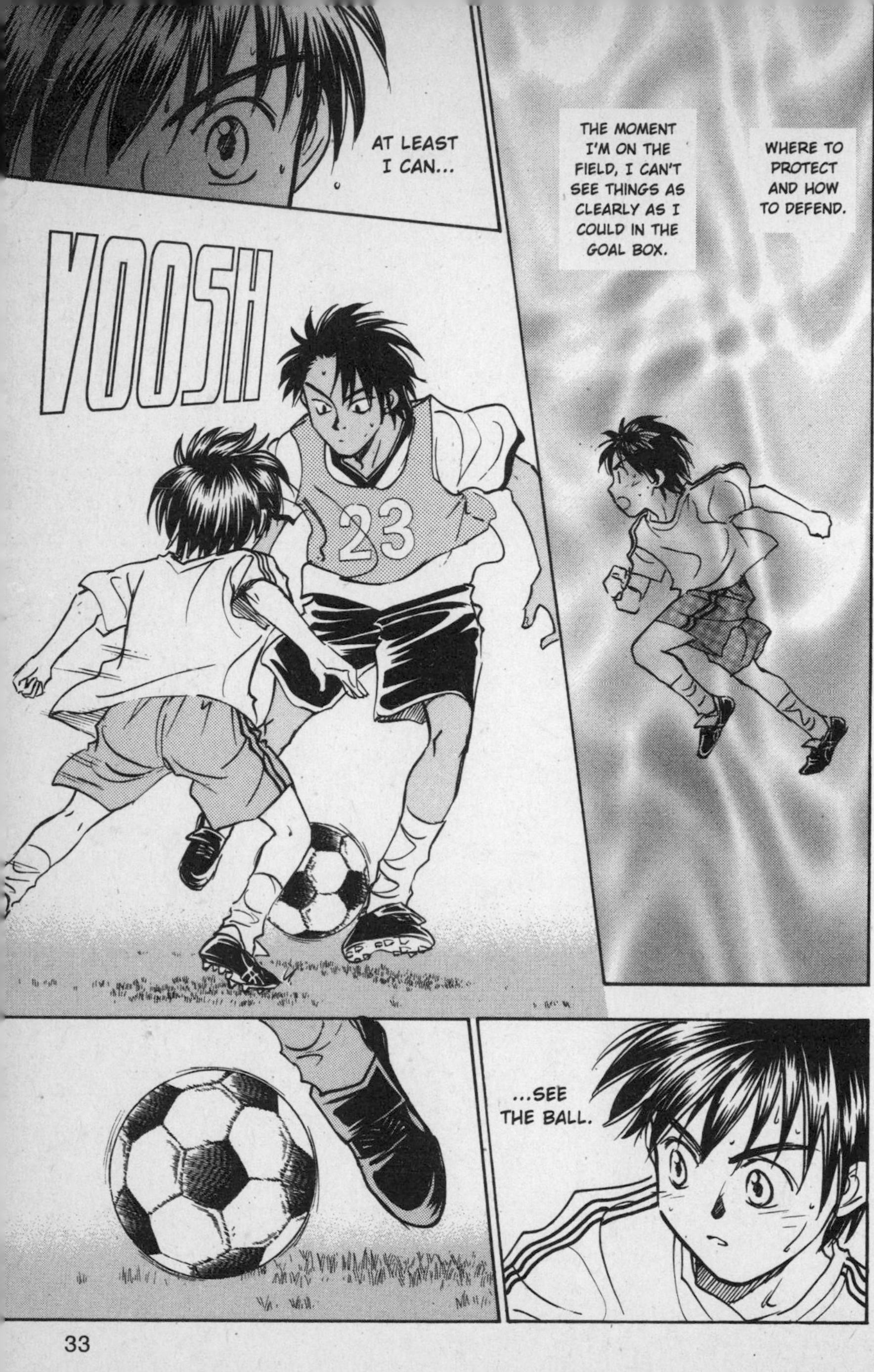
WHERE TO PROTECT AND HOW TO DEFEND.
THE MOMENT I'M ON THE FIELD, I CAN'T SEE THINGS AS CLEARLY AS I COULD IN THE GOAL BOX.
AT LEAST I CAN...
VOOSH
...SEE THE BALL.

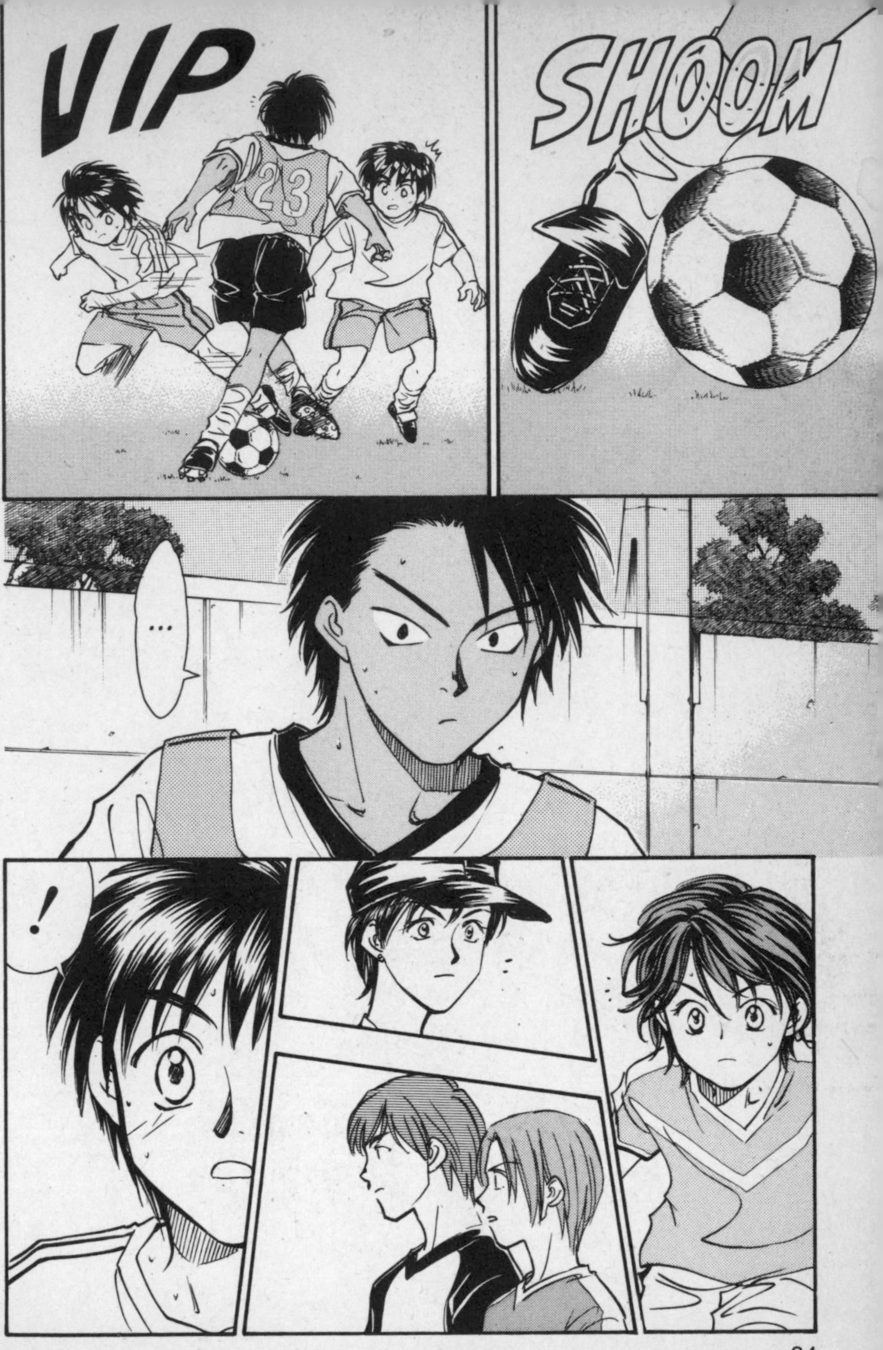
SHOOM
VIP
...
!

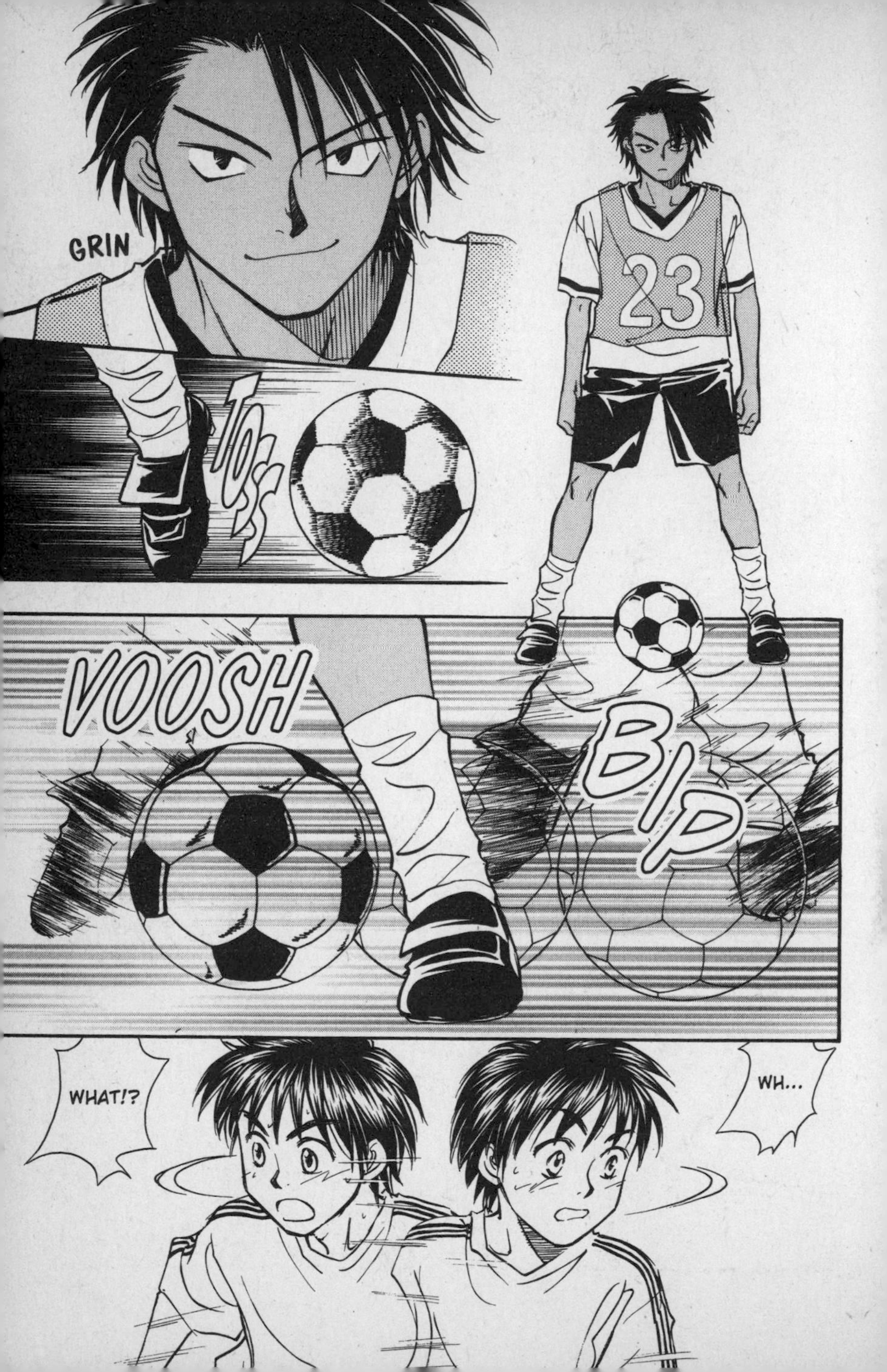
GRIN
TOSS
BIP
VOOSH
WH...
WHAT!?

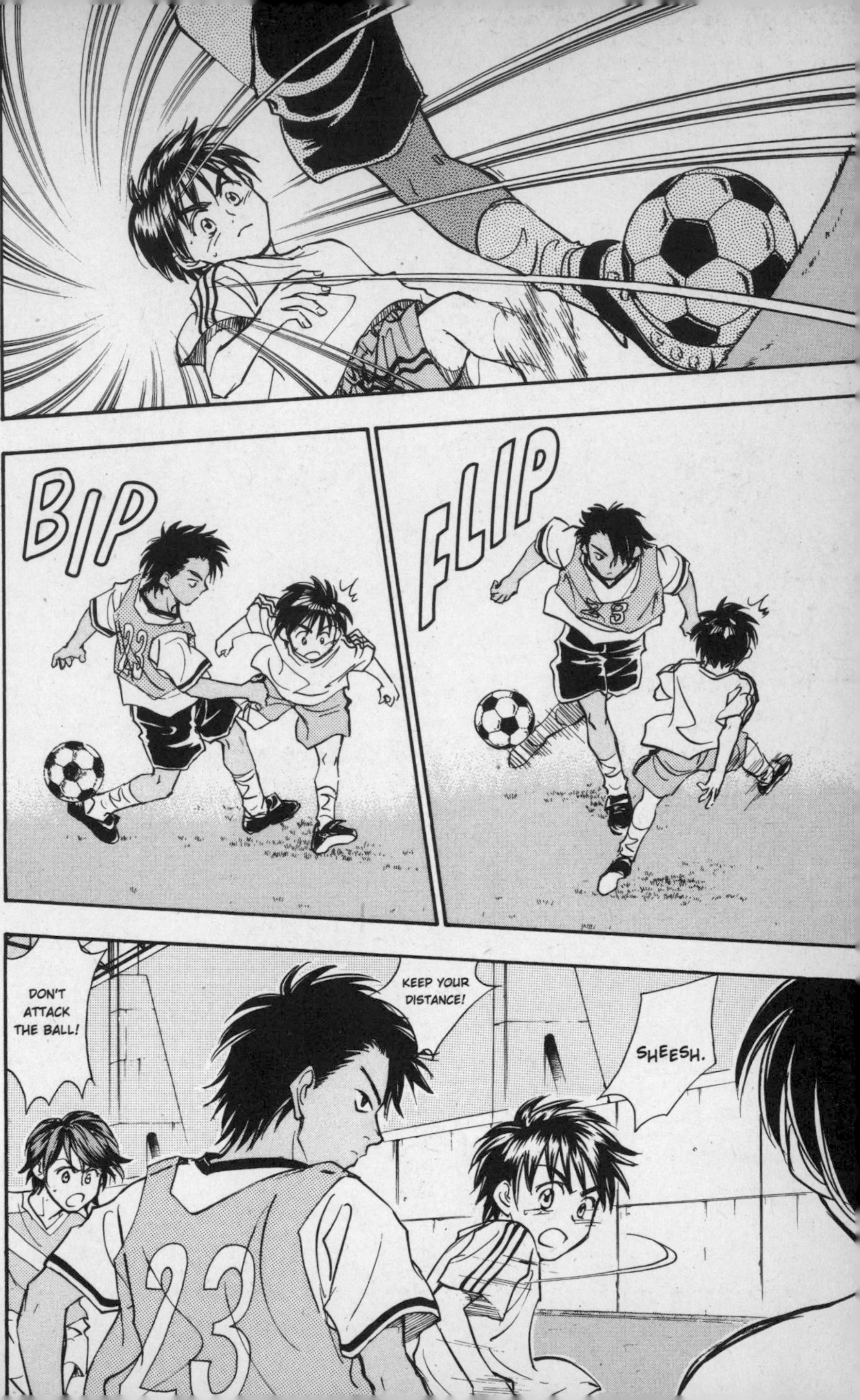
FLIP
BIP
SHEESH.
KEEP YOUR DISTANCE!
DON'T ATTACK THE BALL!

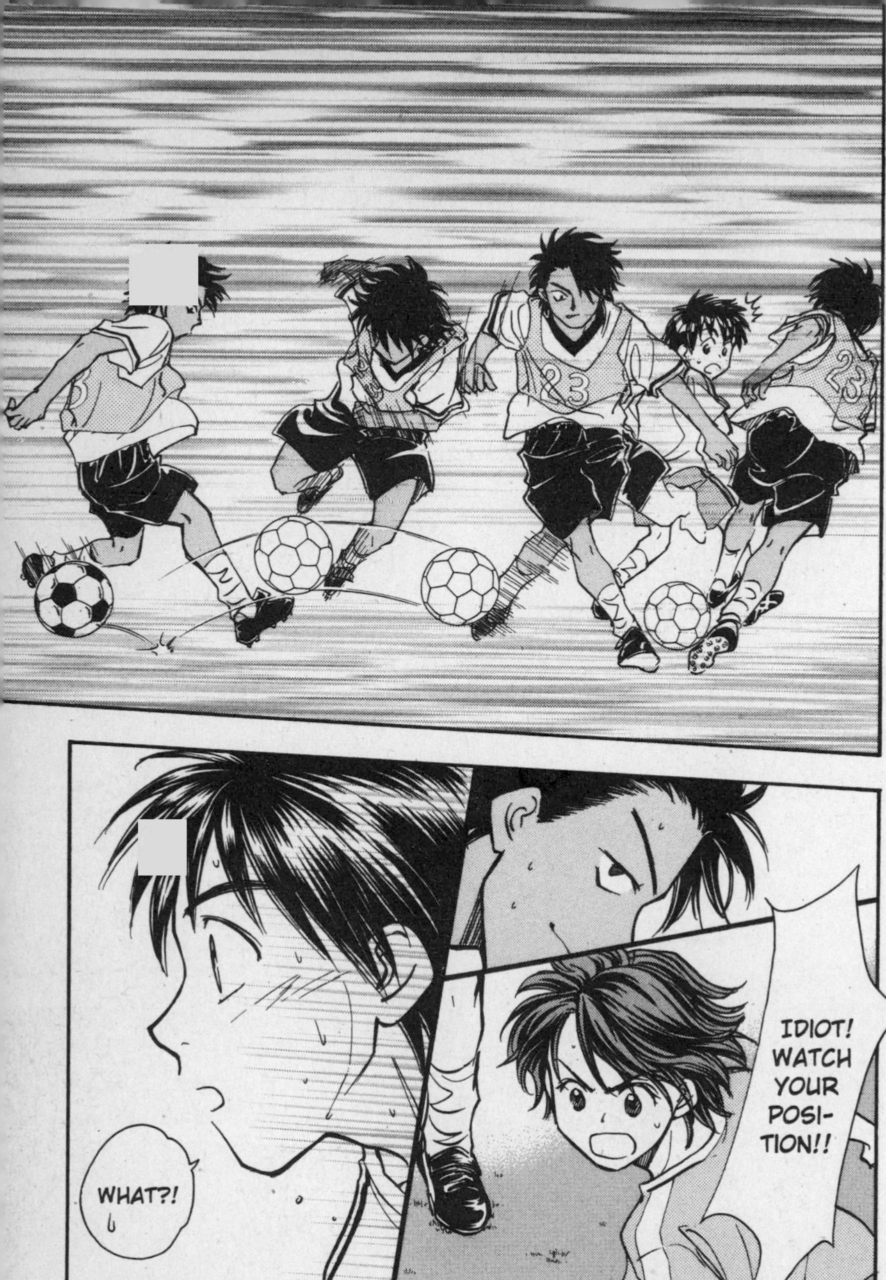
IDIOT! WATCH YOUR POSI- TION!!
WHAT?!

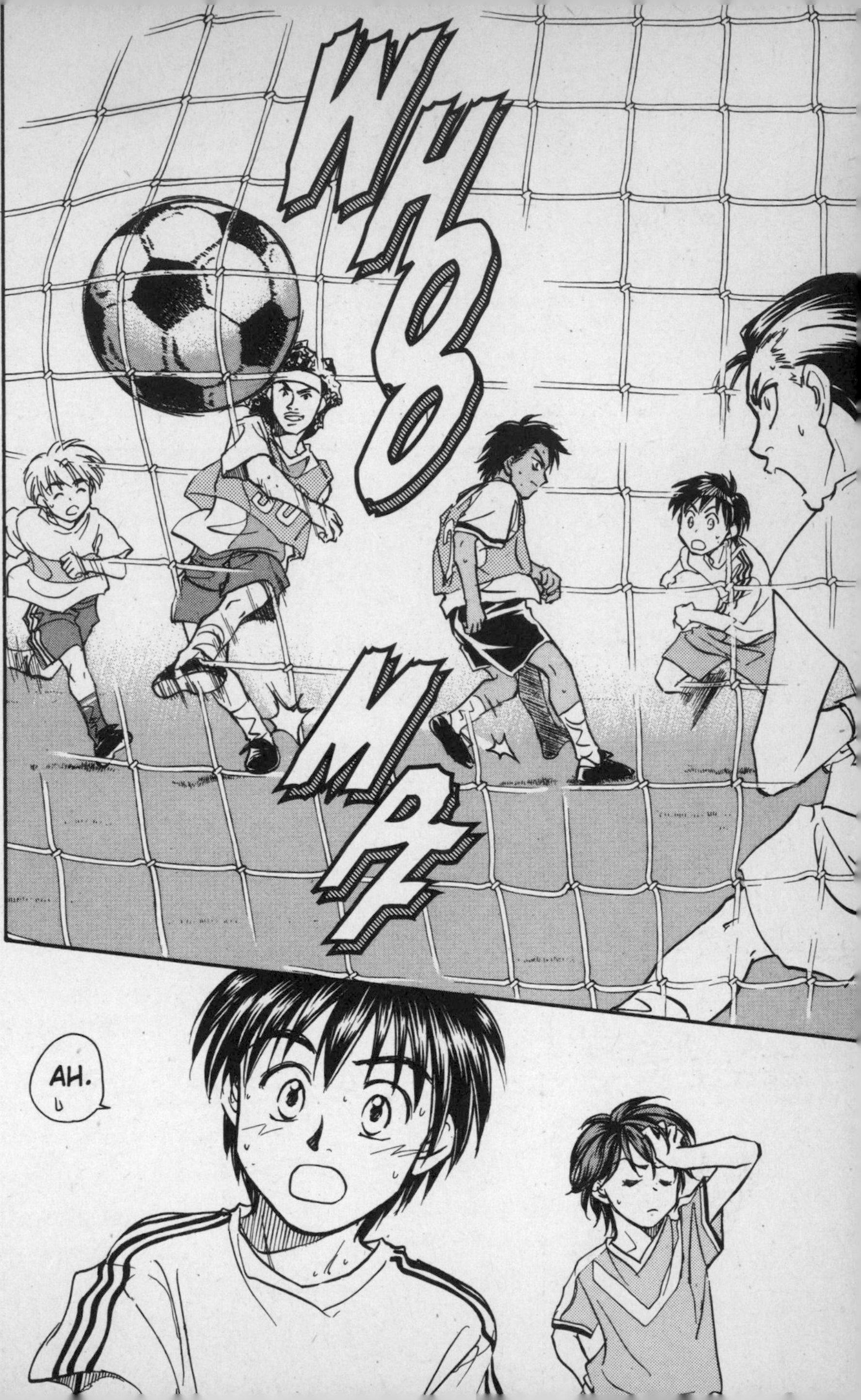
WHOOMP
AH.

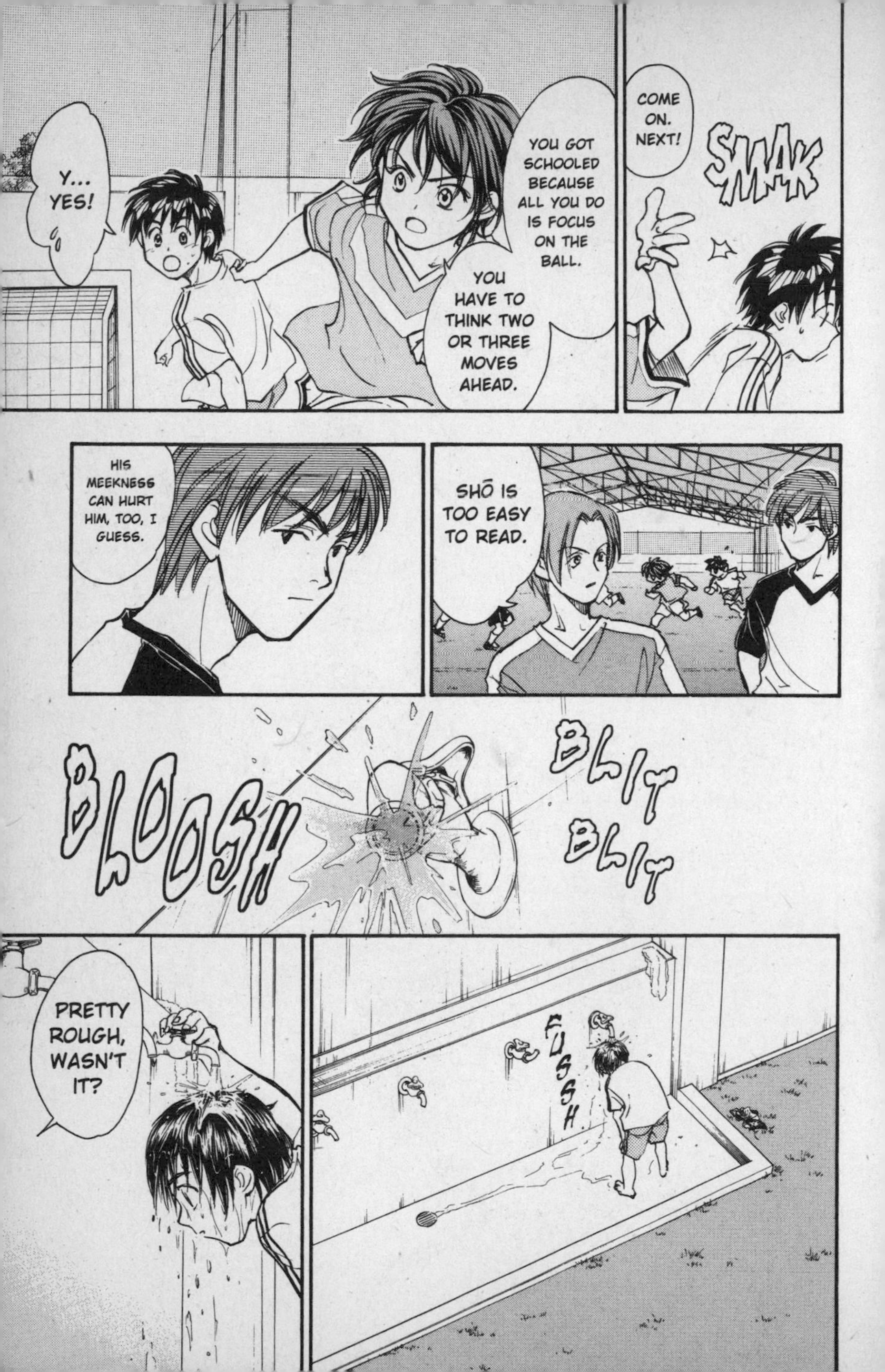
SMAK
COME ON. NEXT!
YOU GOT SCHOOLED BECAUSE ALL YOU DO IS FOCUS ON THE BALL.
YOU HAVE TO THINK TWO OR THREE MOVES AHEAD.
Y... YES!
SHŌ IS TOO EASY TO READ.
HIS MEEKNESS CAN HURT HIM, TOO, I GUESS.
BLIT BLIT
BLOOSH
FUSSH
PRETTY ROUGH, WASN'T IT?

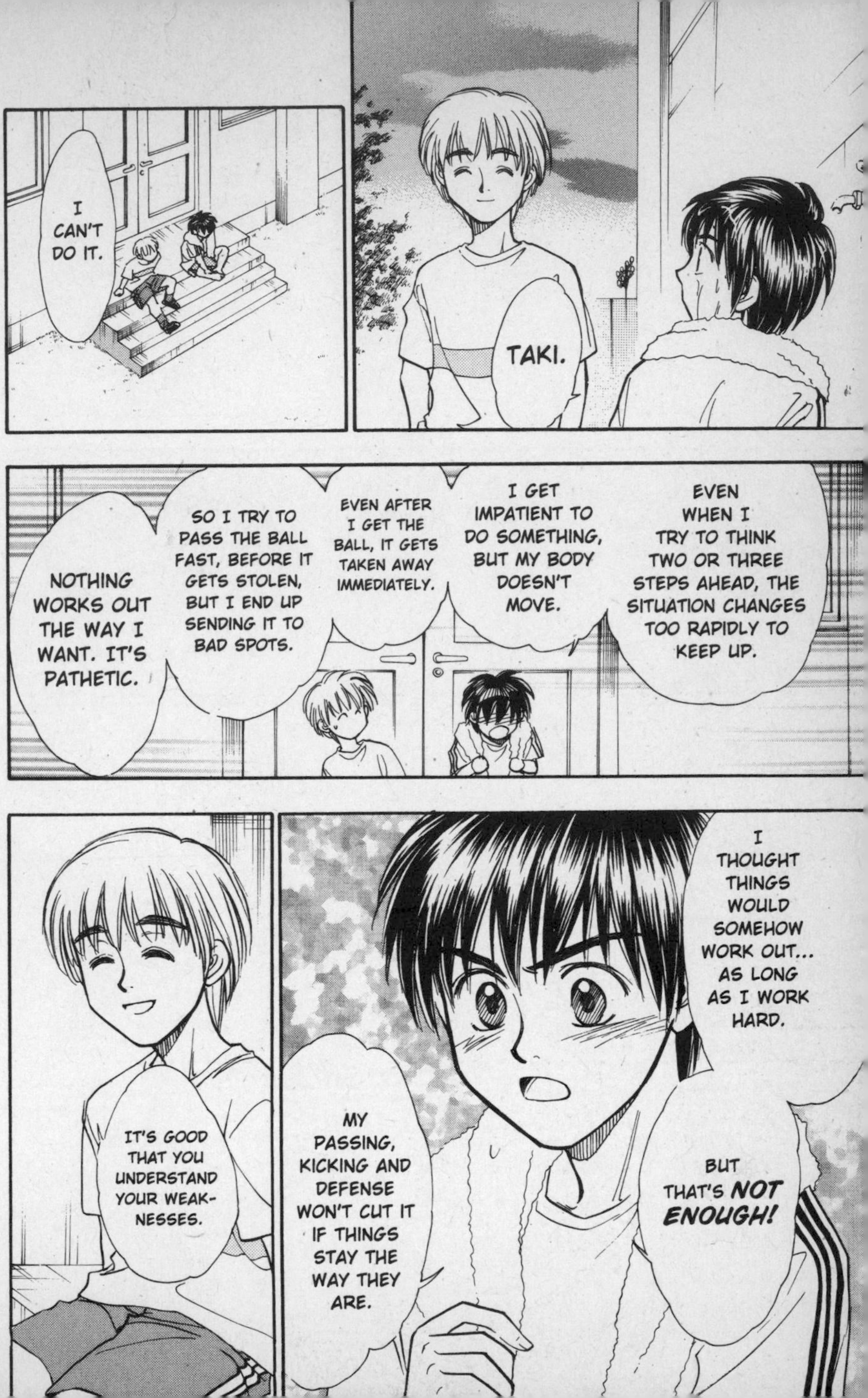
TAKI.
I CAN'T DO IT.
EVEN WHEN I TRY TO THINK TWO OR THREE STEPS AHEAD, THE SITUATION CHANGES TOO RAPIDLY TO KEEP UP.
I GET IMPATIENT TO DO SOMETHING, BUT MY BODY DOESN'T MOVE.
EVEN AFTER I GET THE BALL, IT GETS TAKEN AWAY IMMEDIATELY.
SO I TRY TO PASS THE BALL FAST, BEFORE IT GETS STOLEN, BUT I END UP SENDING IT TO BAD SPOTS.
NOTHING WORKS OUT THE WAY I WANT. IT'S PATHETIC.
I THOUGHT THINGS WOULD SOMEHOW WORK OUT... AS LONG AS I WORK HARD.
BUT THAT'S ***NOT ENOUGH!***
MY PASSING, KICKING AND DEFENSE WON'T CUT IT IF THINGS STAY THE WAY THEY ARE.
IT'S GOOD THAT YOU UNDERSTAND YOUR WEAK-NESSES.

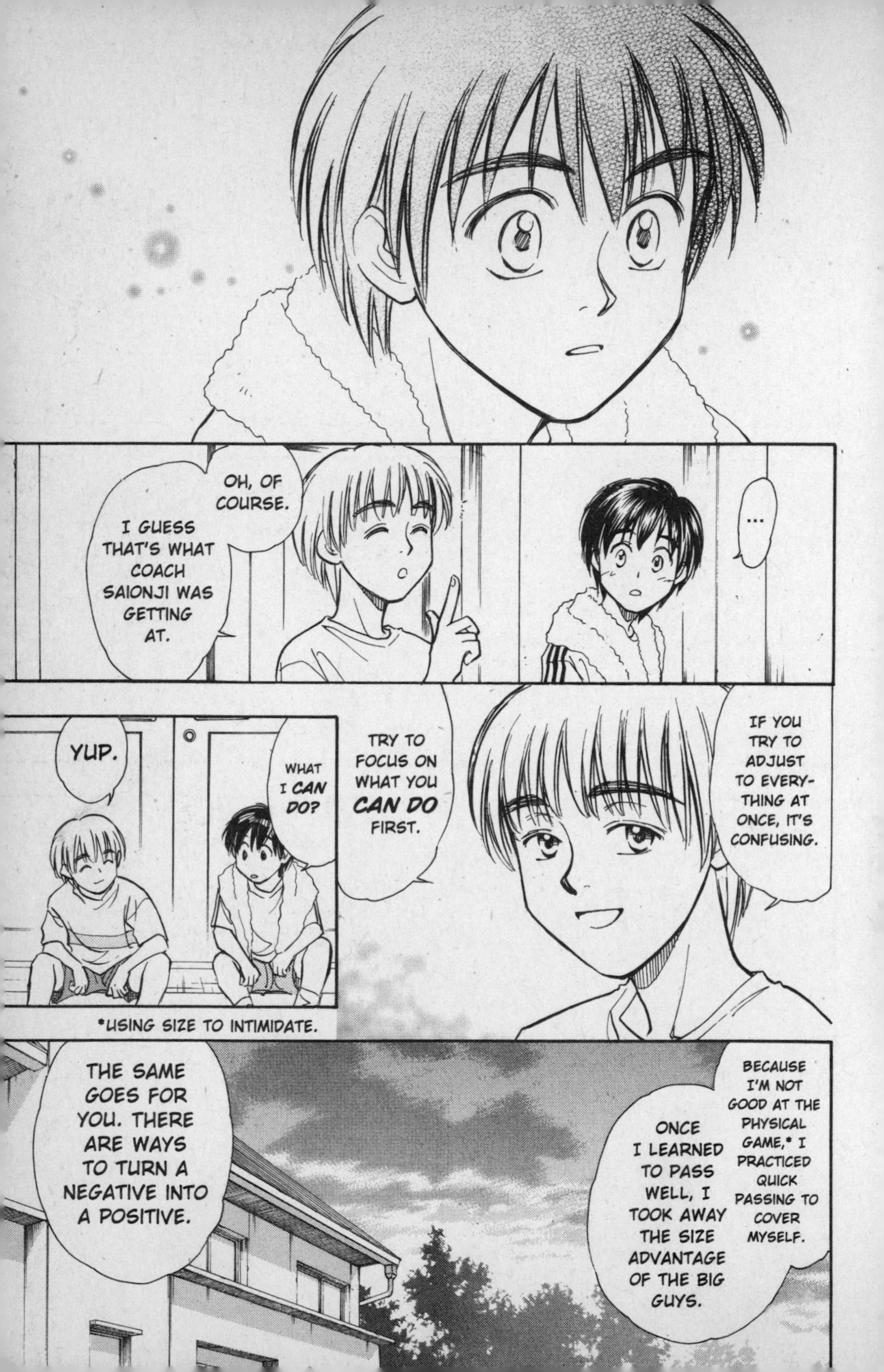
...
OH, OF COURSE.
I GUESS THAT'S WHAT COACH SAIONJI WAS GETTING AT.
IF YOU TRY TO ADJUST TO EVERY-THING AT ONCE, IT'S CONFUSING.
TRY TO FOCUS ON WHAT YOU CAN DO FIRST.
WHAT I CAN DO?
YUP.
*USING SIZE TO INTIMIDATE.
BECAUSE I'M NOT GOOD AT THE PHYSICAL GAME,* I PRACTICED QUICK PASSING TO COVER MYSELF.
ONCE I LEARNED TO PASS WELL, I TOOK AWAY THE SIZE ADVANTAGE OF THE BIG GUYS.
THE SAME GOES FOR YOU. THERE ARE WAYS TO TURN A NEGATIVE INTO A POSITIVE.

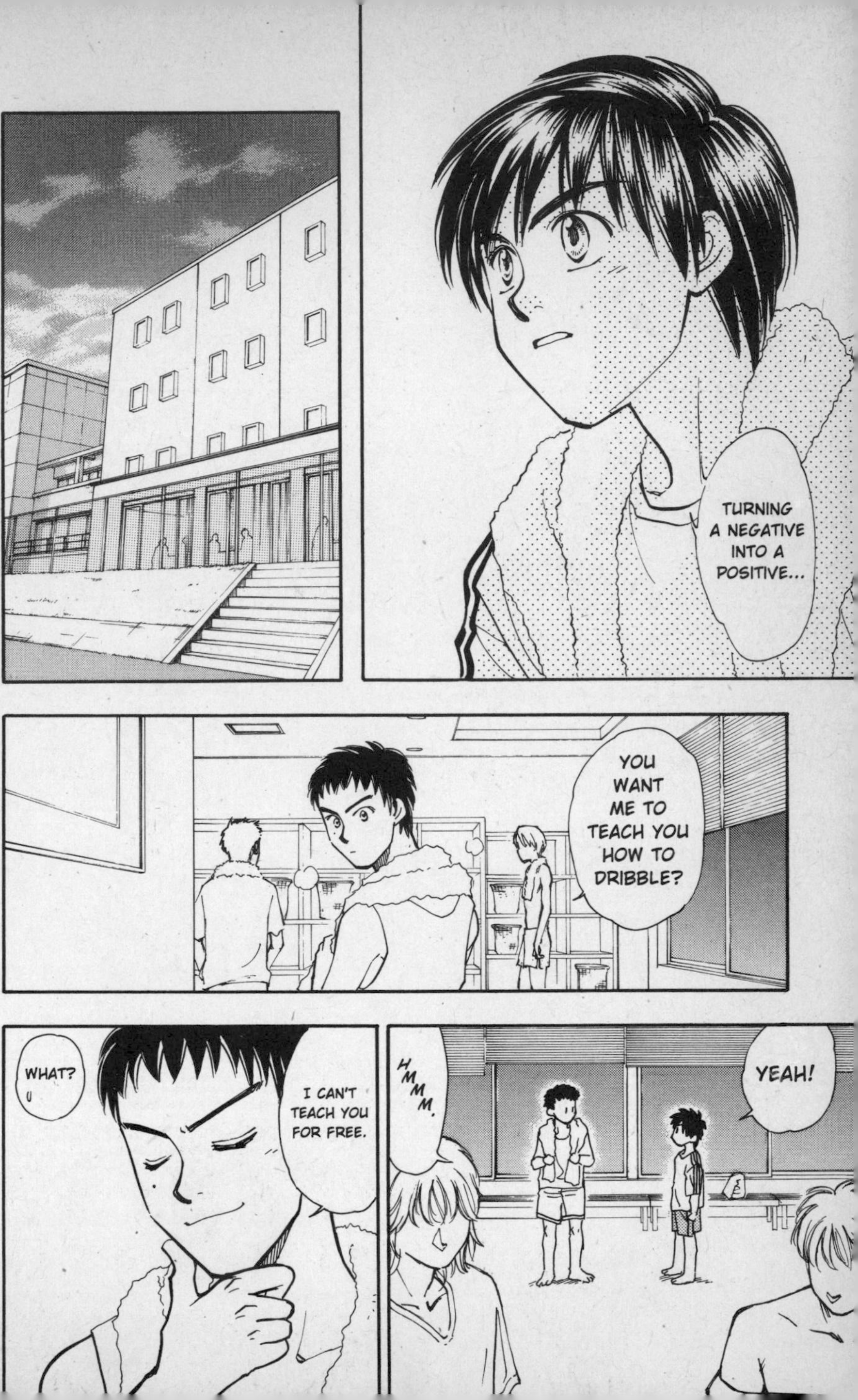
TURNING A NEGATIVE INTO A POSITIVE...
YOU WANT ME TO TEACH YOU HOW TO DRIBBLE?
YEAH!
HMMM.
I CAN'T TEACH YOU FOR FREE.
WHAT?

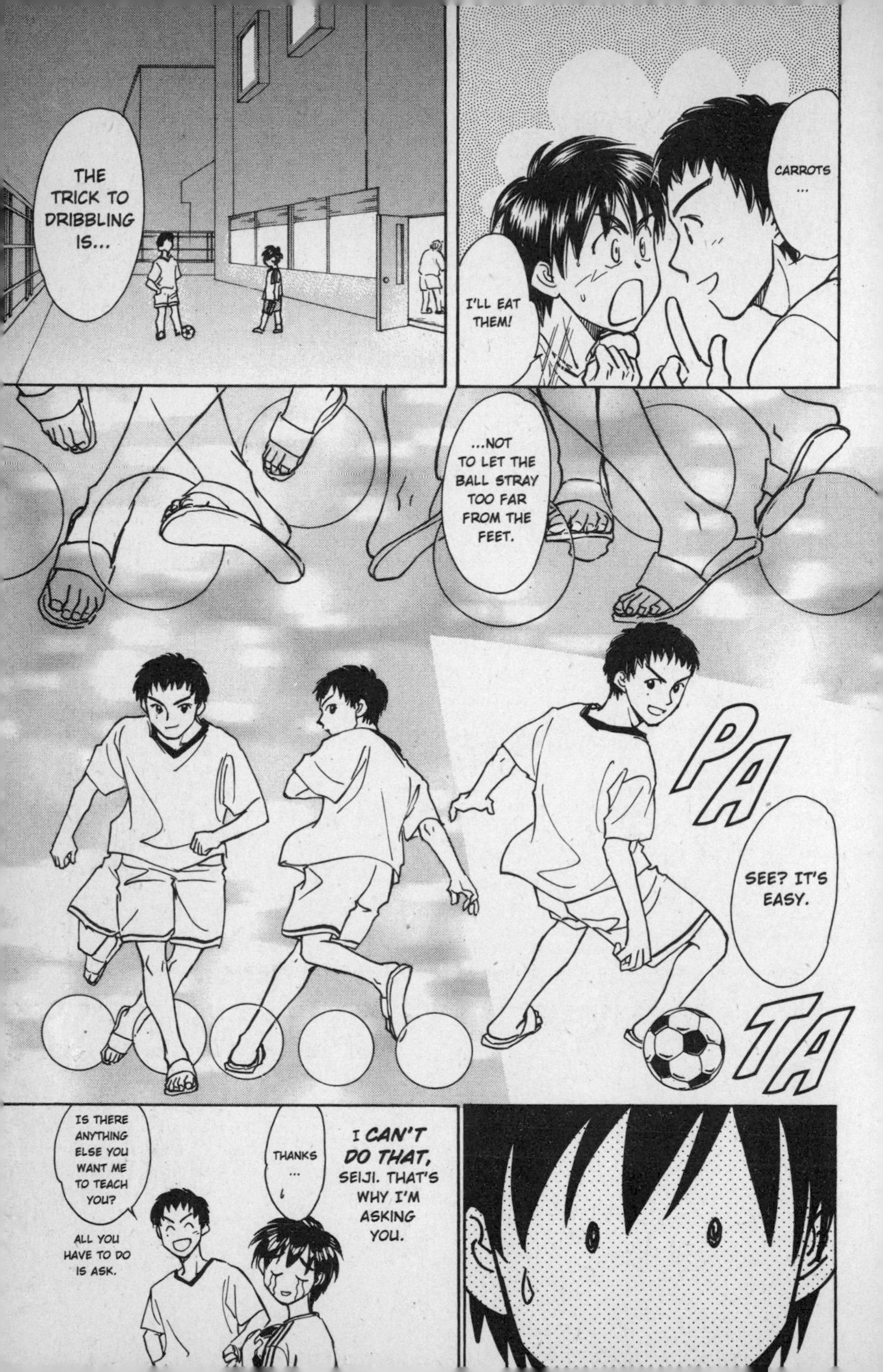
CARROTS ...
I'LL EAT THEM!
THE TRICK TO DRIBBLING IS...
...NOT TO LET THE BALL STRAY TOO FAR FROM THE FEET.
PA
SEE? IT'S EASY.
TA
I CAN'T DO THAT, SEIJI. THAT'S WHY I'M ASKING YOU.
THANKS ...
IS THERE ANYTHING ELSE YOU WANT ME TO TEACH YOU?
ALL YOU HAVE TO DO IS ASK.

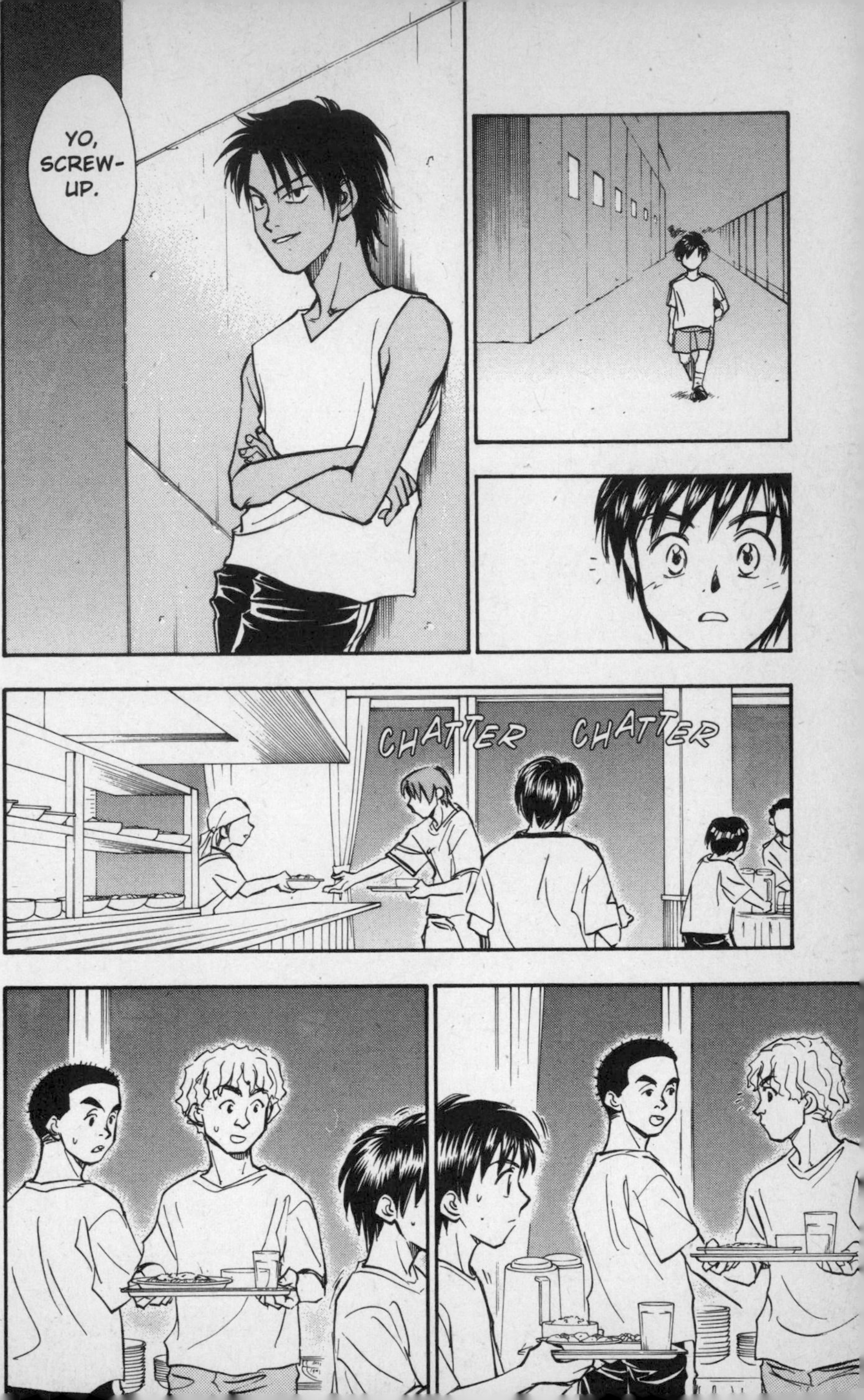
YO, SCREW-UP.
CHATTER CHATTER

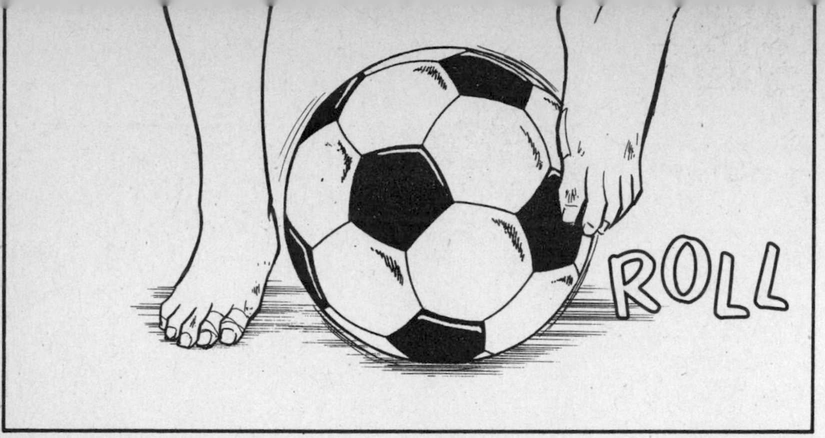
ROLL
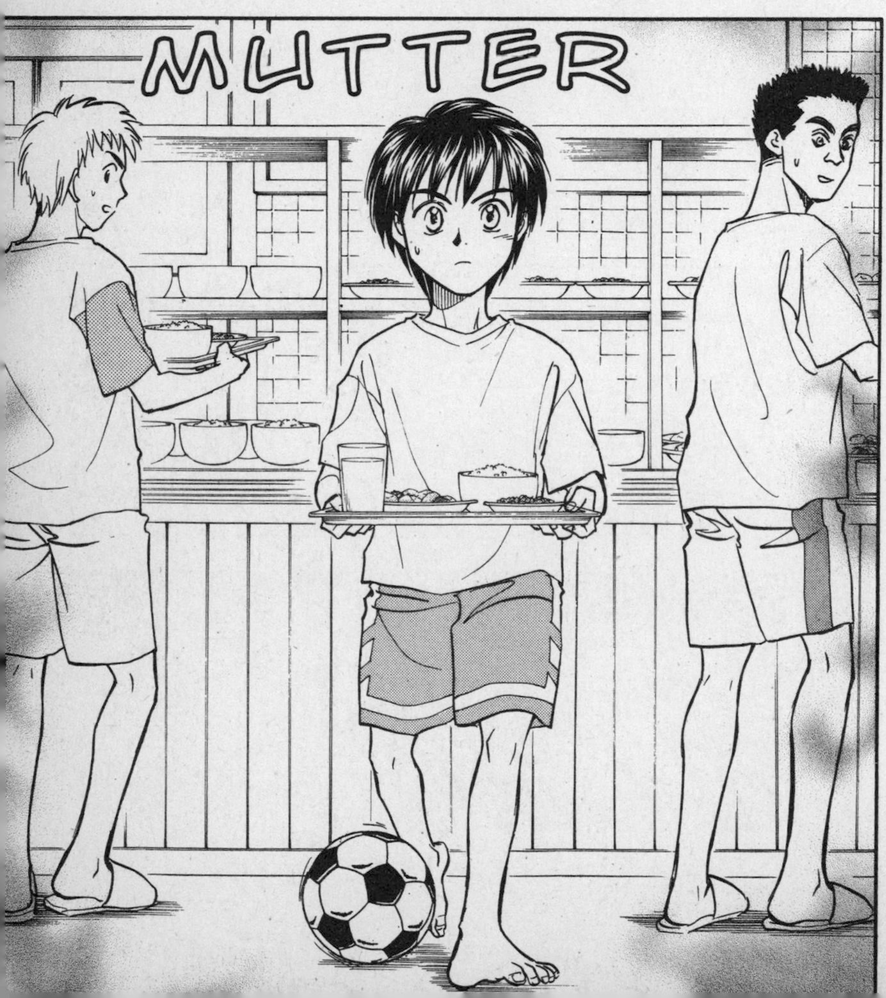
MUTTER

WH**I**STLE!™

STAGE.110 Barefootin' It

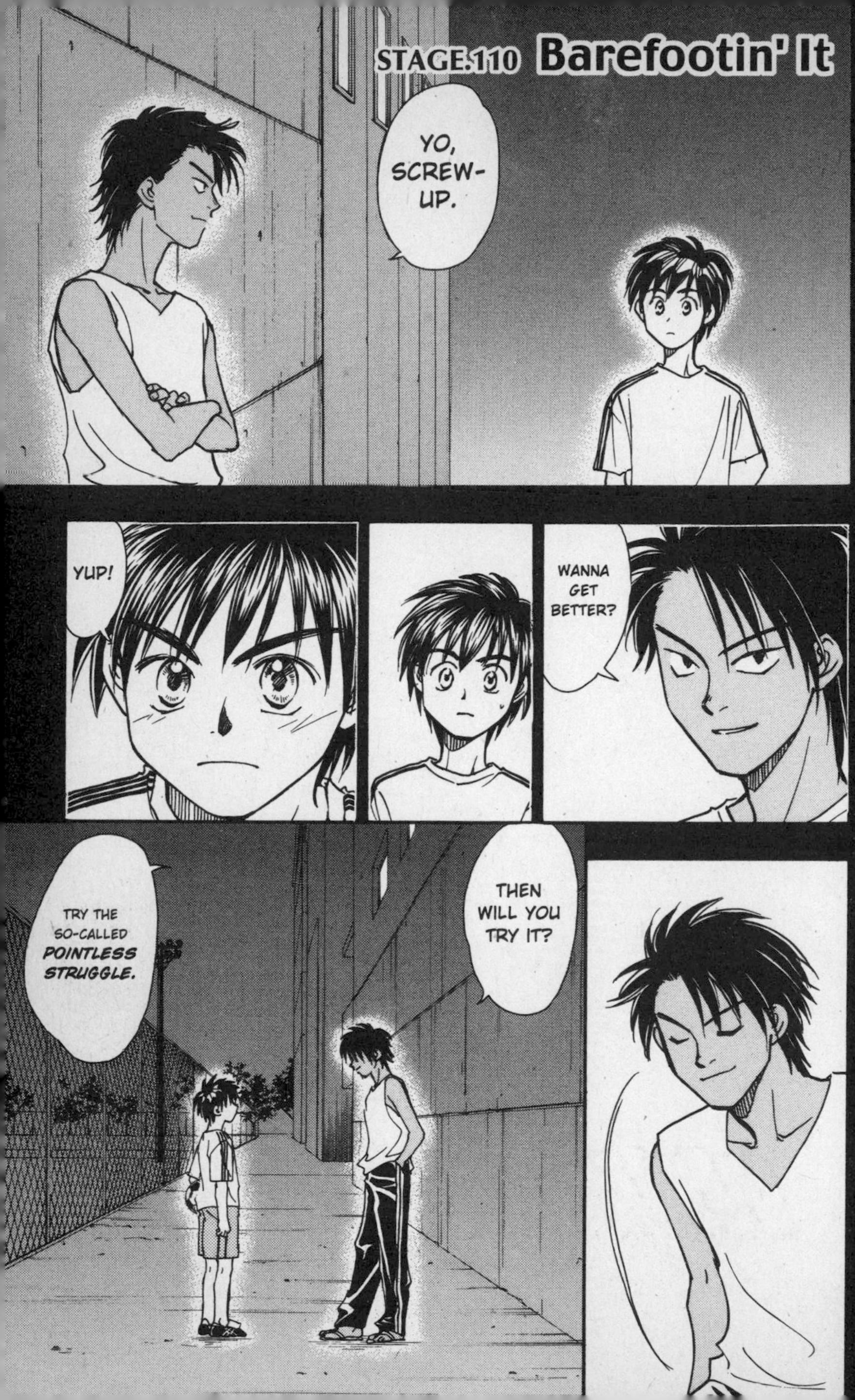
YO, SCREW-UP.
WANNA GET BETTER?
YUP!
THEN WILL YOU TRY IT?
TRY THE SO-CALLED POINTLESS STRUGGLE.

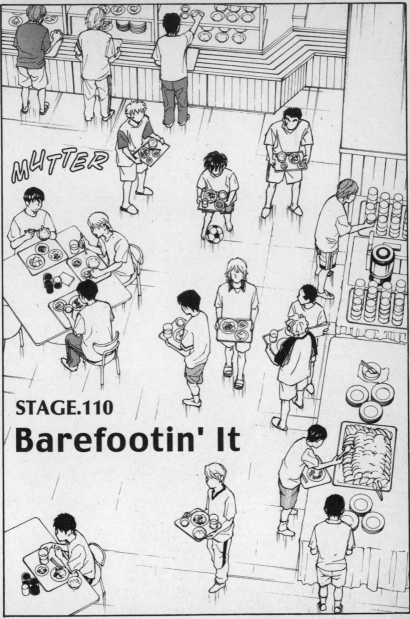

MUTTER

STAGE.110
Barefootin' It

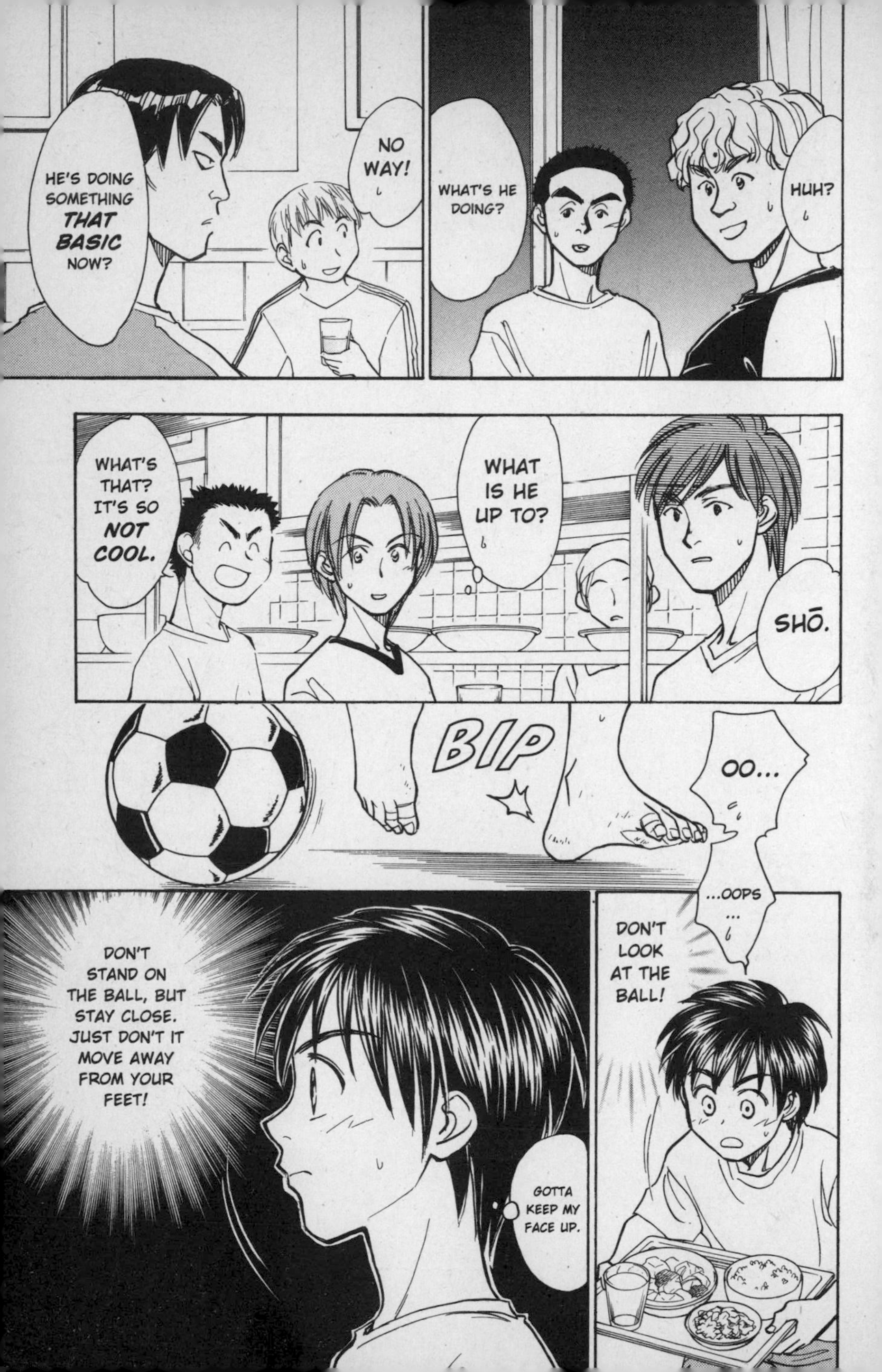
HUH?
WHAT'S HE DOING?
NO WAY!
HE'S DOING SOMETHING THAT BASIC NOW?
SHŌ.
WHAT IS HE UP TO?
WHAT'S THAT? IT'S SO NOT COOL.
OO...
BIP
...OOPS ...
DON'T LOOK AT THE BALL!
DON'T STAND ON THE BALL, BUT STAY CLOSE. JUST DON'T IT MOVE AWAY FROM YOUR FEET!
GOTTA KEEP MY FACE UP.

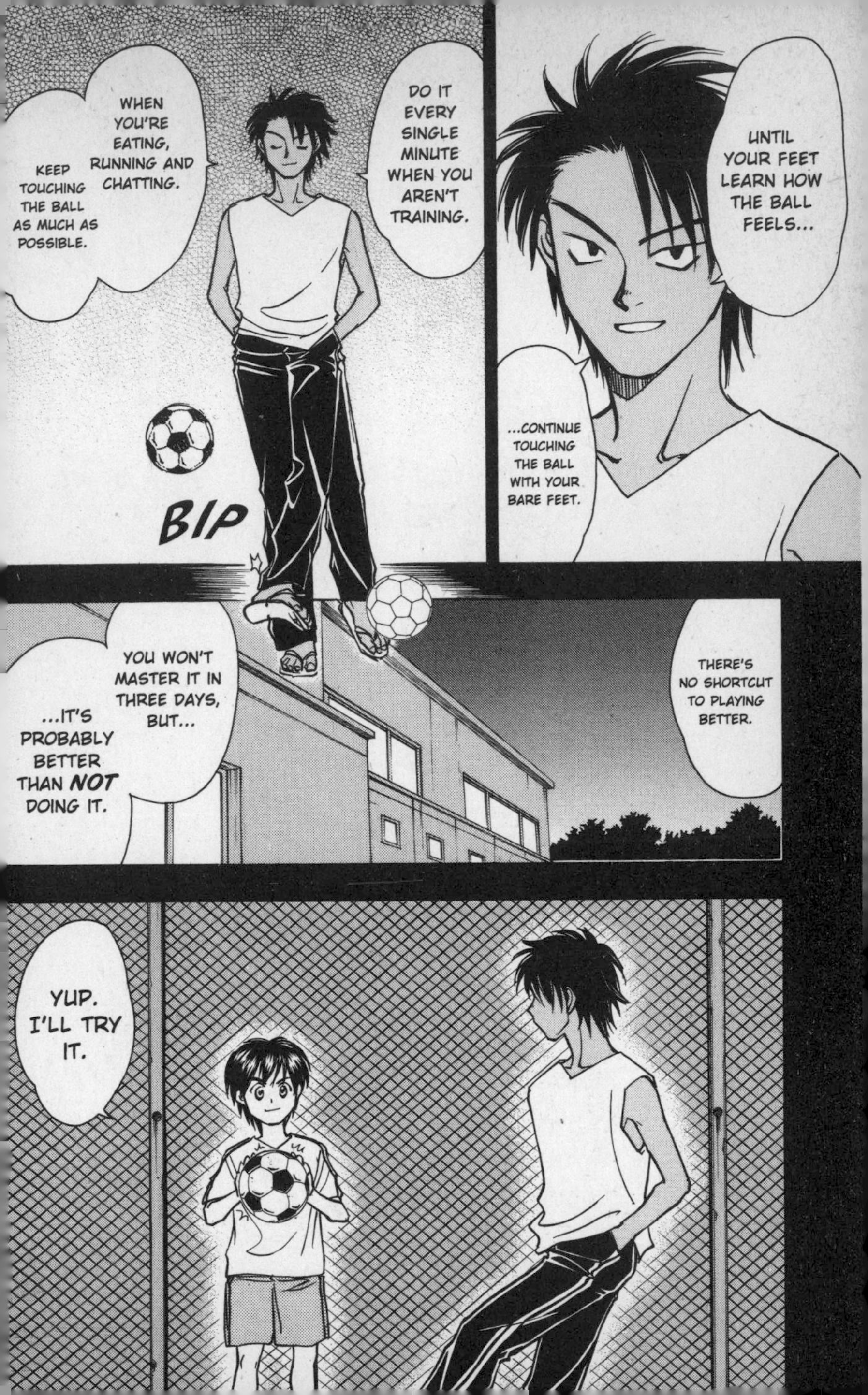
UNTIL YOUR FEET LEARN HOW THE BALL FEELS...
...CONTINUE TOUCHING THE BALL WITH YOUR BARE FEET.
DO IT EVERY SINGLE MINUTE WHEN YOU AREN'T TRAINING.
WHEN YOU'RE EATING, RUNNING AND CHATTING.
KEEP TOUCHING THE BALL AS MUCH AS POSSIBLE.
BIP
THERE'S NO SHORTCUT TO PLAYING BETTER.
YOU WON'T MASTER IT IN THREE DAYS, BUT...
...IT'S PROBABLY BETTER THAN *NOT* DOING IT.
YUP. I'LL TRY IT.

READ THIS WAY

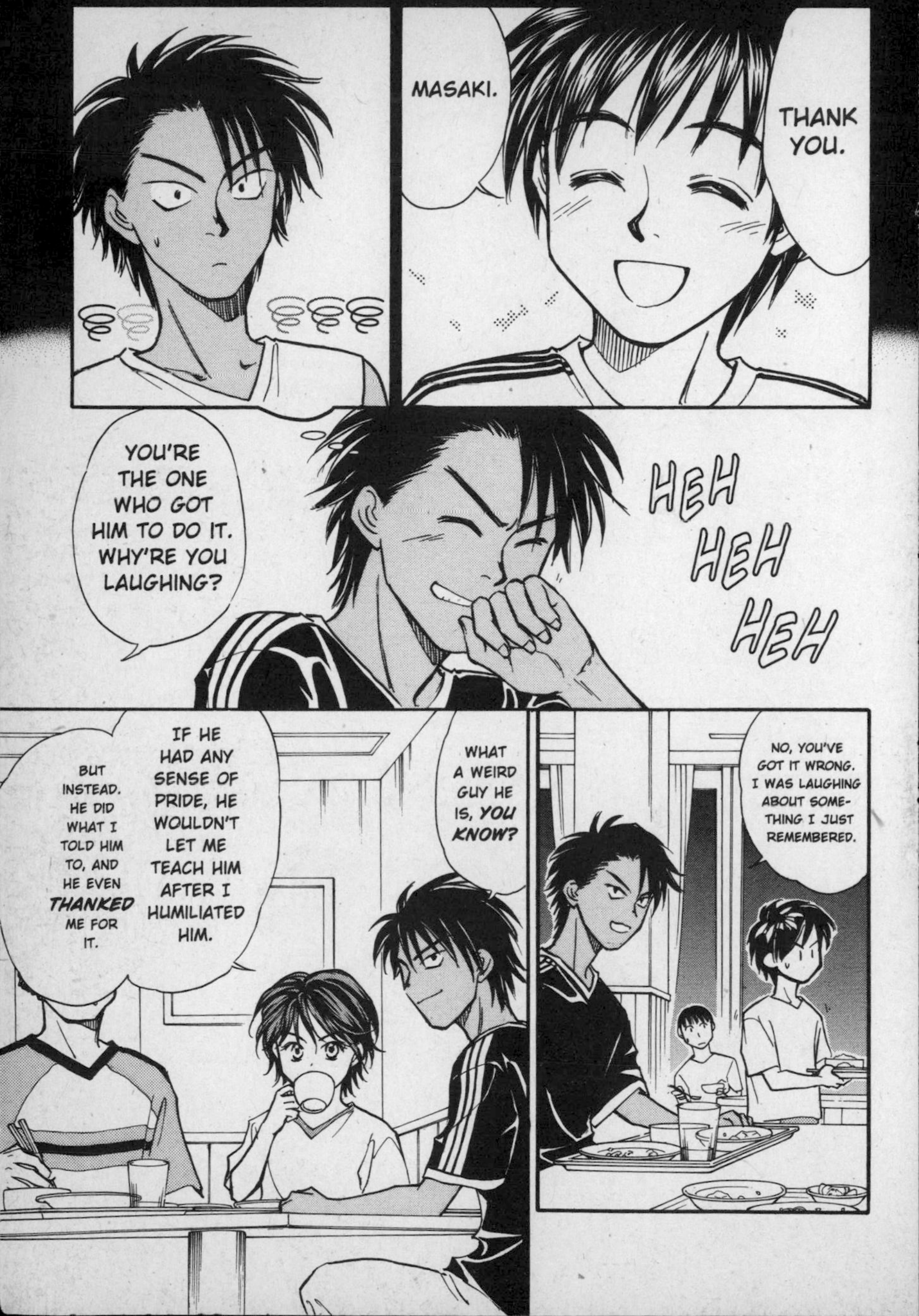
MASAKI.
THANK YOU.
HEH HEH HEH
YOU'RE THE ONE WHO GOT HIM TO DO IT. WHY'RE YOU LAUGHING?
NO, YOU'VE GOT IT WRONG. I WAS LAUGHING ABOUT SOMETHING I JUST REMEMBERED.
WHAT A WEIRD GUY HE IS, *YOU KNOW?*
IF HE HAD ANY SENSE OF PRIDE, HE WOULDN'T LET ME TEACH HIM AFTER I HUMILIATED HIM.
BUT INSTEAD. HE DID WHAT I TOLD HIM TO, AND HE EVEN *THANKED* ME FOR IT.

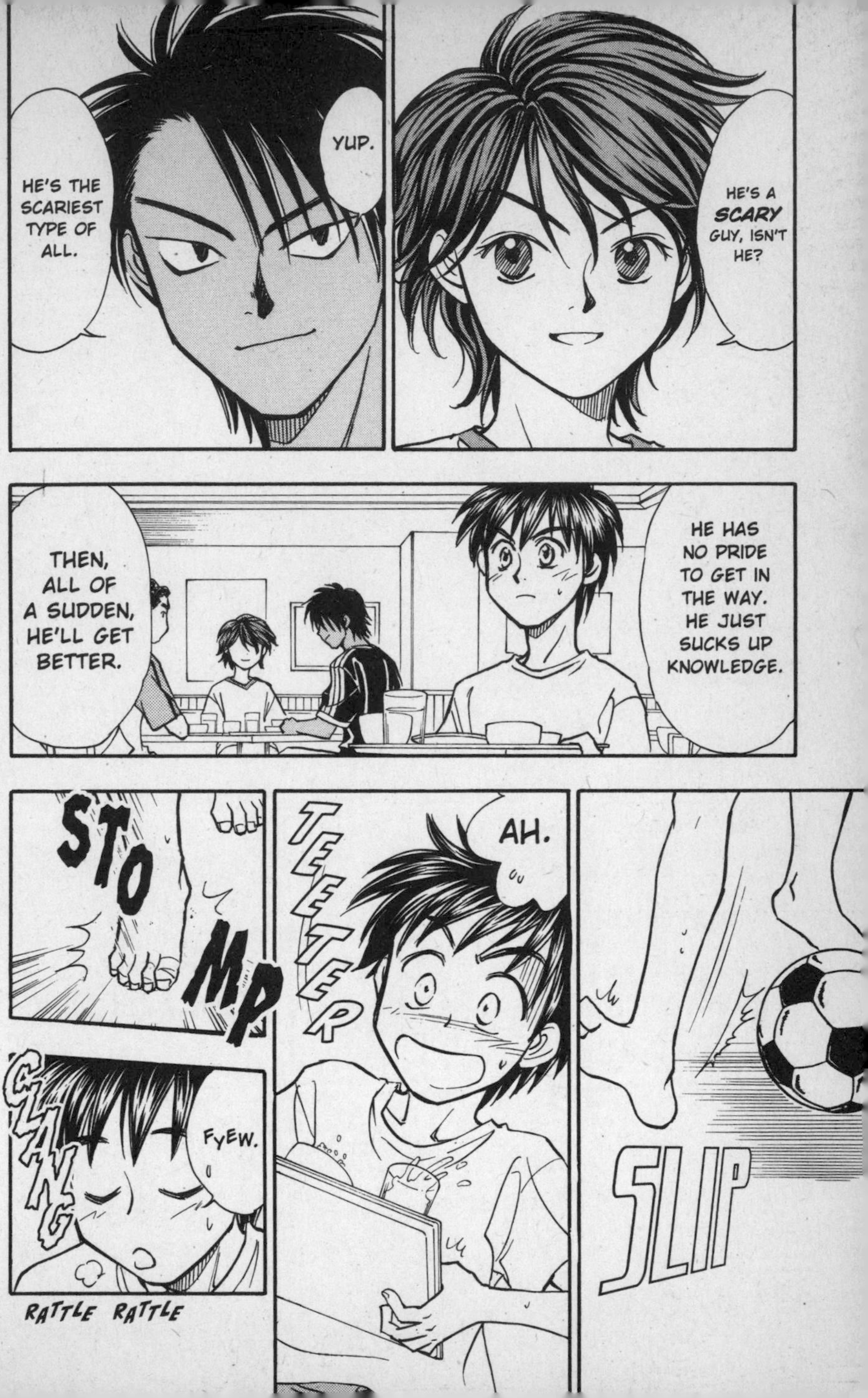
HE'S A SCARY GUY, ISN'T HE?
YUP.
HE'S THE SCARIEST TYPE OF ALL.
HE HAS NO PRIDE TO GET IN THE WAY. HE JUST SUCKS UP KNOWLEDGE.
THEN, ALL OF A SUDDEN, HE'LL GET BETTER.
SLIP
AH.
TEETER
STOMP
CLANG
FYEW.
RATTLE RATTLE

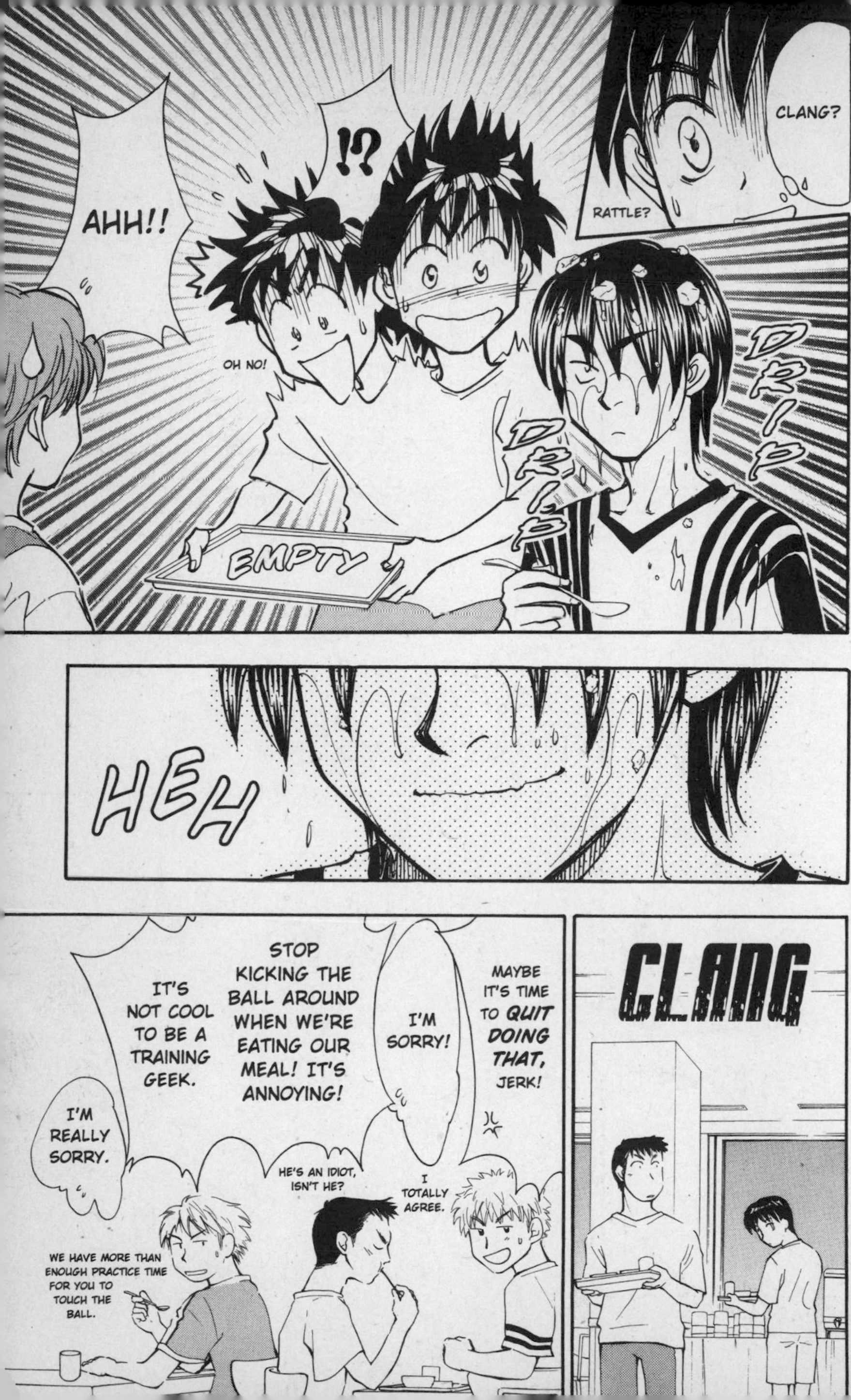
CLANG?
RATTLE?
DRIP
DRIP
!?
AHH!!
OH NO!
EMPTY
HEH
CLANG
MAYBE IT'S TIME TO QUIT DOING THAT, JERK!
I'M SORRY!
STOP KICKING THE BALL AROUND WHEN WE'RE EATING OUR MEAL! IT'S ANNOYING!
IT'S NOT COOL TO BE A TRAINING GEEK.
I'M REALLY SORRY.
I TOTALLY AGREE.
HE'S AN IDIOT, ISN'T HE?
WE HAVE MORE THAN ENOUGH PRACTICE TIME FOR YOU TO TOUCH THE BALL.

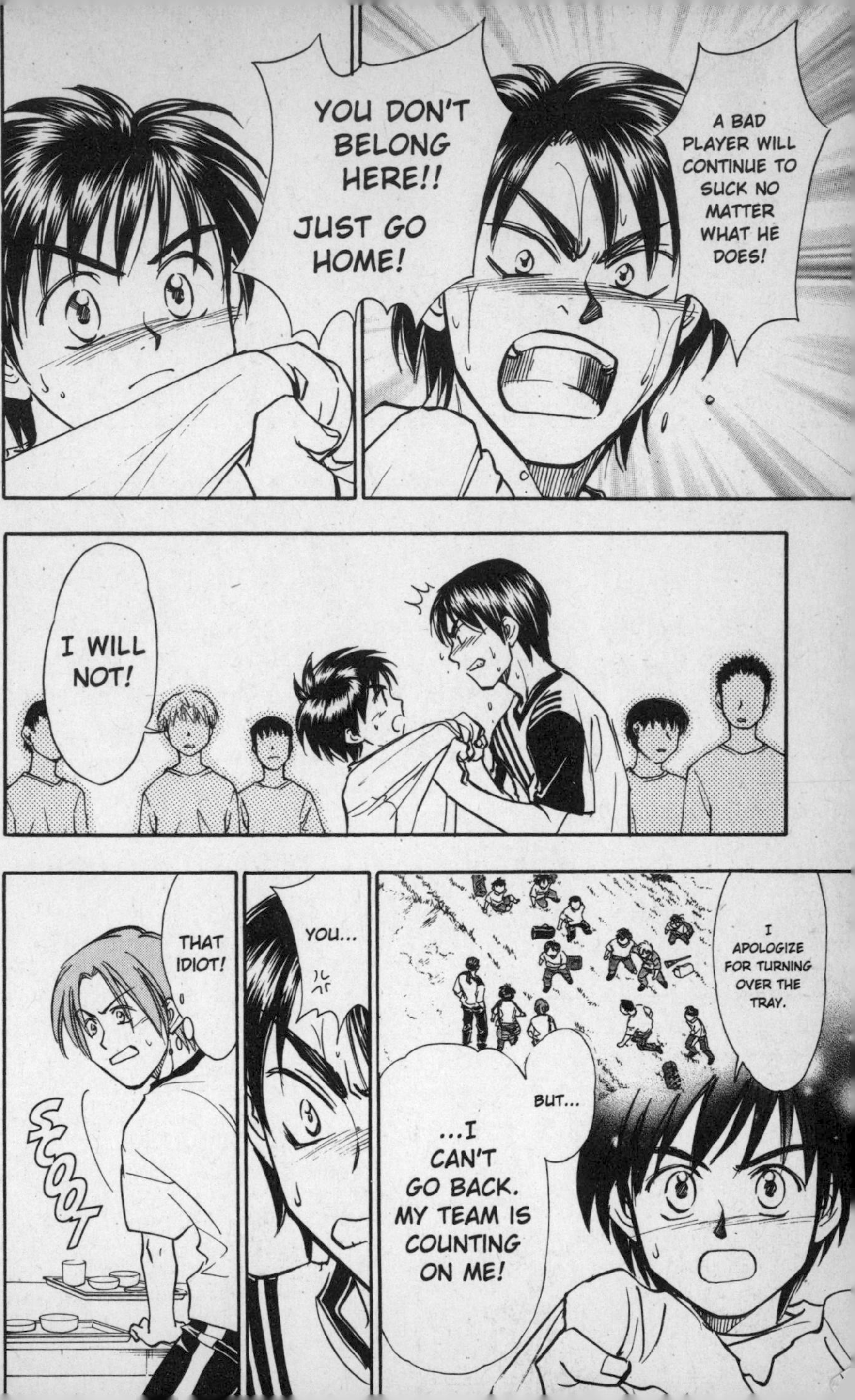
A BAD PLAYER WILL CONTINUE TO SUCK NO MATTER WHAT HE DOES!
YOU DON'T BELONG HERE!!
JUST GO HOME!
I WILL NOT!
I APOLOGIZE FOR TURNING OVER THE TRAY.
BUT...
...I CAN'T GO BACK. MY TEAM IS COUNTING ON ME!
YOU...
THAT IDIOT!
SCOOT

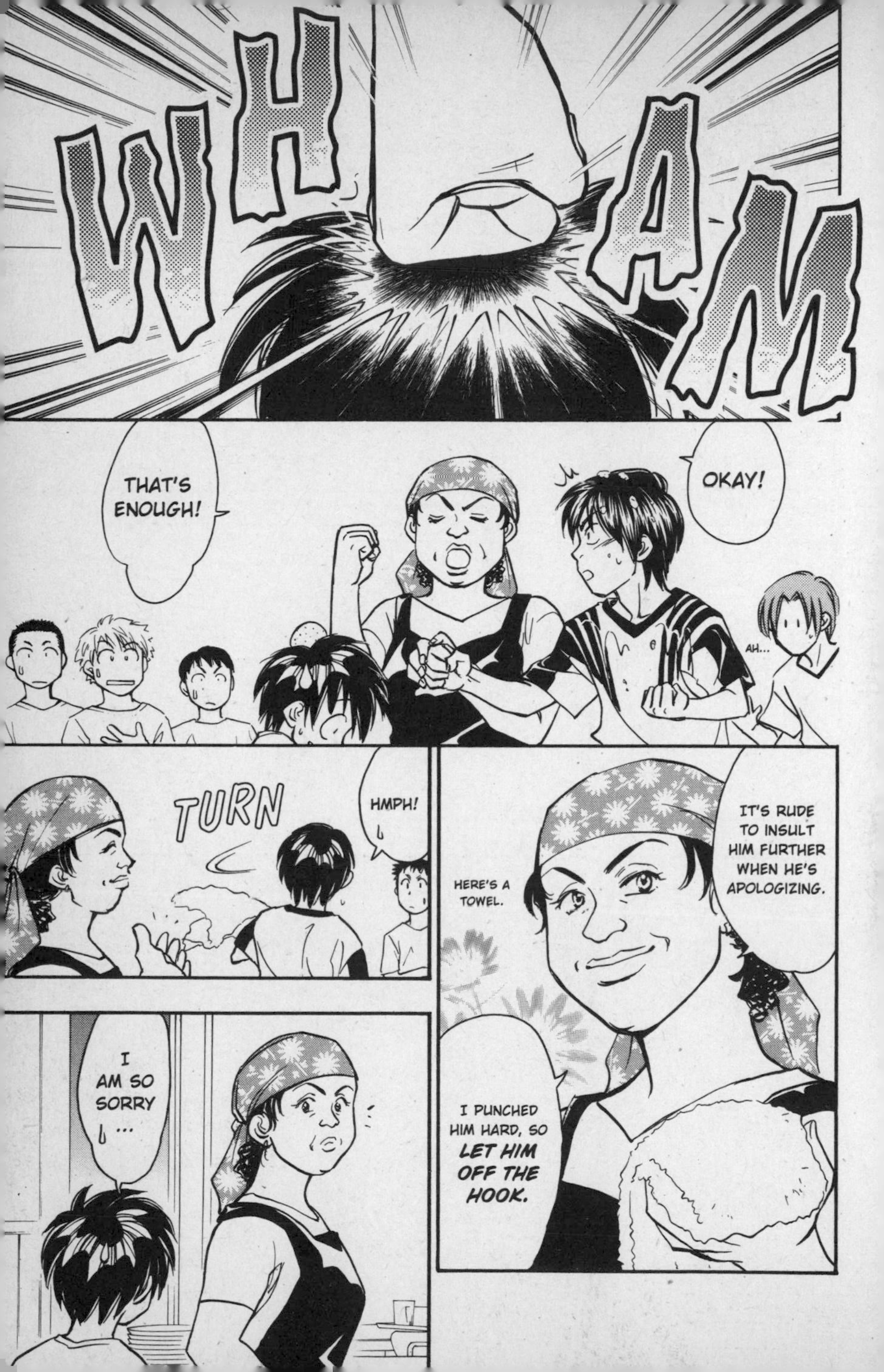
WHAM
OKAY!
THAT'S ENOUGH!
AH...
IT'S RUDE TO INSULT HIM FURTHER WHEN HE'S APOLOGIZING.
HERE'S A TOWEL.
I PUNCHED HIM HARD, SO LET HIM OFF THE HOOK.
HMPH!
TURN
I AM SO SORRY ...

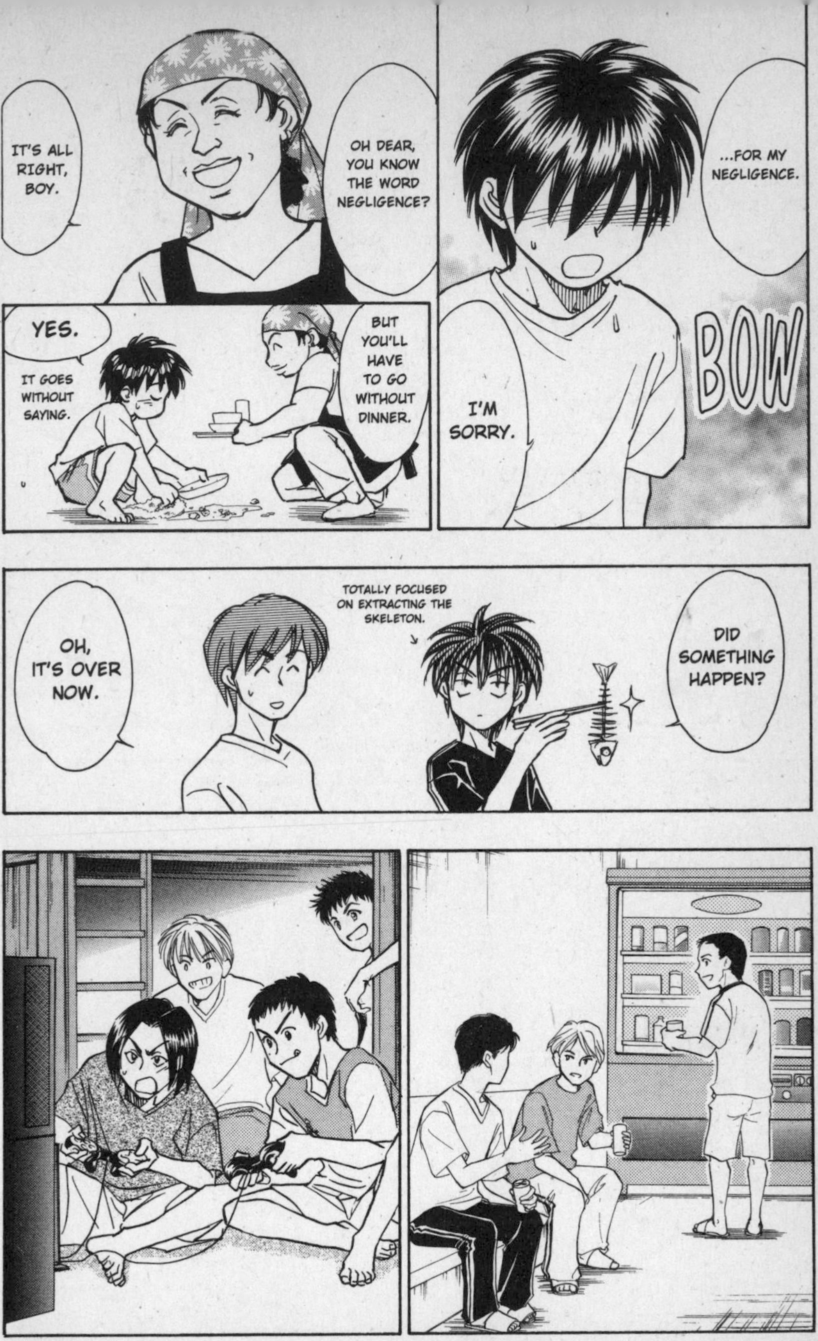
...FOR MY NEGLIGENCE.
I'M SORRY.
BOW
OH DEAR, YOU KNOW THE WORD NEGLIGENCE?
IT'S ALL RIGHT, BOY.
BUT YOU'LL HAVE TO GO WITHOUT DINNER.
YES.
IT GOES WITHOUT SAYING.
DID SOMETHING HAPPEN?
TOTALLY FOCUSED ON EXTRACTING THE SKELETON.
OH, IT'S OVER NOW.

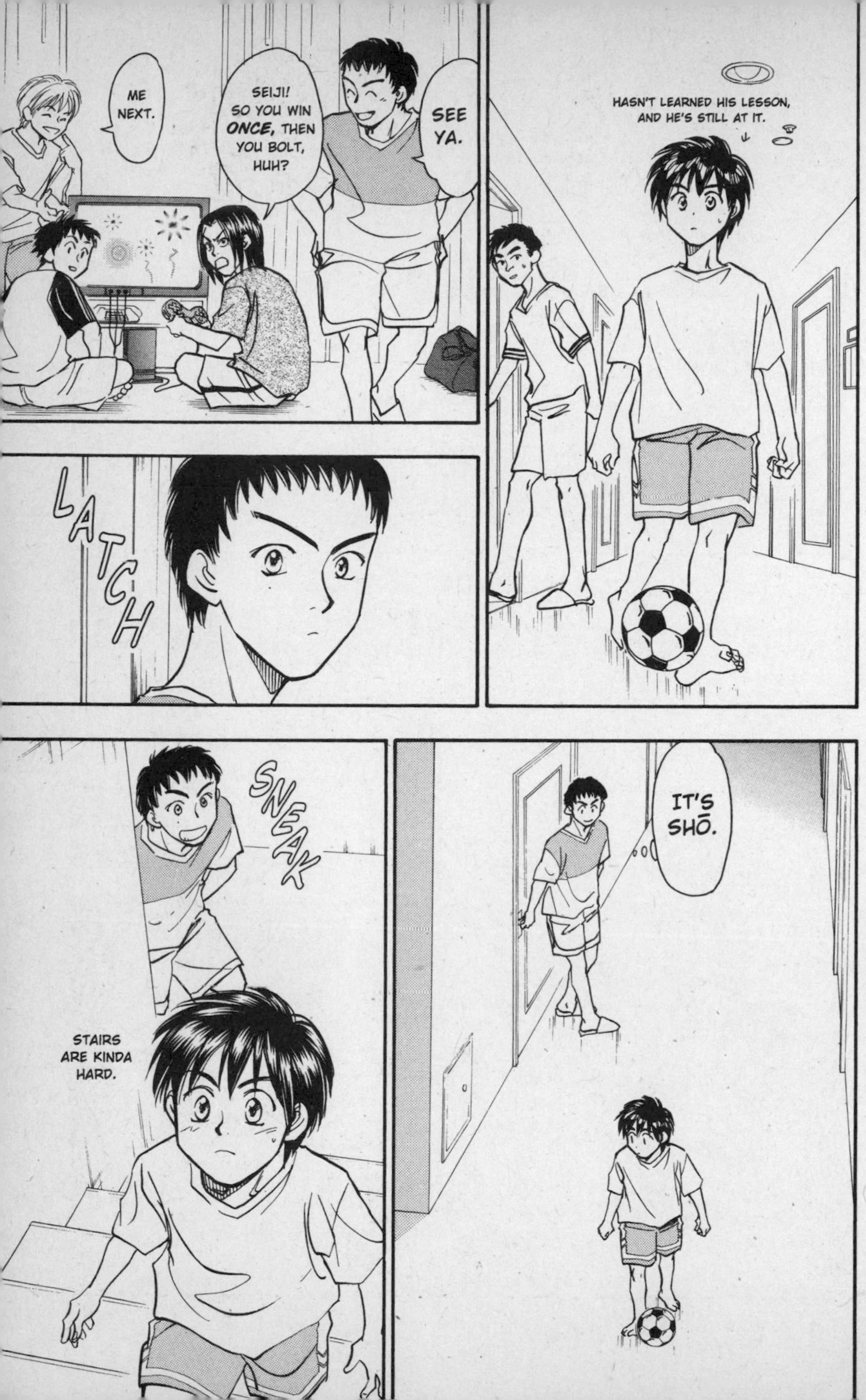
HASN'T LEARNED HIS LESSON, AND HE'S STILL AT IT.
SEE YA.
SEIJI! SO YOU WIN ONCE, THEN YOU BOLT, HUH?
ME NEXT.
LATCH
IT'S SHŌ.
SNEAK
STAIRS ARE KINDA HARD.

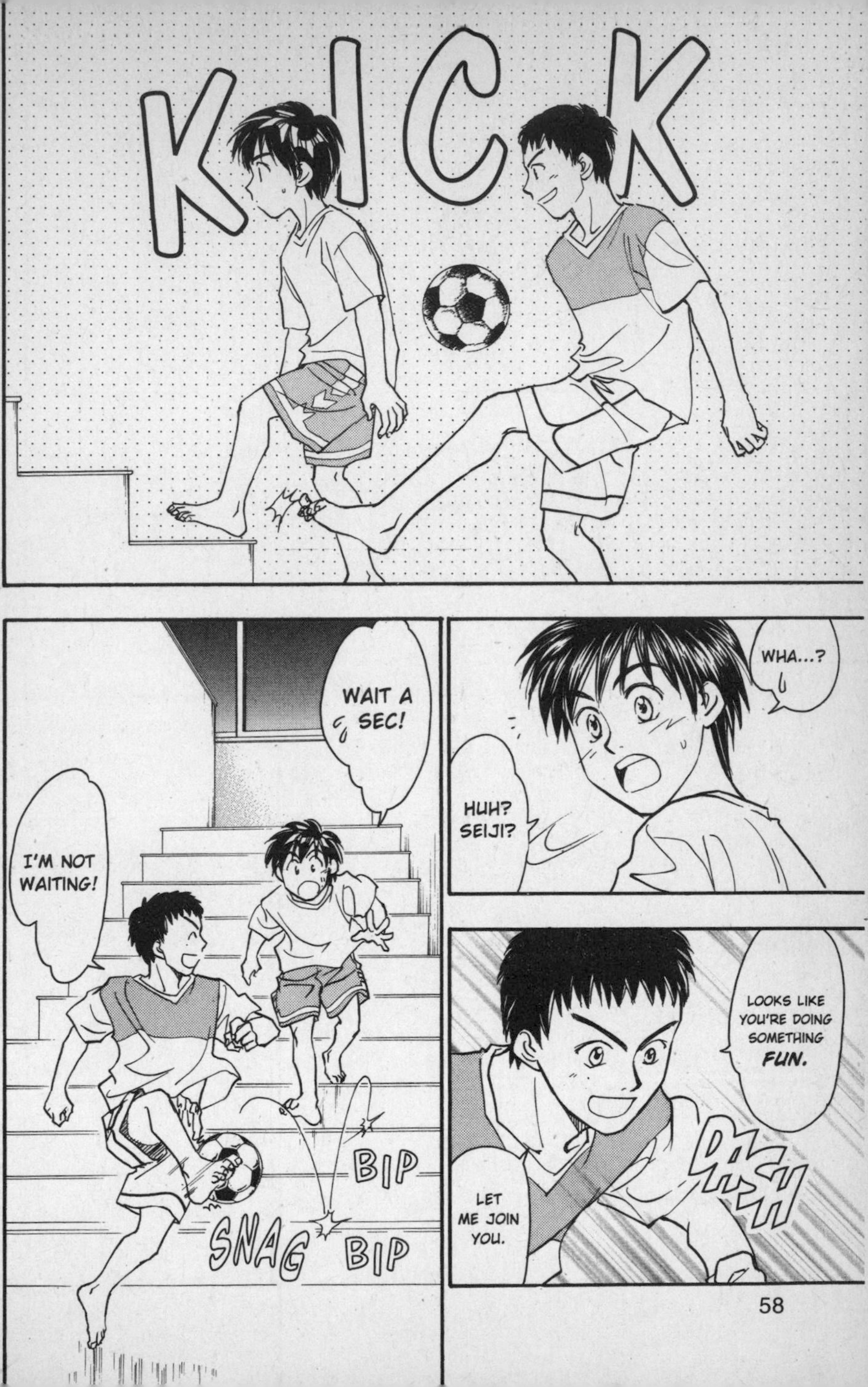
KICK
WHA...?
HUH? SEIJI?
LOOKS LIKE YOU'RE DOING SOMETHING FUN.
DASH
LET ME JOIN YOU.
WAIT A SEC!
I'M NOT WAITING!
BIP
BIP
SNAG

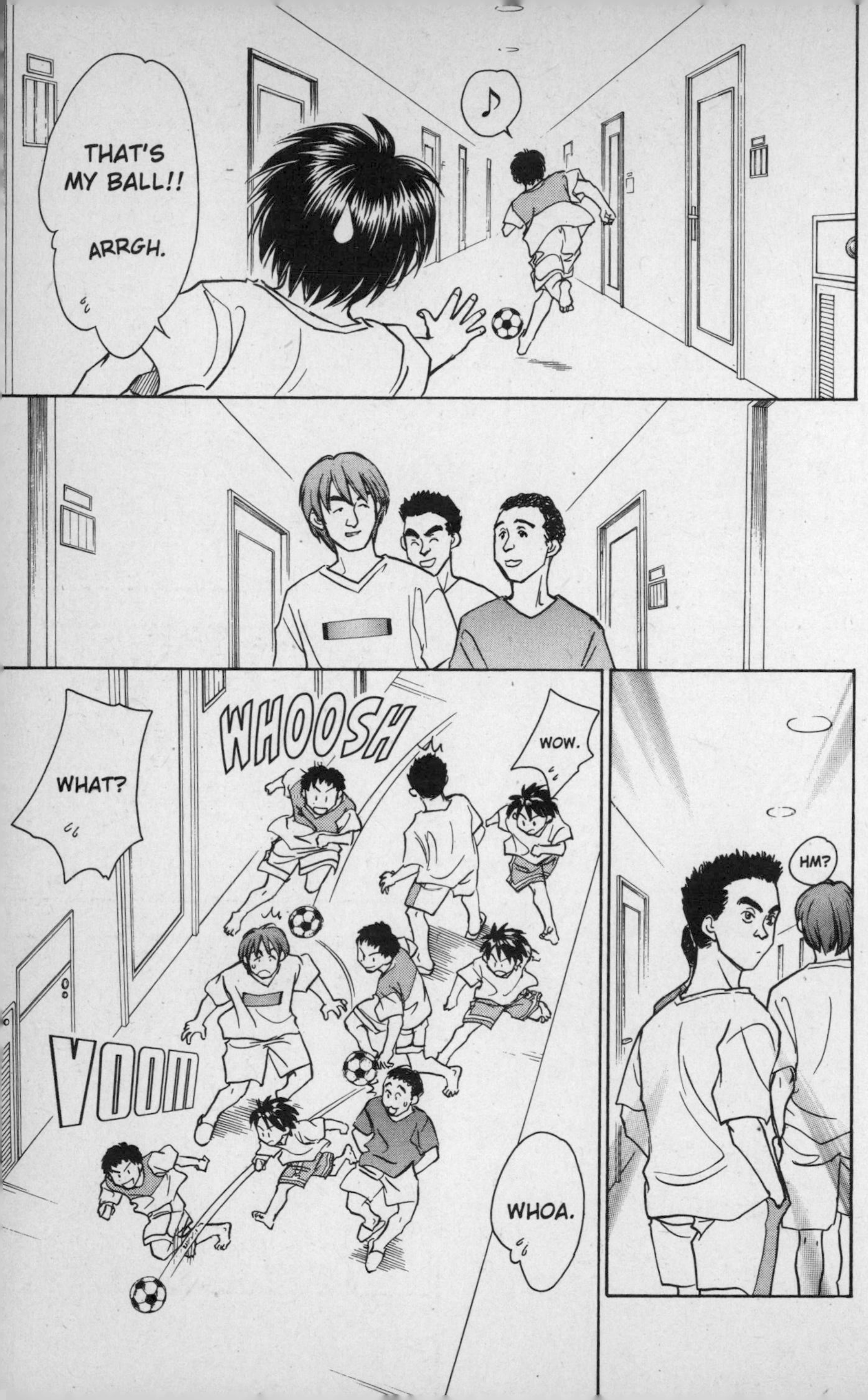
♪
THAT'S MY BALL!!
ARRGH.
HM?
WOW.
WHOOSH
WHAT?
VOOM
WHOA.

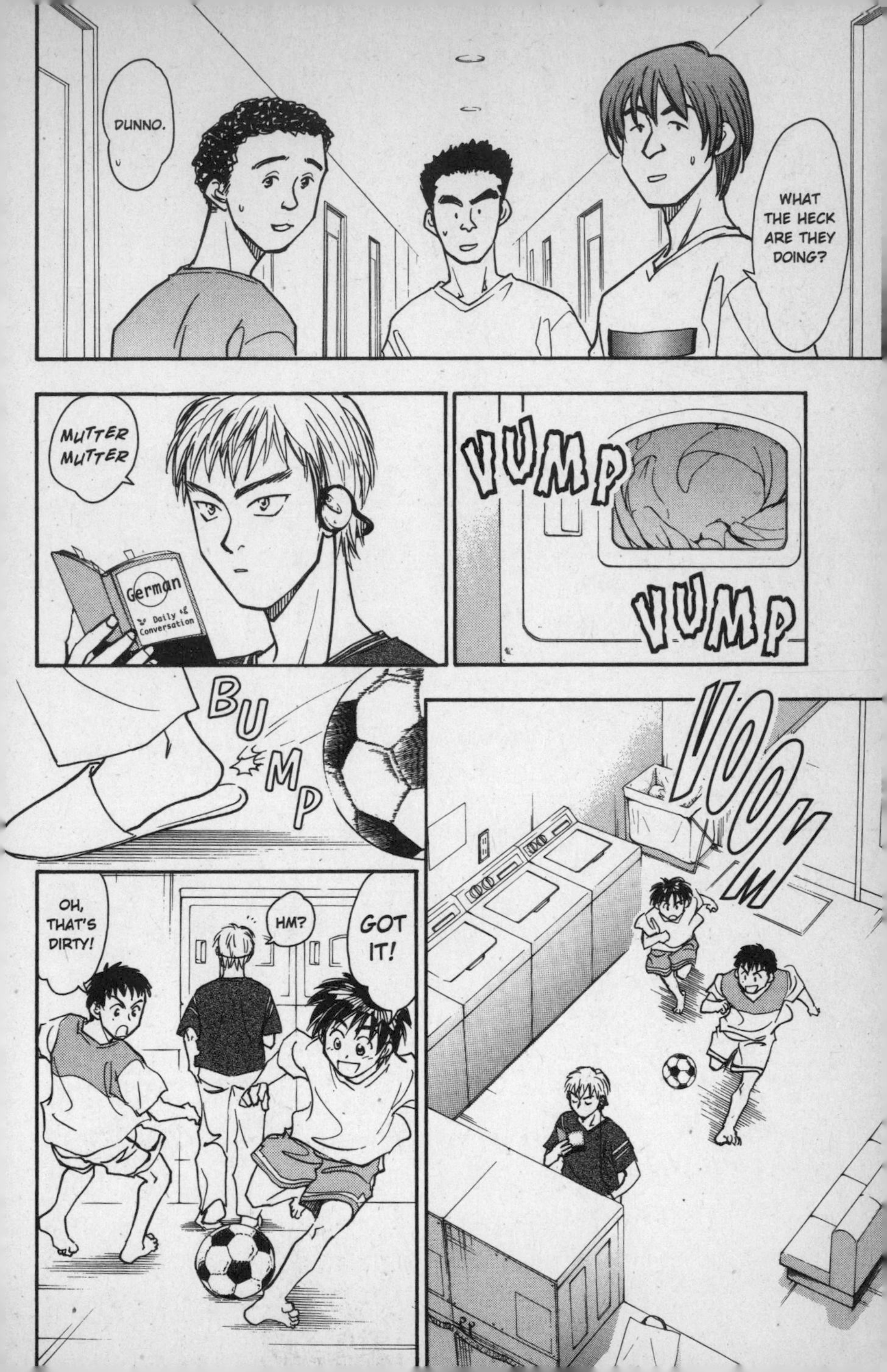

WHAT THE HECK ARE THEY DOING?
DUNNO.
VUMP
VUMP
MUTTER MUTTER
German
Daily Conversation
VOOOM
BUMP
GOT IT!
HM?
OH, THAT'S DIRTY!

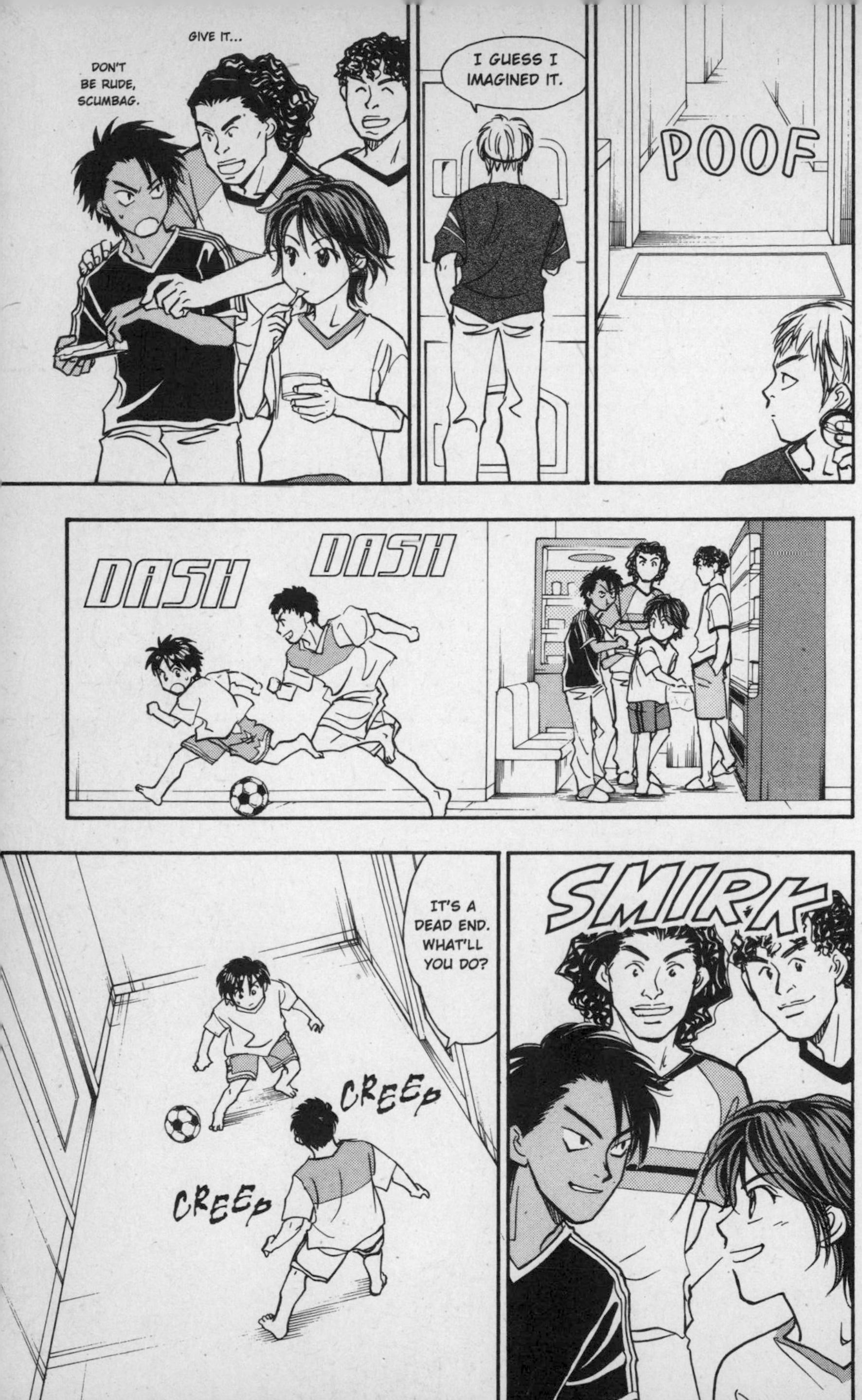
POOF
I GUESS I IMAGINED IT.
GIVE IT...
DON'T BE RUDE, SCUMBAG.
DASH
DASH
SMIRK
IT'S A DEAD END. WHAT'LL YOU DO?
CREEP
CREEP

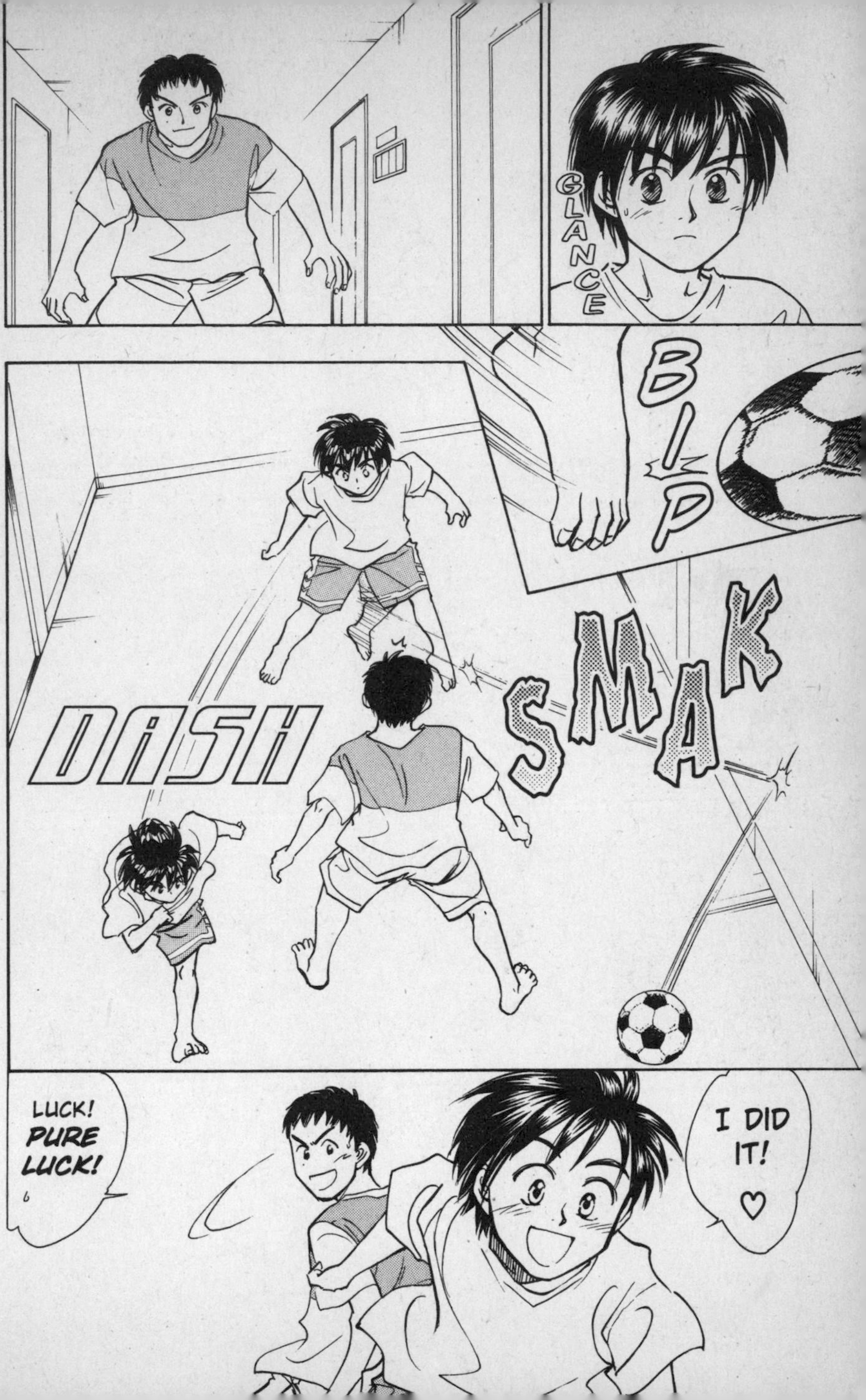
GLANCE
BIP
SMAK
DASH
I DID IT! ♥
LUCK! PURE LUCK!

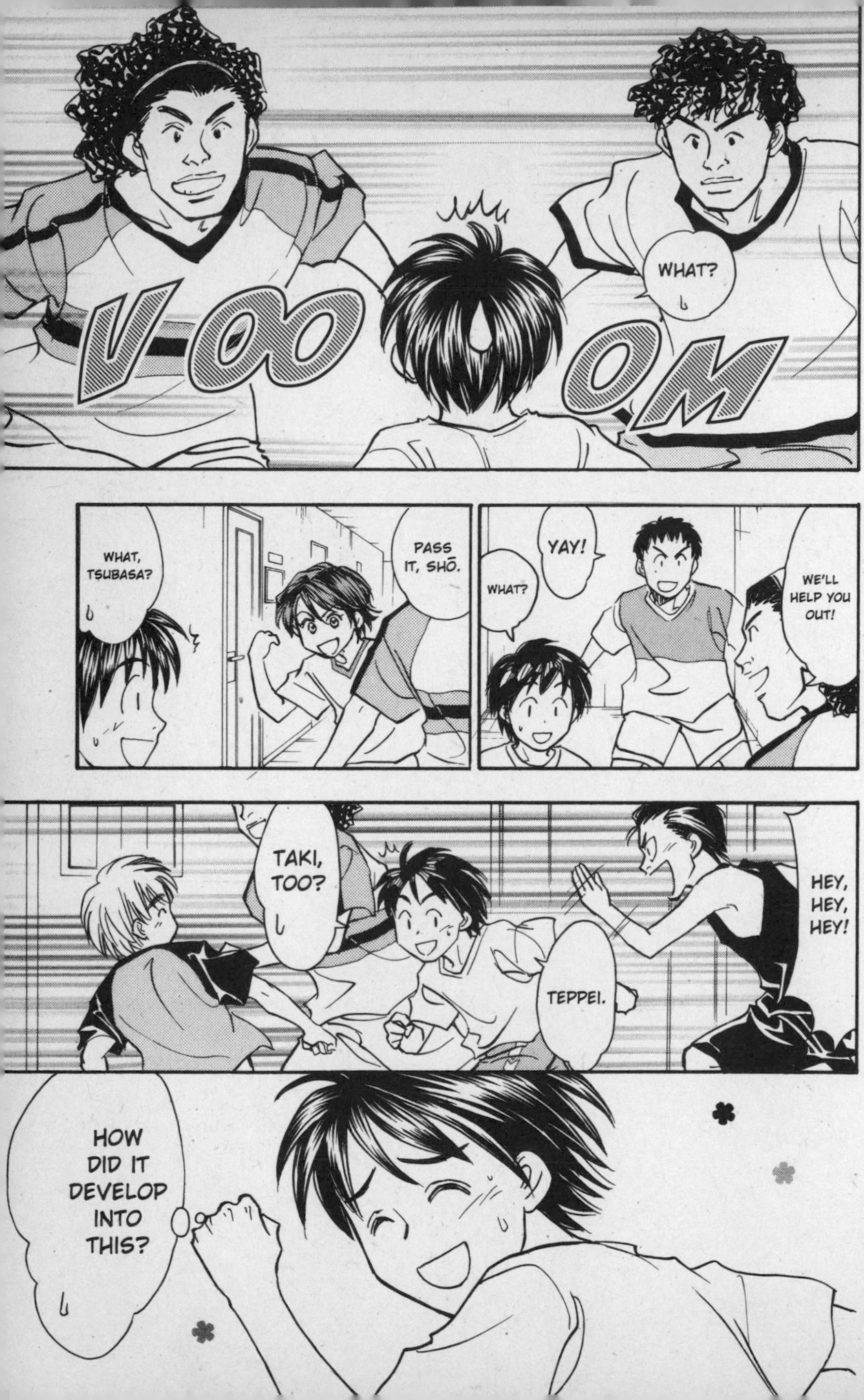
WHAT?
V-OOOM
WE'LL HELP YOU OUT!
YAY!
WHAT?
PASS IT, SHŌ.
WHAT, TSUBASA?
HEY, HEY, HEY!
TEPPEI.
TAKI, TOO?
HOW DID IT DEVELOP INTO THIS?

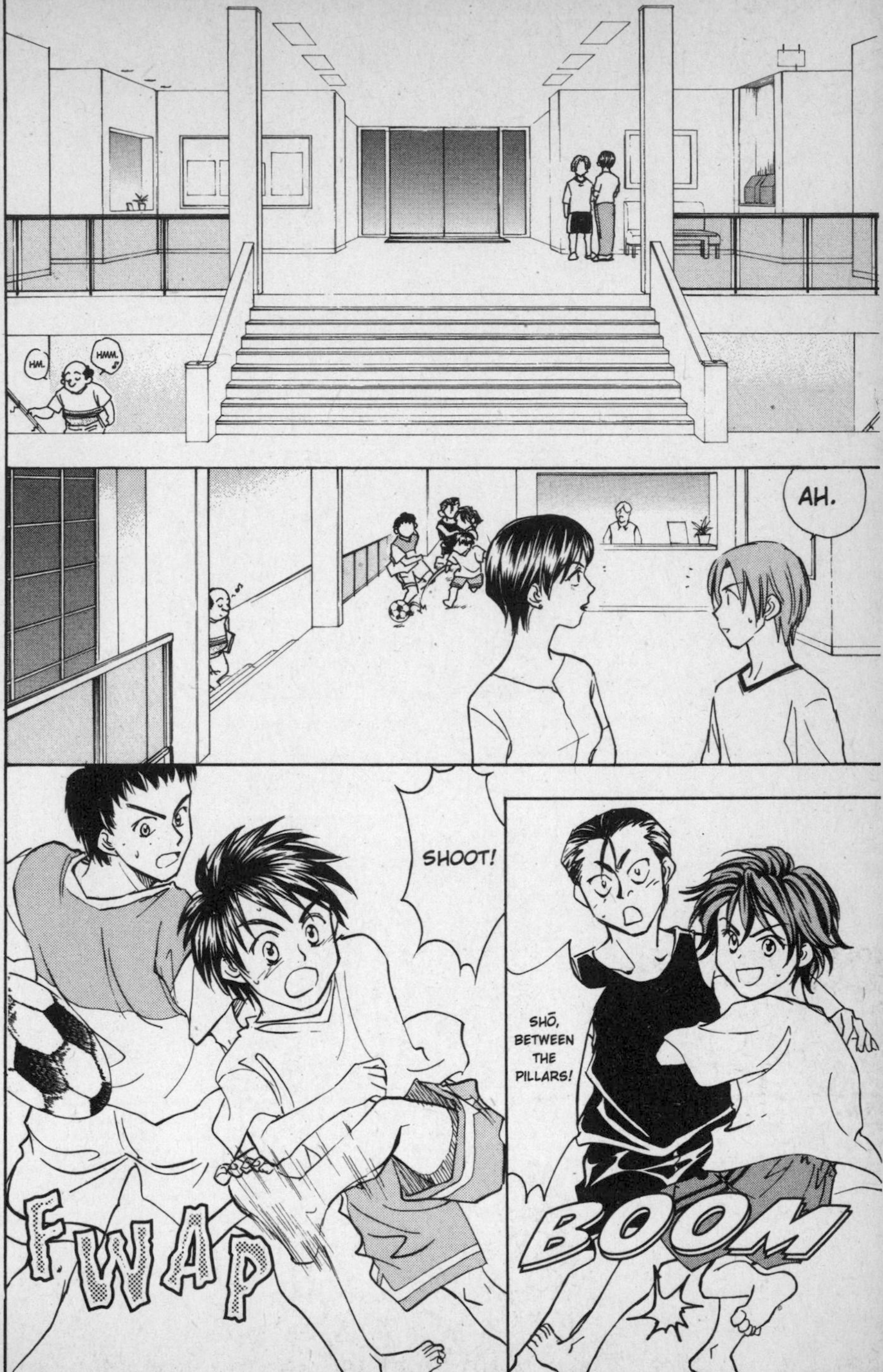
HMM.
HM.
AH.
SHŌ, BETWEEN THE PILLARS!
BOOM
SHOOT!
FWAP

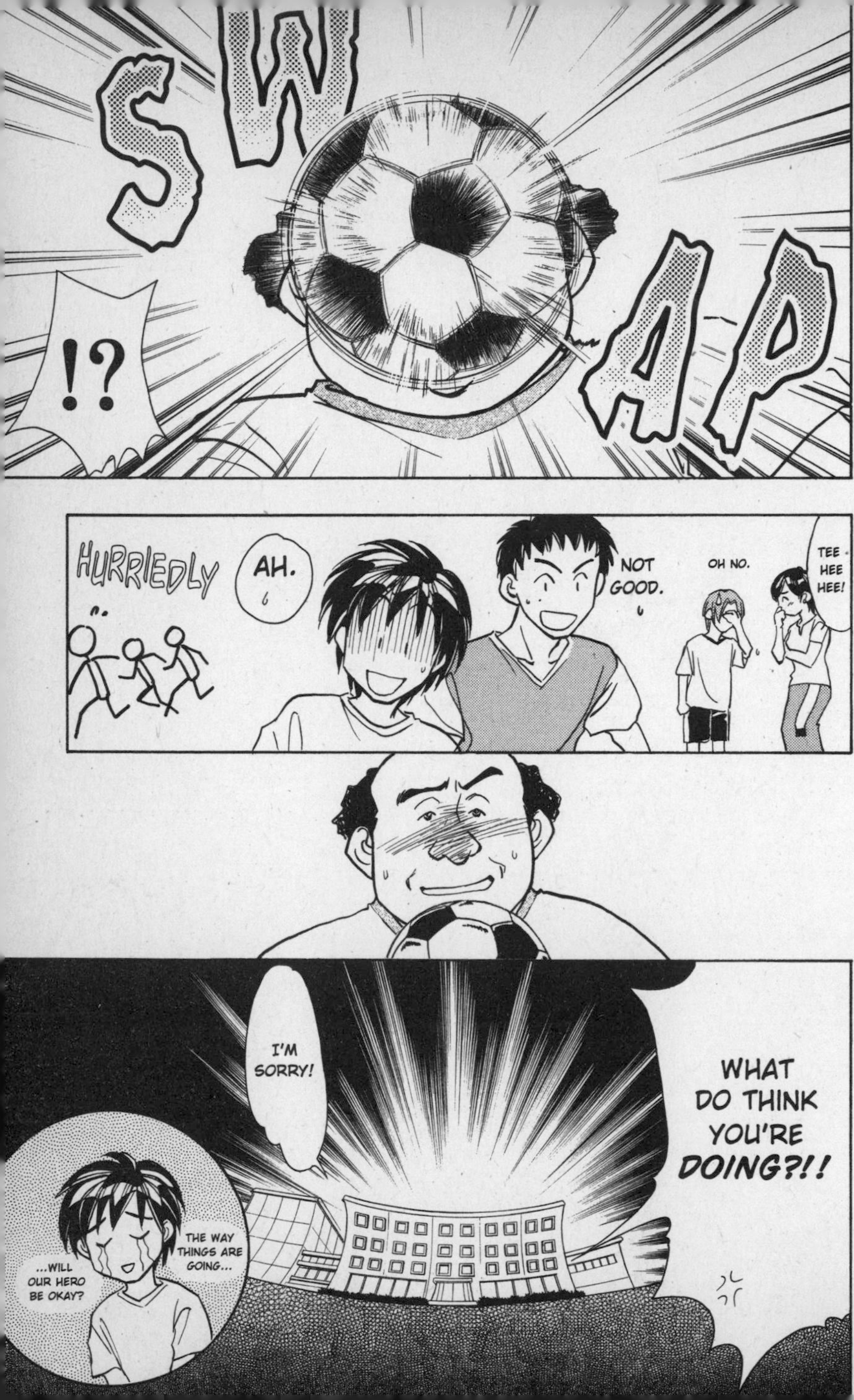
SWAP
!?
TEE HEE HEE!
OH NO.
NOT GOOD.
AH.
HURRIEDLY
WHAT DO THINK YOU'RE DOING?!!
I'M SORRY!
THE WAY THINGS ARE GOING...
...WILL OUR HERO BE OKAY?

WHISTLE! THEATRE!!

MIYUKI IS DRESSED UP A BIT.

MANGA BY SEKI, ASSISTANT S

The Power of Focus
READY.
GO!
CRAK
RATTLE
FWISH
DONG
FWISH
DID SOMETHING HAPPEN?
PERFECT.
OH, IT'S OVER NOW.
WHAT? YOU DIDN'T NOTICE...?

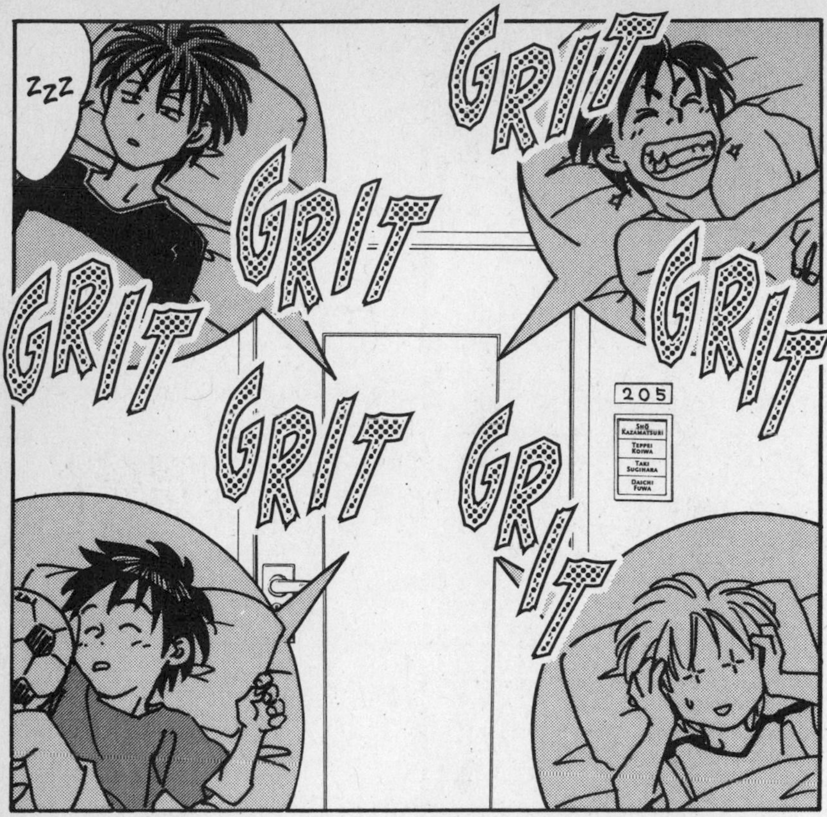
GRIT
GRIT
GRIT
GRIT
GRIT
GRIT
ZZZ
205
SHŌ KAZAMATSURI
TEPPEI KOIWA
TAKI SUGIHARA
DAICHI FUWA

STAGE.111 An Unsettling Feeling

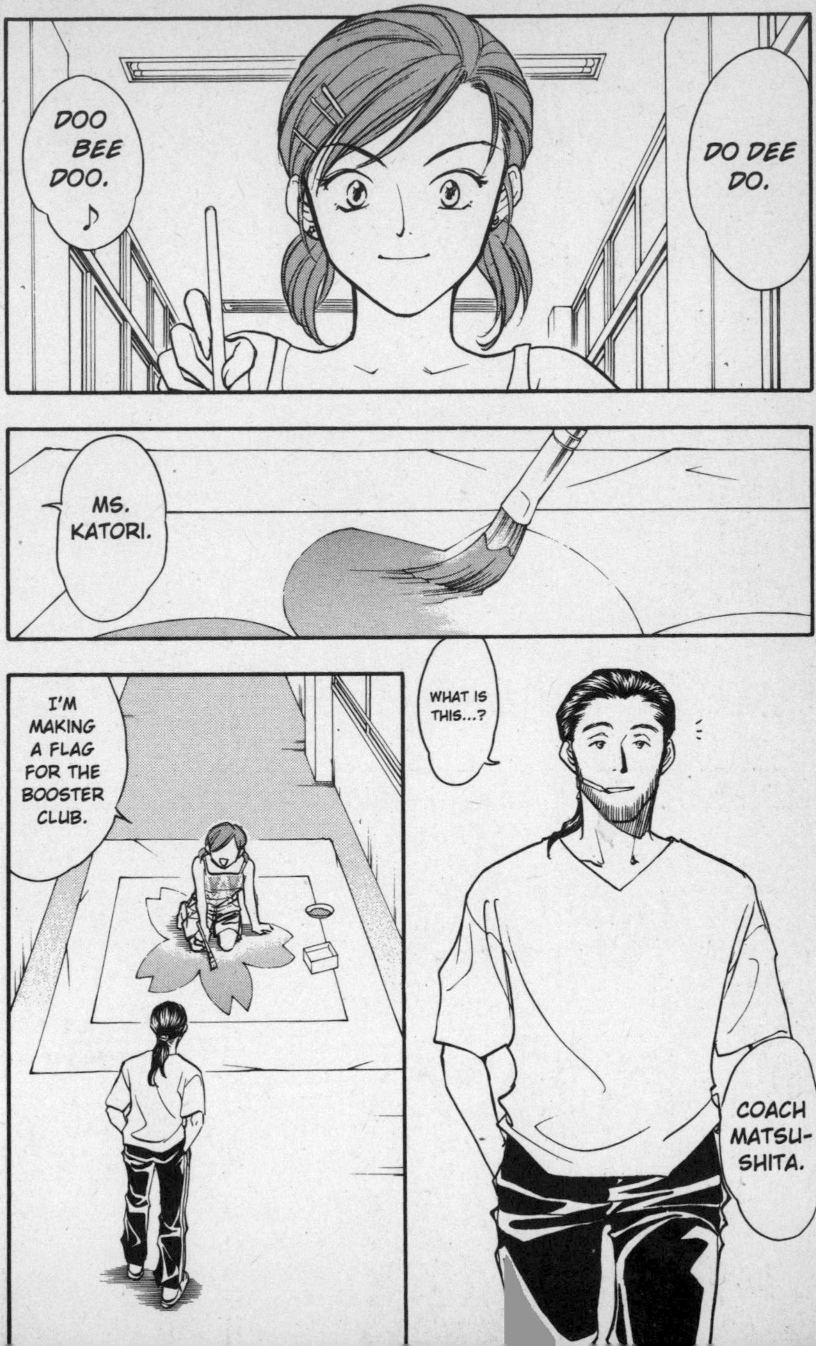
DO DEE DO.
DOO BEE DOO. ♪
MS. KATORI.
WHAT IS THIS...?
COACH MATSU-SHITA.
I'M MAKING A FLAG FOR THE BOOSTER CLUB.

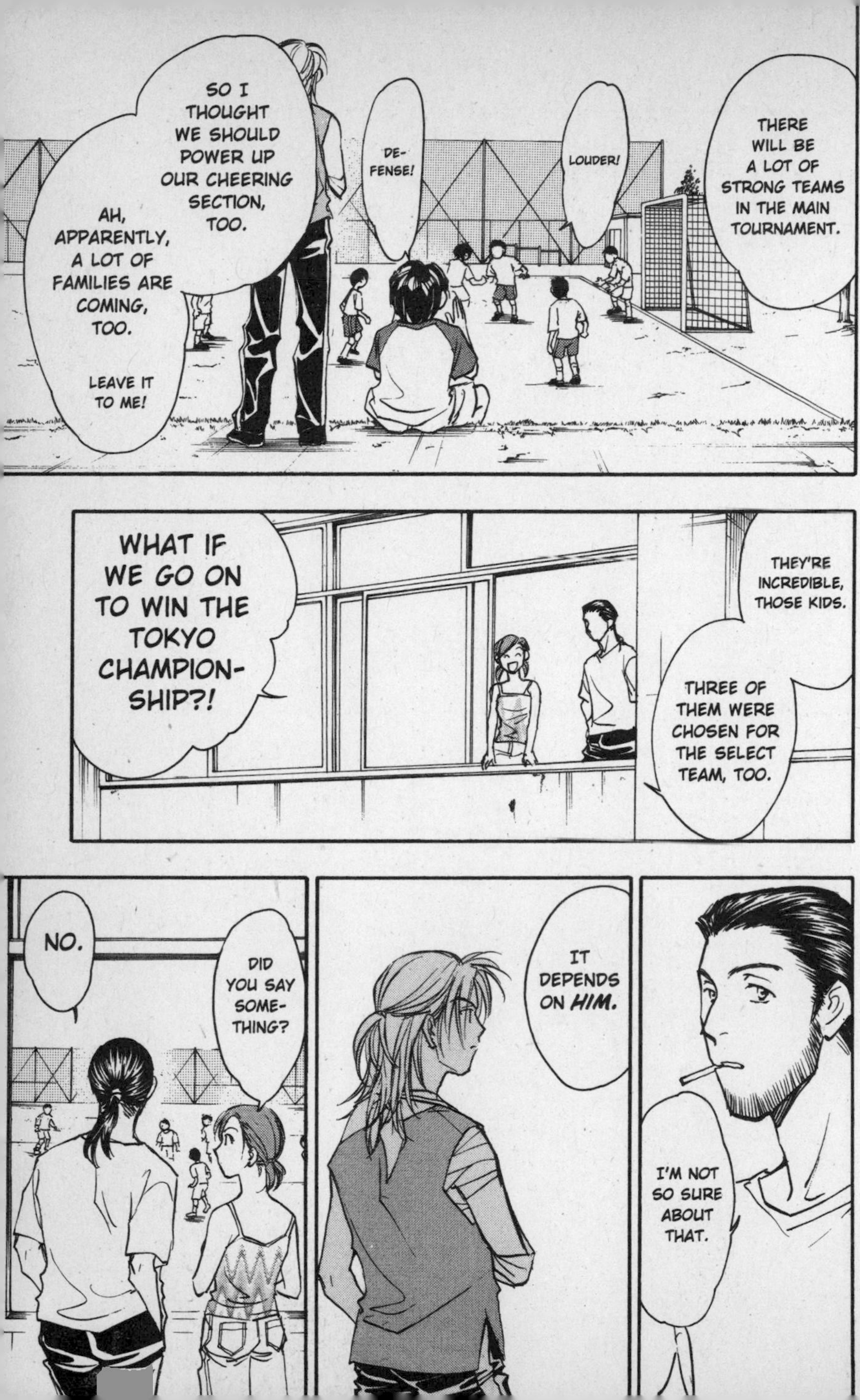
THERE WILL BE A LOT OF STRONG TEAMS IN THE MAIN TOURNAMENT.
LOUDER!
DE-FENSE!
SO I THOUGHT WE SHOULD POWER UP OUR CHEERING SECTION, TOO.
AH, APPARENTLY, A LOT OF FAMILIES ARE COMING, TOO.
LEAVE IT TO ME!
THEY'RE INCREDIBLE, THOSE KIDS.
THREE OF THEM WERE CHOSEN FOR THE SELECT TEAM, TOO.
WHAT IF WE GO ON TO WIN THE TOKYO CHAMPION-SHIP?!
I'M NOT SO SURE ABOUT THAT.
IT DEPENDS ON *HIM*.
DID YOU SAY SOME-THING?
NO.

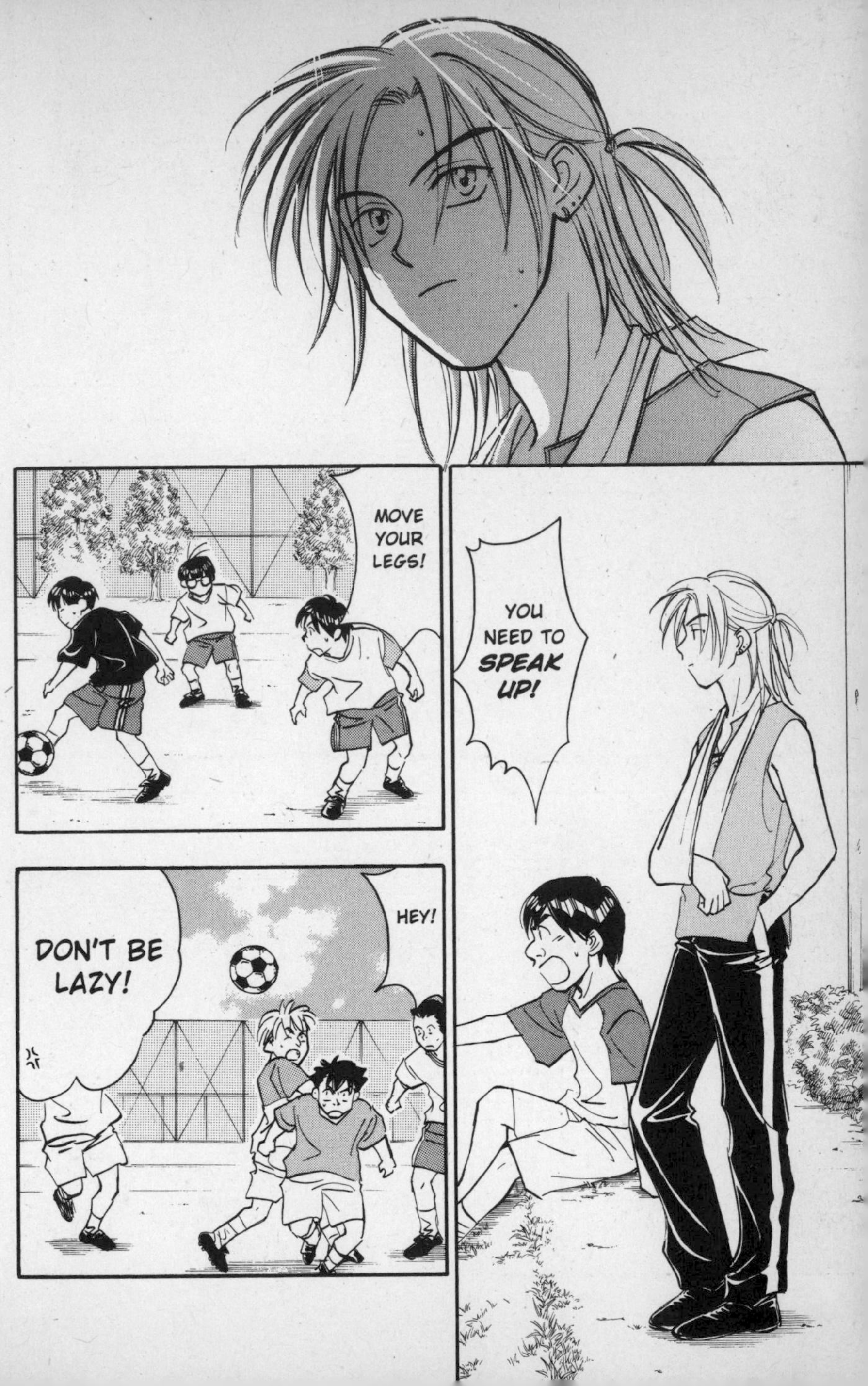
YOU NEED TO SPEAK UP!
MOVE YOUR LEGS!
HEY!
DON'T BE LAZY!

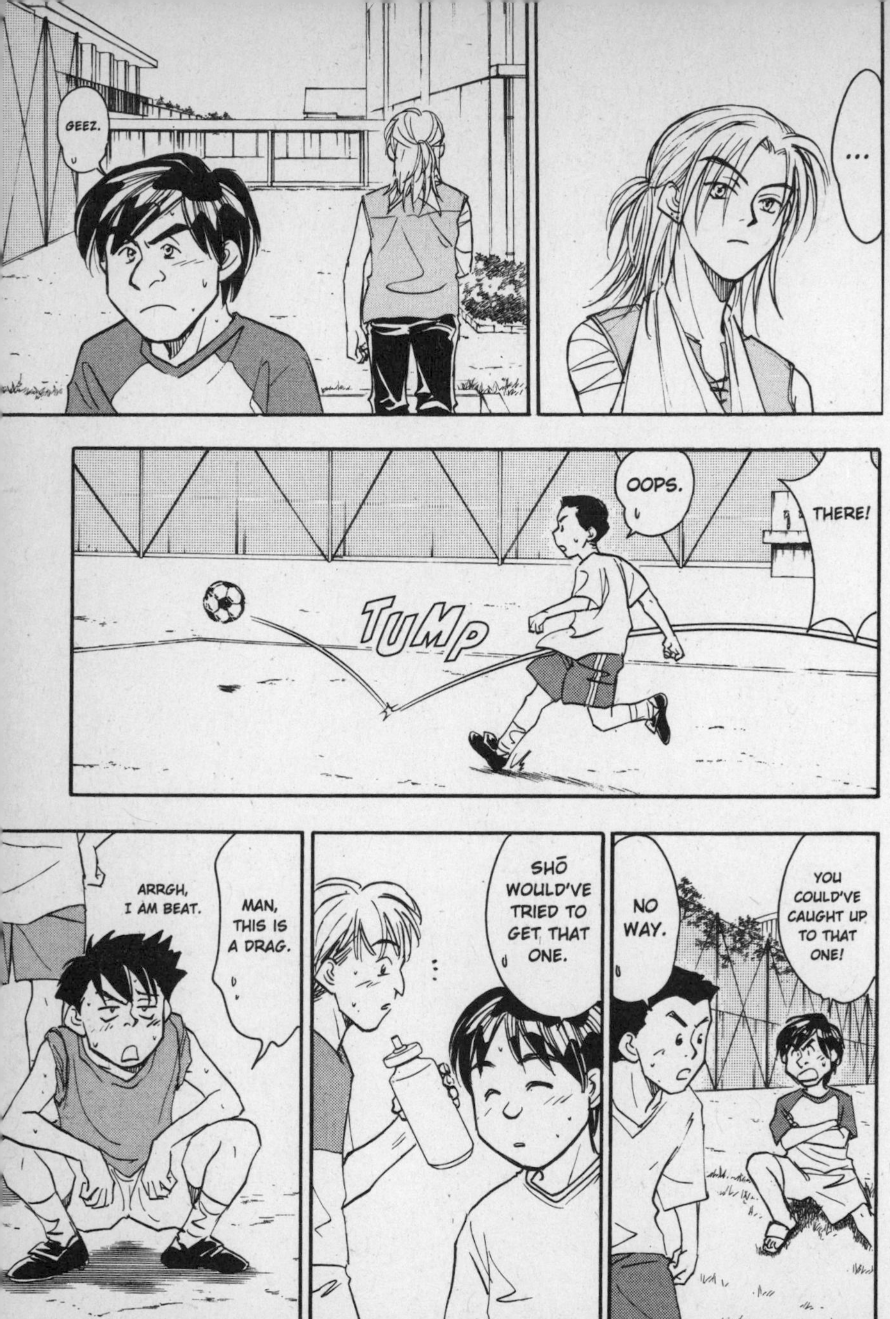
...
GEEZ.
THERE!
OOPS.
TUMP
YOU COULD'VE CAUGHT UP TO THAT ONE!
NO WAY.
SHŌ WOULD'VE TRIED TO GET THAT ONE.
...
MAN, THIS IS A DRAG.
ARRGH, I AM BEAT.

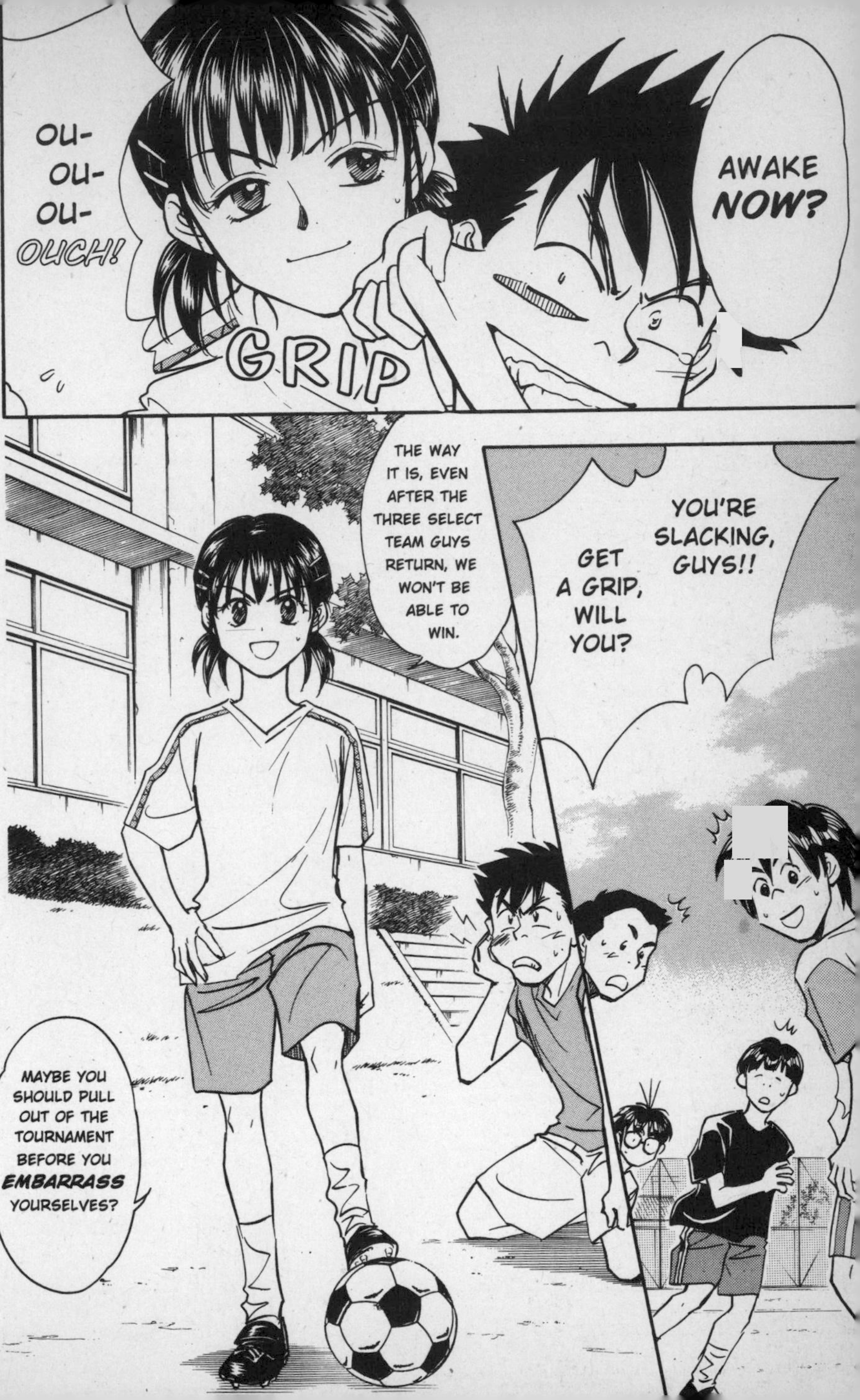
AWAKE NOW?
OU-OU-OU-OUCH!
GRIP
YOU'RE SLACKING, GUYS!!
GET A GRIP, WILL YOU?
THE WAY IT IS, EVEN AFTER THE THREE SELECT TEAM GUYS RETURN, WE WON'T BE ABLE TO WIN.
MAYBE YOU SHOULD PULL OUT OF THE TOURNAMENT BEFORE YOU EMBARRASS YOURSELVES?

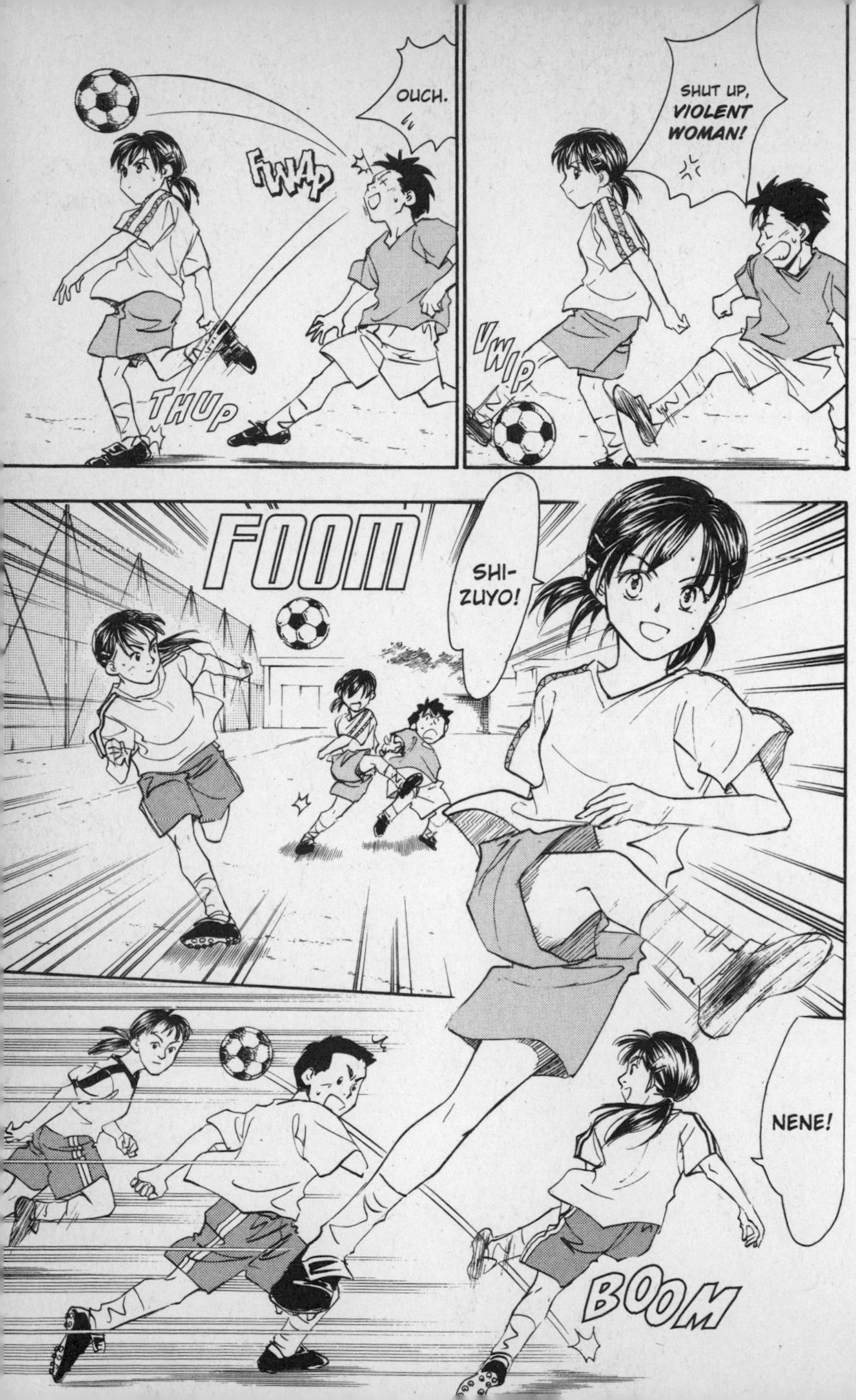
SHUT UP, VIOLENT WOMAN!
VWIP
OUCH.
FWAP
THUP
SHI-ZUYO!
FOOM
NENE!
BOOM

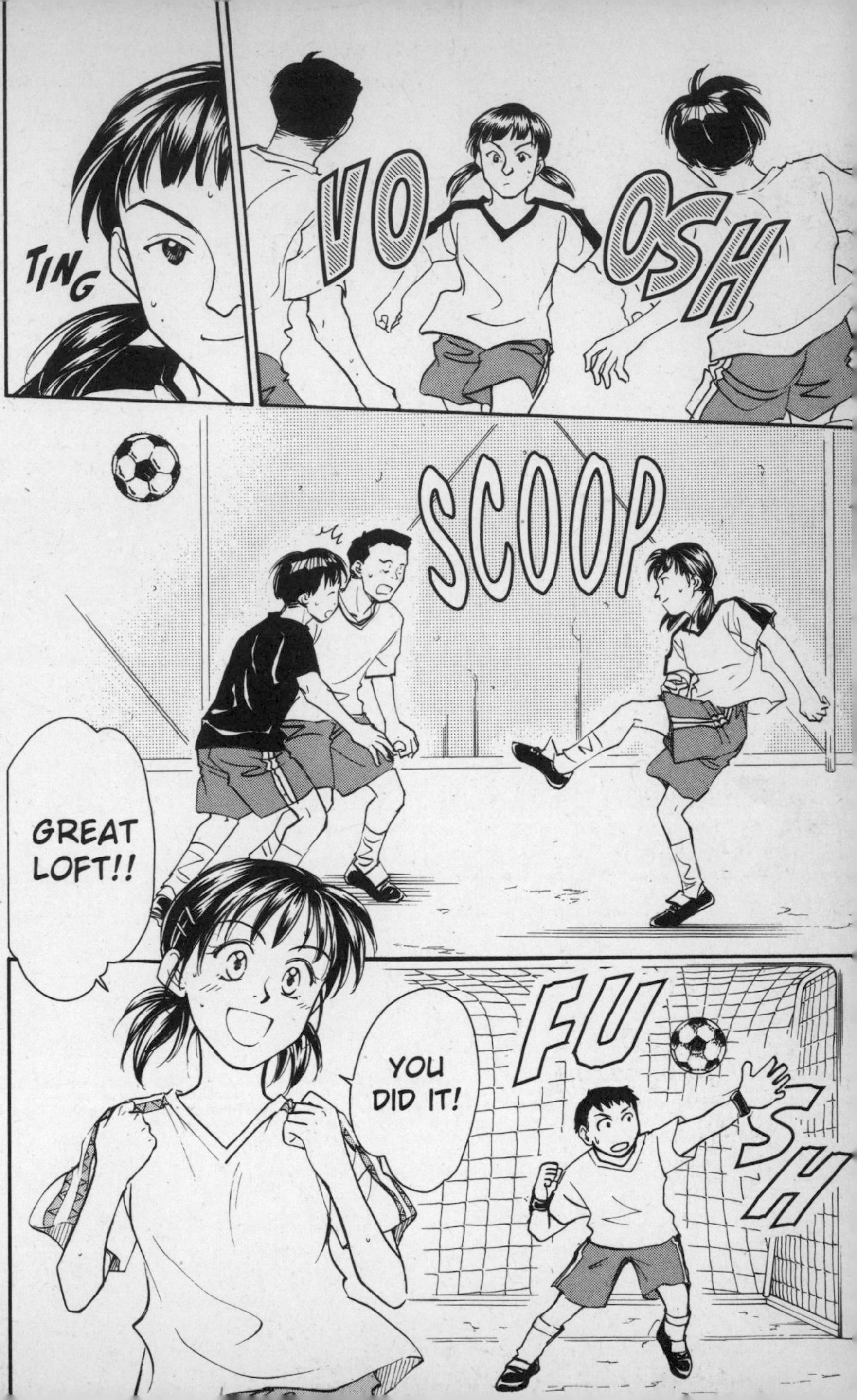
VOOSH
TING
SCOOP
GREAT LOFT!!
FUSH
YOU DID IT!

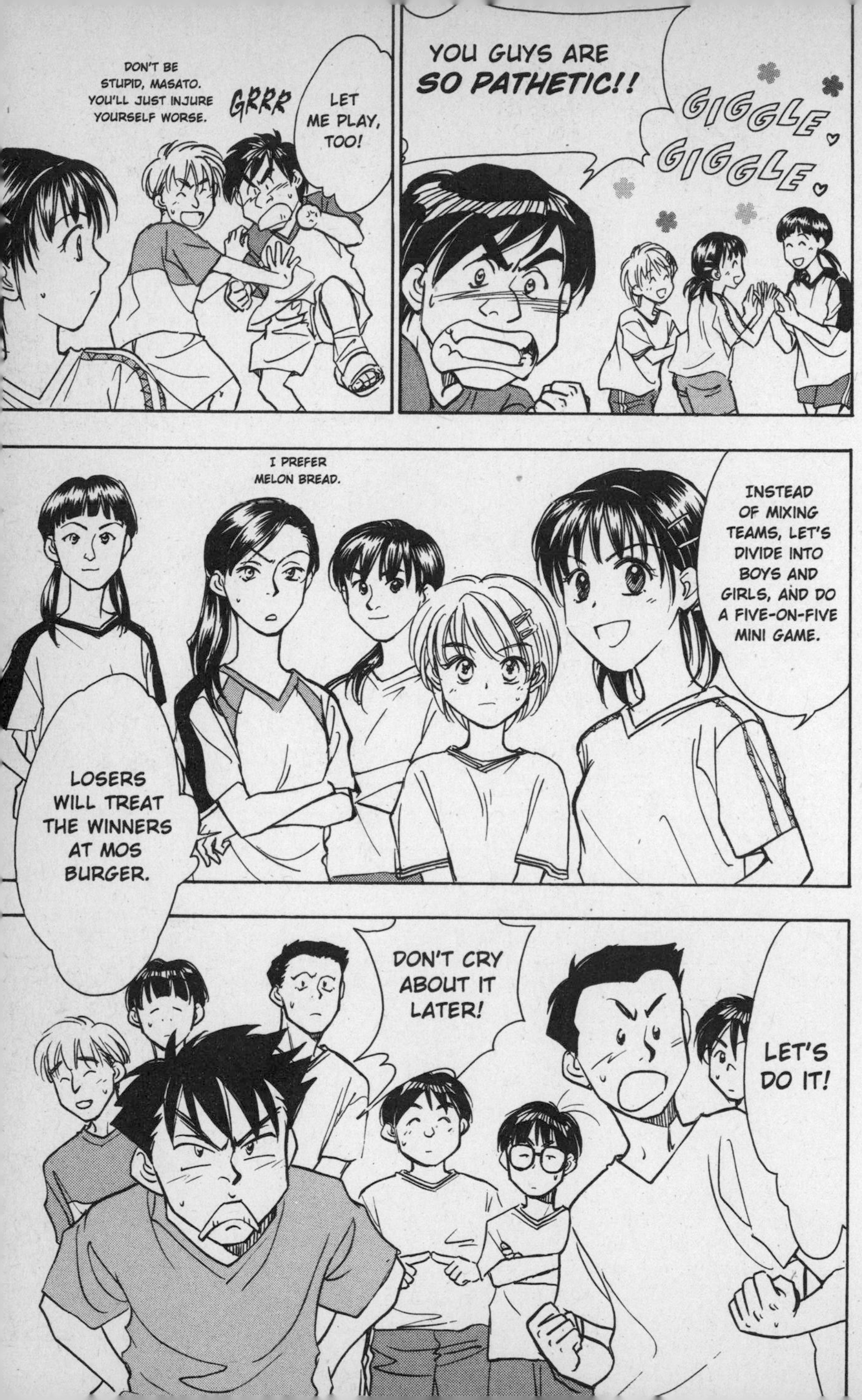
YOU GUYS ARE SO PATHETIC!!
GIGGLE GIGGLE
LET ME PLAY, TOO!
GRRR
DON'T BE STUPID, MASATO. YOU'LL JUST INJURE YOURSELF WORSE.
INSTEAD OF MIXING TEAMS, LET'S DIVIDE INTO BOYS AND GIRLS, AND DO A FIVE-ON-FIVE MINI GAME.
I PREFER MELON BREAD.
LOSERS WILL TREAT THE WINNERS AT MOS BURGER.
LET'S DO IT!
DON'T CRY ABOUT IT LATER!

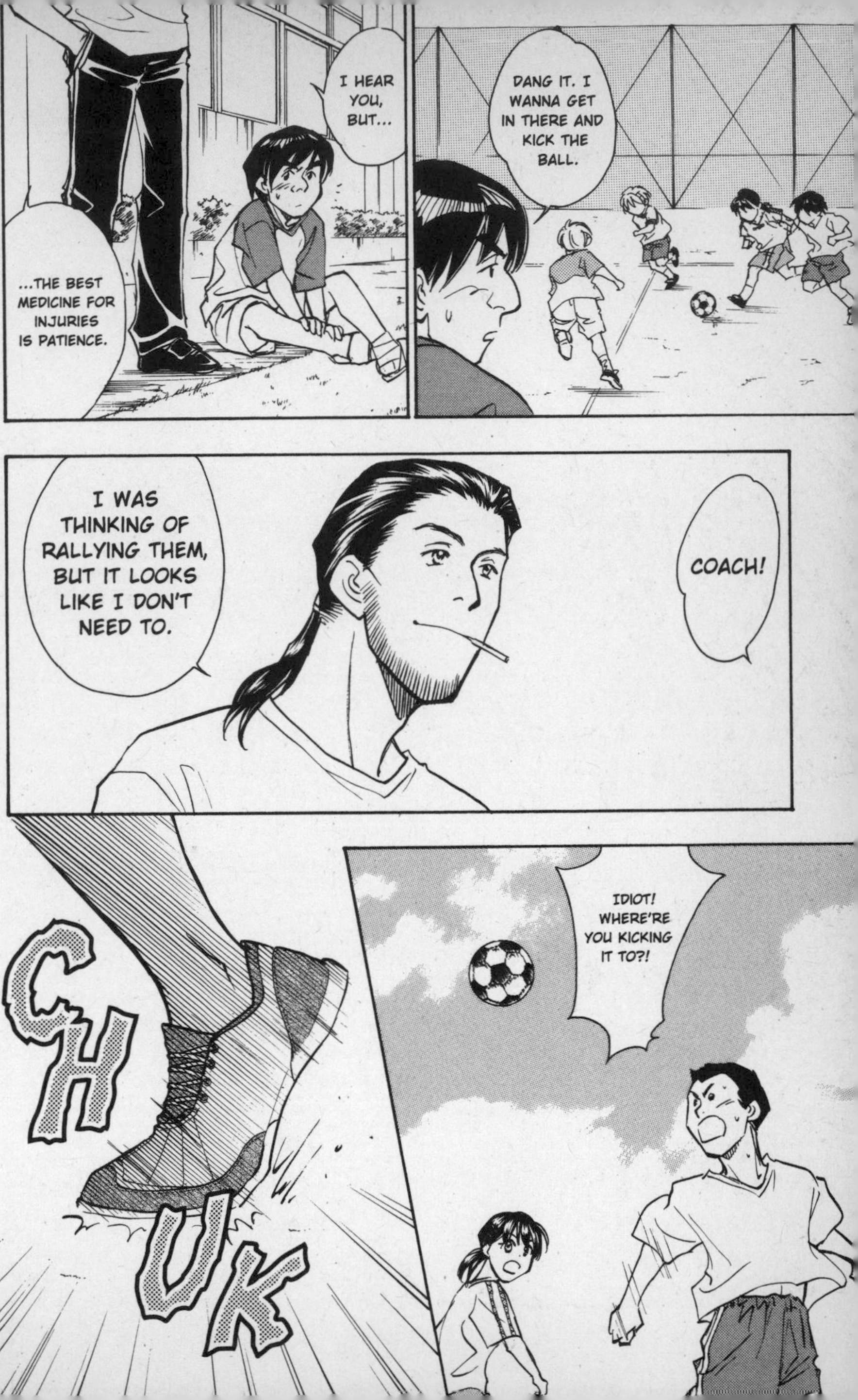
DANG IT. I WANNA GET IN THERE AND KICK THE BALL.
I HEAR YOU, BUT...
...THE BEST MEDICINE FOR INJURIES IS PATIENCE.
COACH!
I WAS THINKING OF RALLYING THEM, BUT IT LOOKS LIKE I DON'T NEED TO.
IDIOT! WHERE'RE YOU KICKING IT TO?!
CHUK

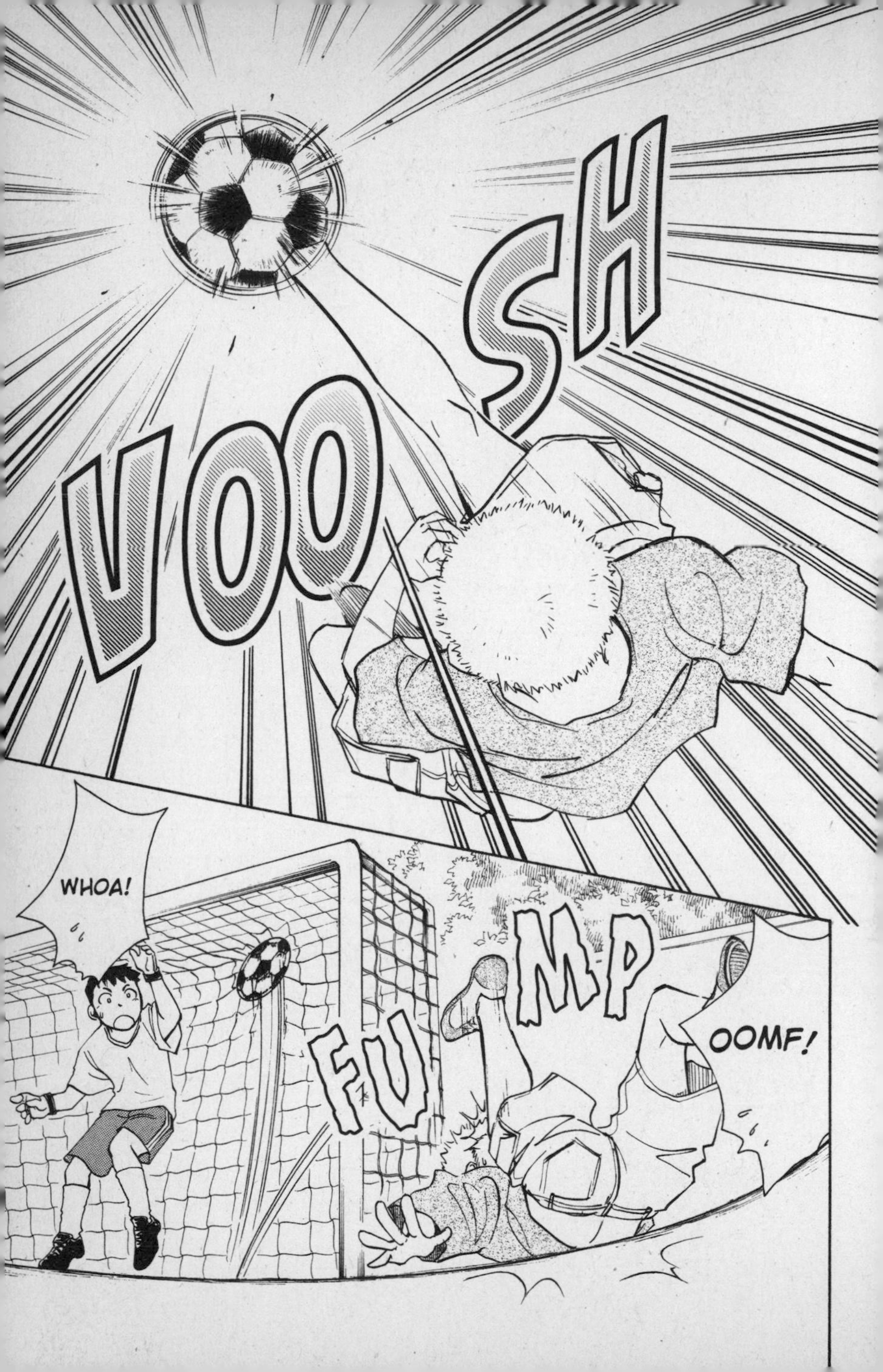
VOOSH
OOMF!
FUMP
WHOA!

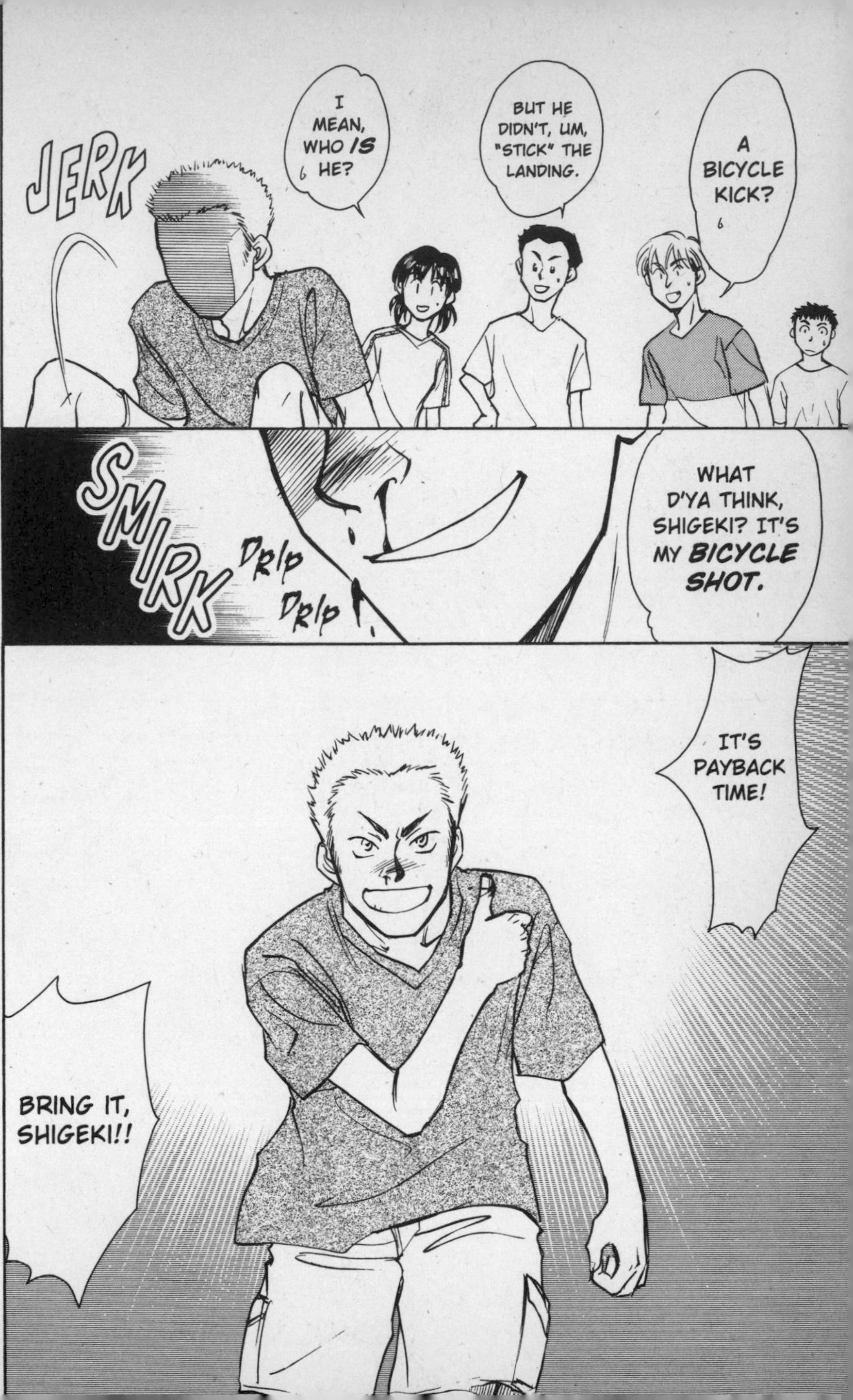
A BICYCLE KICK?
BUT HE DIDN'T, UM, "STICK" THE LANDING.
I MEAN, WHO IS HE?
JERK
WHAT D'YA THINK, SHIGEKI? IT'S MY BICYCLE SHOT.
DRIP DRIP
SMIRK
IT'S PAYBACK TIME!
BRING IT, SHIGEKI!!

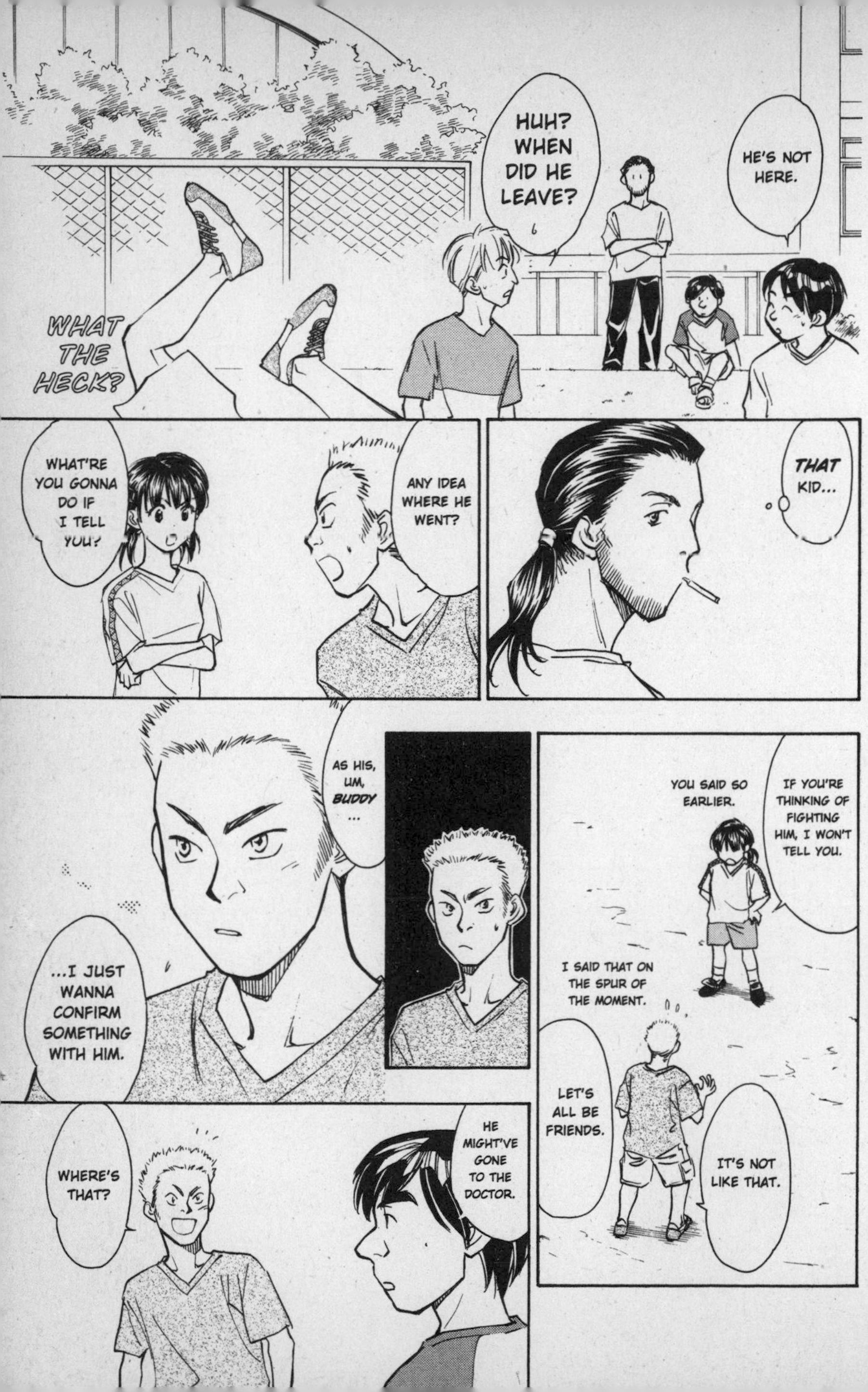
HE'S NOT HERE.
HUH? WHEN DID HE LEAVE?
WHAT THE HECK?
THAT KID...
ANY IDEA WHERE HE WENT?
WHAT'RE YOU GONNA DO IF I TELL YOU?
IF YOU'RE THINKING OF FIGHTING HIM, I WON'T TELL YOU.
YOU SAID SO EARLIER.
I SAID THAT ON THE SPUR OF THE MOMENT.
IT'S NOT LIKE THAT.
LET'S ALL BE FRIENDS.
AS HIS, UM, *BUDDY* ...
...I JUST WANNA CONFIRM SOMETHING WITH HIM.
HE MIGHT'VE GONE TO THE DOCTOR.
WHERE'S THAT?

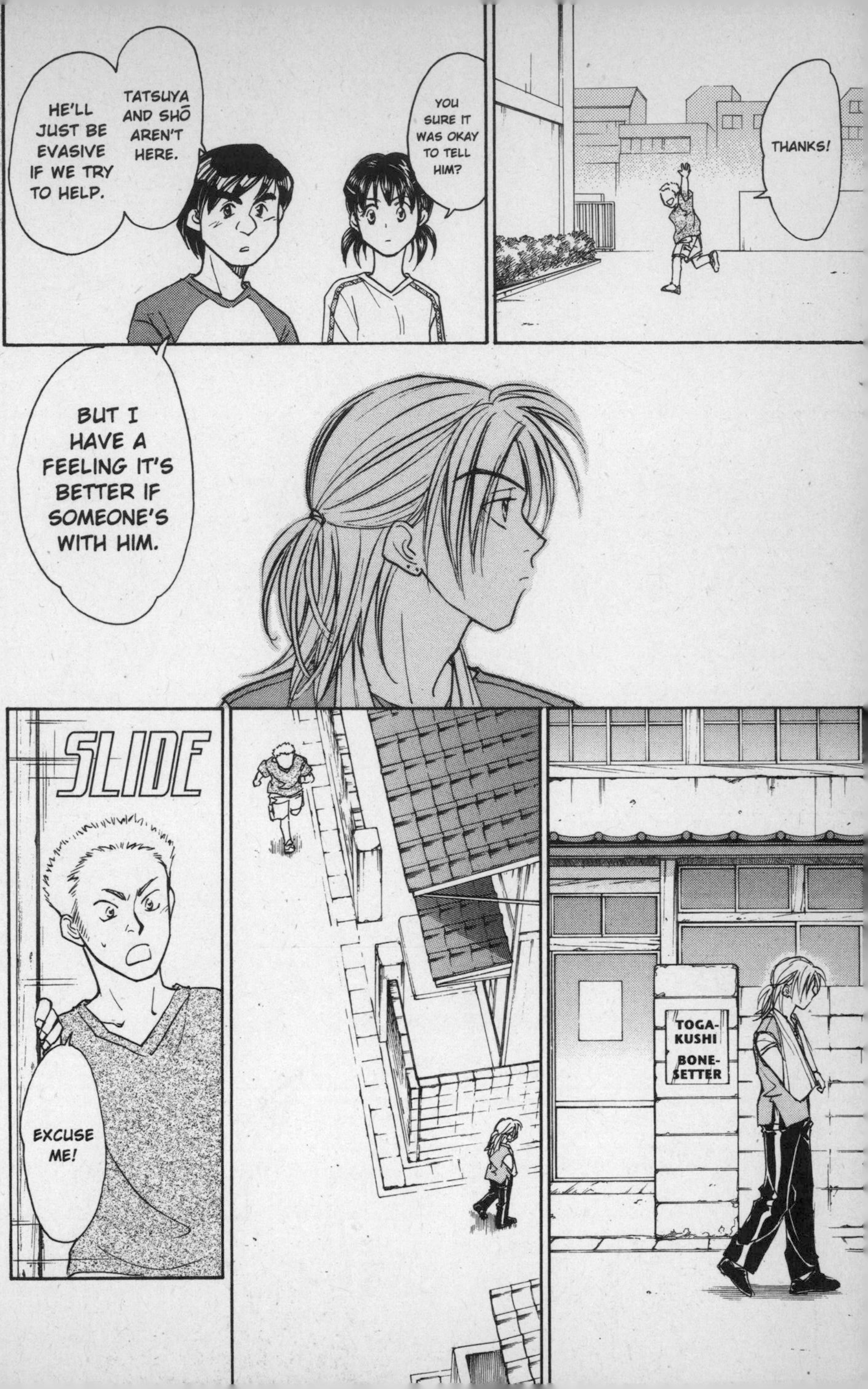
THANKS!
YOU SURE IT WAS OKAY TO TELL HIM?
TATSUYA AND SHŌ AREN'T HERE.
HE'LL JUST BE EVASIVE IF WE TRY TO HELP.
BUT I HAVE A FEELING IT'S BETTER IF SOMEONE'S WITH HIM.
TOGA-KUSHI BONE-SETTER
SLIDE
EXCUSE ME!

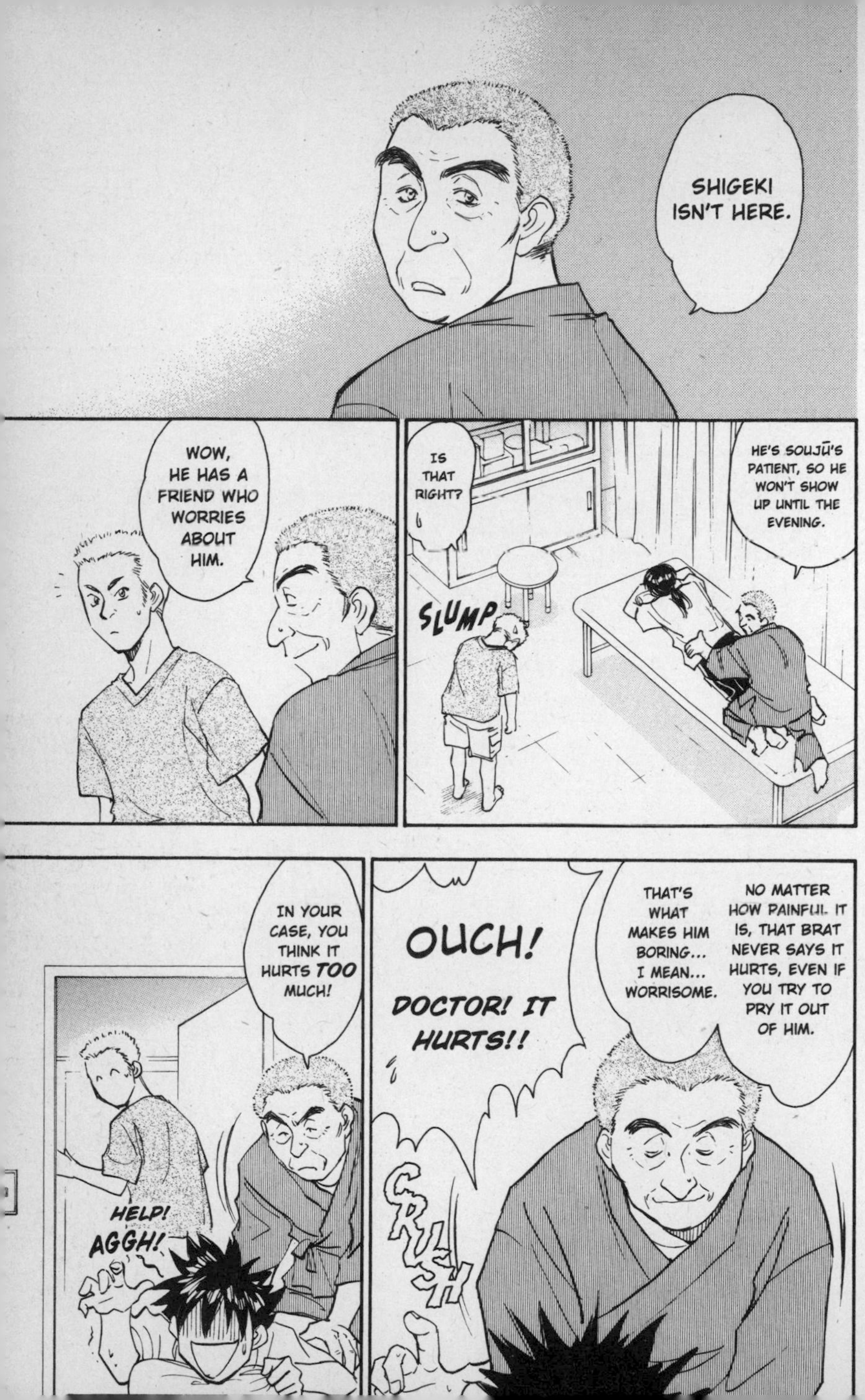
SHIGEKI ISN'T HERE.
HE'S SOUJŪ'S PATIENT, SO HE WON'T SHOW UP UNTIL THE EVENING.
IS THAT RIGHT?
SLUMP
WOW, HE HAS A FRIEND WHO WORRIES ABOUT HIM.
NO MATTER HOW PAINFUL IT IS, THAT BRAT NEVER SAYS IT HURTS, EVEN IF YOU TRY TO PRY IT OUT OF HIM.
THAT'S WHAT MAKES HIM BORING... I MEAN... WORRISOME.
OUCH!
DOCTOR! IT HURTS!!
CRUSH
IN YOUR CASE, YOU THINK IT HURTS TOO MUCH!
HELP! AGGH!

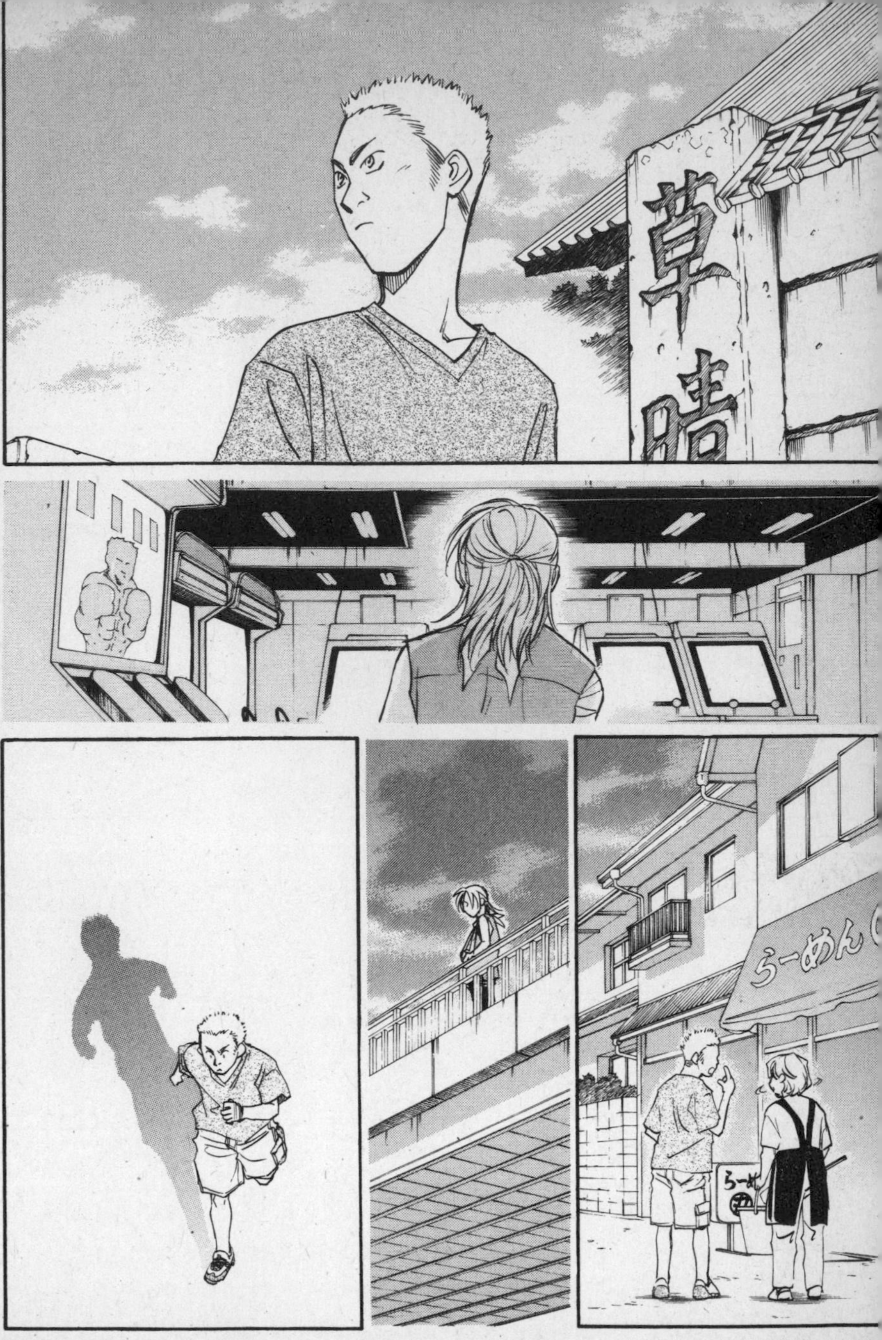
草晴
らーめん
らーめ

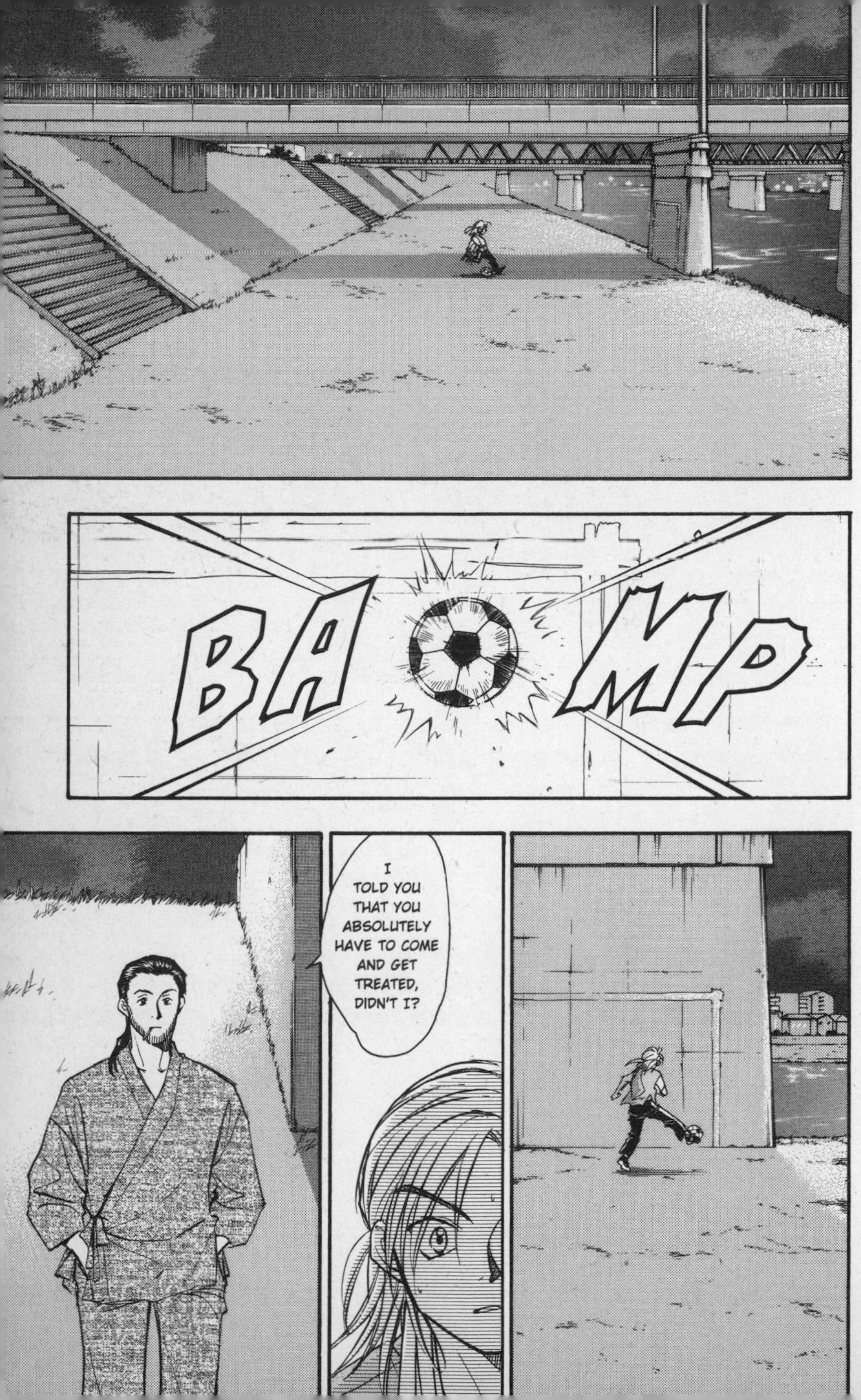
BAMP
I TOLD YOU THAT YOU ABSOLUTELY HAVE TO COME AND GET TREATED, DIDN'T I?

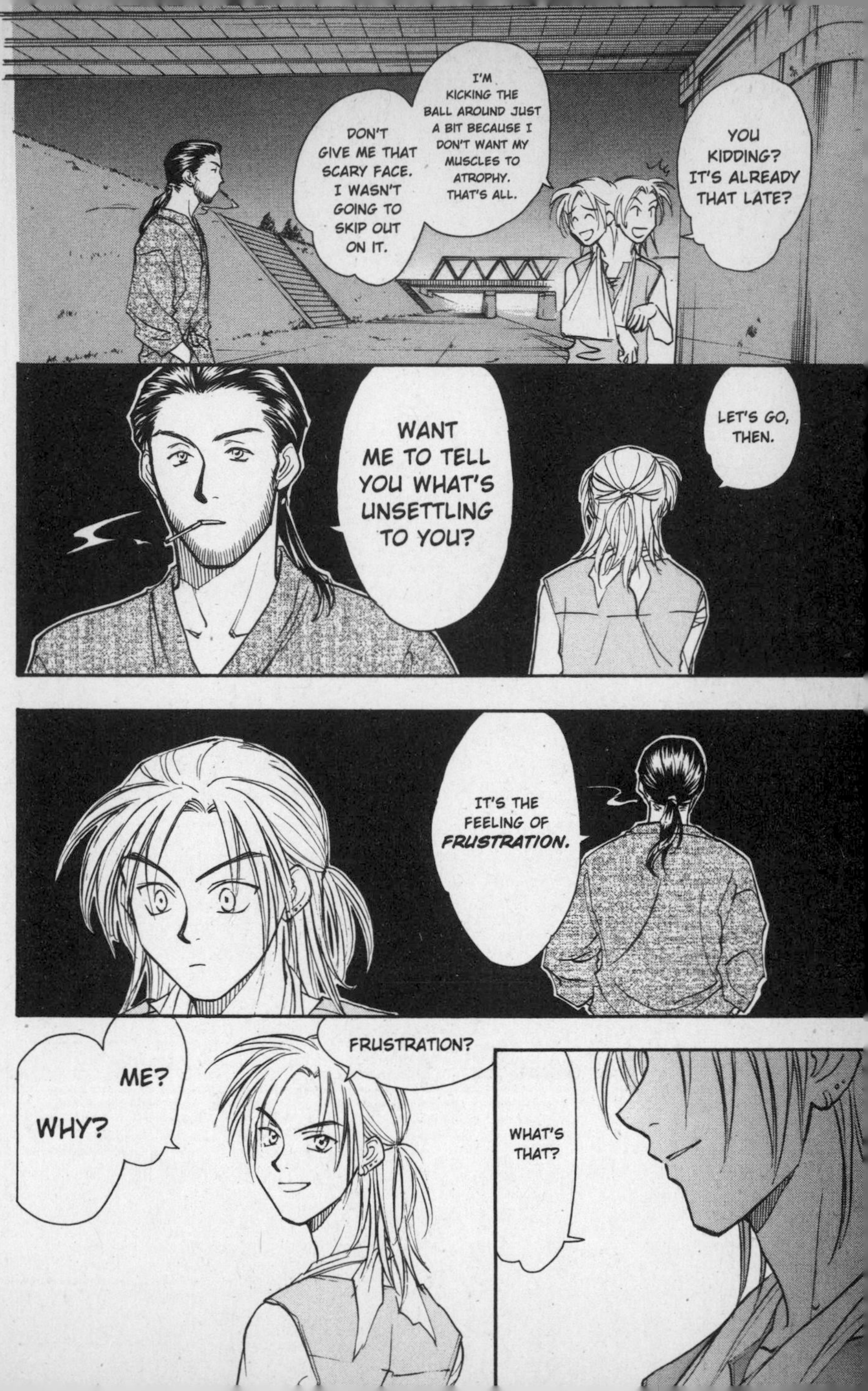
YOU KIDDING? IT'S ALREADY THAT LATE?
I'M KICKING THE BALL AROUND JUST A BIT BECAUSE I DON'T WANT MY MUSCLES TO ATROPHY. THAT'S ALL.
DON'T GIVE ME THAT SCARY FACE. I WASN'T GOING TO SKIP OUT ON IT.
LET'S GO, THEN.
WANT ME TO TELL YOU WHAT'S UNSETTLING TO YOU?
IT'S THE FEELING OF *FRUSTRATION.*
WHAT'S THAT?
FRUSTRATION?
ME?
WHY?

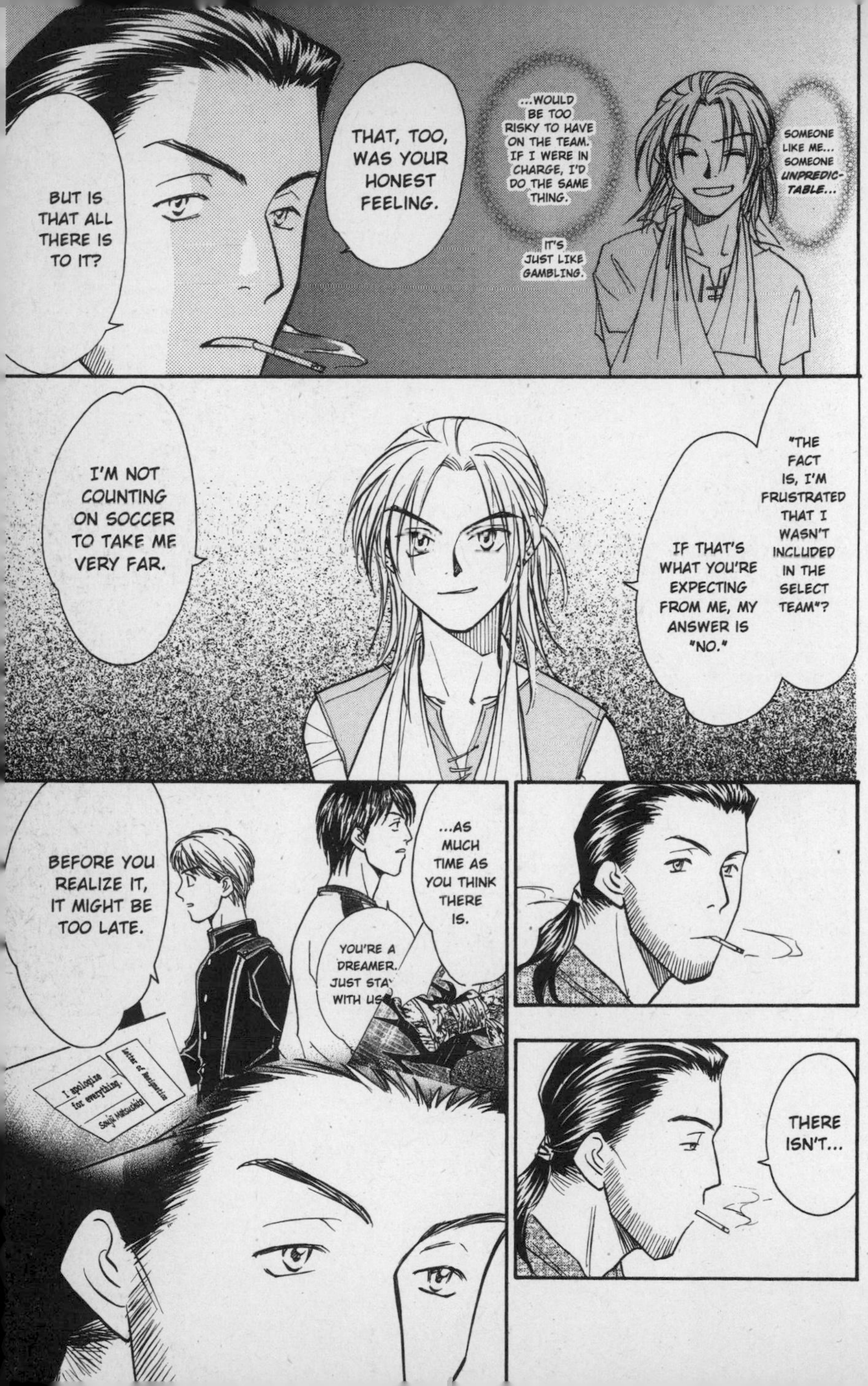
SOMEONE LIKE ME... SOMEONE UNPREDICTABLE...
...WOULD BE TOO RISKY TO HAVE ON THE TEAM. IF I WERE IN CHARGE, I'D DO THE SAME THING.
IT'S JUST LIKE GAMBLING.
THAT, TOO, WAS YOUR HONEST FEELING.
BUT IS THAT ALL THERE IS TO IT?
"THE FACT IS, I'M FRUSTRATED THAT I WASN'T INCLUDED IN THE SELECT TEAM"?
IF THAT'S WHAT YOU'RE EXPECTING FROM ME, MY ANSWER IS "NO."
I'M NOT COUNTING ON SOCCER TO TAKE ME VERY FAR.
THERE ISN'T...
...AS MUCH TIME AS YOU THINK THERE IS.
YOU'RE A DREAMER. JUST STAY WITH US
BEFORE YOU REALIZE IT, IT MIGHT BE TOO LATE.
Letter of Resignation
I apologize for everything.
Souji Matsushita

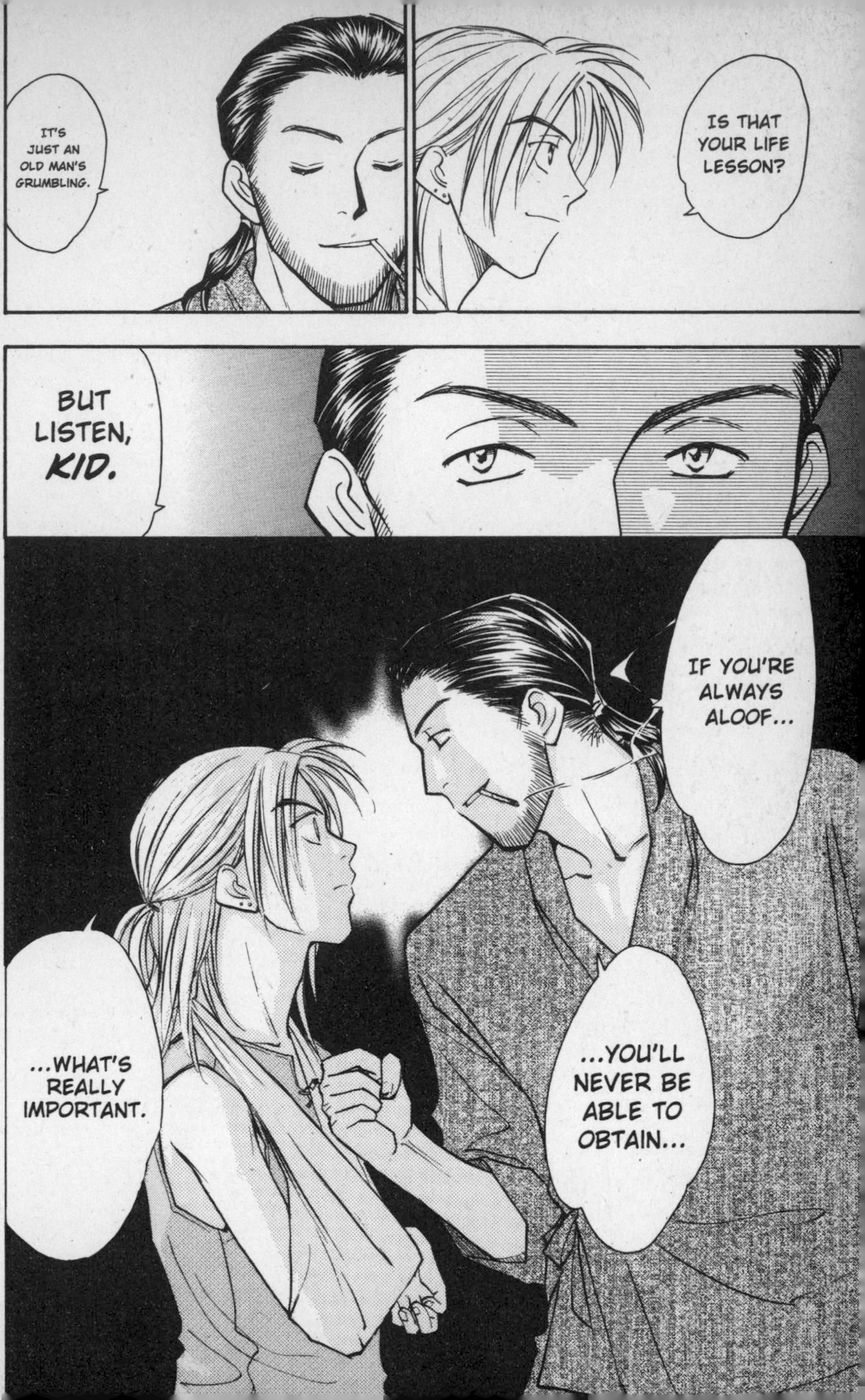
IS THAT YOUR LIFE LESSON?
IT'S JUST AN OLD MAN'S GRUMBLING.
BUT LISTEN, *KID.*
IF YOU'RE ALWAYS ALOOF...
...YOU'LL NEVER BE ABLE TO OBTAIN...
...WHAT'S REALLY IMPORTANT.

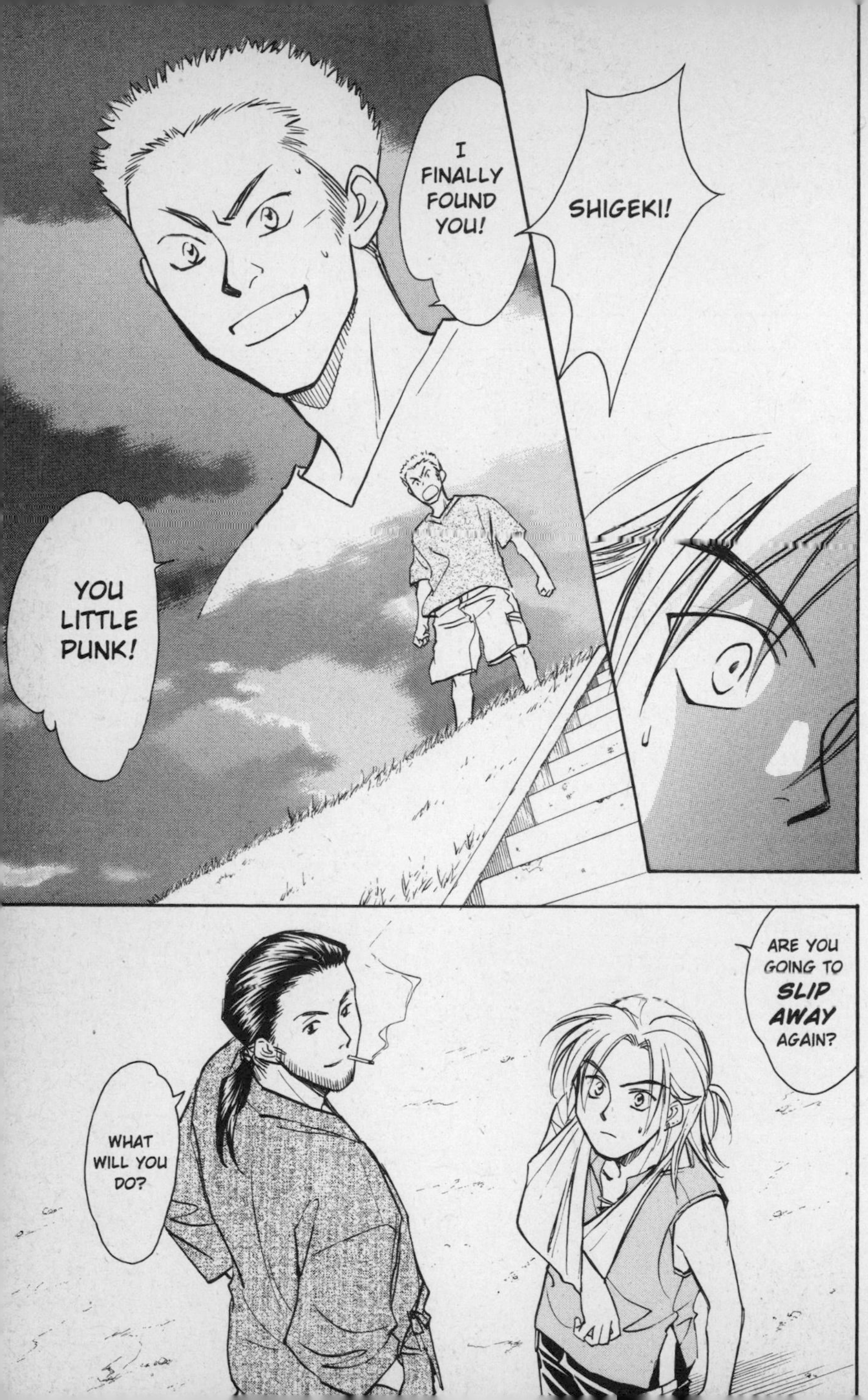
SHIGEKI!
I FINALLY FOUND YOU!
YOU LITTLE PUNK!
ARE YOU GOING TO SLIP AWAY AGAIN?
WHAT WILL YOU DO?

WHISTLE!™

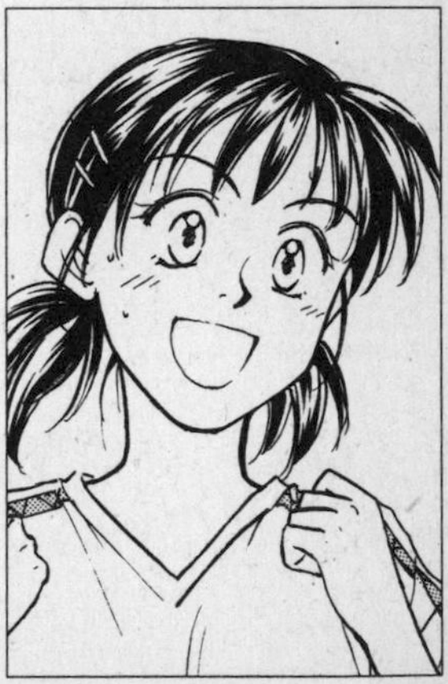

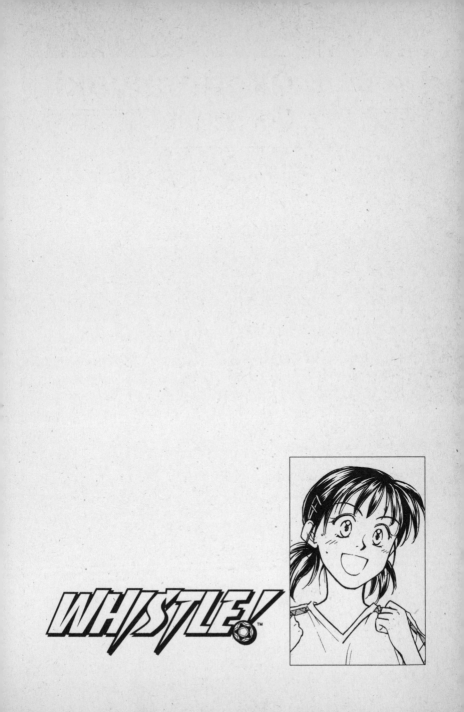

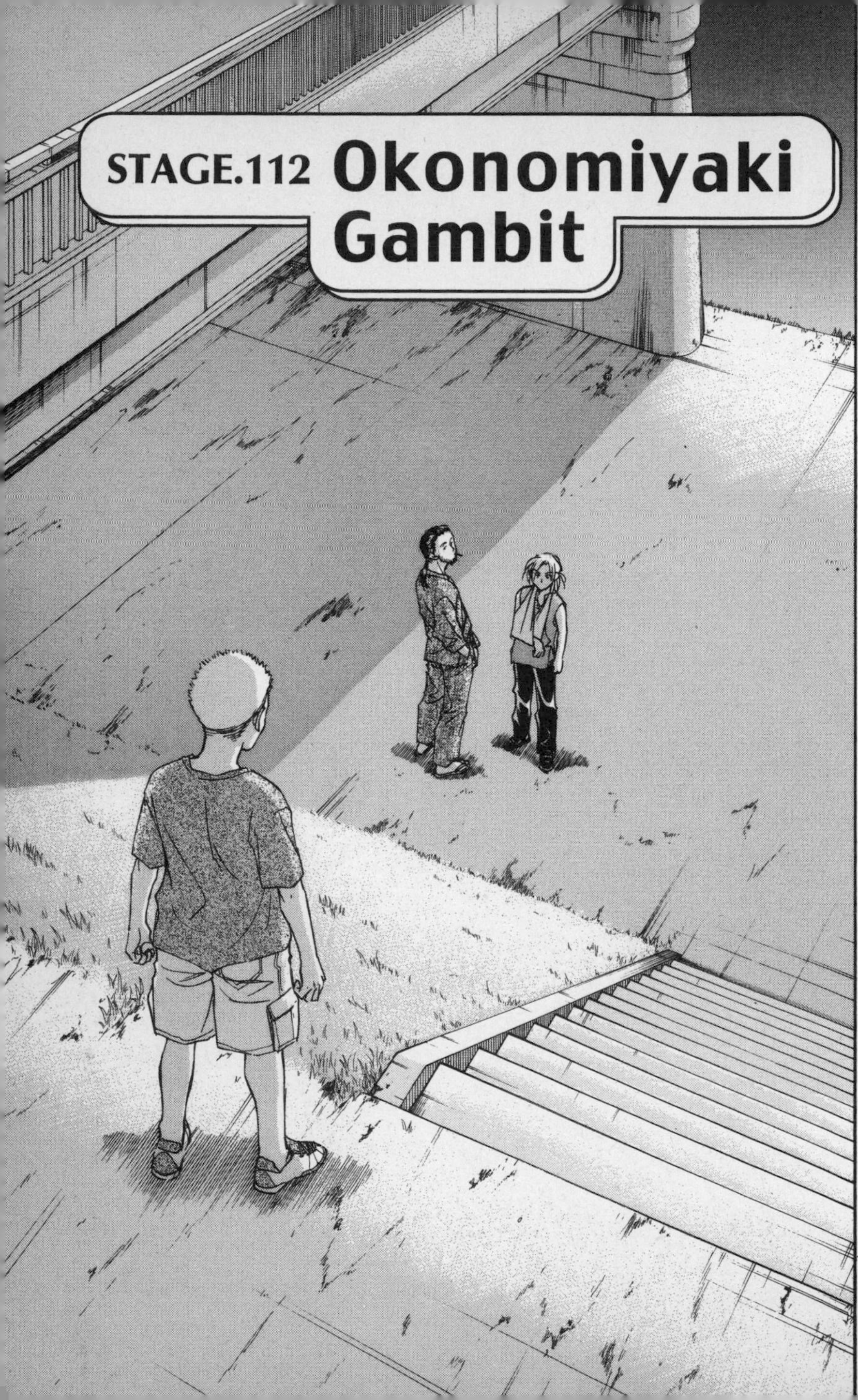
STAGE.112 Okonomiyaki Gambit

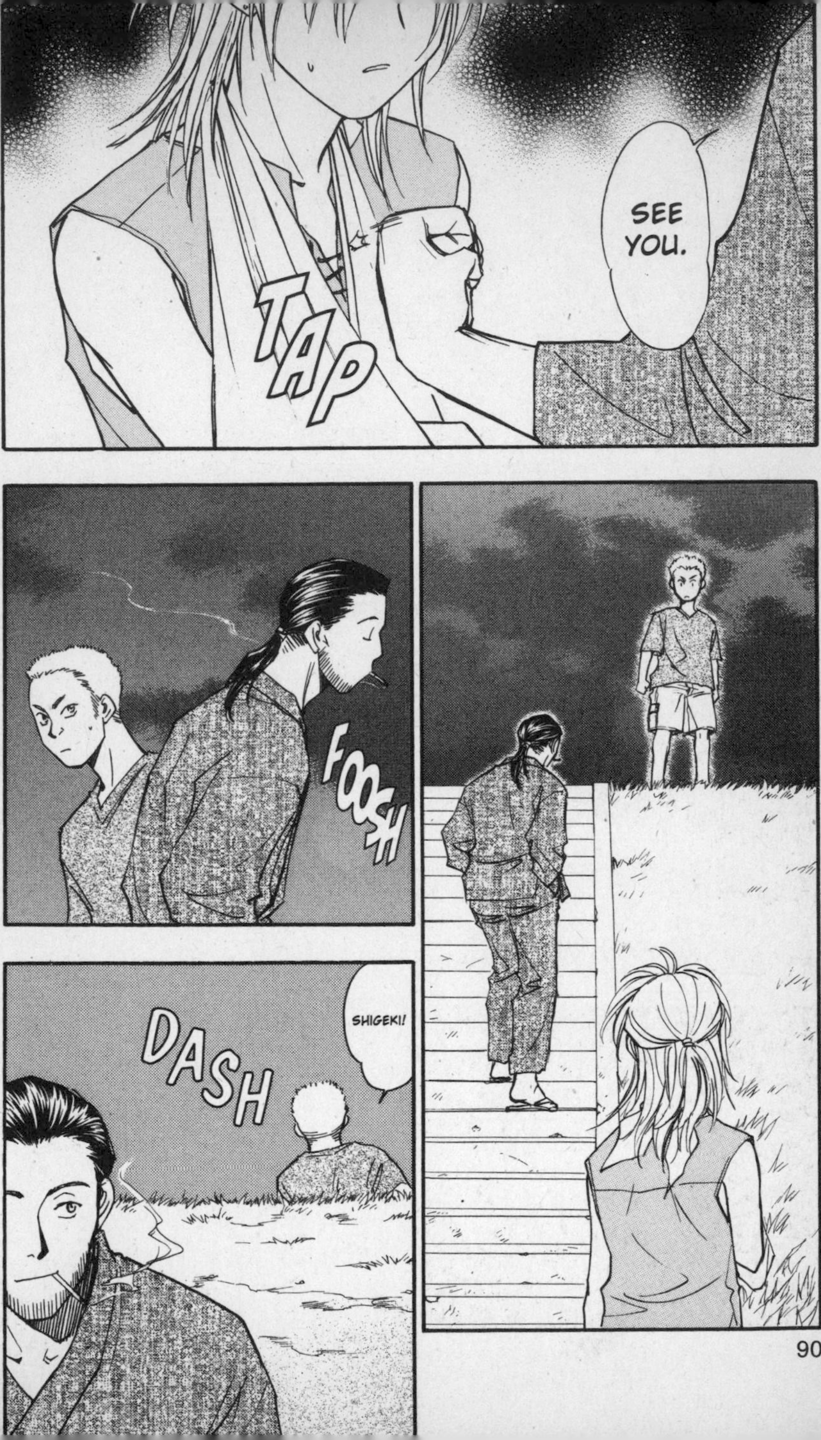
SEE YOU.
TAP
FOOSH
SHIGEKI!
DASH

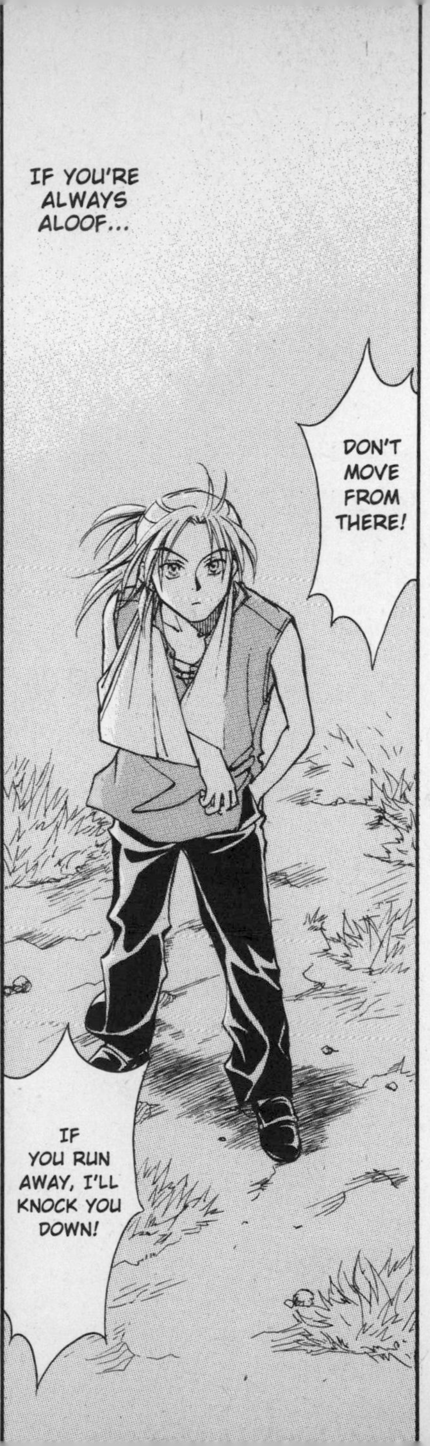
IF YOU'RE ALWAYS ALOOF...
DON'T MOVE FROM THERE!
IF YOU RUN AWAY, I'LL KNOCK YOU DOWN!

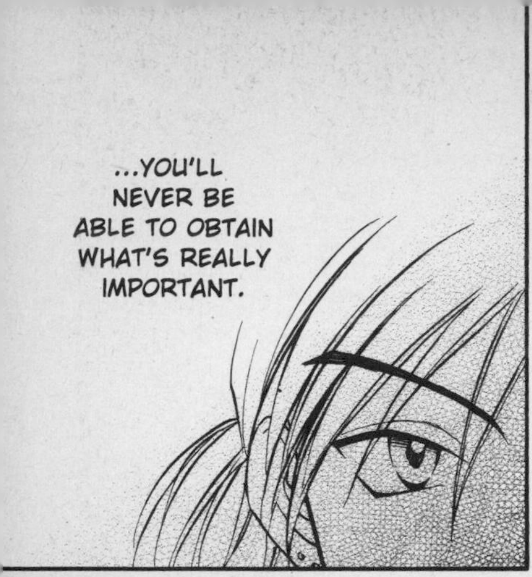
...YOU'LL NEVER BE ABLE TO OBTAIN WHAT'S REALLY IMPORTANT.

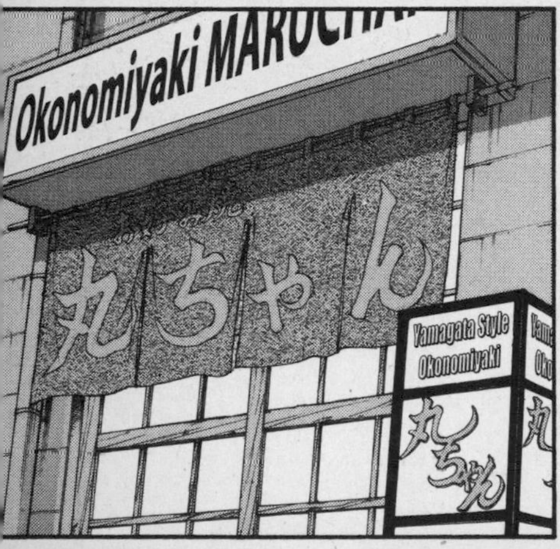
Okonomiyaki MAROCHA
丸ちゃん
Yamagata Style Okonomiyaki
丸ちゃん

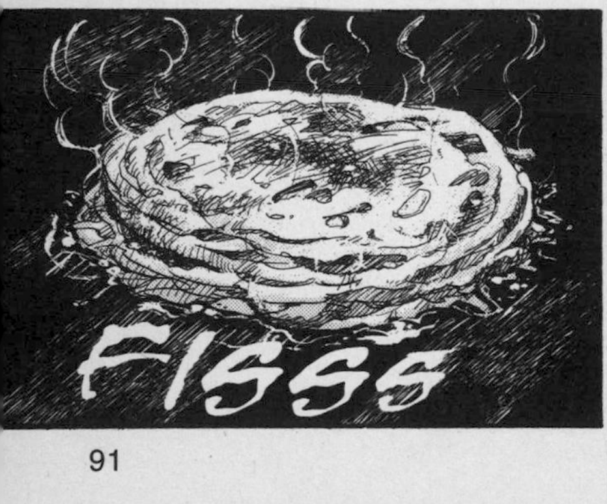
FISSS

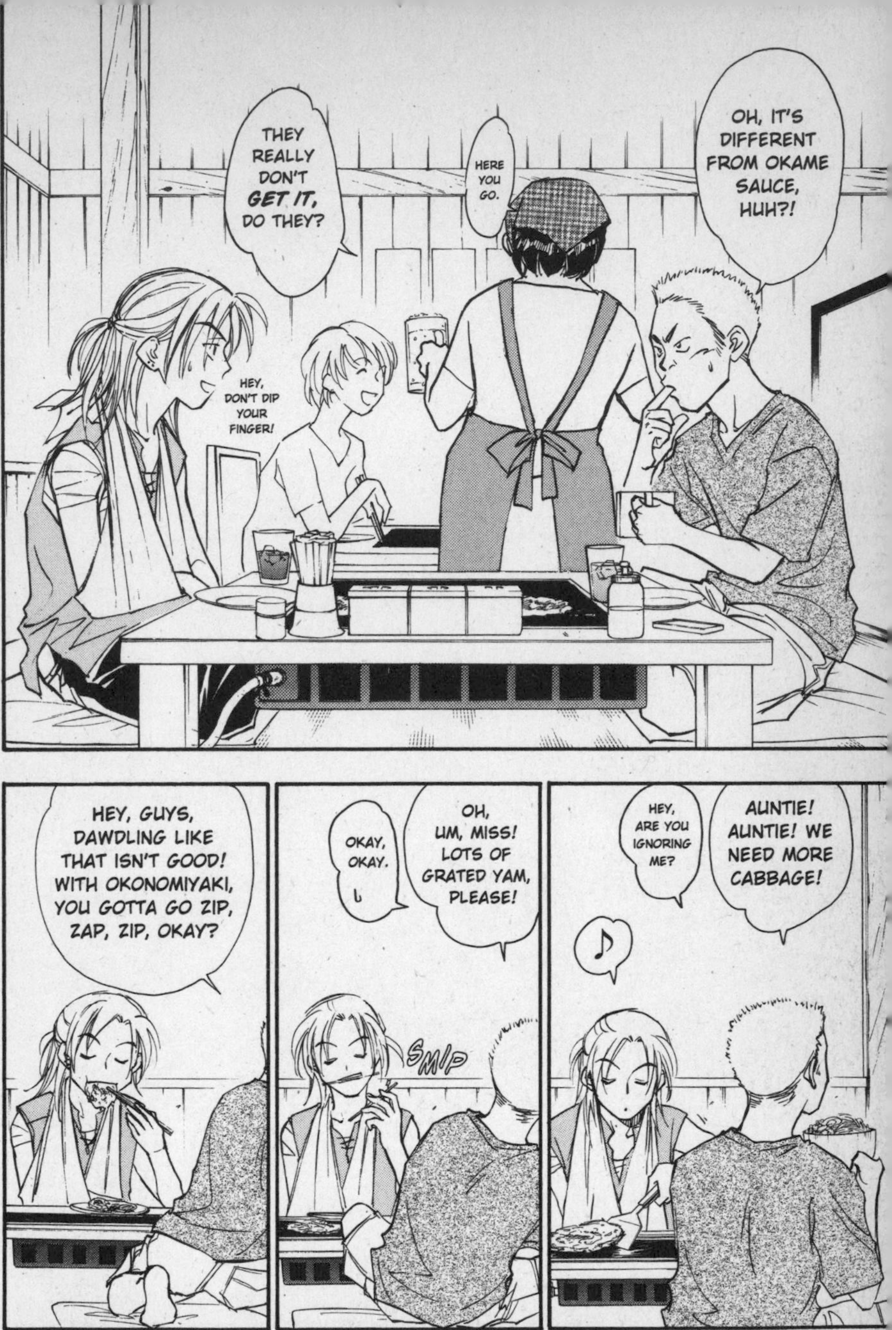
OH, IT'S DIFFERENT FROM OKAME SAUCE, HUH?!
HERE YOU GO.
THEY REALLY DON'T GET IT, DO THEY?
HEY, DON'T DIP YOUR FINGER!
AUNTIE! AUNTIE! WE NEED MORE CABBAGE!
HEY, ARE YOU IGNORING ME?
♪
OH, UM, MISS! LOTS OF GRATED YAM, PLEASE!
OKAY, OKAY.
SMIP
HEY, GUYS, DAWDLING LIKE THAT ISN'T GOOD! WITH OKONOMIYAKI, YOU GOTTA GO ZIP, ZAP, ZIP, OKAY?

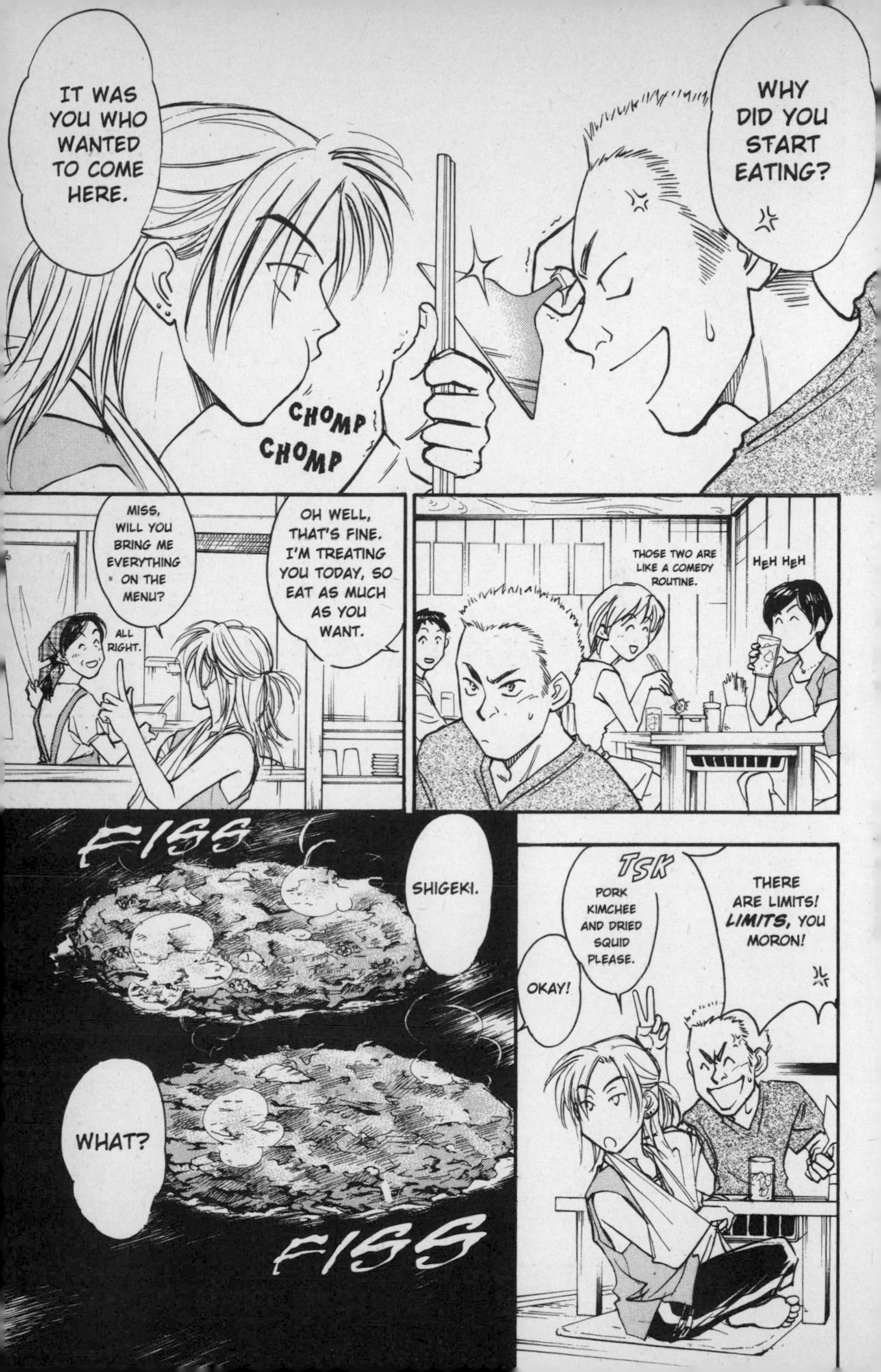
WHY DID YOU START EATING?
IT WAS YOU WHO WANTED TO COME HERE.
CHOMP CHOMP
HEH HEH
THOSE TWO ARE LIKE A COMEDY ROUTINE.
OH WELL, THAT'S FINE. I'M TREATING YOU TODAY, SO EAT AS MUCH AS YOU WANT.
MISS, WILL YOU BRING ME EVERYTHING ON THE MENU?
ALL RIGHT.
THERE ARE LIMITS! LIMITS, YOU MORON!
TSK
PORK KIMCHEE AND DRIED SQUID PLEASE.
OKAY!
FISS
SHIGEKI.
WHAT?
FISS

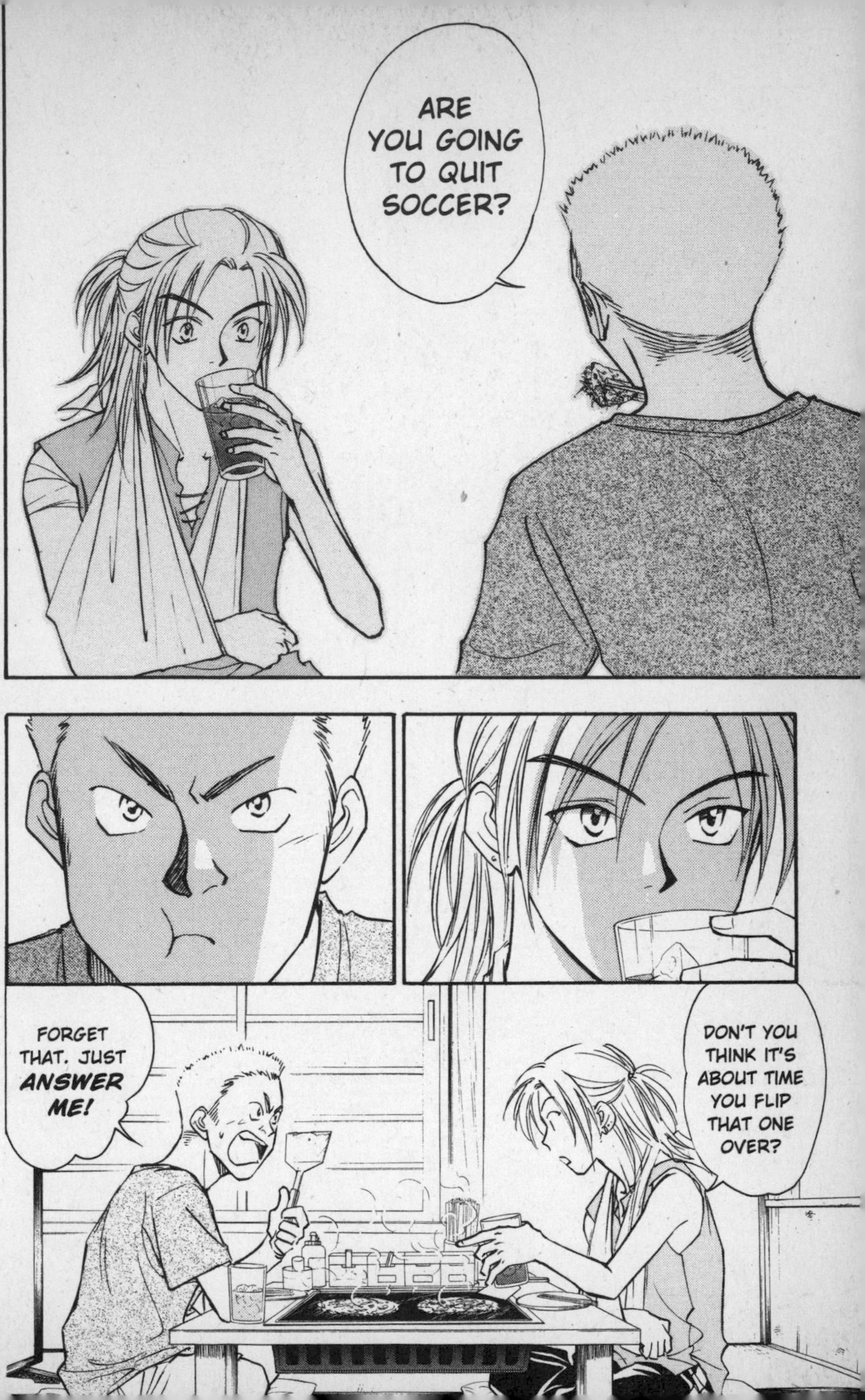
ARE YOU GOING TO QUIT SOCCER?
DON'T YOU THINK IT'S ABOUT TIME YOU FLIP THAT ONE OVER?
FORGET THAT. JUST ANSWER ME!

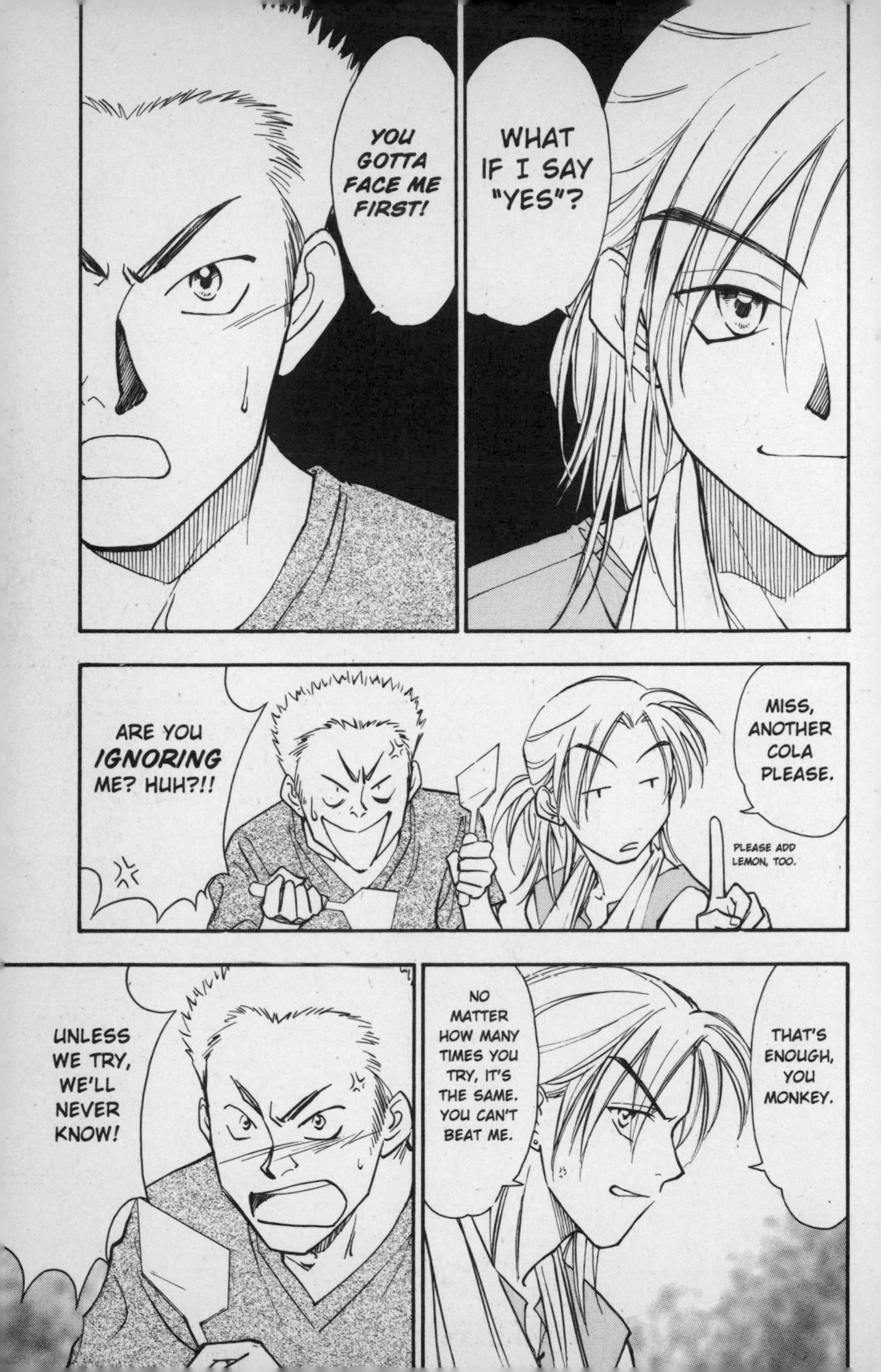
WHAT IF I SAY "YES"?
YOU GOTTA FACE ME FIRST!
MISS, ANOTHER COLA PLEASE.
PLEASE ADD LEMON, TOO.
ARE YOU *IGNORING* ME? HUH?!!
THAT'S ENOUGH, YOU MONKEY.
NO MATTER HOW MANY TIMES YOU TRY, IT'S THE SAME. YOU CAN'T BEAT ME.
UNLESS WE TRY, WE'LL NEVER KNOW!

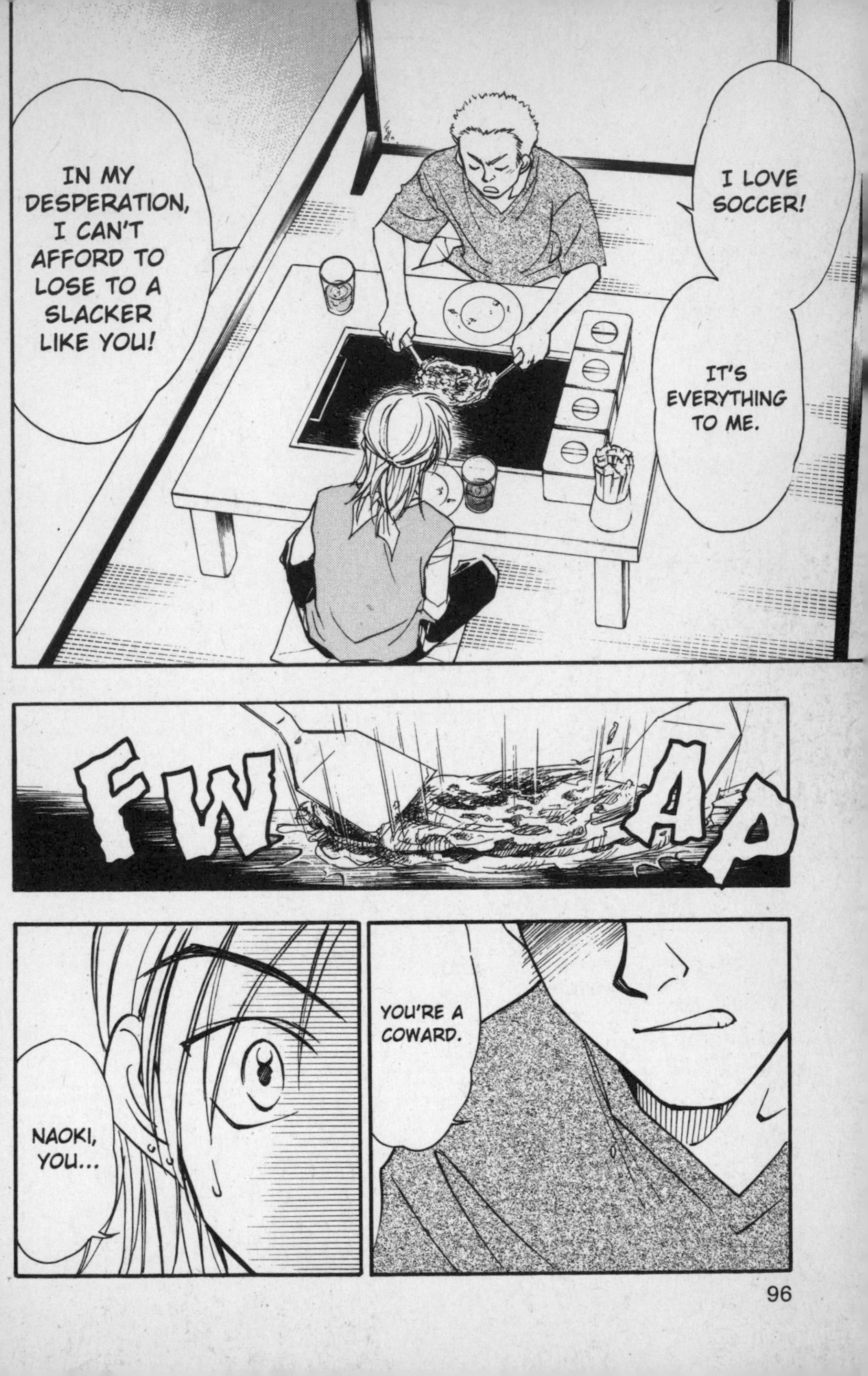
I LOVE SOCCER!
IT'S EVERYTHING TO ME.
IN MY DESPERATION, I CAN'T AFFORD TO LOSE TO A SLACKER LIKE YOU!
FWAP
YOU'RE A COWARD.
NAOKI, YOU...

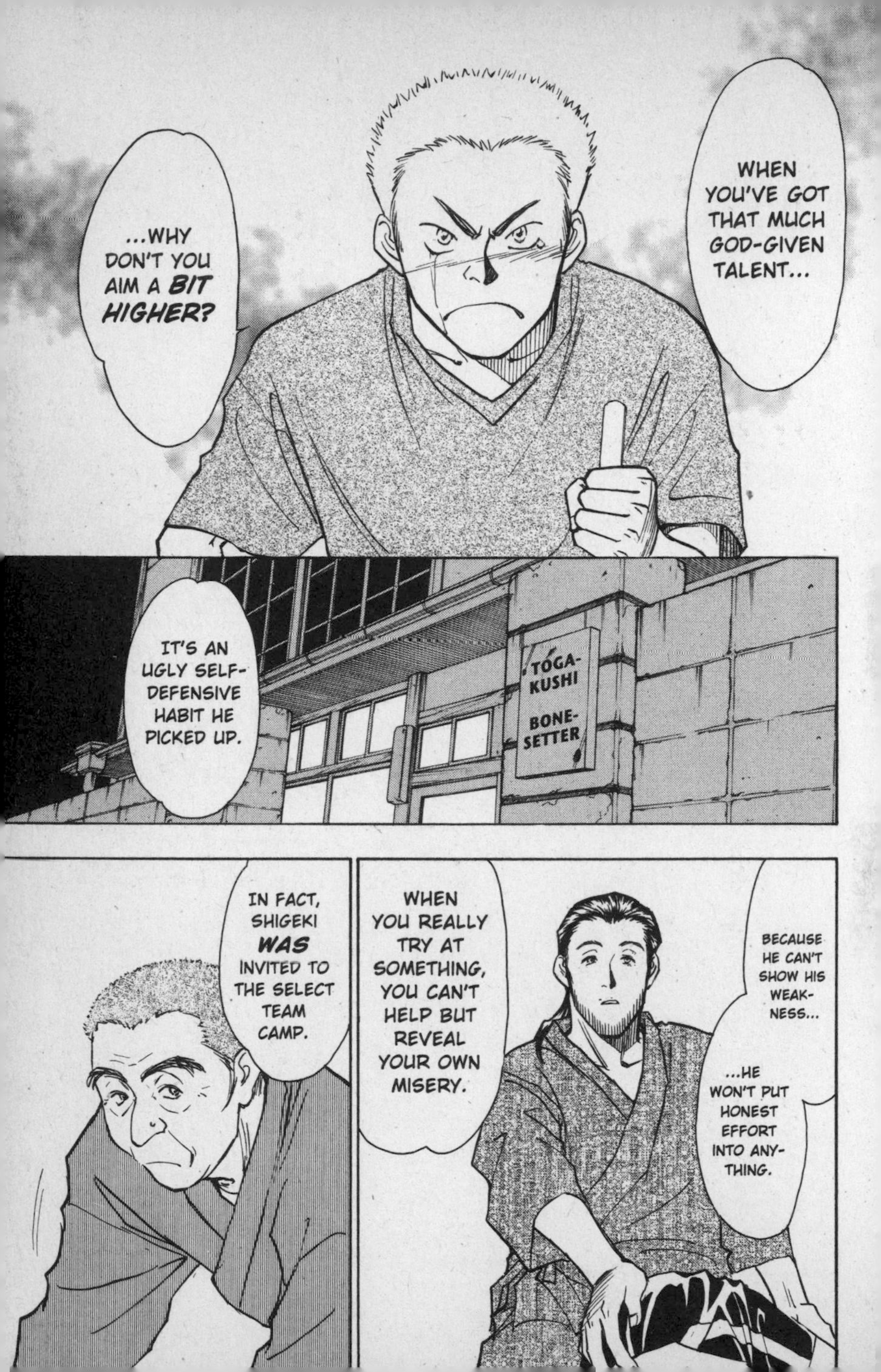
WHEN YOU'VE GOT THAT MUCH GOD-GIVEN TALENT...
...WHY DON'T YOU AIM A BIT HIGHER?
TOGA-KUSHI BONE-SETTER
IT'S AN UGLY SELF-DEFENSIVE HABIT HE PICKED UP.
BECAUSE HE CAN'T SHOW HIS WEAK-NESS...
...HE WON'T PUT HONEST EFFORT INTO ANY-THING.
WHEN YOU REALLY TRY AT SOMETHING, YOU CAN'T HELP BUT REVEAL YOUR OWN MISERY.
IN FACT, SHIGEKI WAS INVITED TO THE SELECT TEAM CAMP.

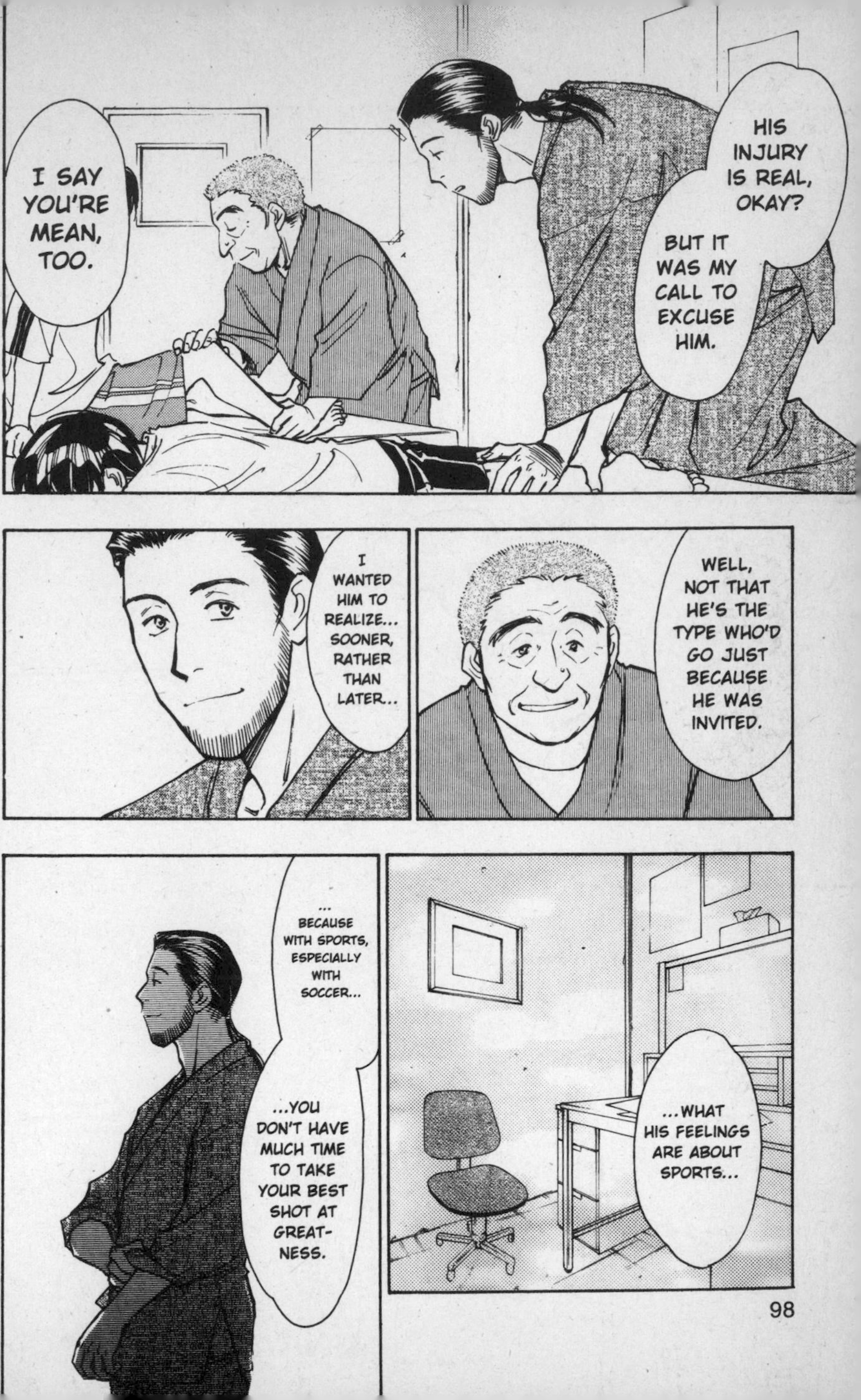
HIS INJURY IS REAL, OKAY?
BUT IT WAS MY CALL TO EXCUSE HIM.
I SAY YOU'RE MEAN, TOO.
WELL, NOT THAT HE'S THE TYPE WHO'D GO JUST BECAUSE HE WAS INVITED.
I WANTED HIM TO REALIZE... SOONER, RATHER THAN LATER...
...WHAT HIS FEELINGS ARE ABOUT SPORTS...
...BECAUSE WITH SPORTS, ESPECIALLY WITH SOCCER...
...YOU DON'T HAVE MUCH TIME TO TAKE YOUR BEST SHOT AT GREAT-NESS.

READ THIS WAY

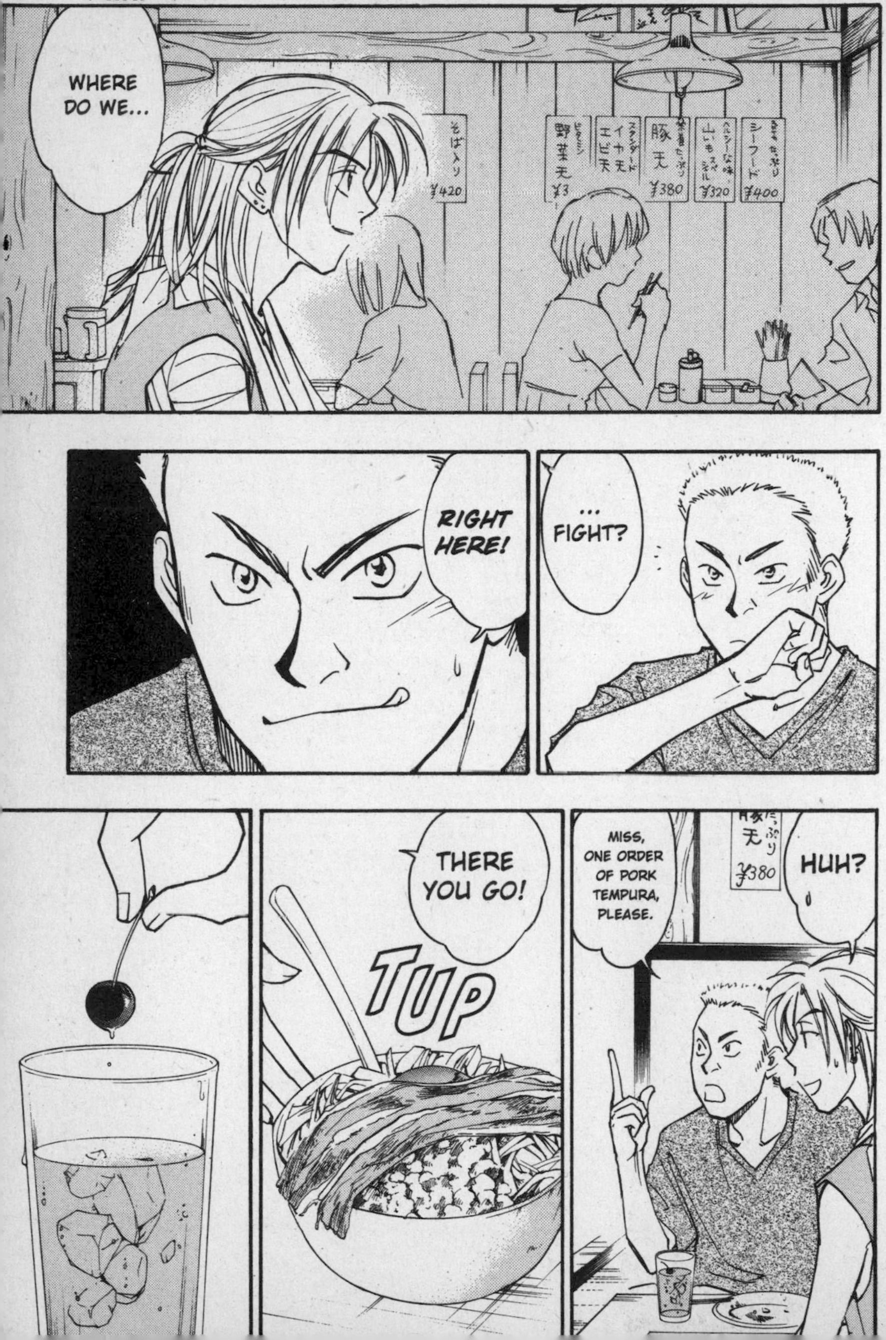
WHERE DO WE...
...FIGHT?
RIGHT HERE!
HUH?
MISS, ONE ORDER OF PORK TEMPURA, PLEASE.
THERE YOU GO!
TUP

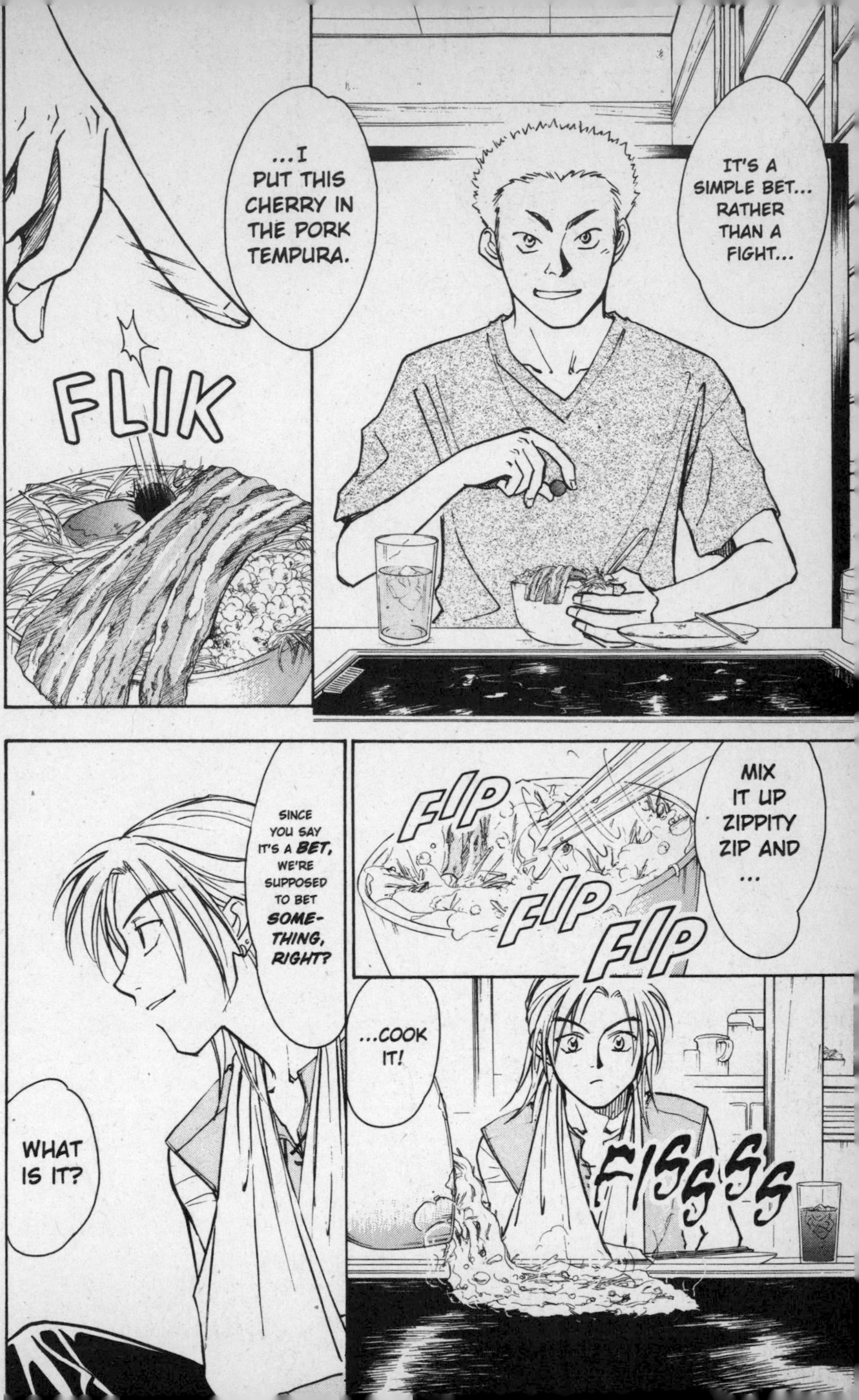
IT'S A SIMPLE BET... RATHER THAN A FIGHT...
...I PUT THIS CHERRY IN THE PORK TEMPURA.
FLIK
MIX IT UP ZIPPITY ZIP AND ...
FLIP
FLIP
FLIP
...COOK IT!
FISSSS
SINCE YOU SAY IT'S A **BET,** WE'RE SUPPOSED TO BET ***SOMETHING, RIGHT?***
WHAT IS IT?

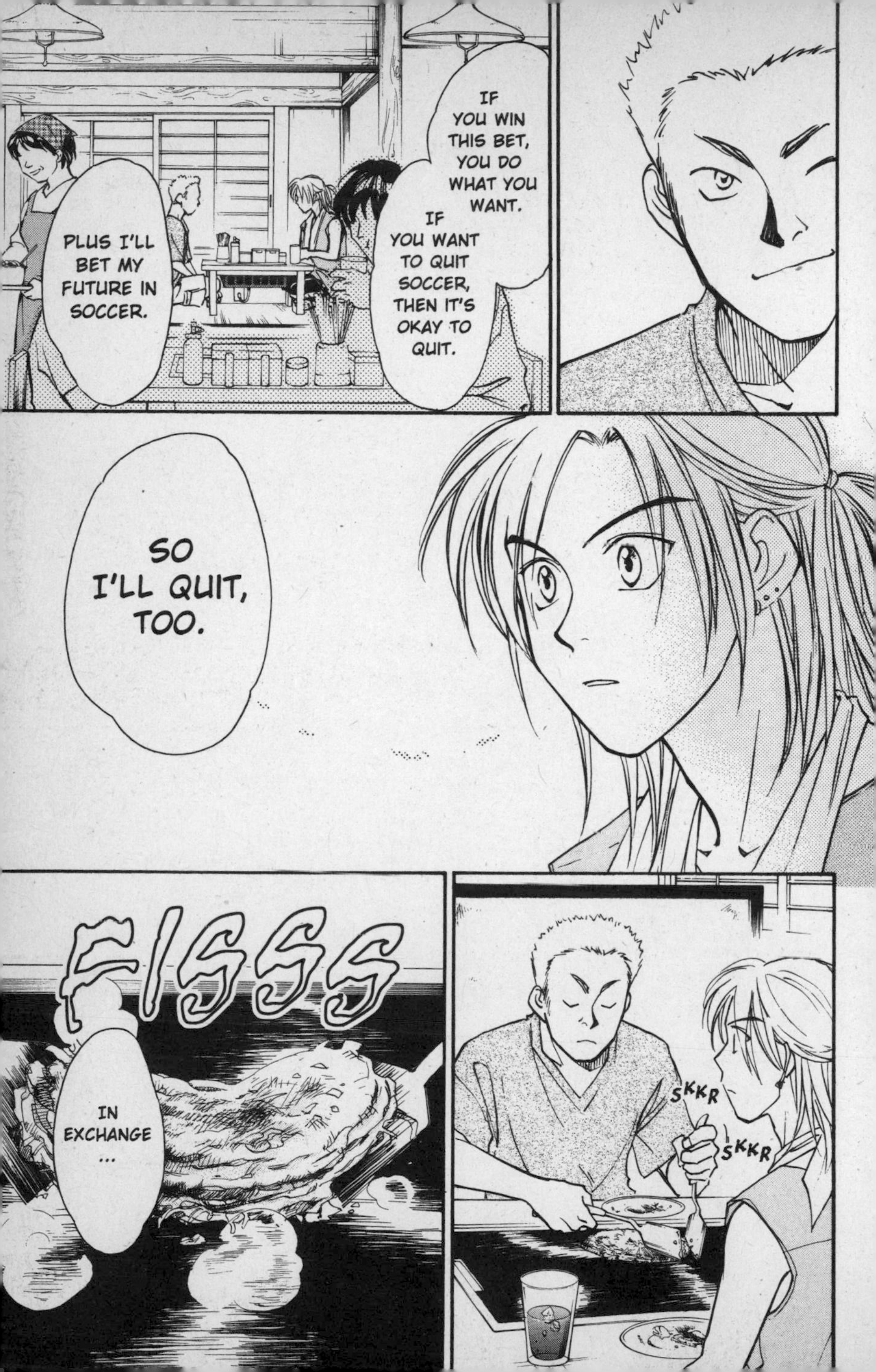
IF YOU WIN THIS BET, YOU DO WHAT YOU WANT.
IF YOU WANT TO QUIT SOCCER, THEN IT'S OKAY TO QUIT.
PLUS I'LL BET MY FUTURE IN SOCCER.
SO I'LL QUIT, TOO.
SKKR
SKKR
FISSS
IN EXCHANGE ...

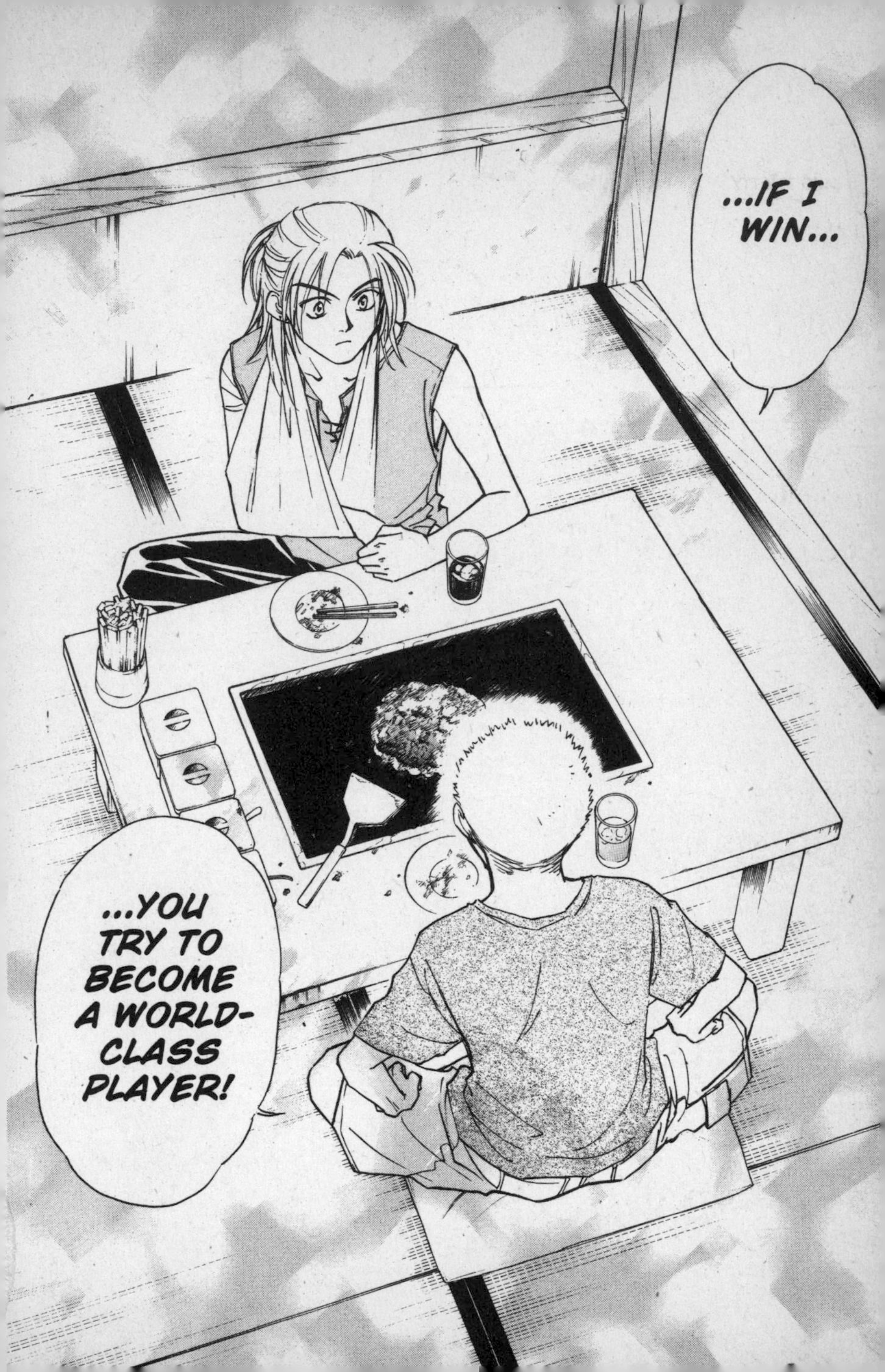
...IF I WIN...
...YOU TRY TO BECOME A WORLD-CLASS PLAYER!

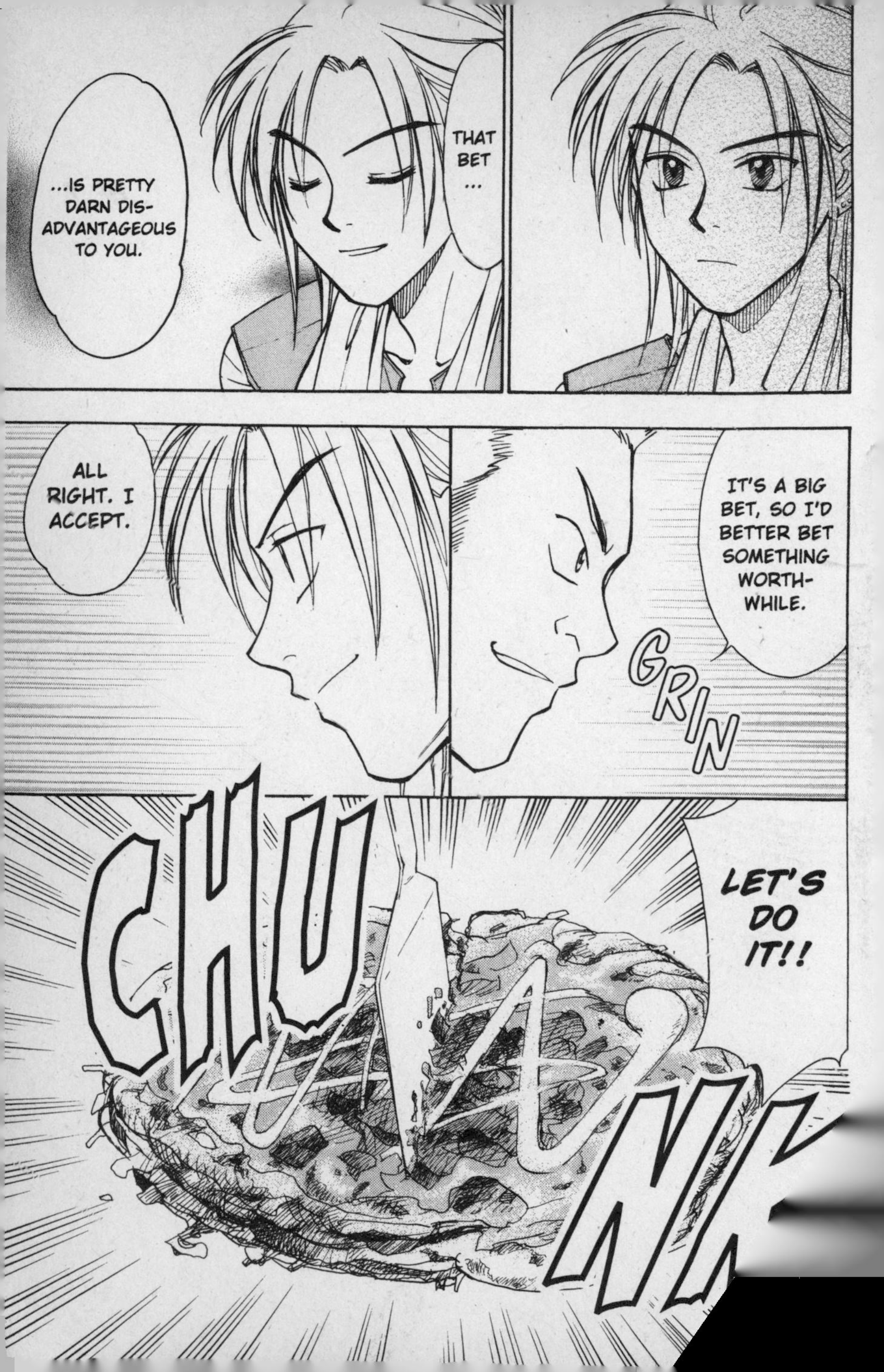
THAT BET ...
...IS PRETTY DARN DIS-ADVANTAGEOUS TO YOU.
IT'S A BIG BET, SO I'D BETTER BET SOMETHING WORTH-WHILE.
GRIN
ALL RIGHT. I ACCEPT.
LET'S DO IT!!
CHU

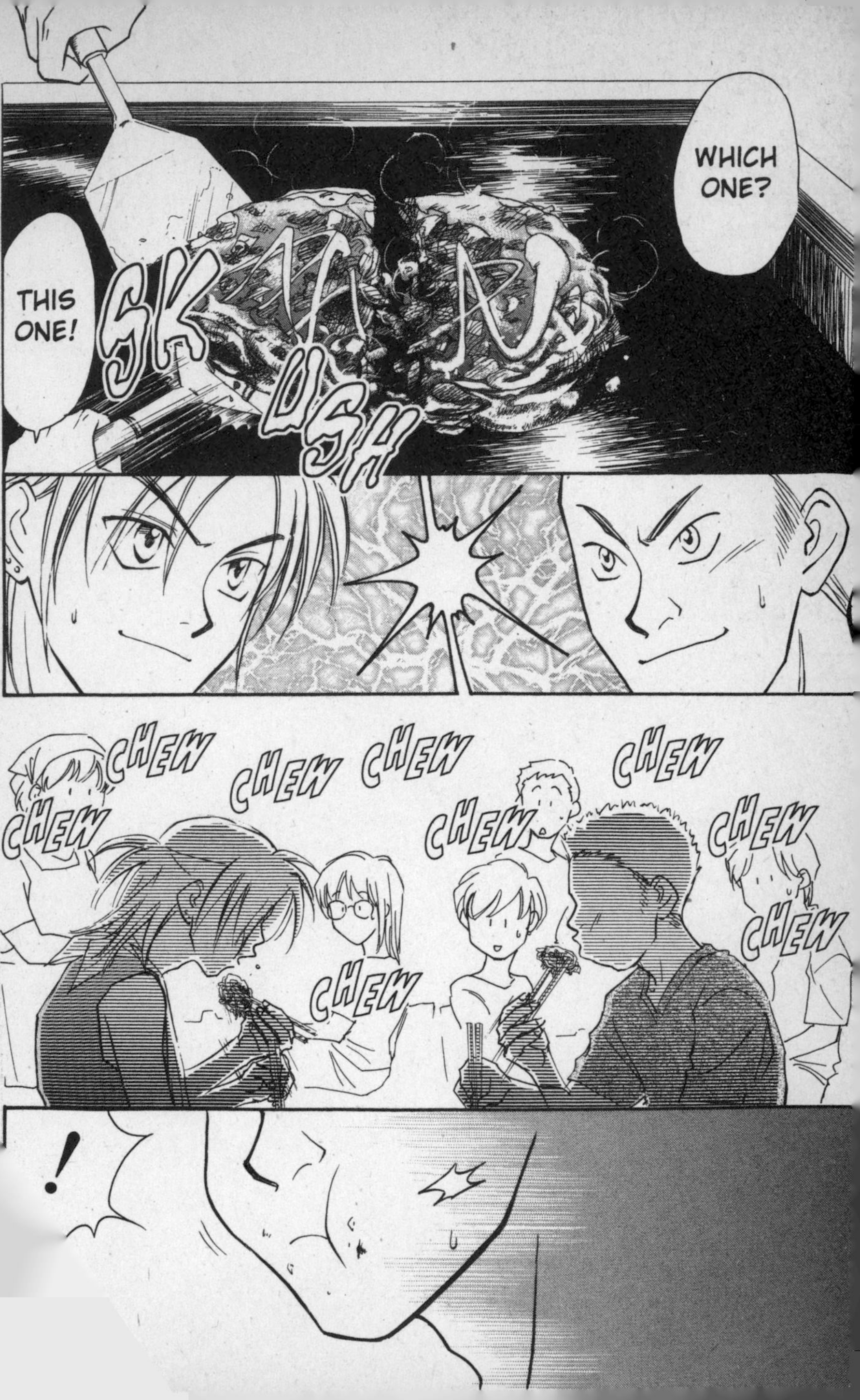
WHICH ONE?
THIS ONE!
SKUSH
CHEW
CHEW
CHEW
CHEW
CHEW
CHEW
CHEW
CHEW
CHEW
!

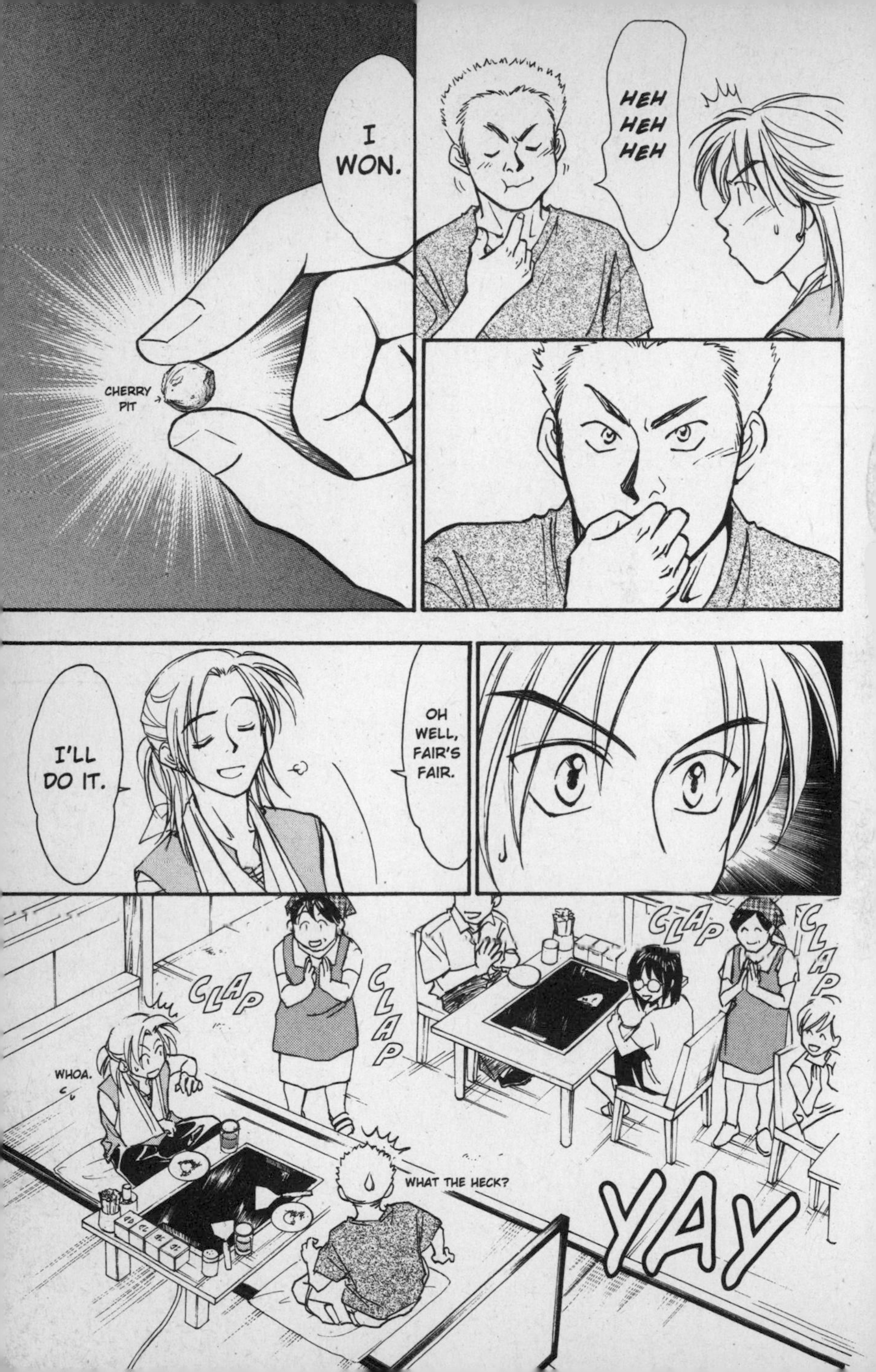
HEH HEH HEH
I WON.
CHERRY PIT
OH WELL, FAIR'S FAIR.
I'LL DO IT.
CLAP CLAP
YAY
CLAP
CLAP
WHAT THE HECK?
WHOA.

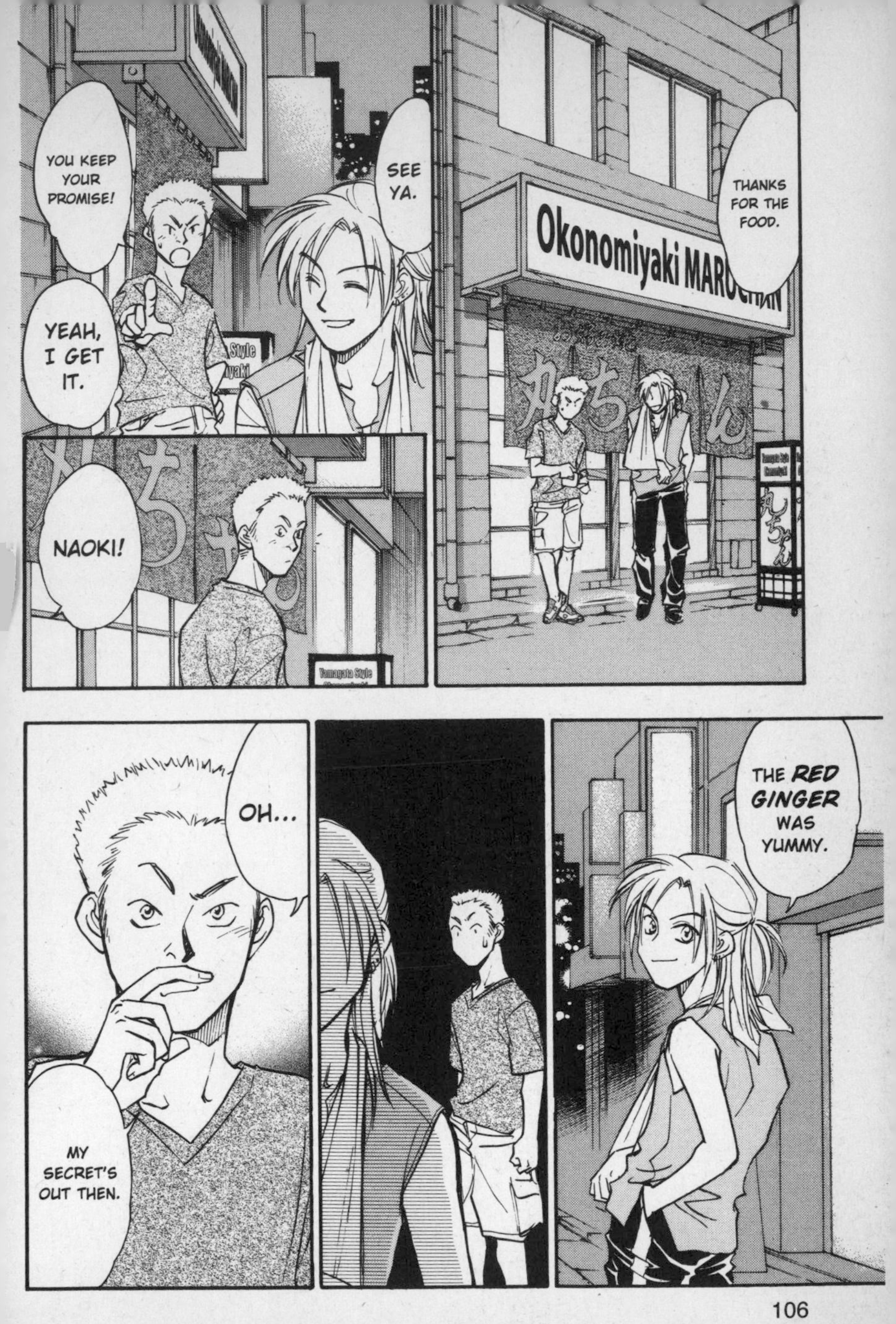
Okonomiyaki MAROCHAN
THANKS FOR THE FOOD.
SEE YA.
YOU KEEP YOUR PROMISE!
YEAH, I GET IT.
NAOKI!
THE *RED GINGER* WAS YUMMY.
OH...
MY SECRET'S OUT THEN.

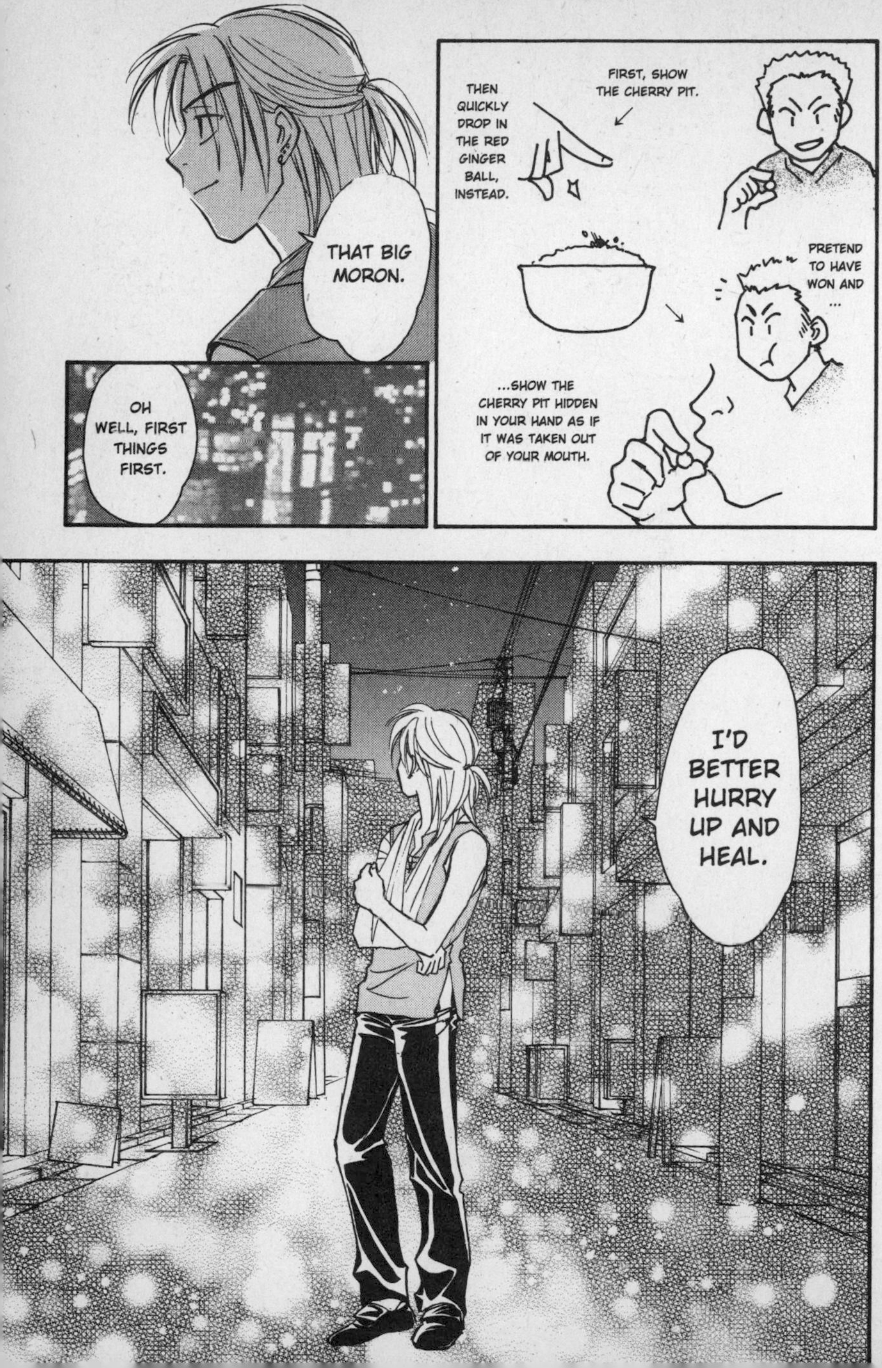
FIRST, SHOW THE CHERRY PIT.
THEN QUICKLY DROP IN THE RED GINGER BALL, INSTEAD.
PRETEND TO HAVE WON AND ...
...SHOW THE CHERRY PIT HIDDEN IN YOUR HAND AS IF IT WAS TAKEN OUT OF YOUR MOUTH.
THAT BIG MORON.
OH WELL, FIRST THINGS FIRST.
I'D BETTER HURRY UP AND HEAL.

WHISTLE!™

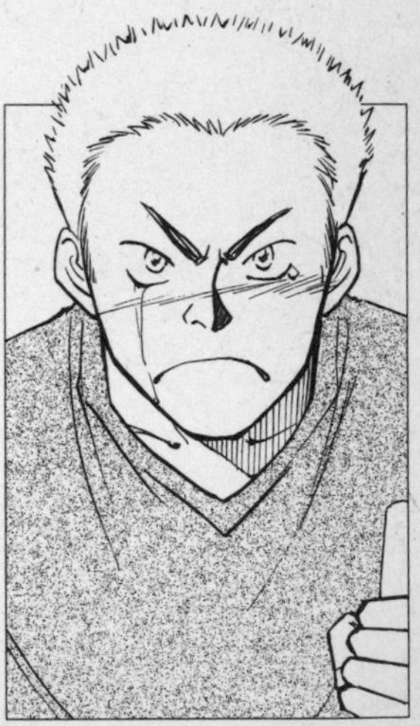

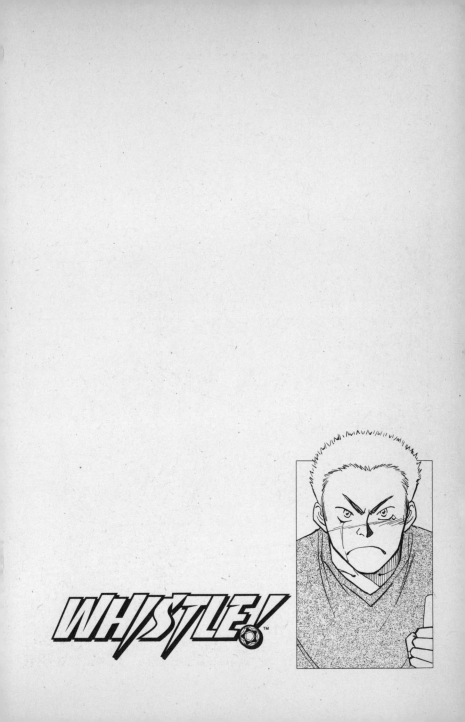

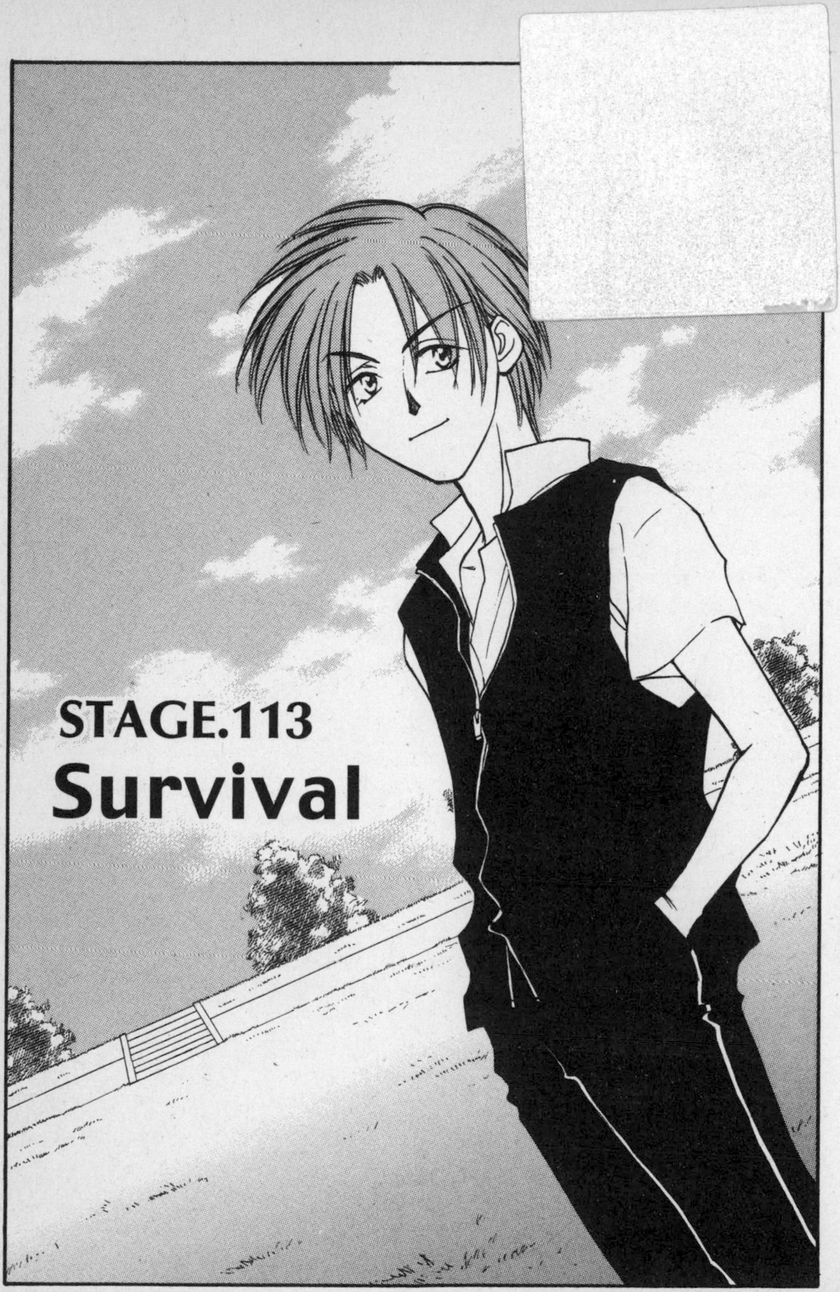
STAGE.113
Survival

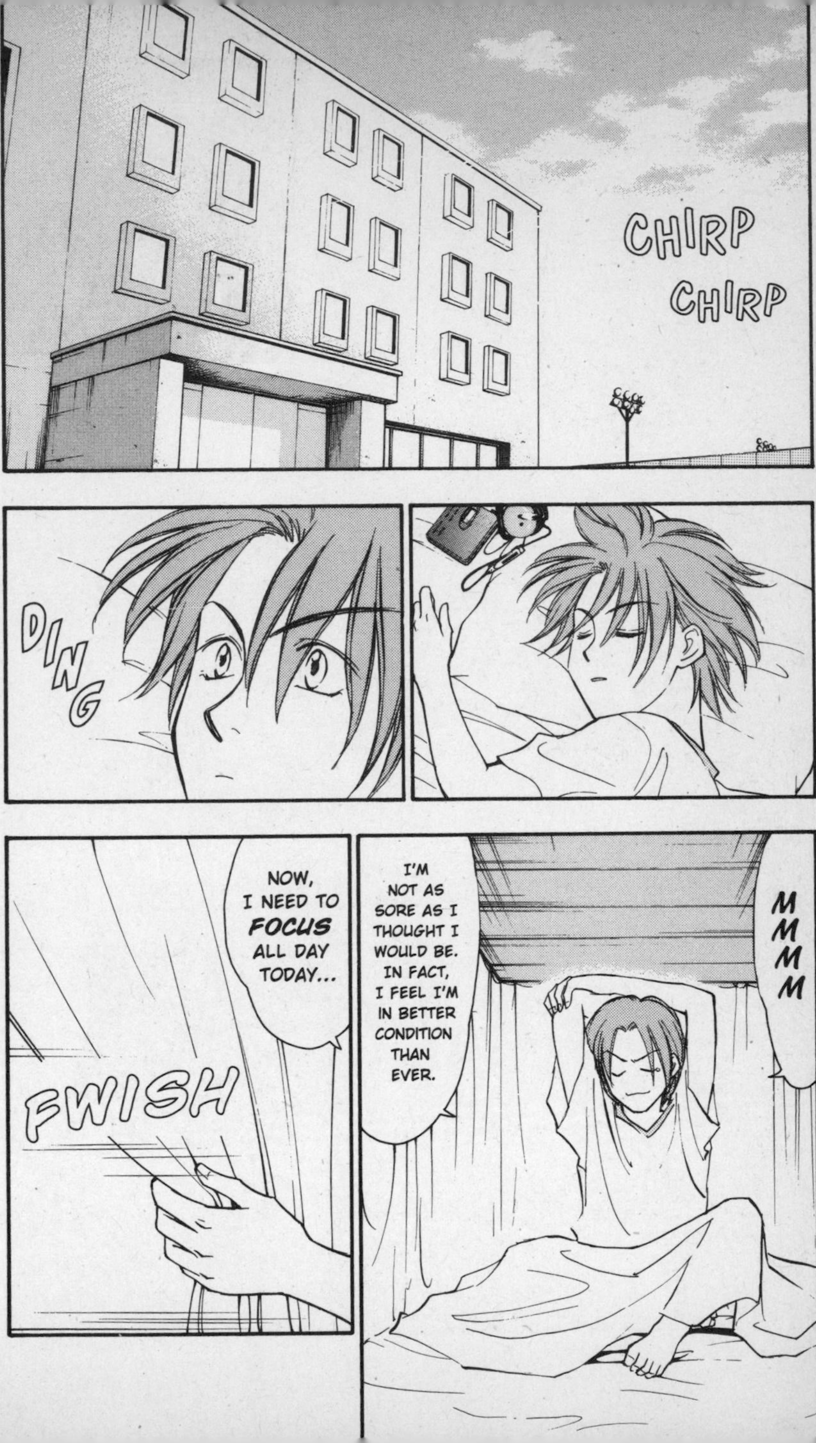
CHIRP
CHIRP
DING
MMMM
I'M NOT AS SORE AS I THOUGHT I WOULD BE. IN FACT, I FEEL I'M IN BETTER CONDITION THAN EVER.
NOW, I NEED TO **FOCUS** ALL DAY TODAY...
FWISH

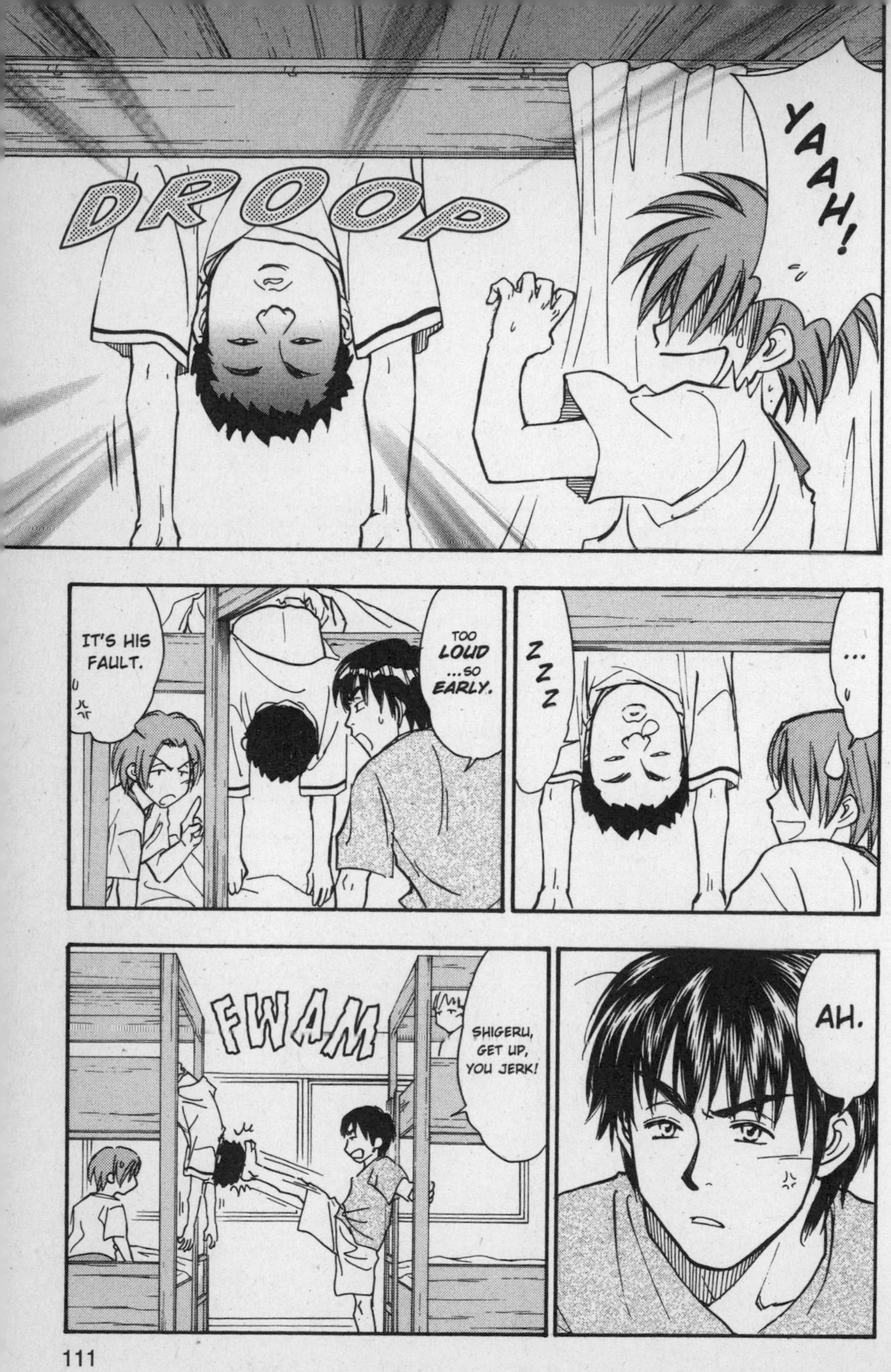
YAAH!
DROOP
...
ZZZ
TOO LOUD ...SO EARLY.
IT'S HIS FAULT.
AH.
SHIGERU, GET UP, YOU JERK!
FWAM

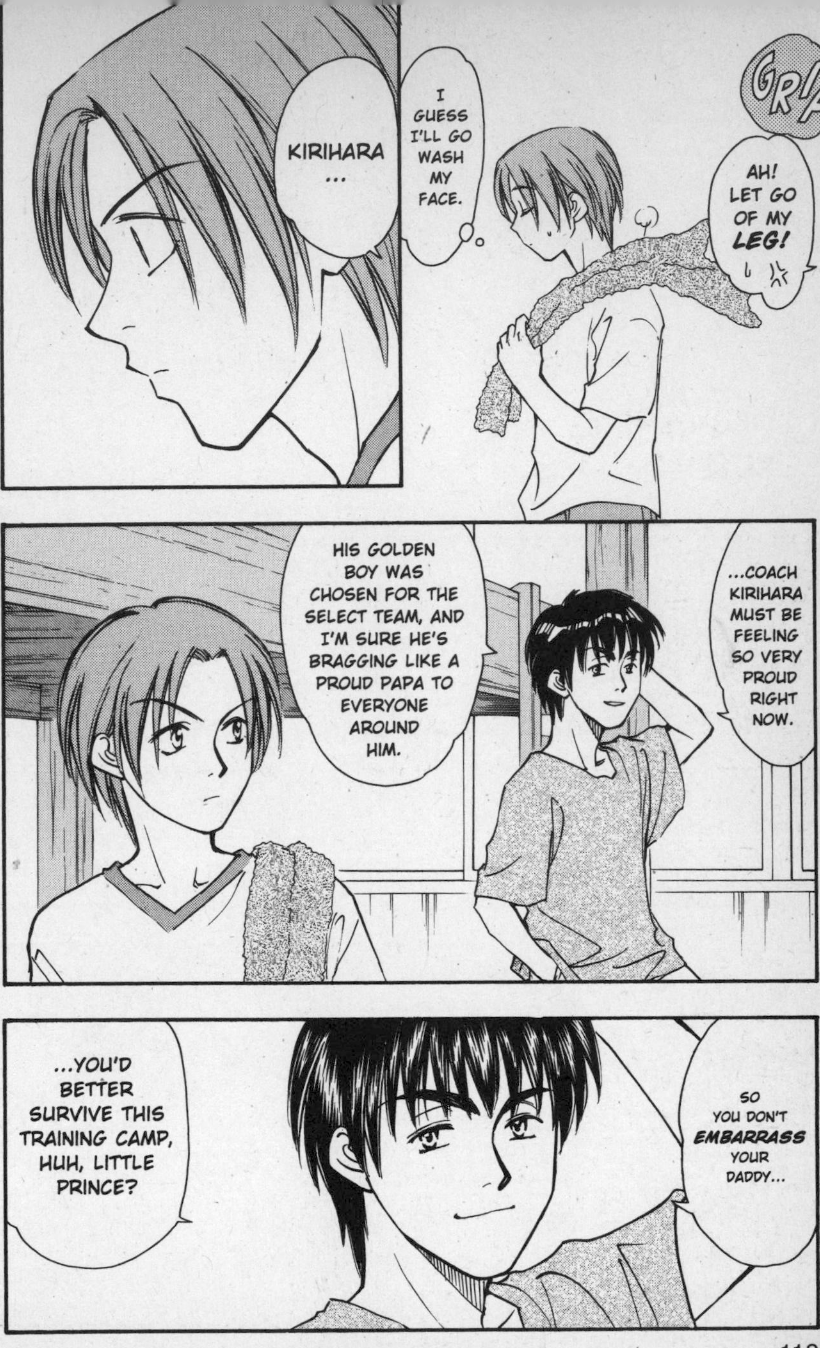
GRIP
AH! LET GO OF MY LEG!
I GUESS I'LL GO WASH MY FACE.
KIRIHARA ...
...COACH KIRIHARA MUST BE FEELING SO VERY PROUD RIGHT NOW.
HIS GOLDEN BOY WAS CHOSEN FOR THE SELECT TEAM, AND I'M SURE HE'S BRAGGING LIKE A PROUD PAPA TO EVERYONE AROUND HIM.
SO YOU DON'T EMBARRASS YOUR DADDY...
...YOU'D BETTER SURVIVE THIS TRAINING CAMP, HUH, LITTLE PRINCE?

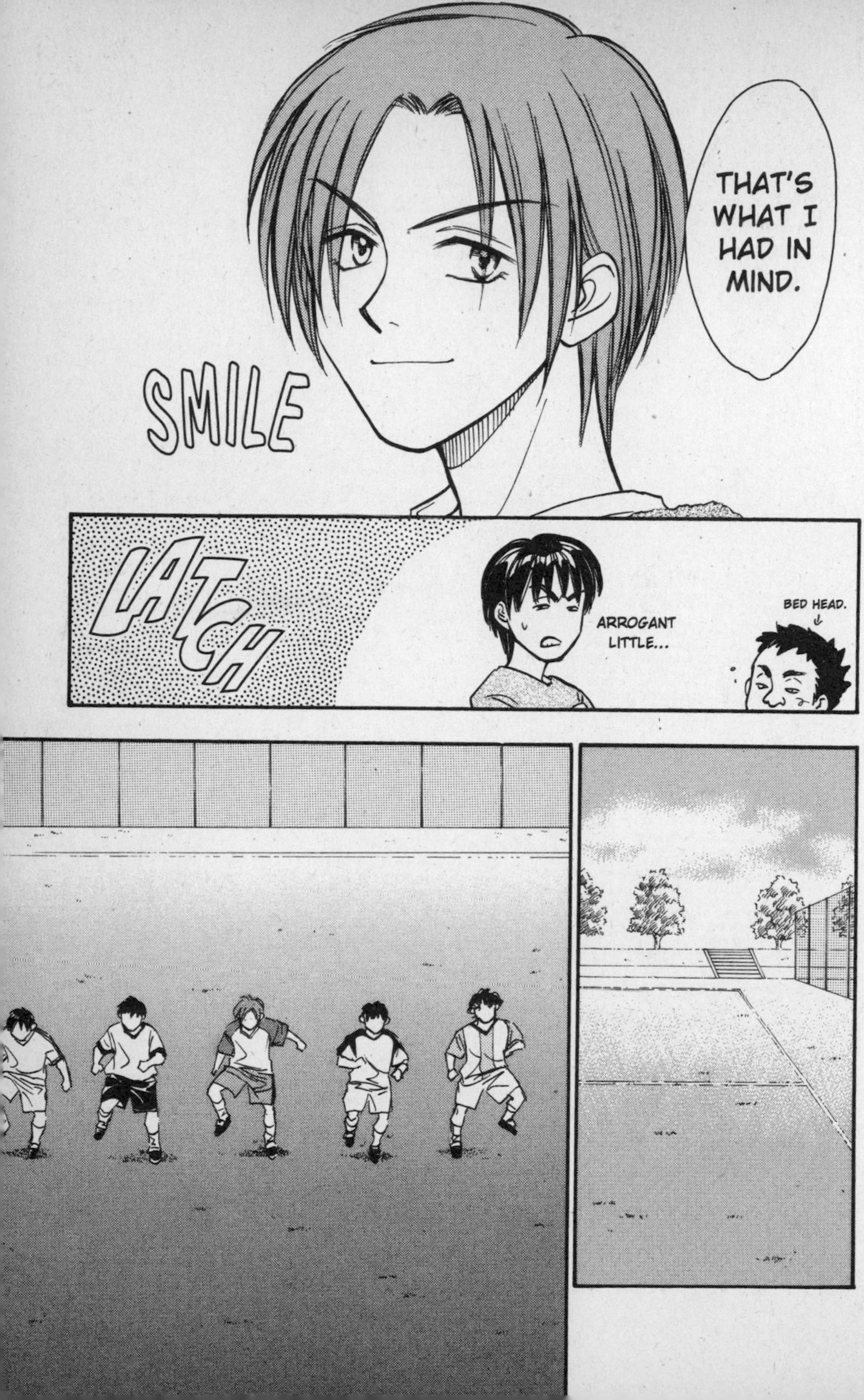
THAT'S WHAT I HAD IN MIND.
SMILE
BED HEAD.
ARROGANT LITTLE...
LATCH

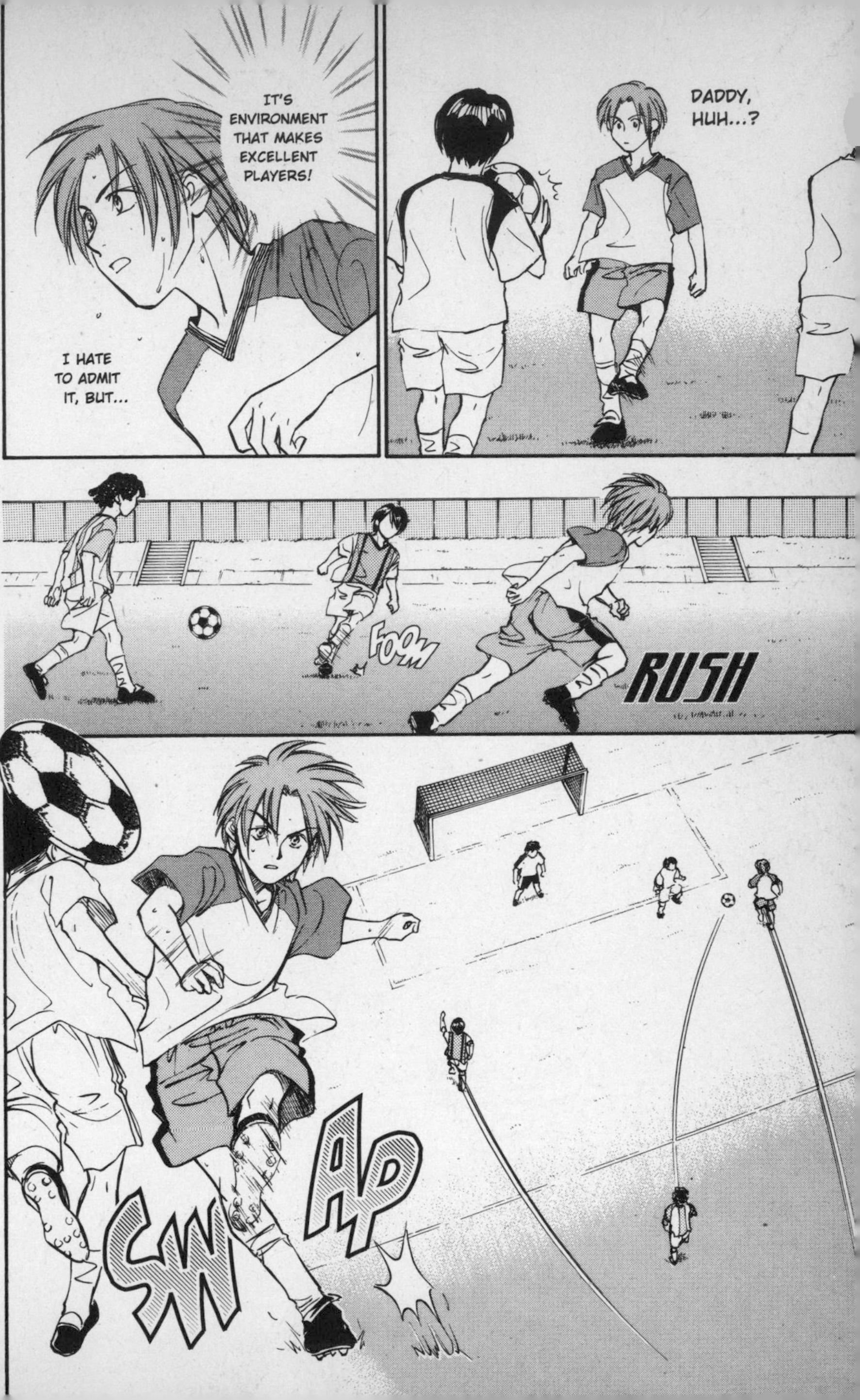
DADDY, HUH...?
I HATE TO ADMIT IT, BUT...
IT'S ENVIRONMENT THAT MAKES EXCELLENT PLAYERS!
RUSH
FOOM
SWAP

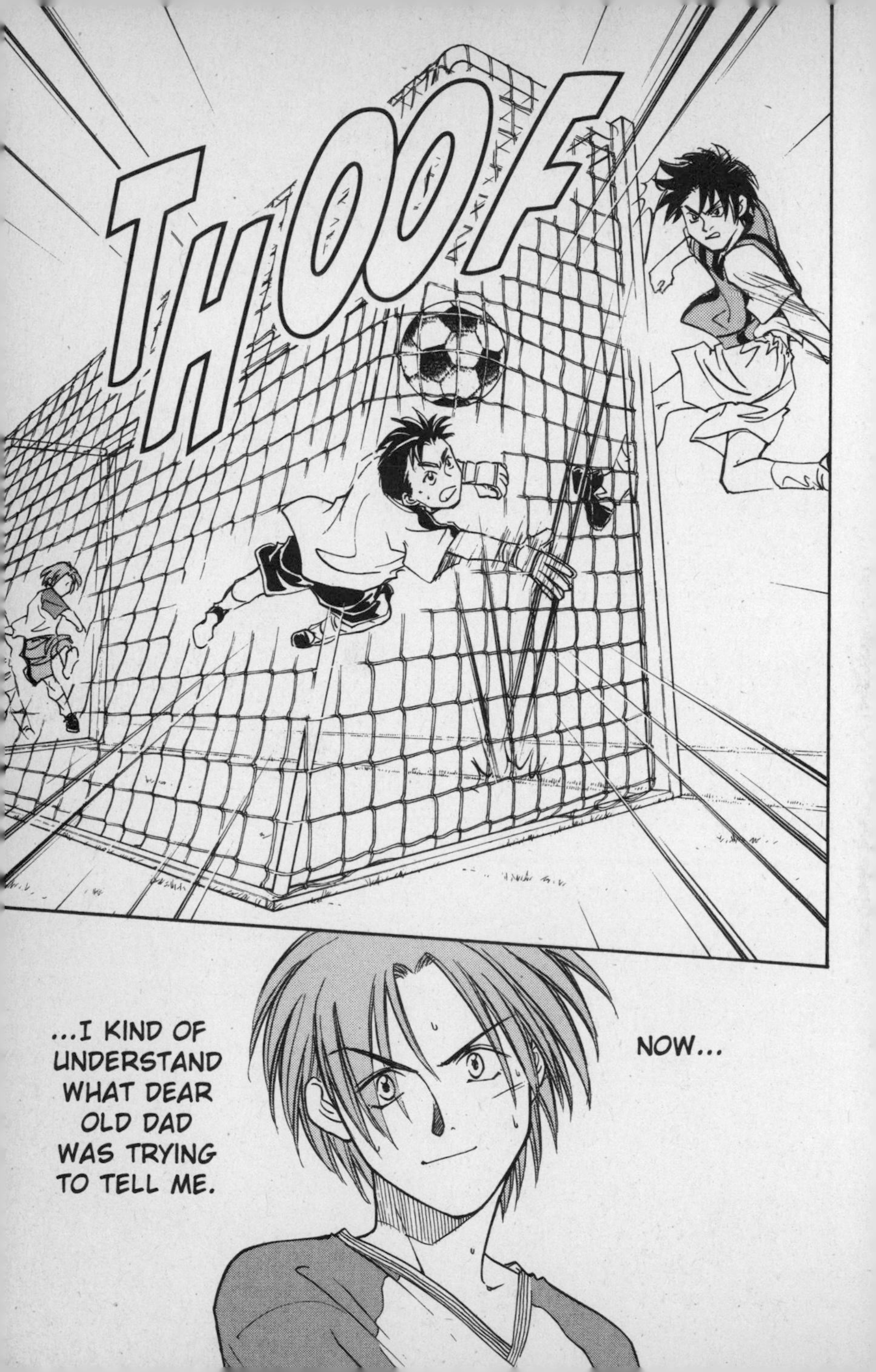
THOOF
NOW...
...I KIND OF UNDERSTAND WHAT DEAR OLD DAD WAS TRYING TO TELL ME.

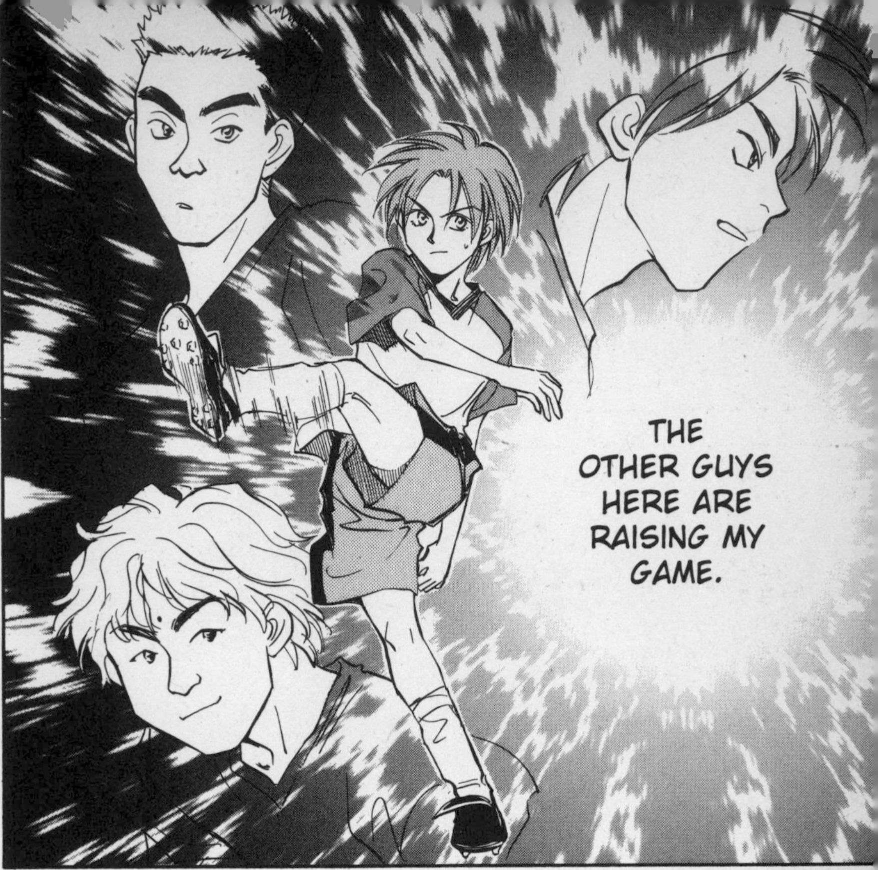
THE OTHER GUYS HERE ARE RAISING MY GAME.

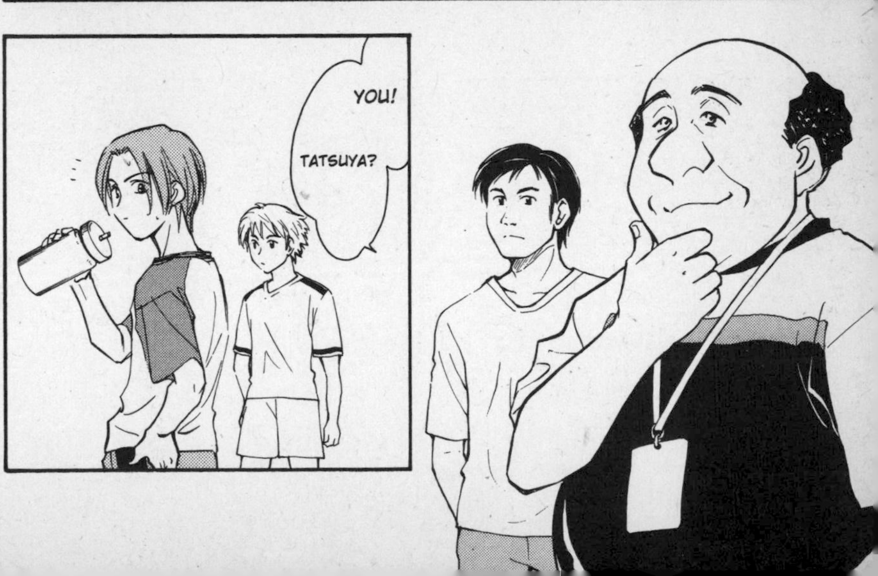
YOU!
TATSUYA?

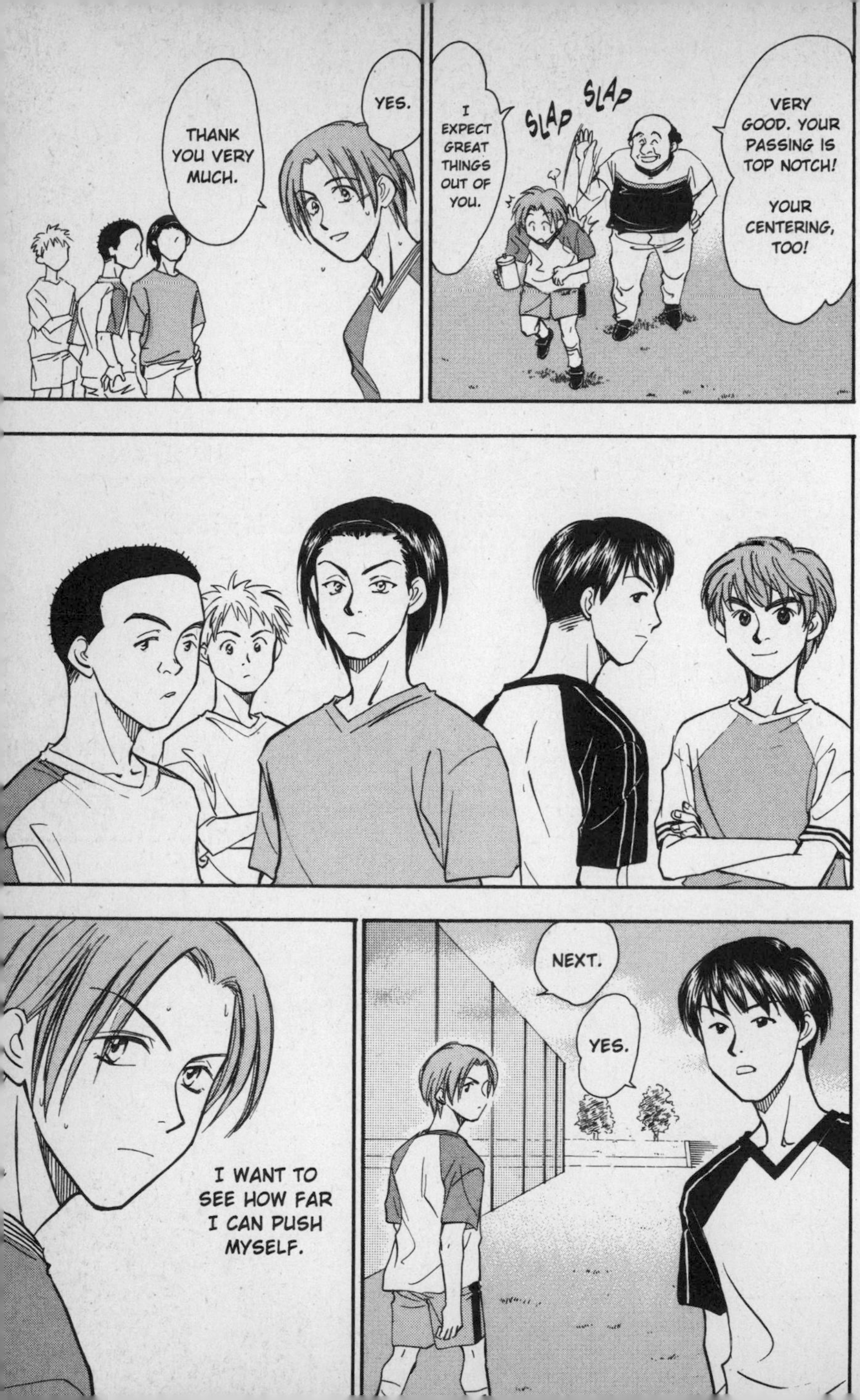
VERY GOOD. YOUR PASSING IS TOP NOTCH!
YOUR CENTERING, TOO!
SLAP
SLAP
I EXPECT GREAT THINGS OUT OF YOU.
YES.
THANK YOU VERY MUCH.
NEXT.
YES.
I WANT TO SEE HOW FAR I CAN PUSH MYSELF.

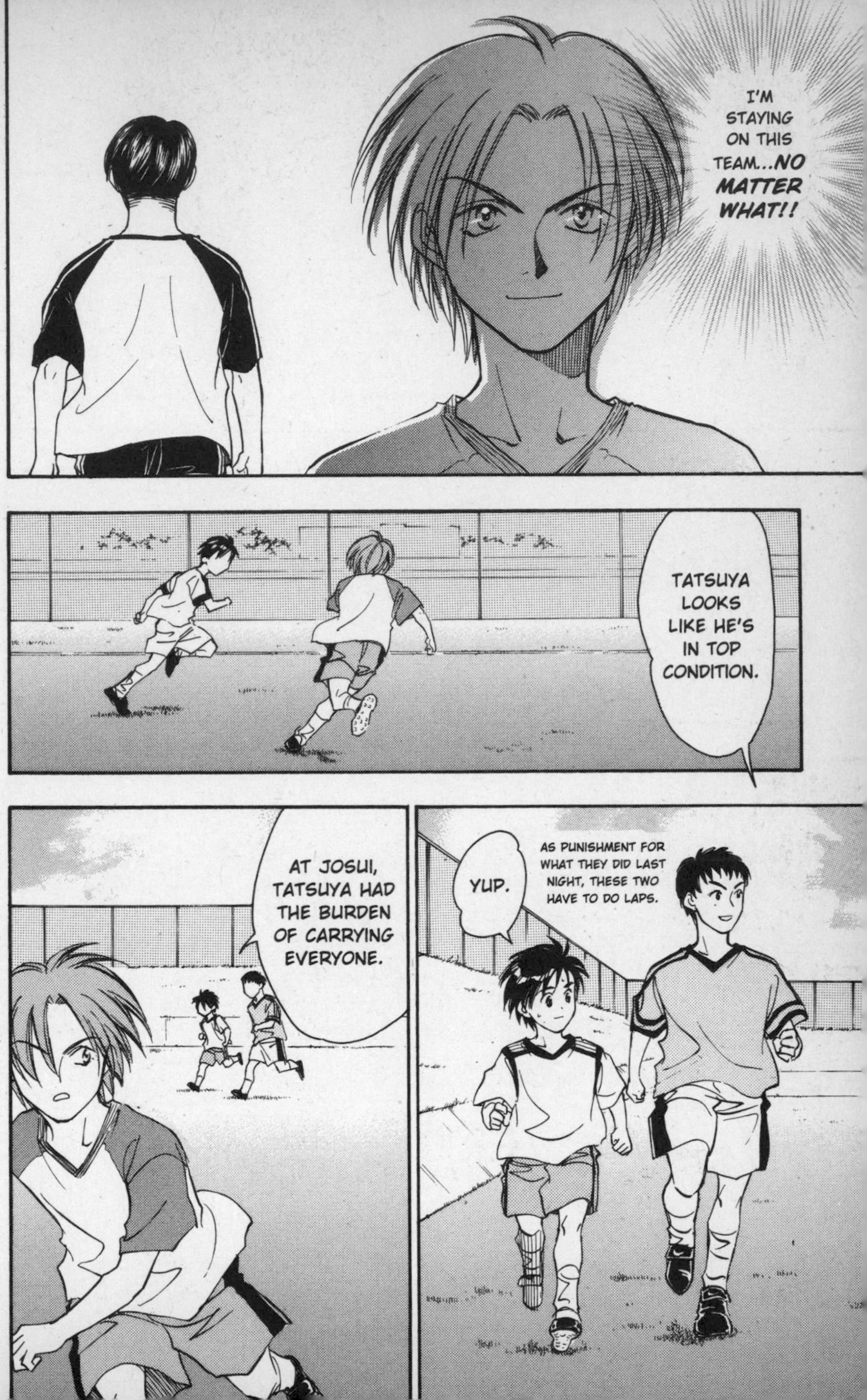
I'M STAYING ON THIS TEAM...NO MATTER WHAT!!
TATSUYA LOOKS LIKE HE'S IN TOP CONDITION.
AS PUNISHMENT FOR WHAT THEY DID LAST NIGHT, THESE TWO HAVE TO DO LAPS.
YUP.
AT JOSUI, TATSUYA HAD THE BURDEN OF CARRYING EVERYONE.

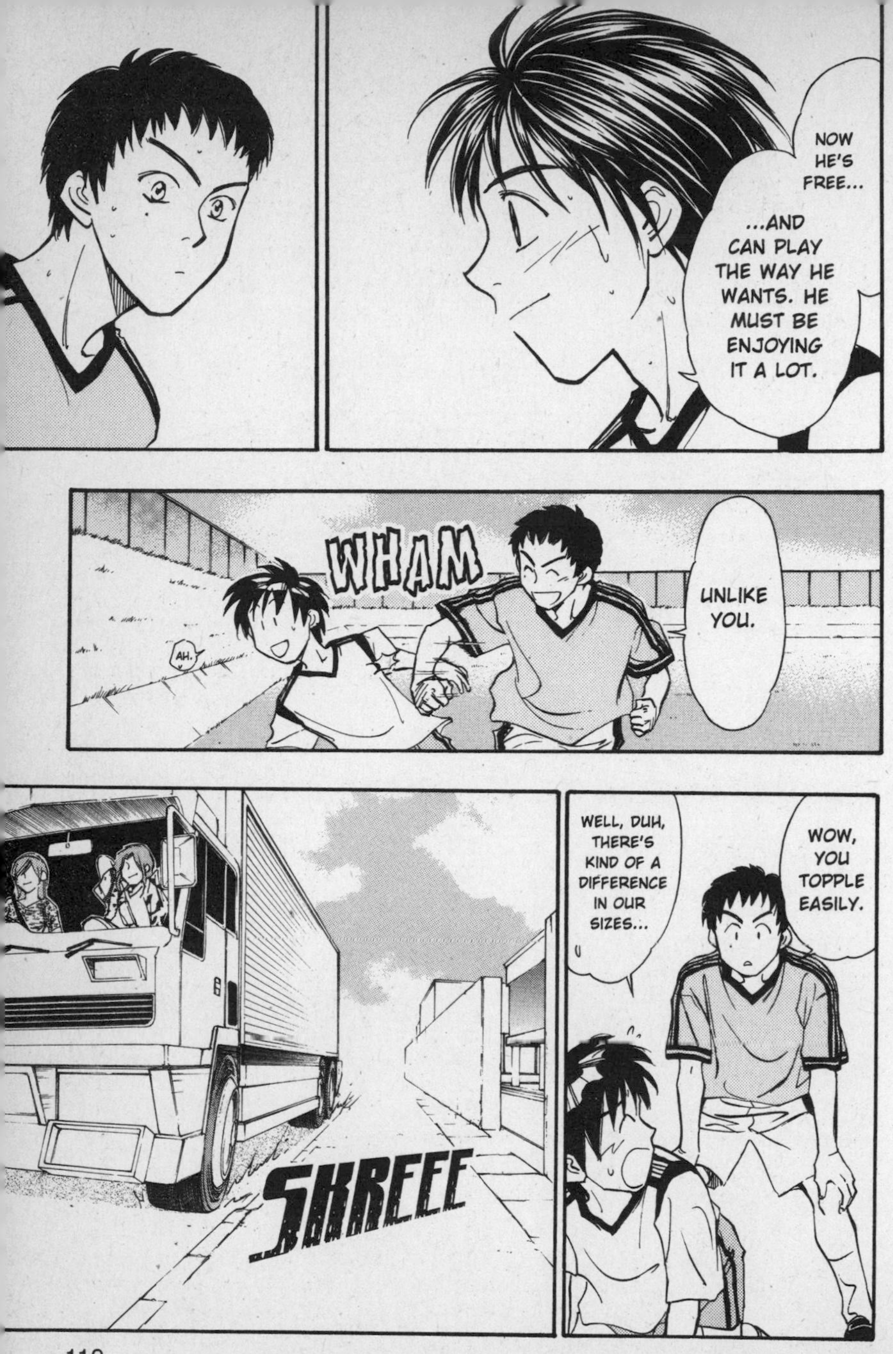
NOW HE'S FREE...
...AND CAN PLAY THE WAY HE WANTS. HE MUST BE ENJOYING IT A LOT.
UNLIKE YOU.
WHAM
AH.
WOW, YOU TOPPLE EASILY.
WELL, DUH, THERE'S KIND OF A DIFFERENCE IN OUR SIZES...
SKREEE

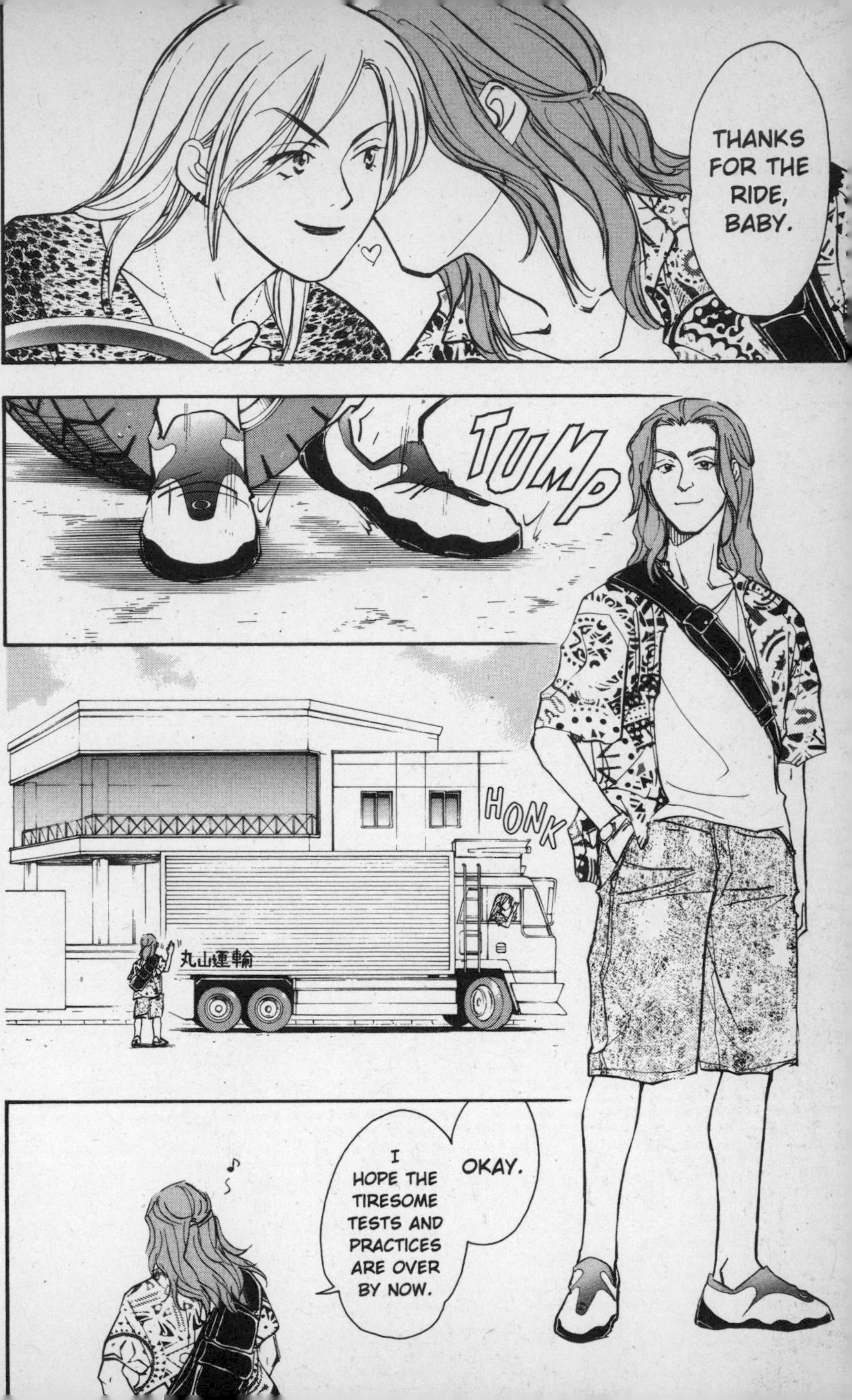
THANKS FOR THE RIDE, BABY.
TUMP
HONK
丸山運輸
OKAY.
I HOPE THE TIRESOME TESTS AND PRACTICES ARE OVER BY NOW.

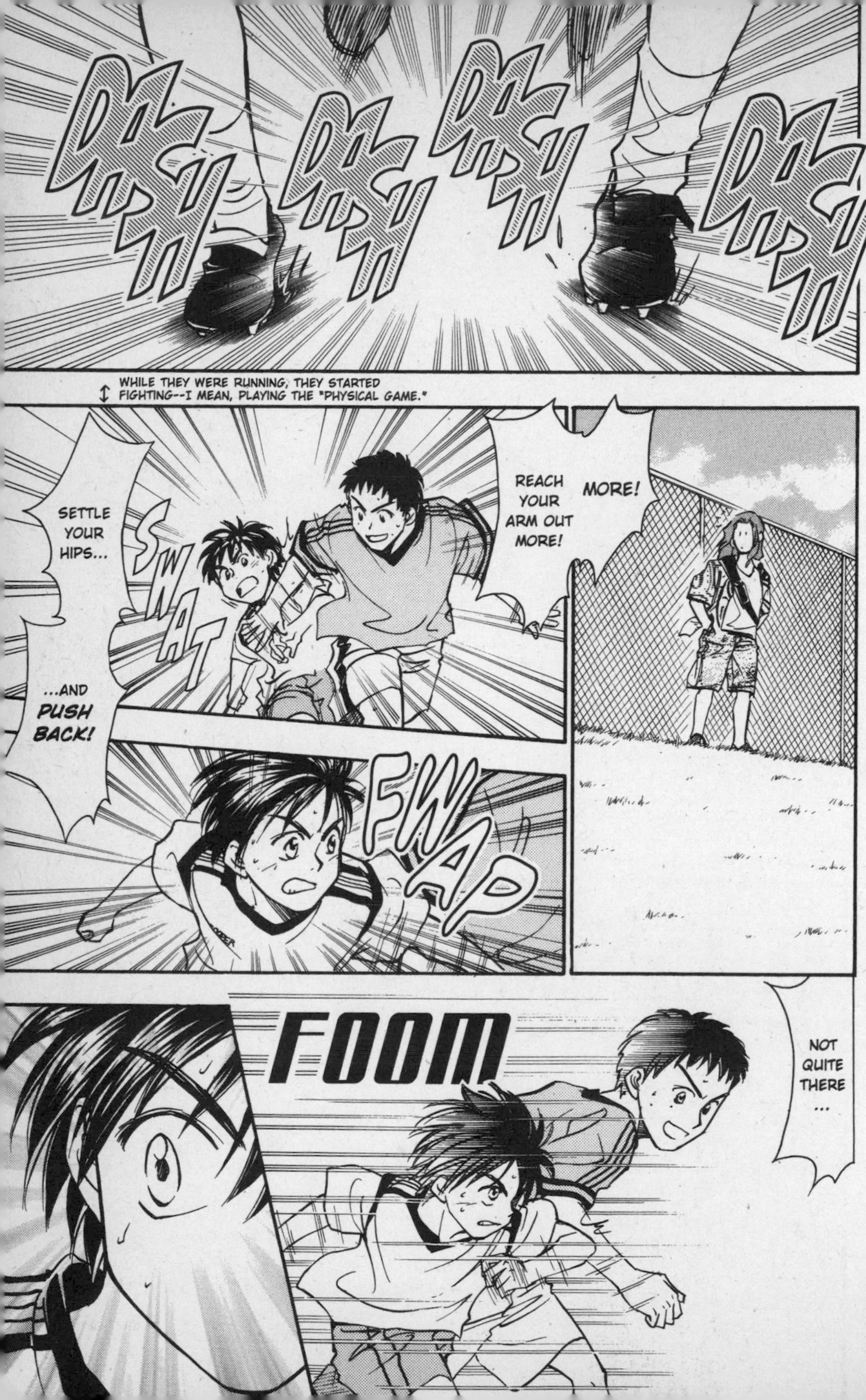
DASH
DASH
DASH
DASH
WHILE THEY WERE RUNNING, THEY STARTED FIGHTING--I MEAN, PLAYING THE "PHYSICAL GAME."
REACH YOUR ARM OUT MORE! MORE!
SWAT
SETTLE YOUR HIPS...
...AND PUSH BACK!
FWAP
NOT QUITE THERE...
FOOM

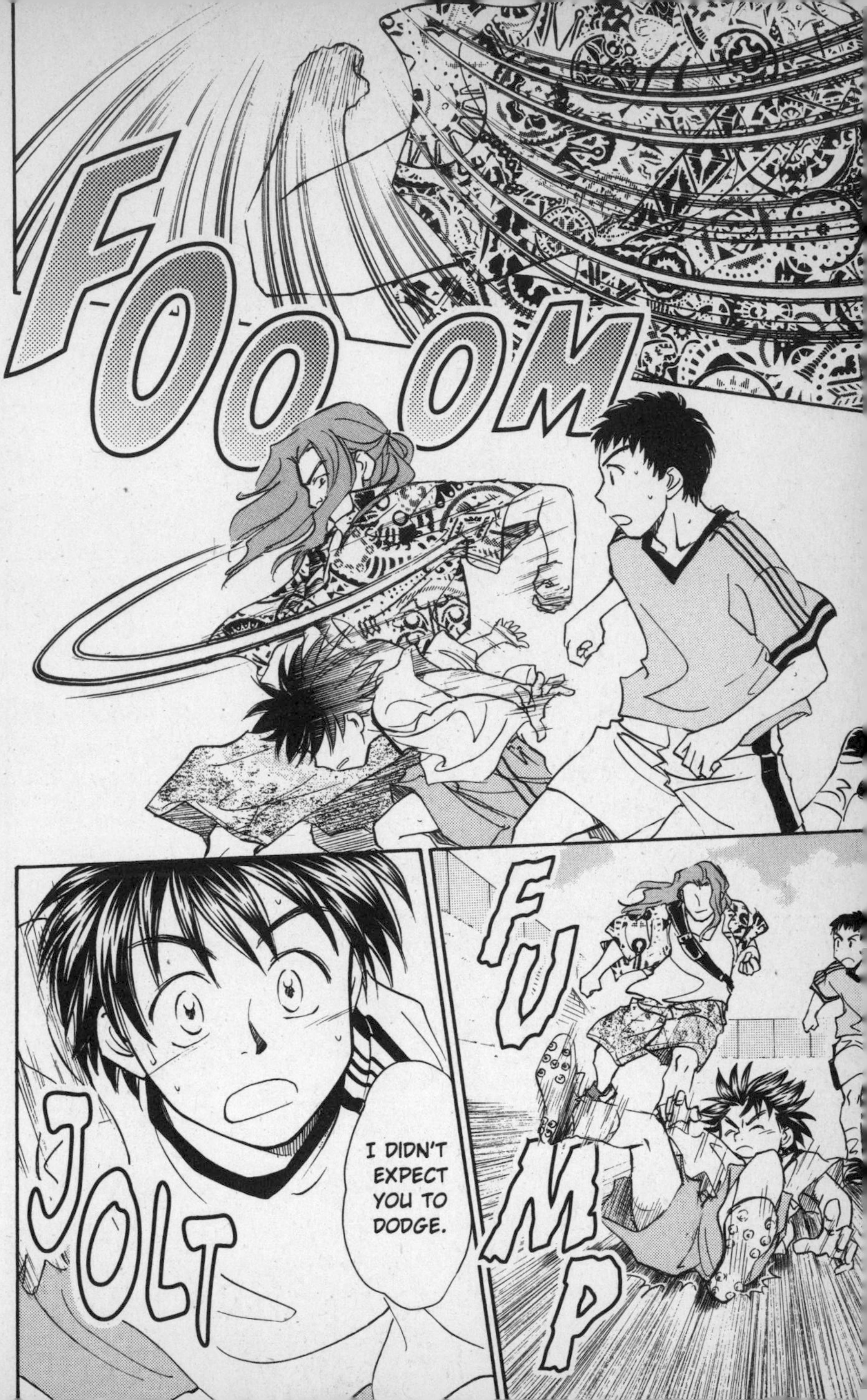
FOOOM
FUMP
JOLT
I DIDN'T EXPECT YOU TO DODGE.

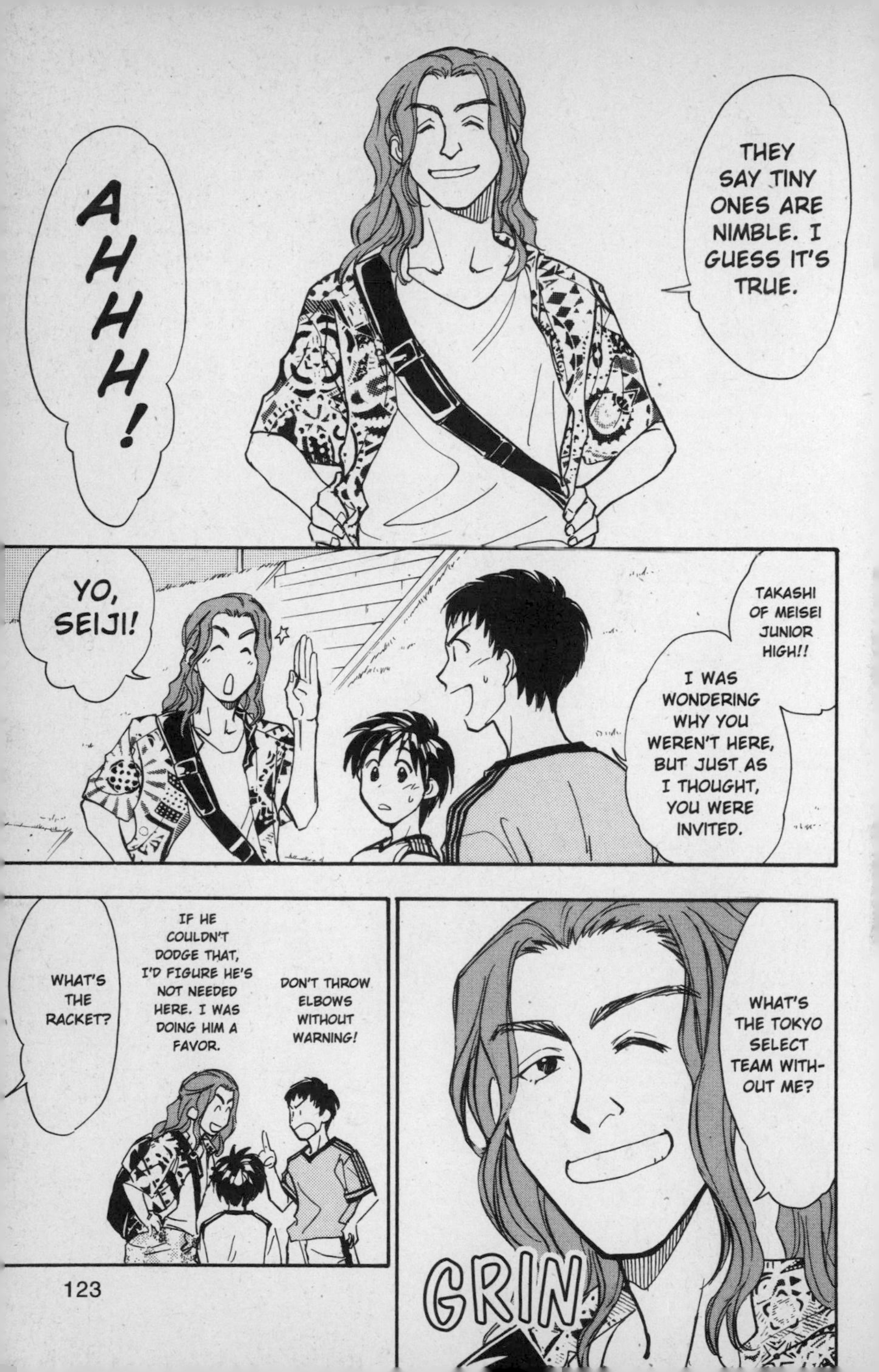
THEY SAY TINY ONES ARE NIMBLE. I GUESS IT'S TRUE.
AHHH!
TAKASHI OF MEISEI JUNIOR HIGH!!
I WAS WONDERING WHY YOU WEREN'T HERE, BUT JUST AS I THOUGHT, YOU WERE INVITED.
YO, SEIJI!
DON'T THROW ELBOWS WITHOUT WARNING!
IF HE COULDN'T DODGE THAT, I'D FIGURE HE'S NOT NEEDED HERE. I WAS DOING HIM A FAVOR.
WHAT'S THE RACKET?
WHAT'S THE TOKYO SELECT TEAM WITH-OUT ME?
GRIN

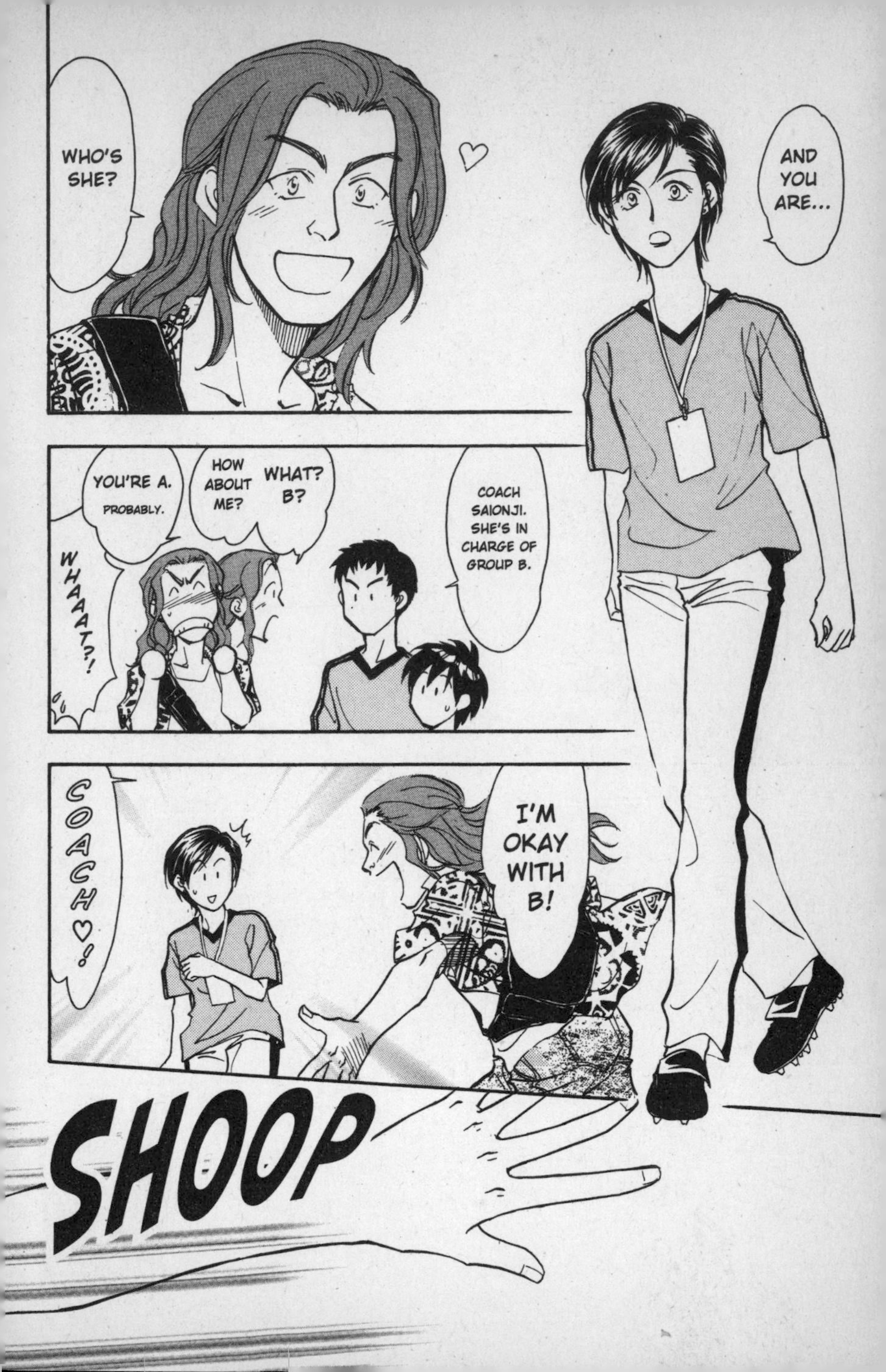
AND YOU ARE...
WHO'S SHE?
COACH SAIONJI. SHE'S IN CHARGE OF GROUP B.
WHAT? B?
HOW ABOUT ME?
YOU'RE A. PROBABLY.
WHAAAAT?!
I'M OKAY WITH B!
COACH♡!
SHOOP

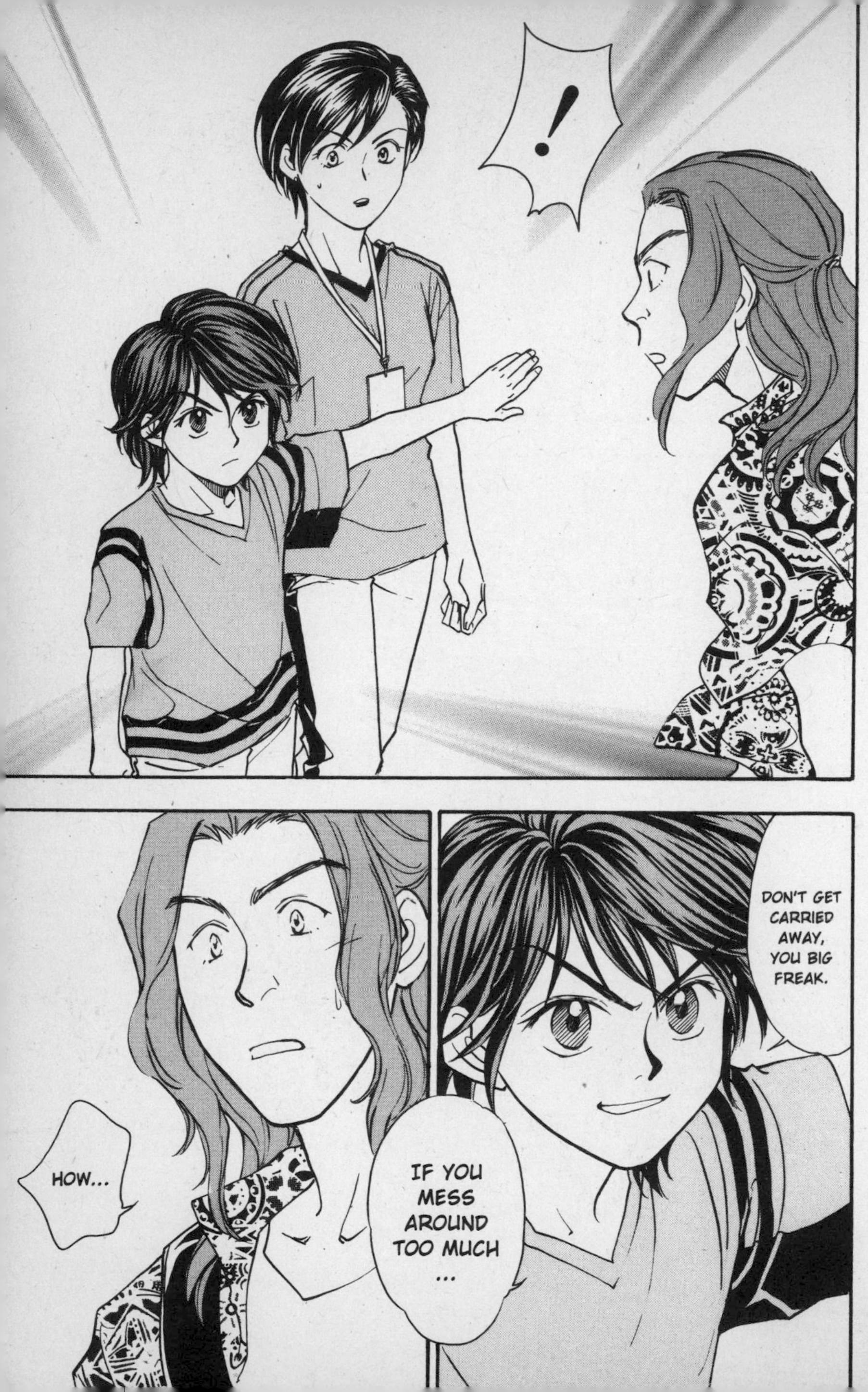
!
DON'T GET CARRIED AWAY, YOU BIG FREAK.
IF YOU MESS AROUND TOO MUCH ...
HOW...

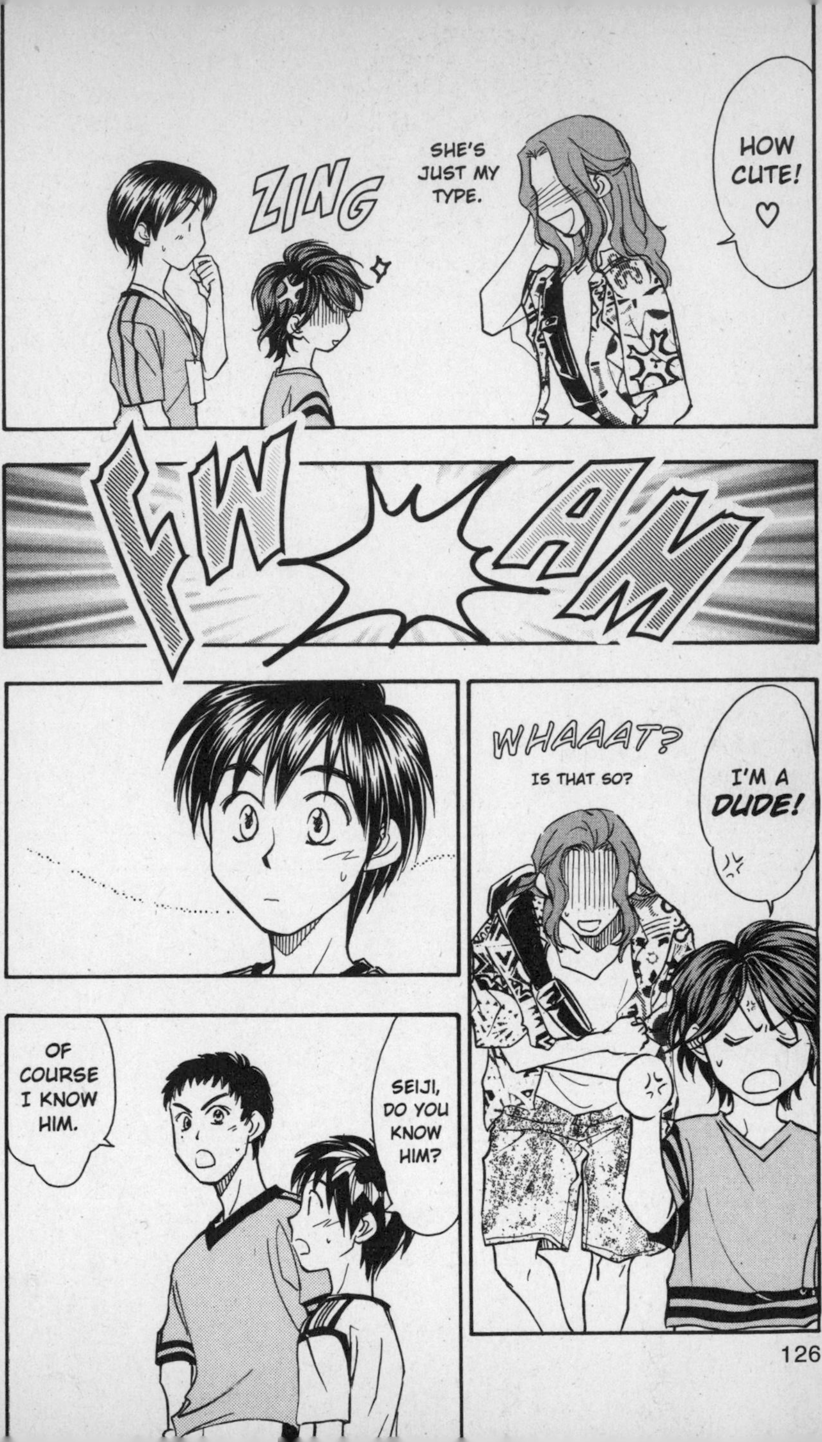
HOW CUTE! ♡
SHE'S JUST MY TYPE.
ZING
FWAM
I'M A **DUDE!**
WHAAAT?
IS THAT SO?
SEIJI, DO YOU KNOW HIM?
OF COURSE I KNOW HIM.

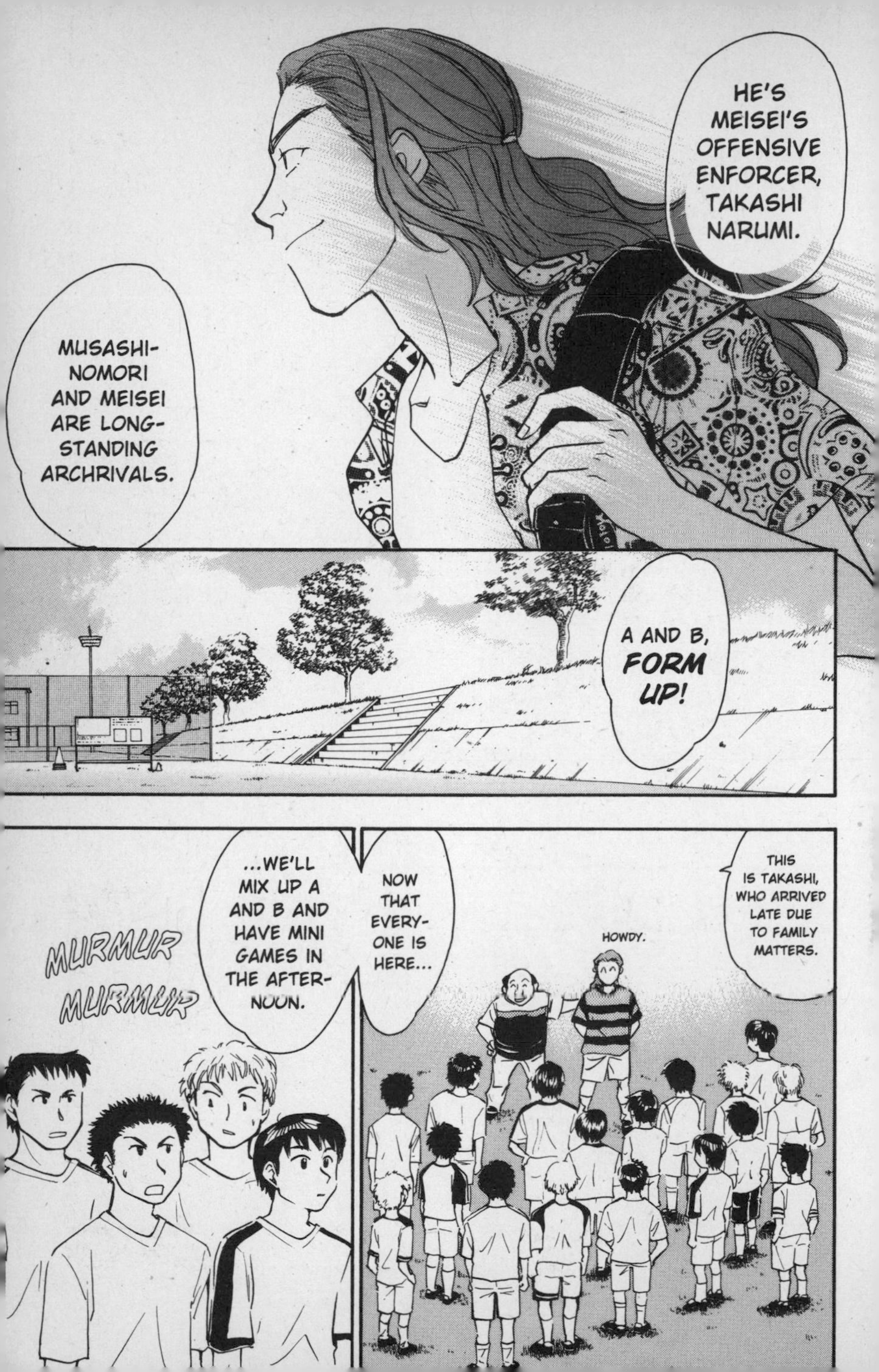
HE'S MEISEI'S OFFENSIVE ENFORCER, TAKASHI NARUMI.
MUSASHI-NOMORI AND MEISEI ARE LONG-STANDING ARCHRIVALS.
A AND B, FORM UP!
THIS IS TAKASHI, WHO ARRIVED LATE DUE TO FAMILY MATTERS.
HOWDY.
NOW THAT EVERY-ONE IS HERE...
...WE'LL MIX UP A AND B AND HAVE MINI GAMES IN THE AFTER-NOON.
MURMUR MURMUR

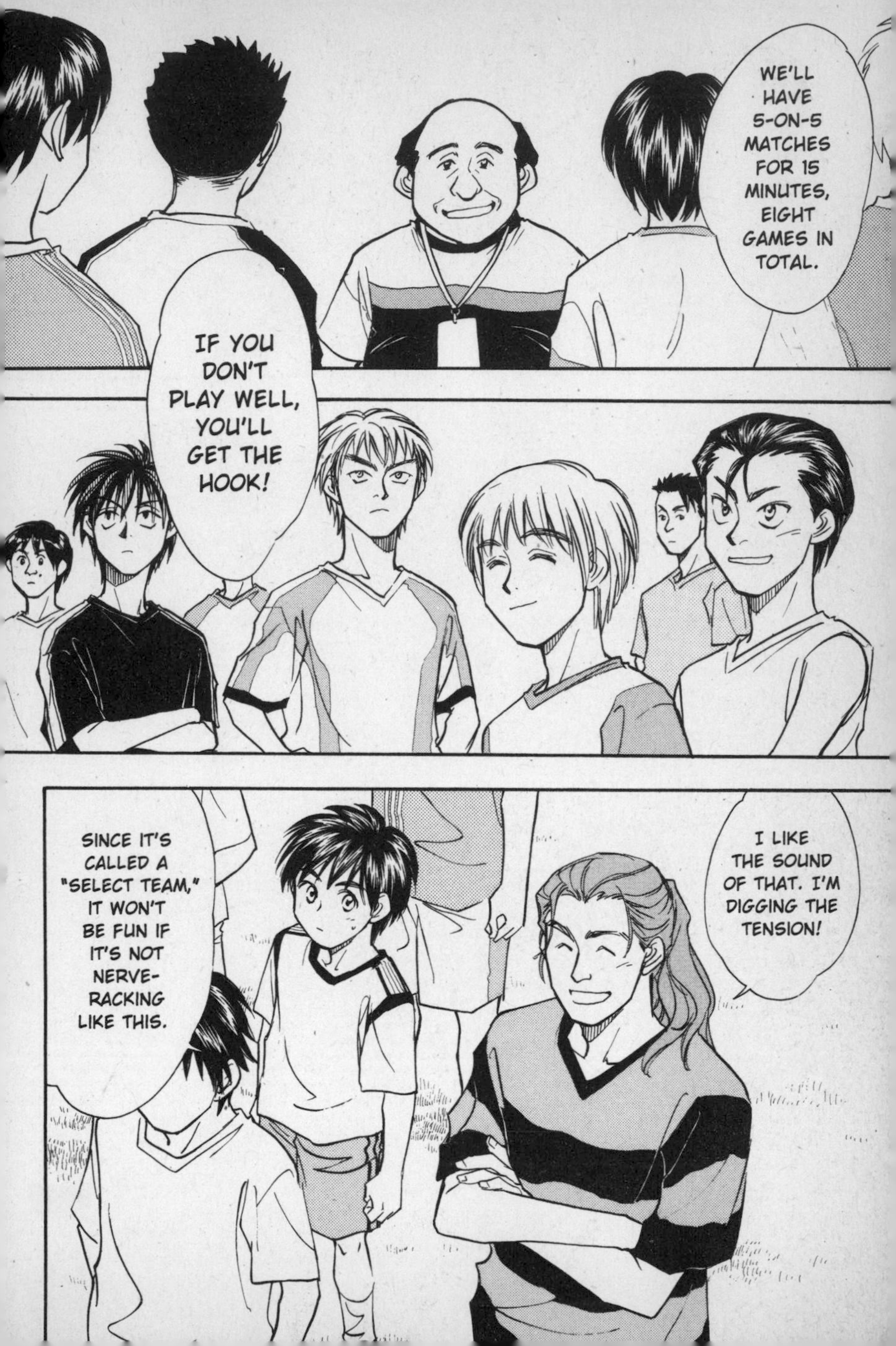
WE'LL HAVE 5-ON-5 MATCHES FOR 15 MINUTES, EIGHT GAMES IN TOTAL.
IF YOU DON'T PLAY WELL, YOU'LL GET THE HOOK!
I LIKE THE SOUND OF THAT. I'M DIGGING THE TENSION!
SINCE IT'S CALLED A "SELECT TEAM," IT WON'T BE FUN IF IT'S NOT NERVE-RACKING LIKE THIS.

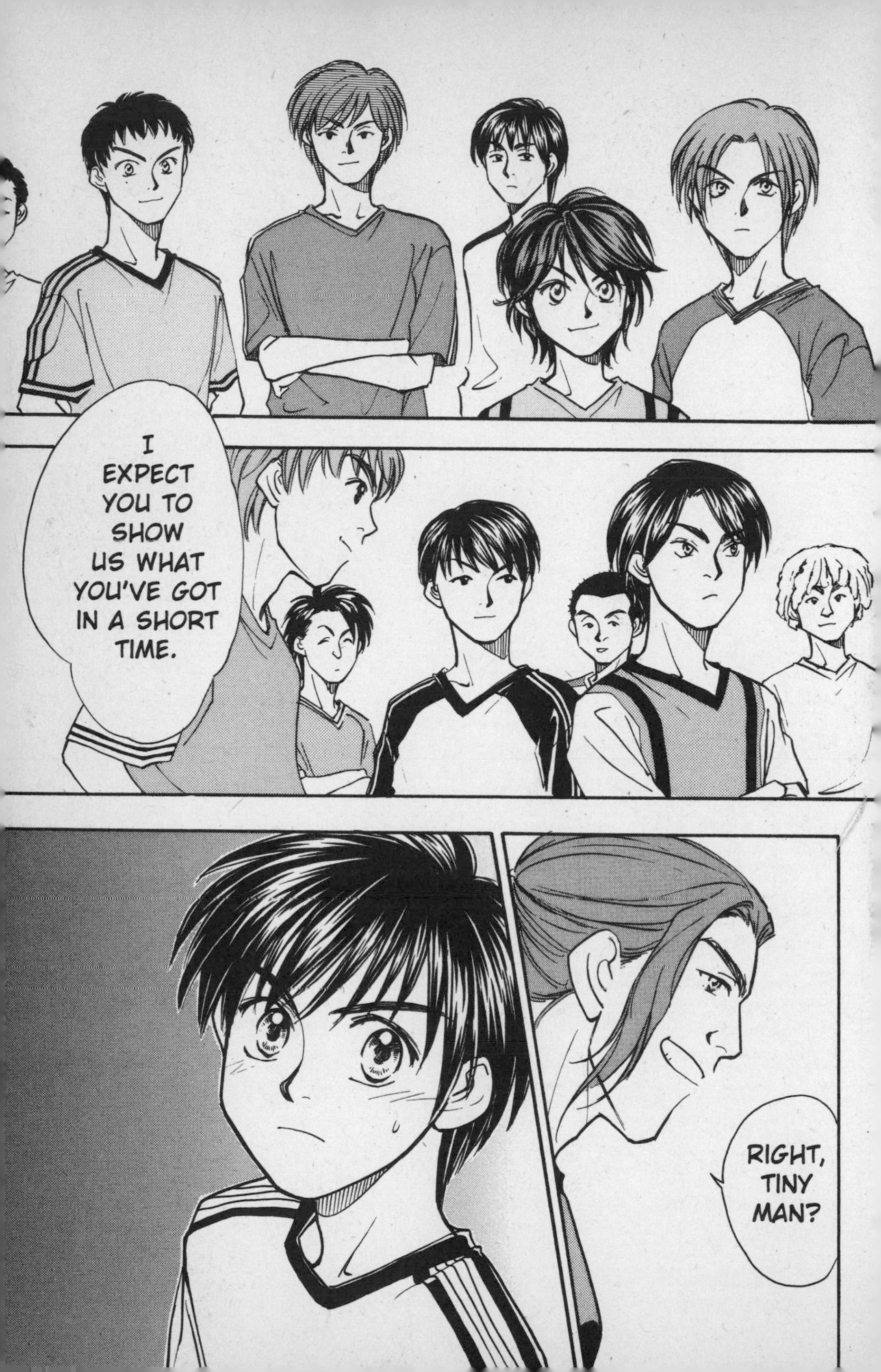
I EXPECT YOU TO SHOW US WHAT YOU'VE GOT IN A SHORT TIME.
RIGHT, TINY MAN?

WEE-STYLE! THEATRE!!

Snapping Turtle

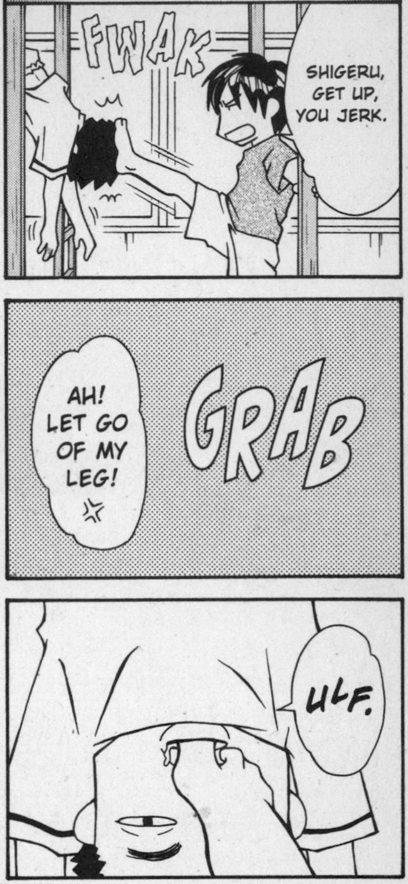
FWAK
SHIGERU, GET UP, YOU JERK.
AH! LET GO OF MY LEG!
GRAB
ULF.
SMIRK
EEEK! WAKE UP, FREAK!!

Another one?

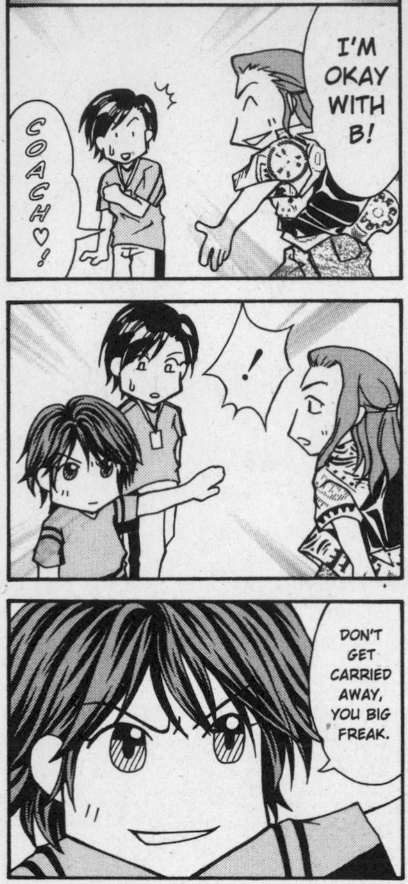
I'M OKAY WITH B!
COACH♡!
!
DON'T GET CARRIED AWAY, YOU BIG FREAK.
AND HERE'S A FREAK, TOO...
SIZZLE SIZZLE
HUH?

MANGA BY SEKI, ASSISTANT S

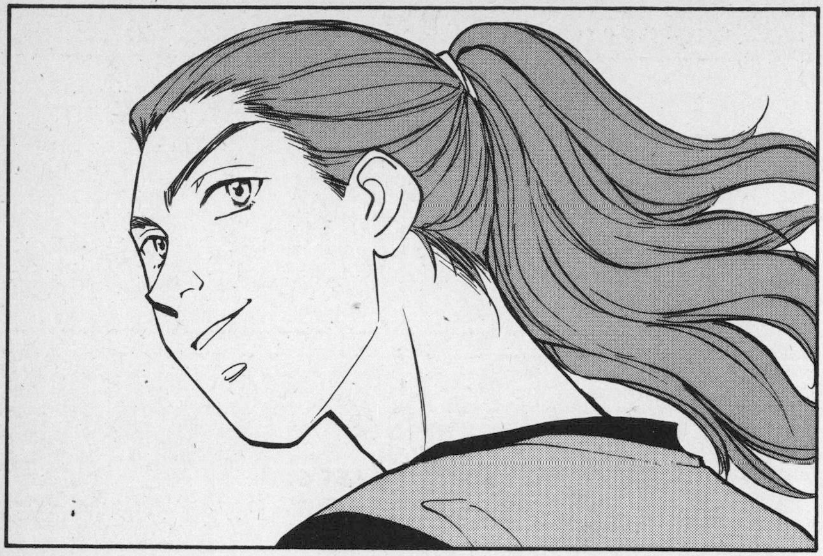

STAGE.114 Mini Games Begin

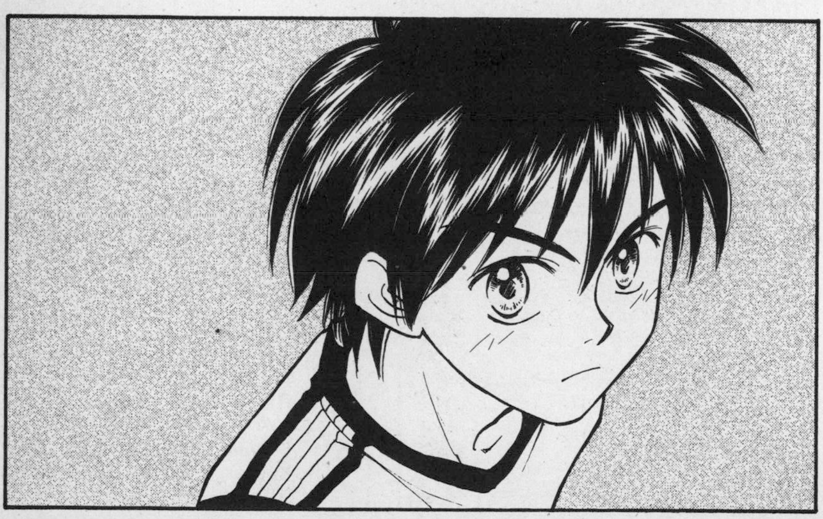

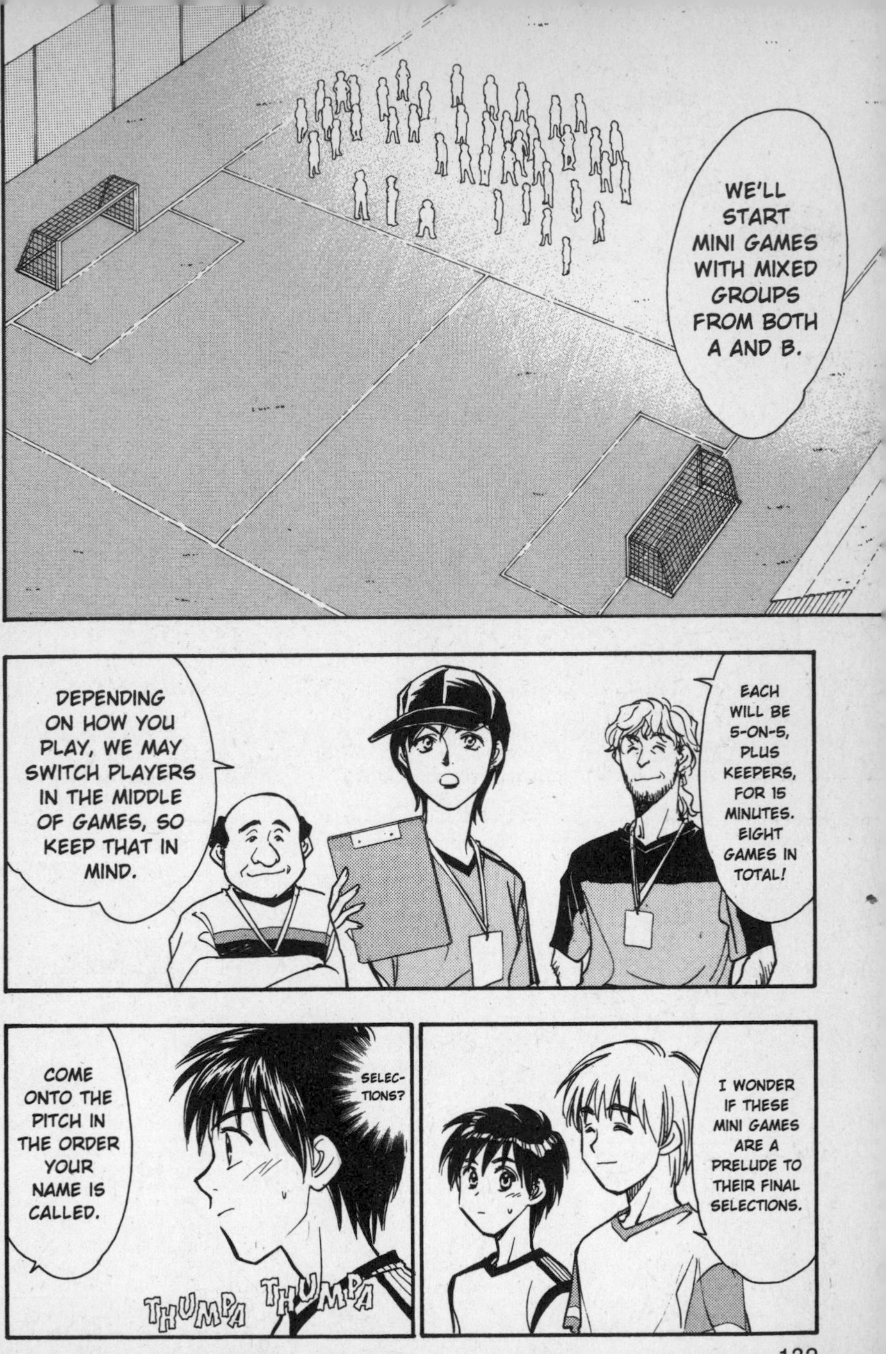
WE'LL START MINI GAMES WITH MIXED GROUPS FROM BOTH A AND B.
EACH WILL BE 5-ON-5, PLUS KEEPERS, FOR 15 MINUTES. EIGHT GAMES IN TOTAL!
DEPENDING ON HOW YOU PLAY, WE MAY SWITCH PLAYERS IN THE MIDDLE OF GAMES, SO KEEP THAT IN MIND.
I WONDER IF THESE MINI GAMES ARE A PRELUDE TO THEIR FINAL SELECTIONS.
SELECTIONS?
COME ONTO THE PITCH IN THE ORDER YOUR NAME IS CALLED.
THUMPA THUMPA

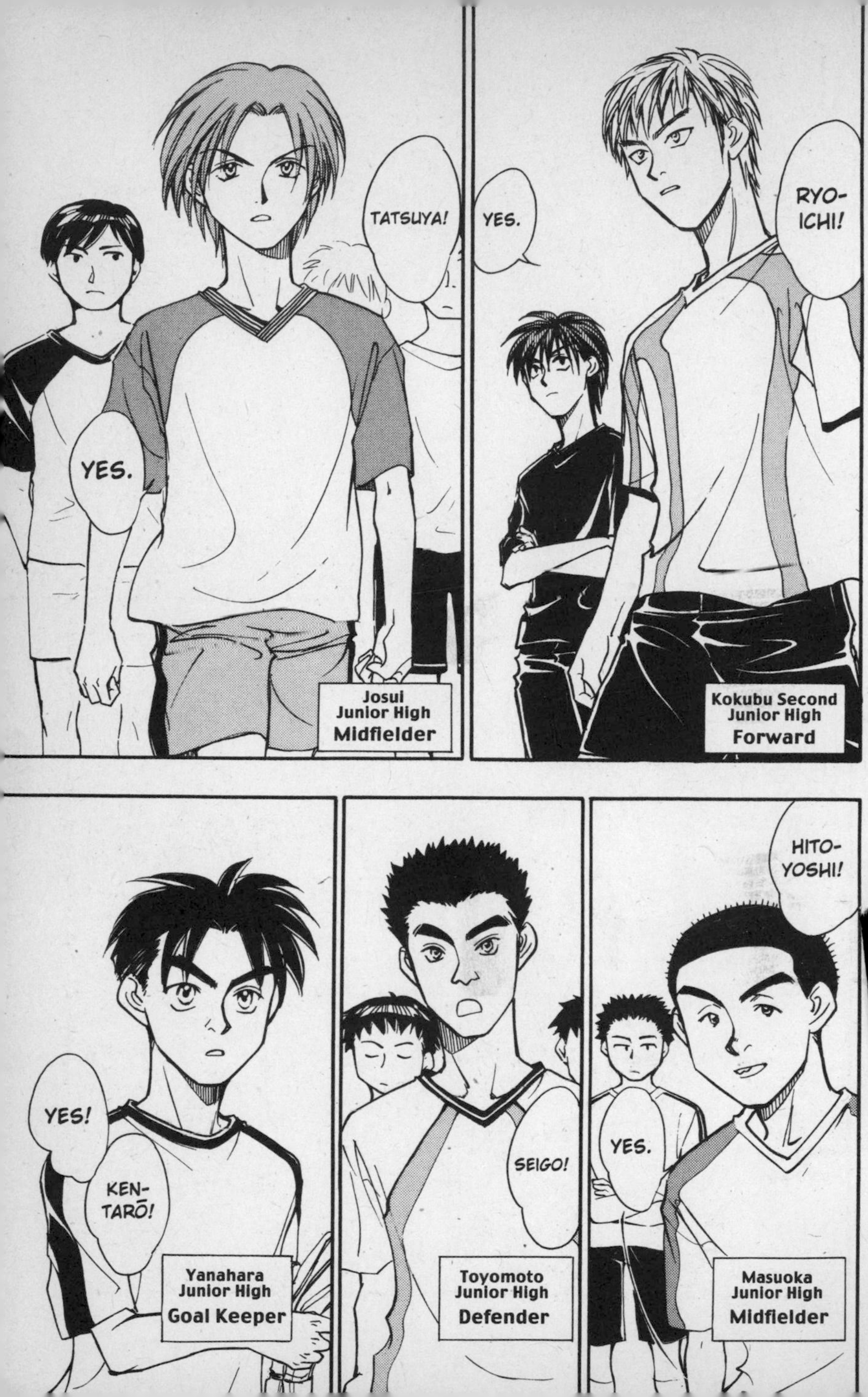
RYO-ICHI!
YES.
Kokubu Second Junior High Forward
TATSUYA!
YES.
Josui Junior High Midfielder
HITO-YOSHI!
YES.
Masuoka Junior High Midfielder
SEIGO!
Toyomoto Junior High Defender
KEN-TARŌ!
YES!
Yanahara Junior High Goal Keeper

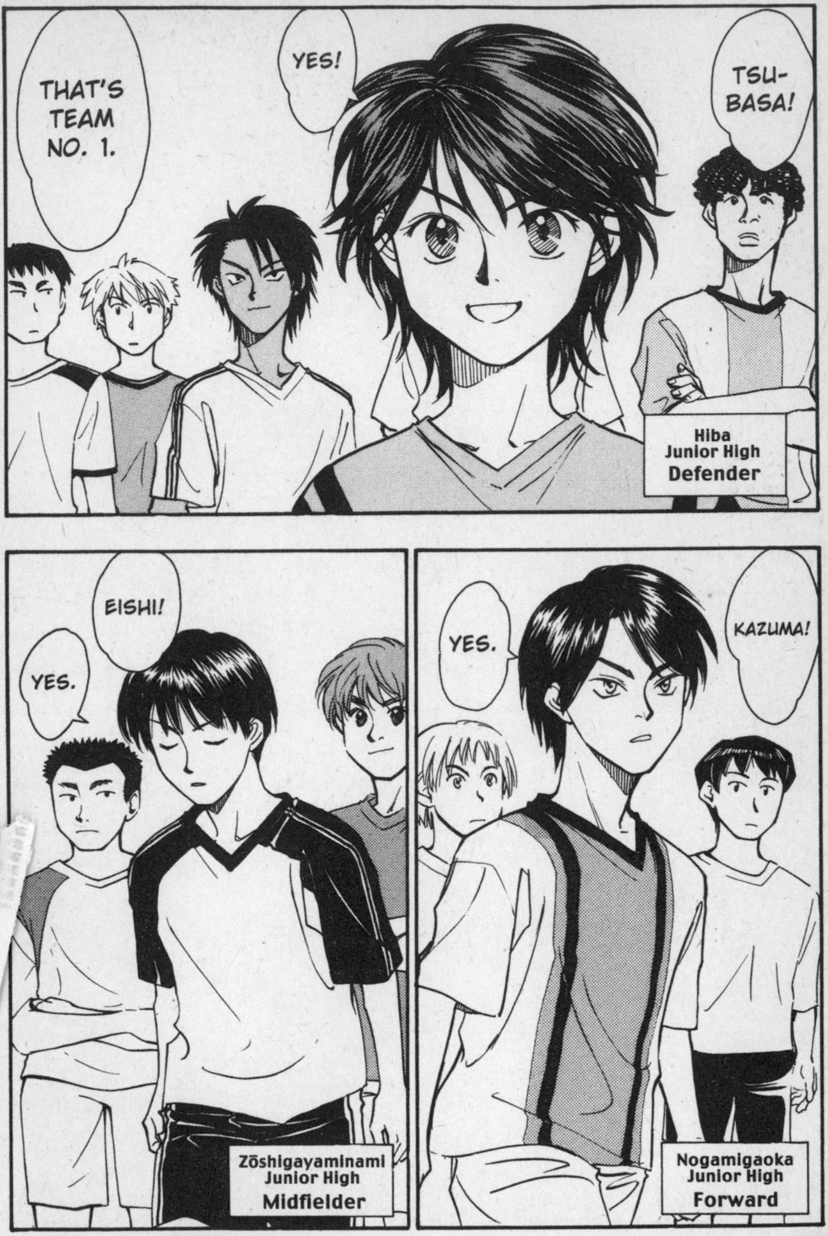
TSU-BASA!
YES!
THAT'S TEAM NO. 1.
Hiba Junior High Defender
KAZUMA!
YES.
Nogamigaoka Junior High Forward
EISHI!
YES.
Zōshigayaminami Junior High Midfielder

READ THIS WAY

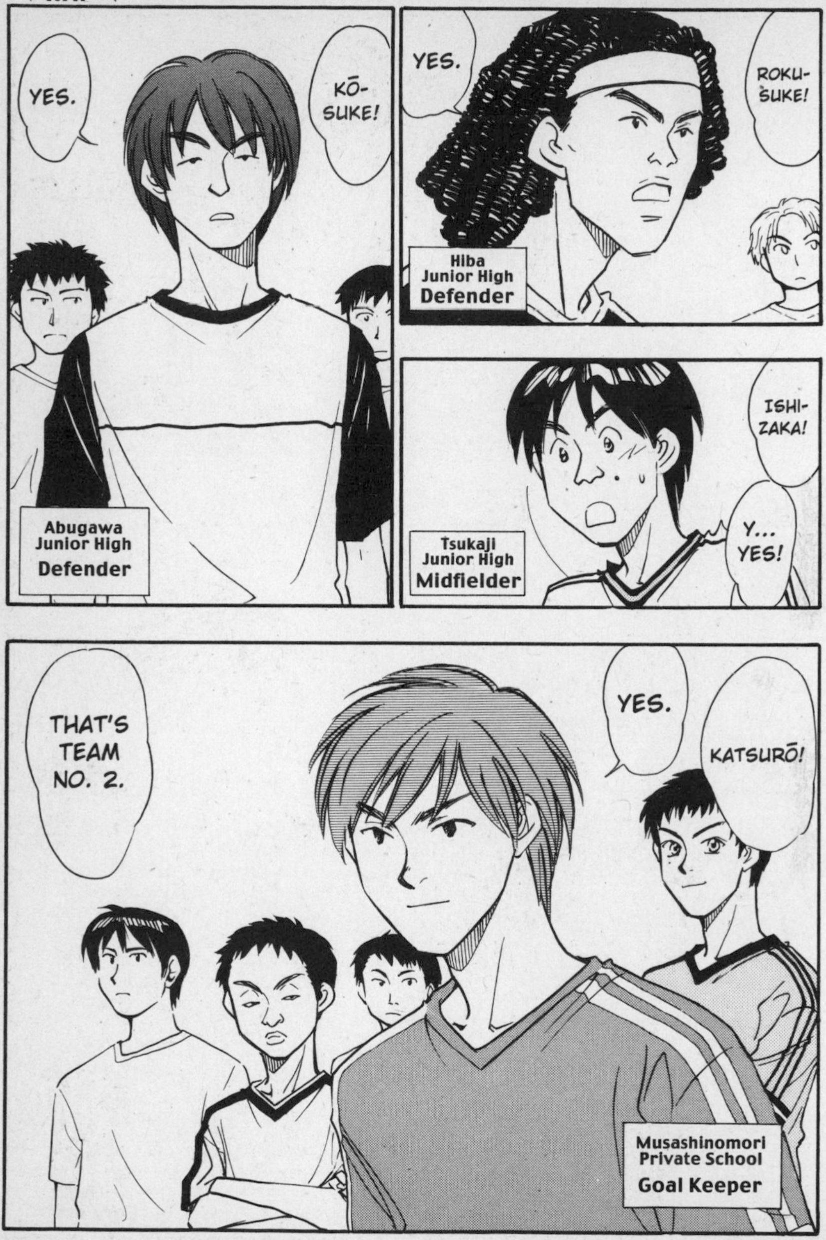
ROKU-SUKE!
YES.
Hiba Junior High Defender
ISHI-ZAKA!
Y... YES!
Tsukaji Junior High Midfielder
KŌ-SUKE!
YES.
Abugawa Junior High Defender
KATSURŌ!
YES.
THAT'S TEAM NO. 2.
Musashinomori Private School Goal Keeper

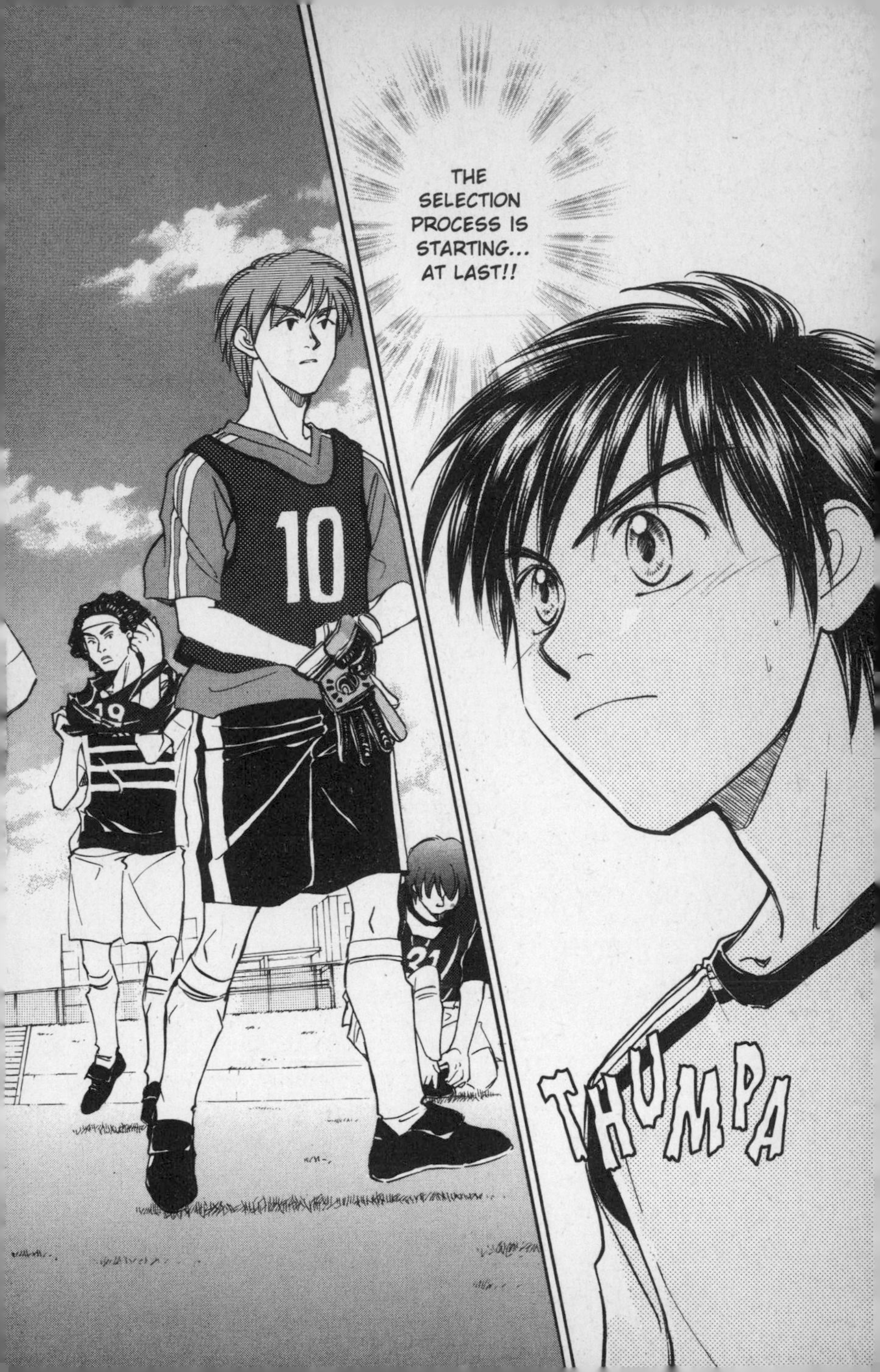
THE SELECTION PROCESS IS STARTING... AT LAST!!
THUMPA

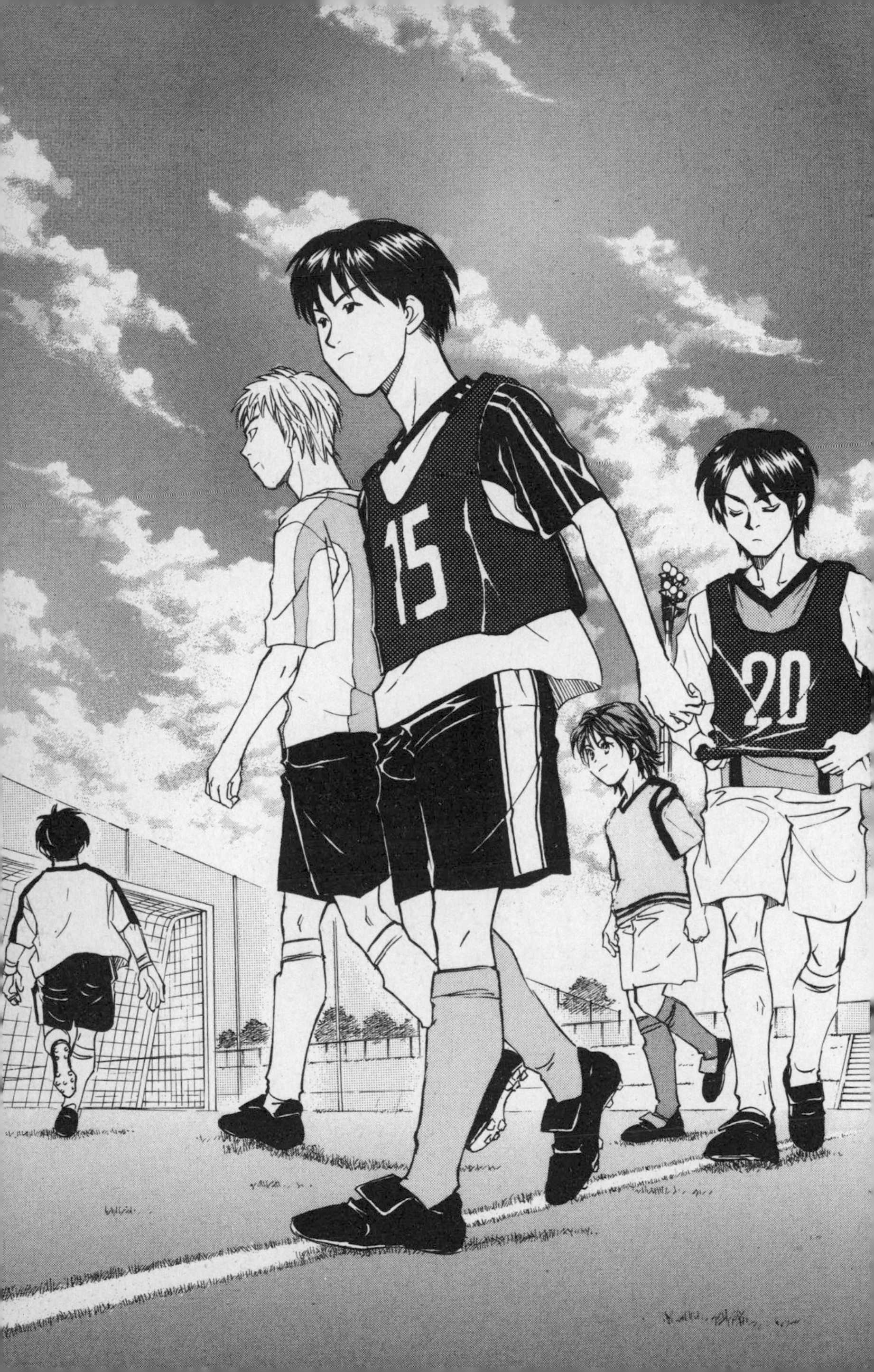
15
20

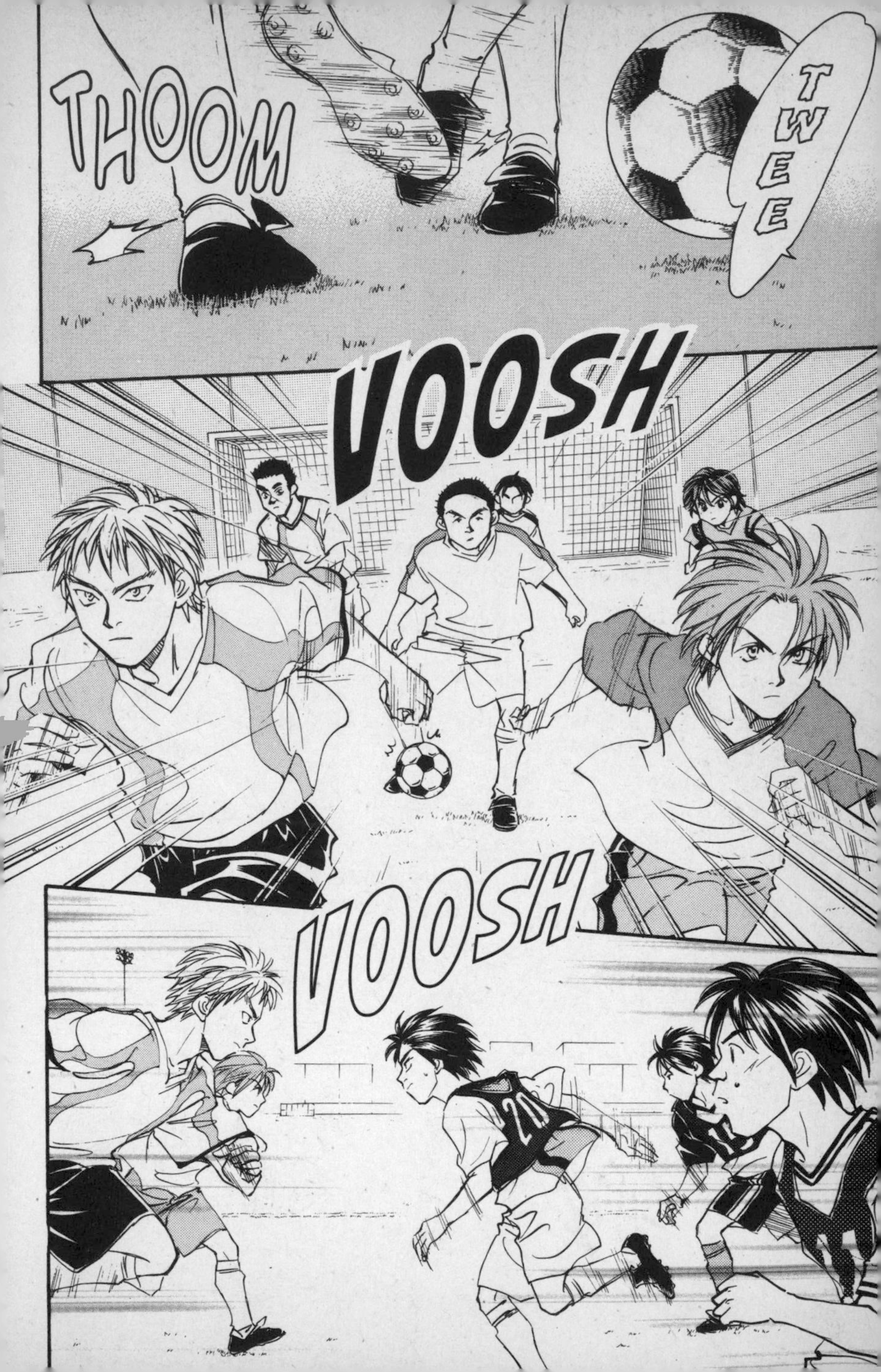
TWEE
THOOM
VOOSH
VOOSH

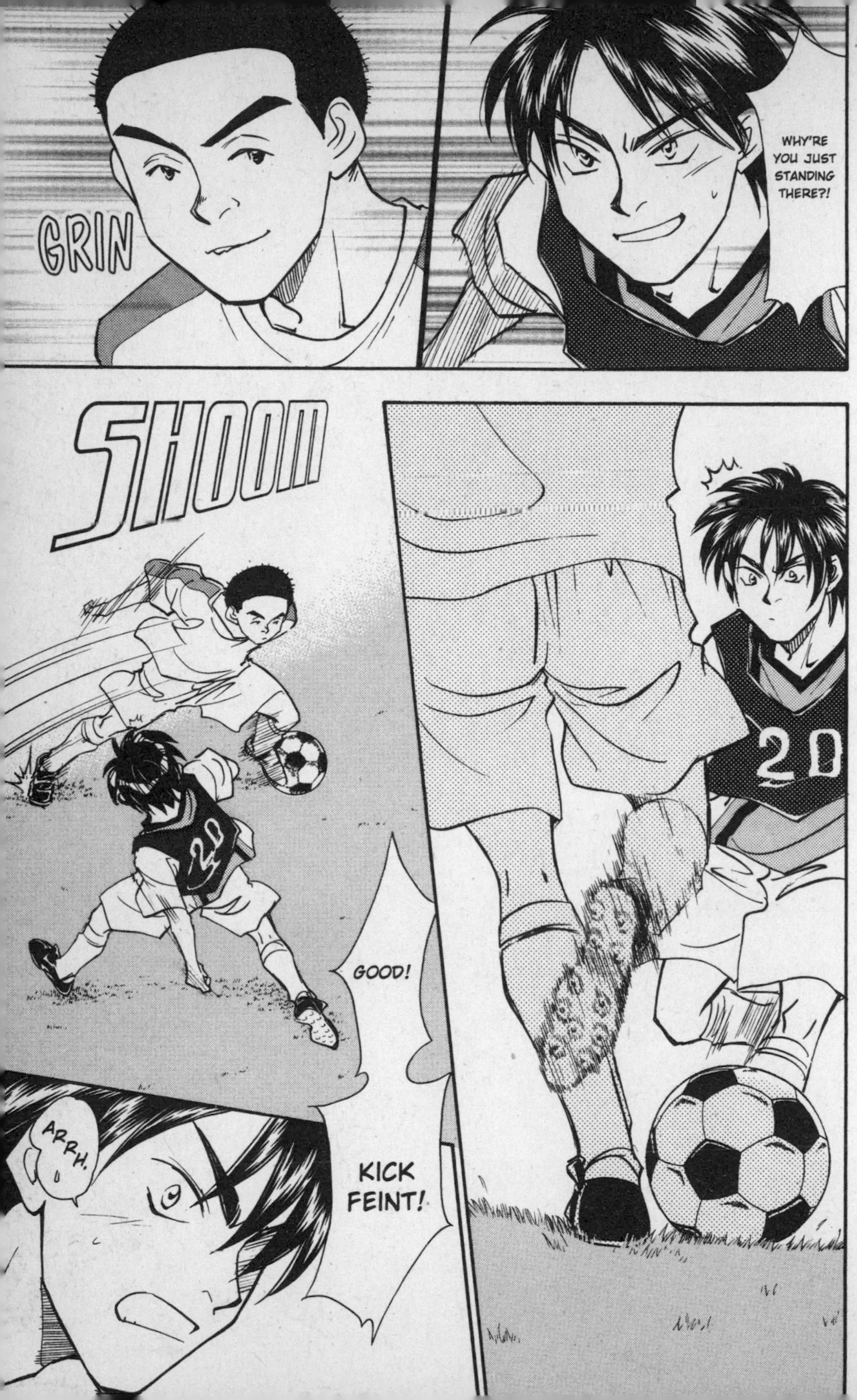
WHY'RE YOU JUST STANDING THERE?!
GRIN
SHOOM
GOOD!
ARRH.
KICK FEINT!

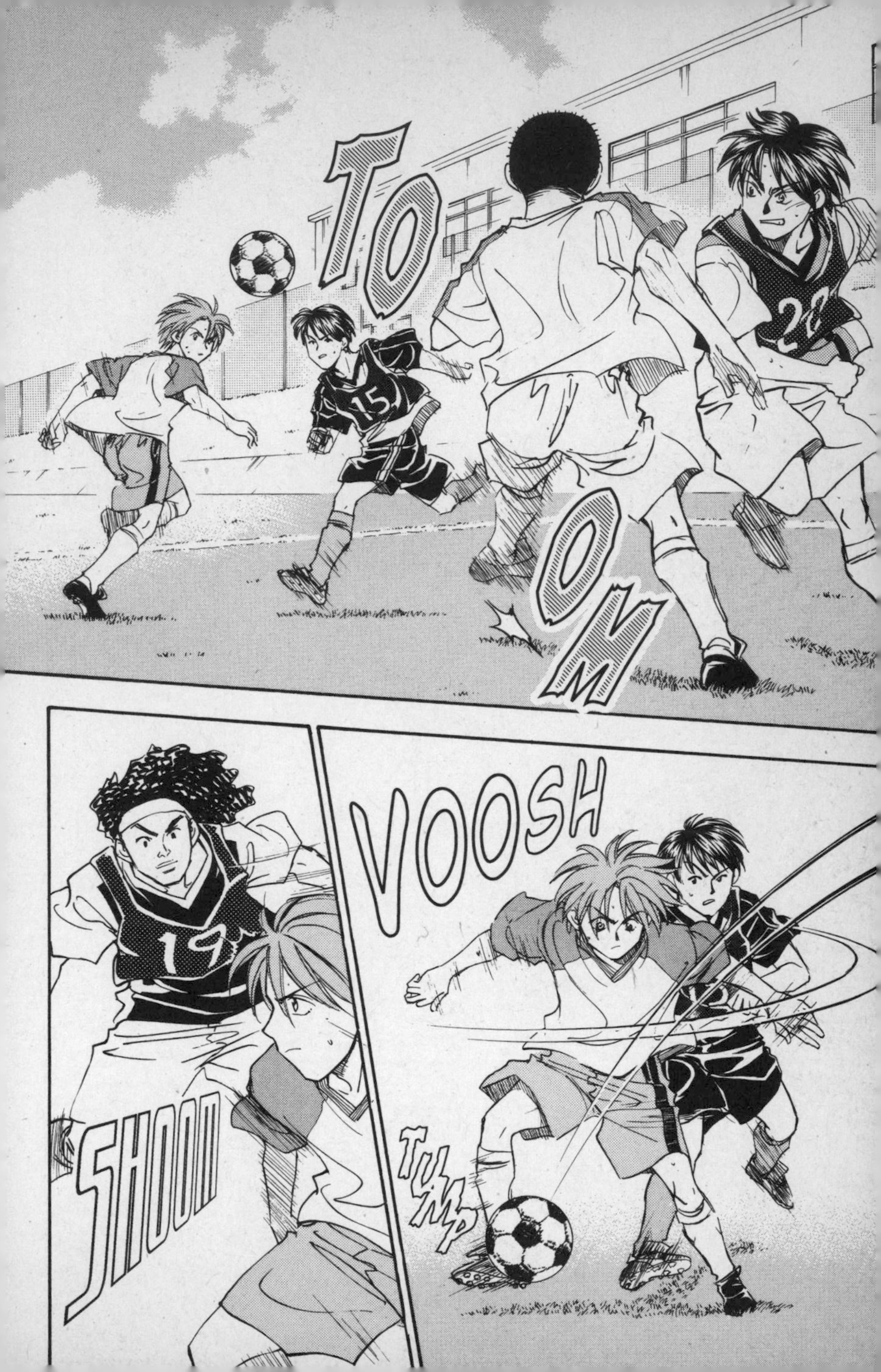
TO
OM
VOOSH
TUMP
SHOOM

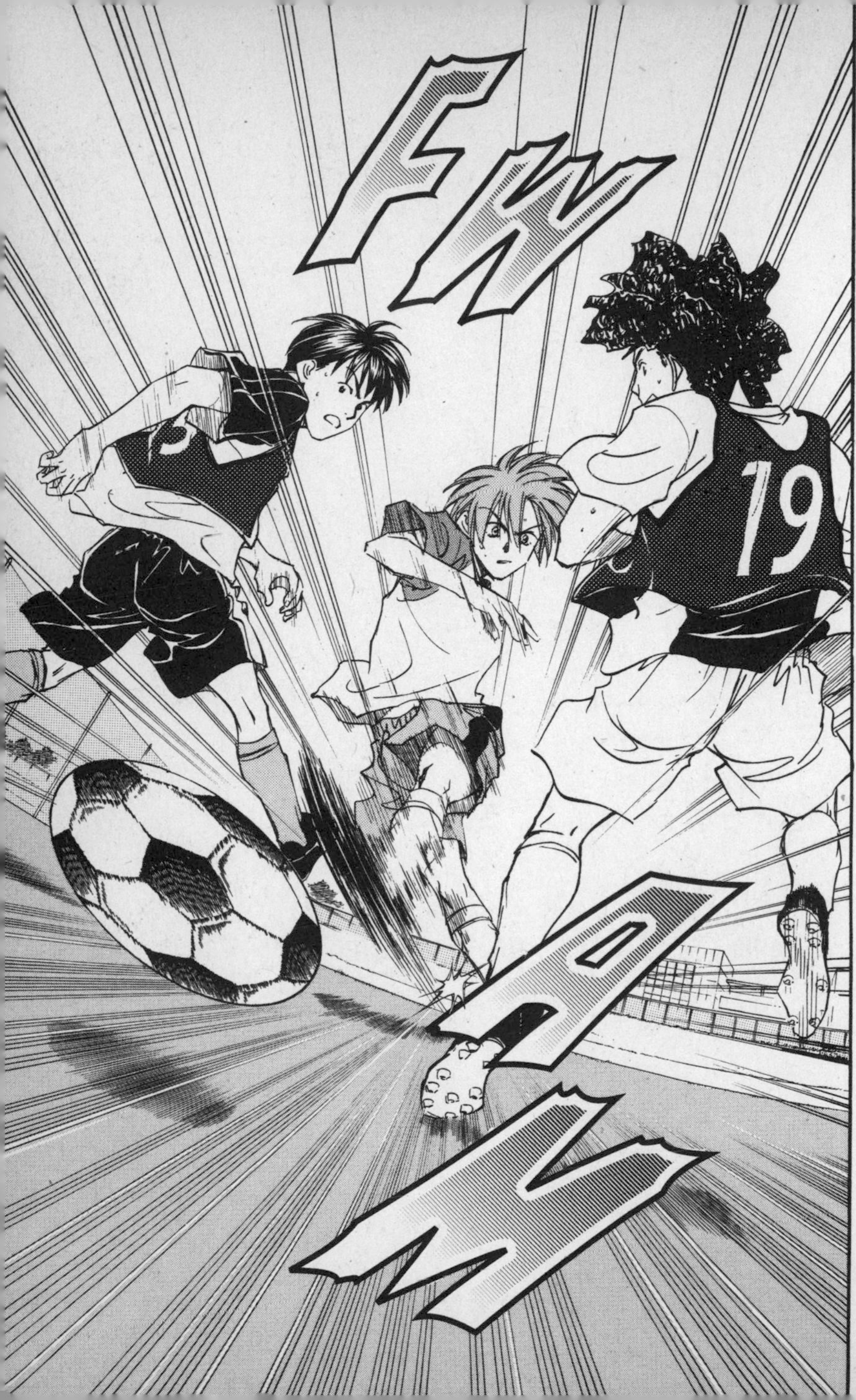
19

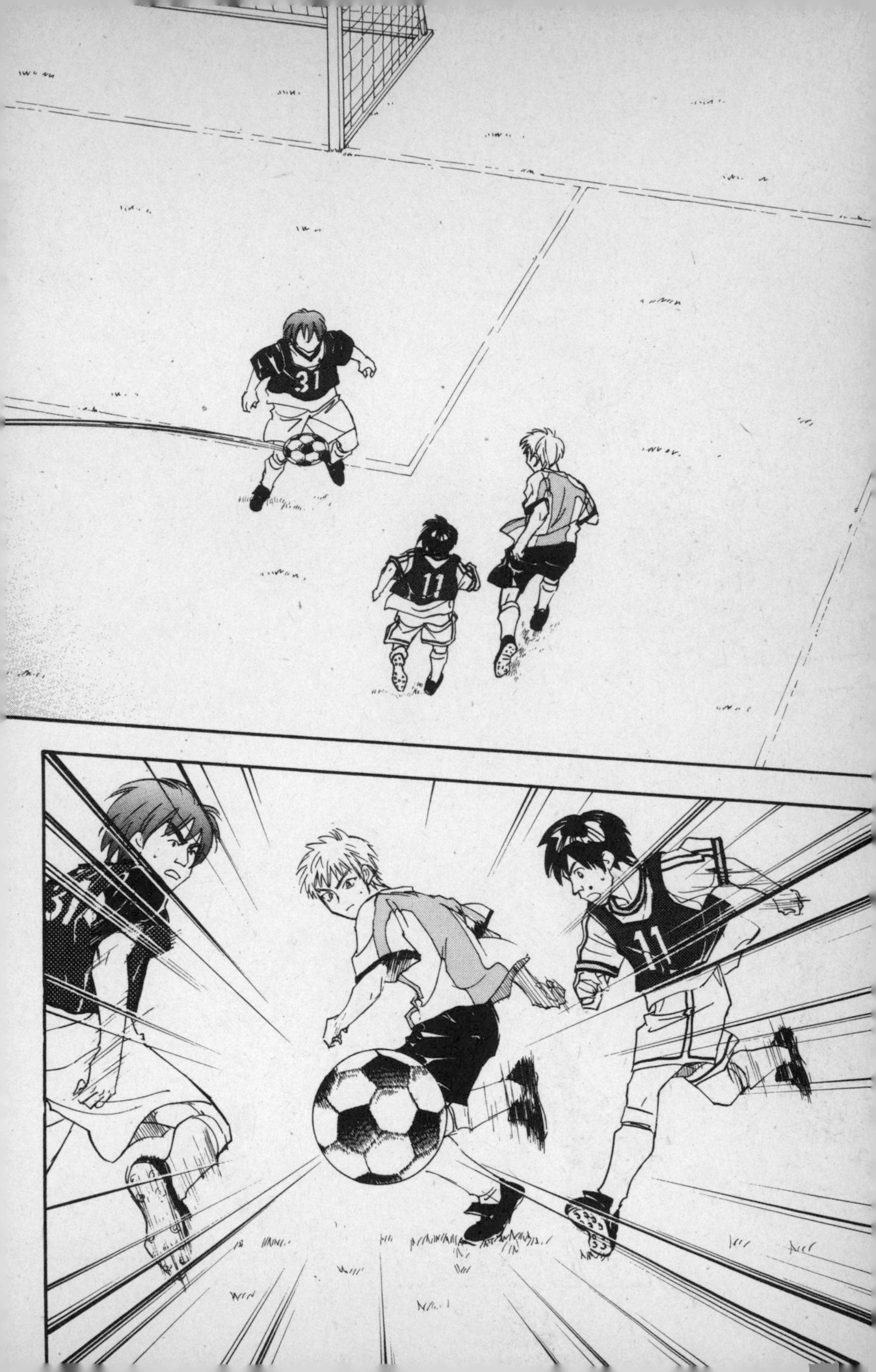

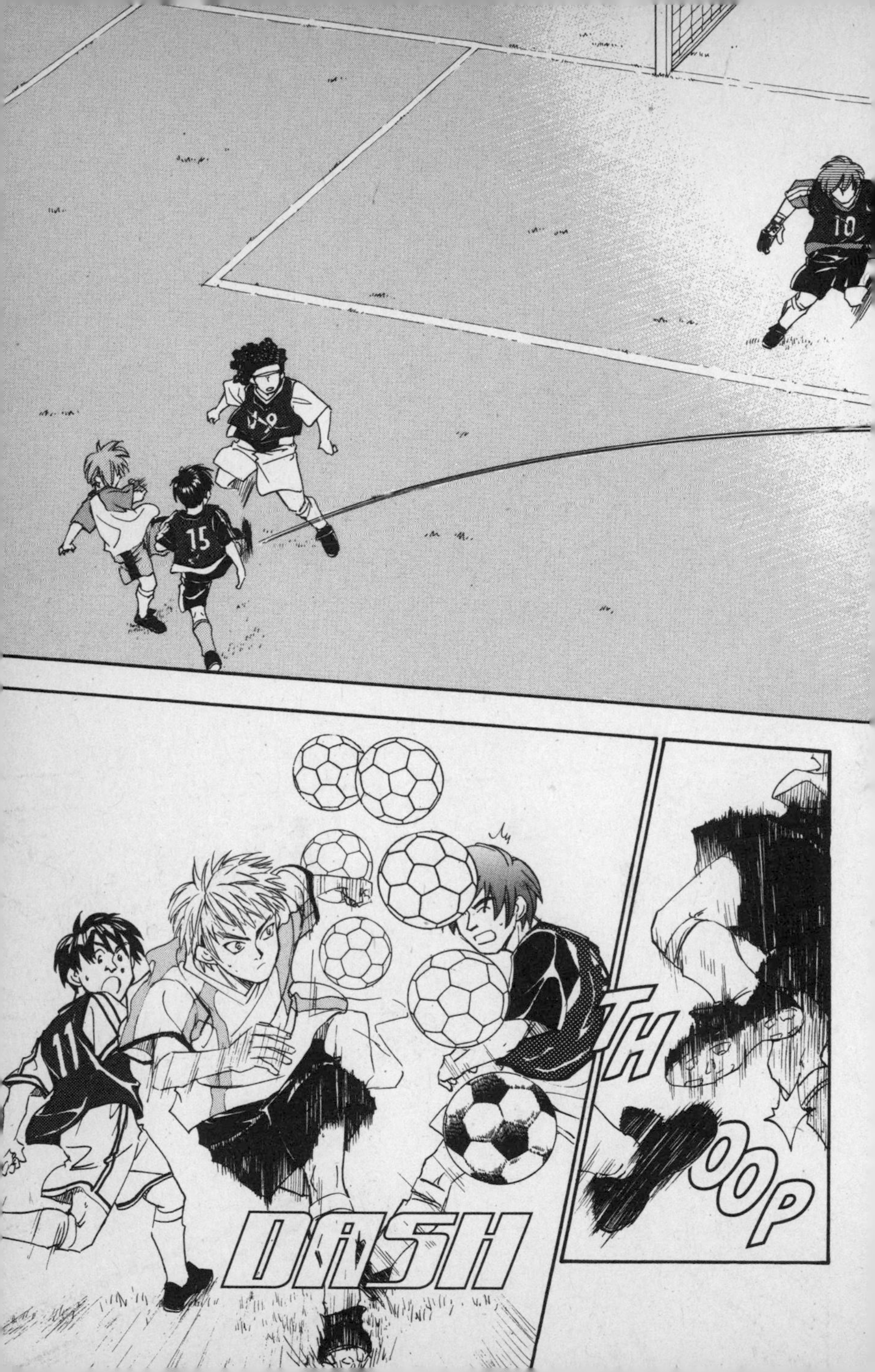
THOOP
DASH

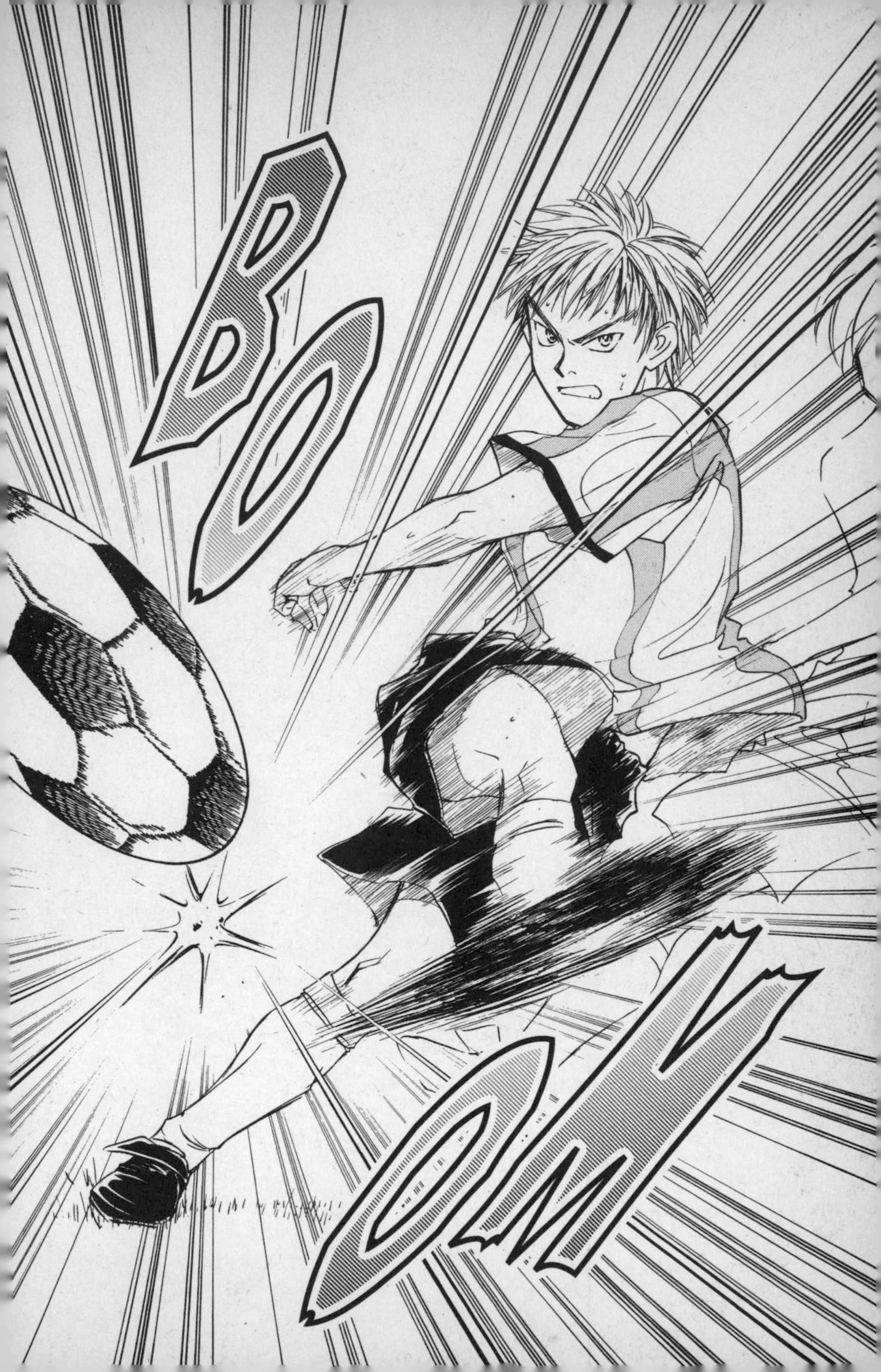
BOOM

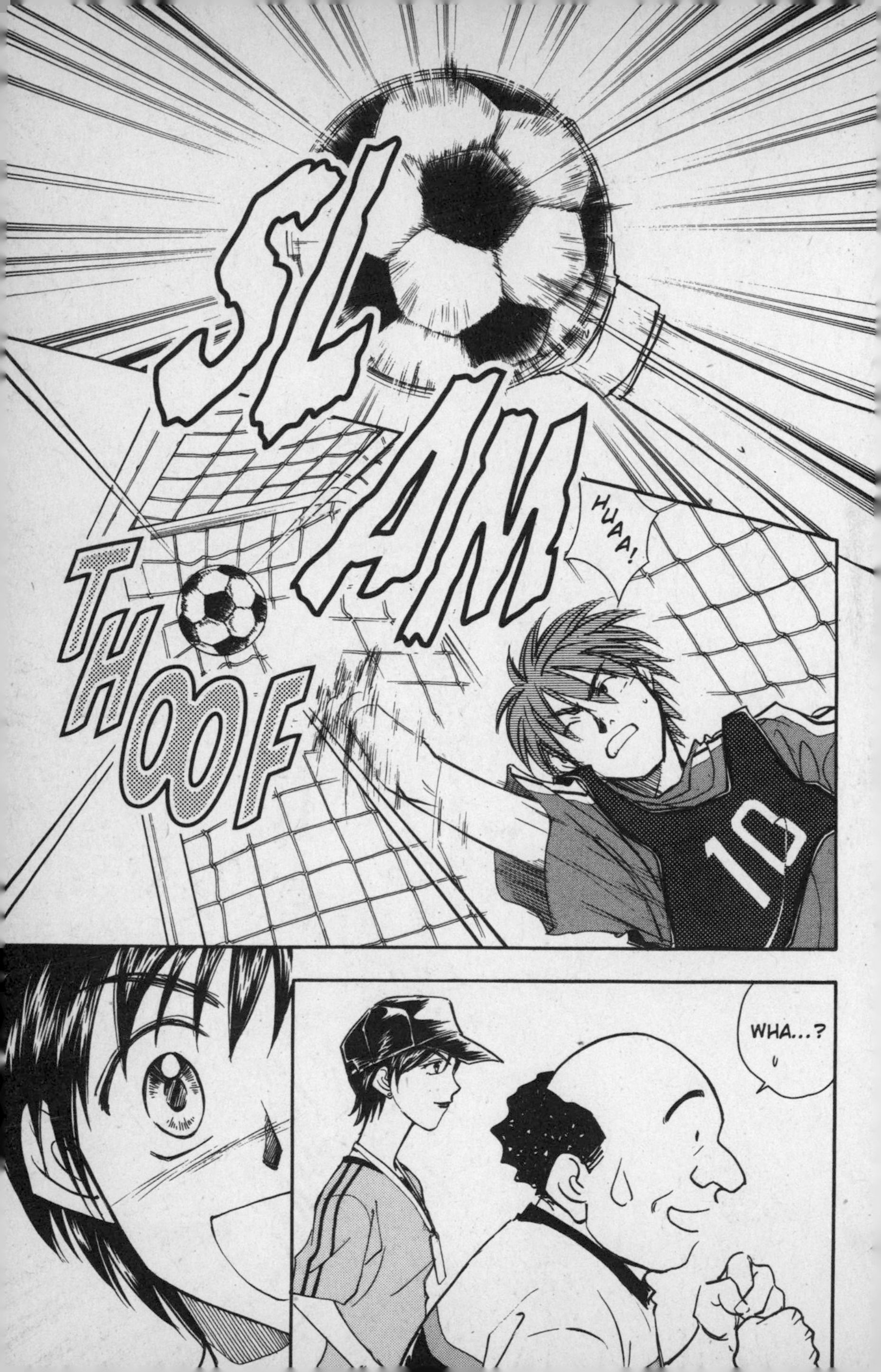
SLAM
THOOF
HUAA!
WHA...?

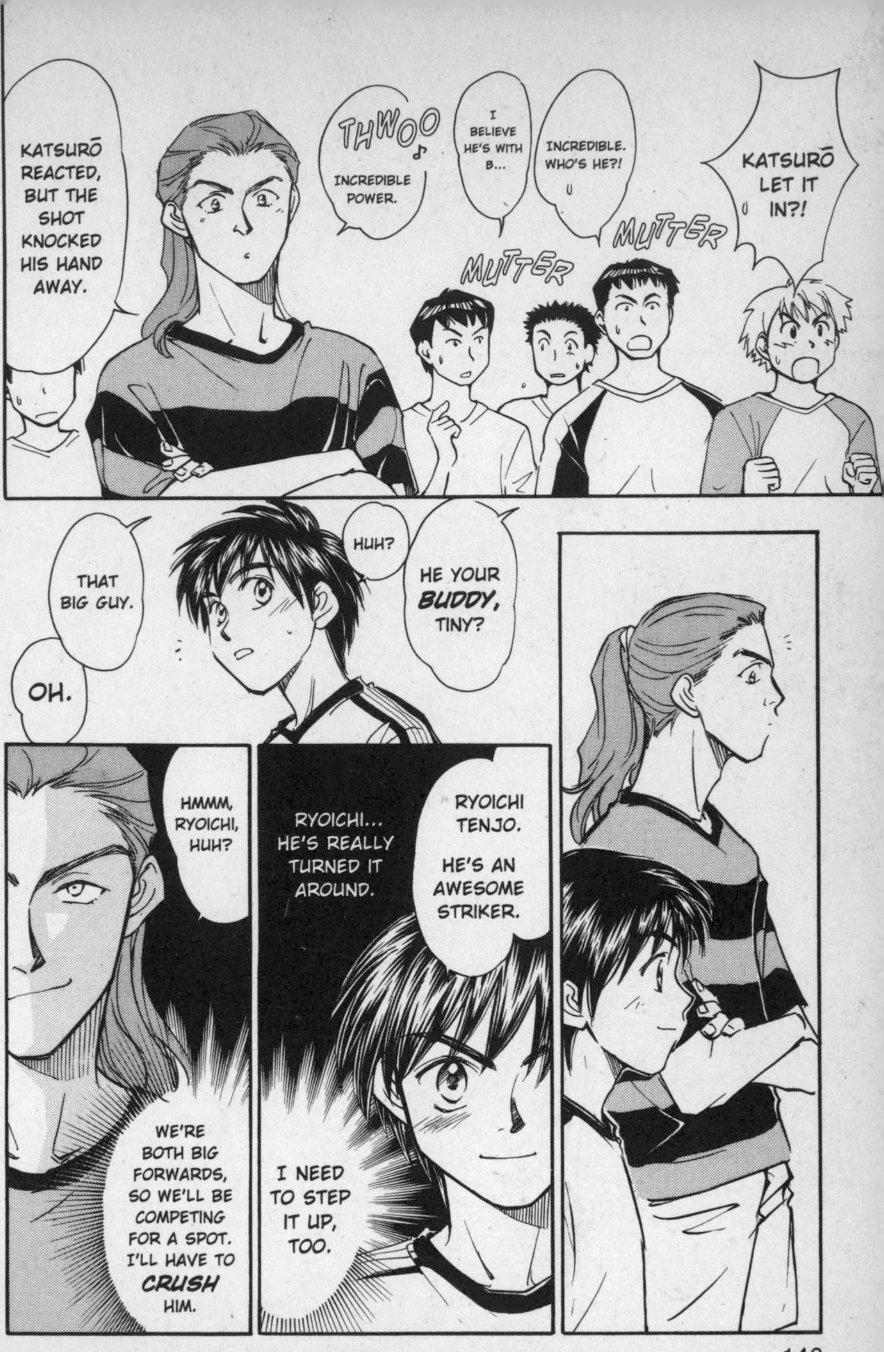
KATSURŌ LET IT IN?!
MUTTER
INCREDIBLE. WHO'S HE?!
I BELIEVE HE'S WITH B...
MUTTER
THWOO ♪
INCREDIBLE POWER.
KATSURŌ REACTED, BUT THE SHOT KNOCKED HIS HAND AWAY.
HE YOUR BUDDY, TINY?
HUH?
THAT BIG GUY.
OH.
RYOICHI TENJO.
HE'S AN AWESOME STRIKER.
RYOICHI... HE'S REALLY TURNED IT AROUND.
I NEED TO STEP IT UP, TOO.
HMMM, RYOICHI, HUH?
WE'RE BOTH BIG FORWARDS, SO WE'LL BE COMPETING FOR A SPOT. I'LL HAVE TO CRUSH HIM.

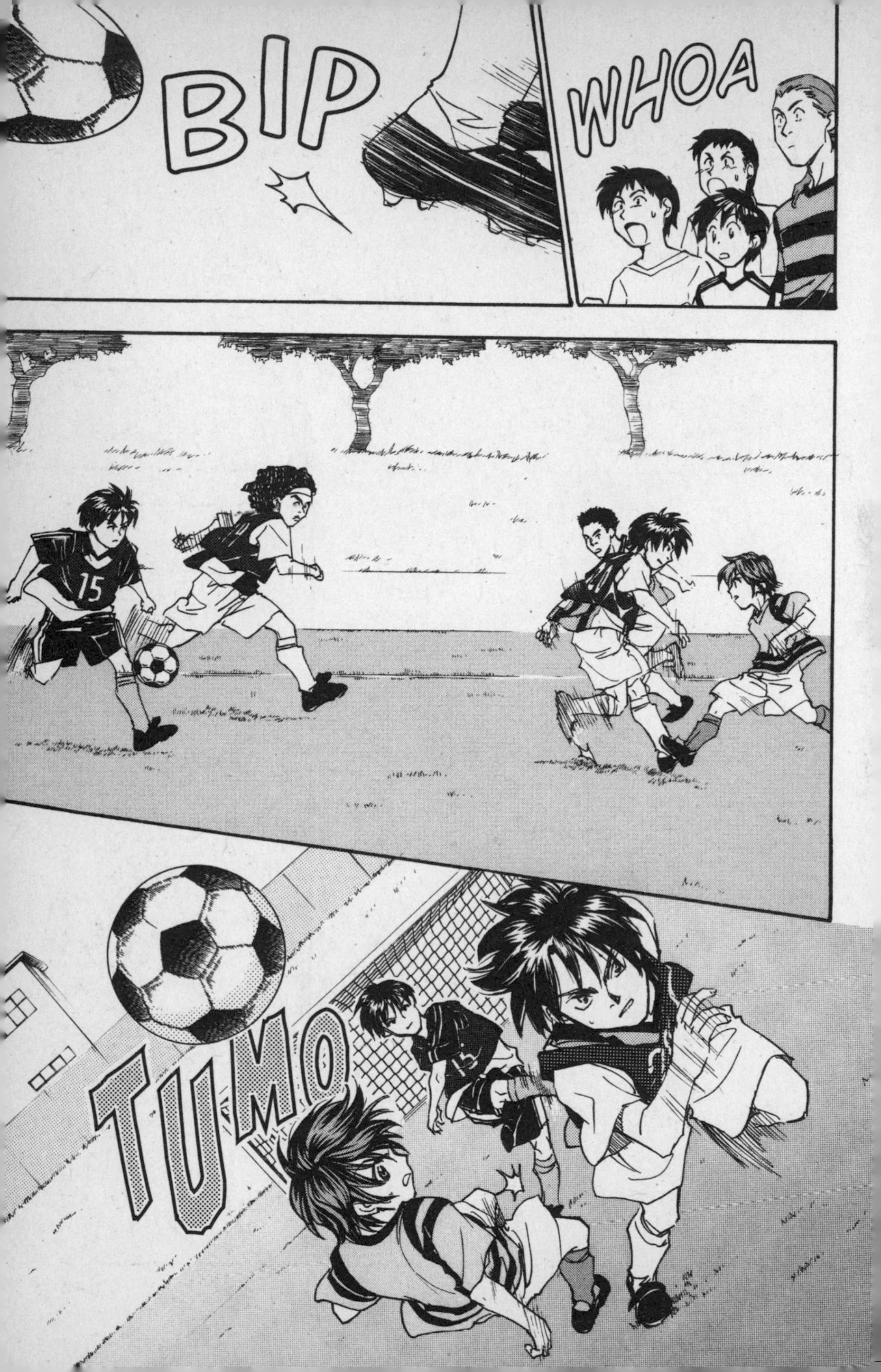
WHOA
BIP
15
TUMO

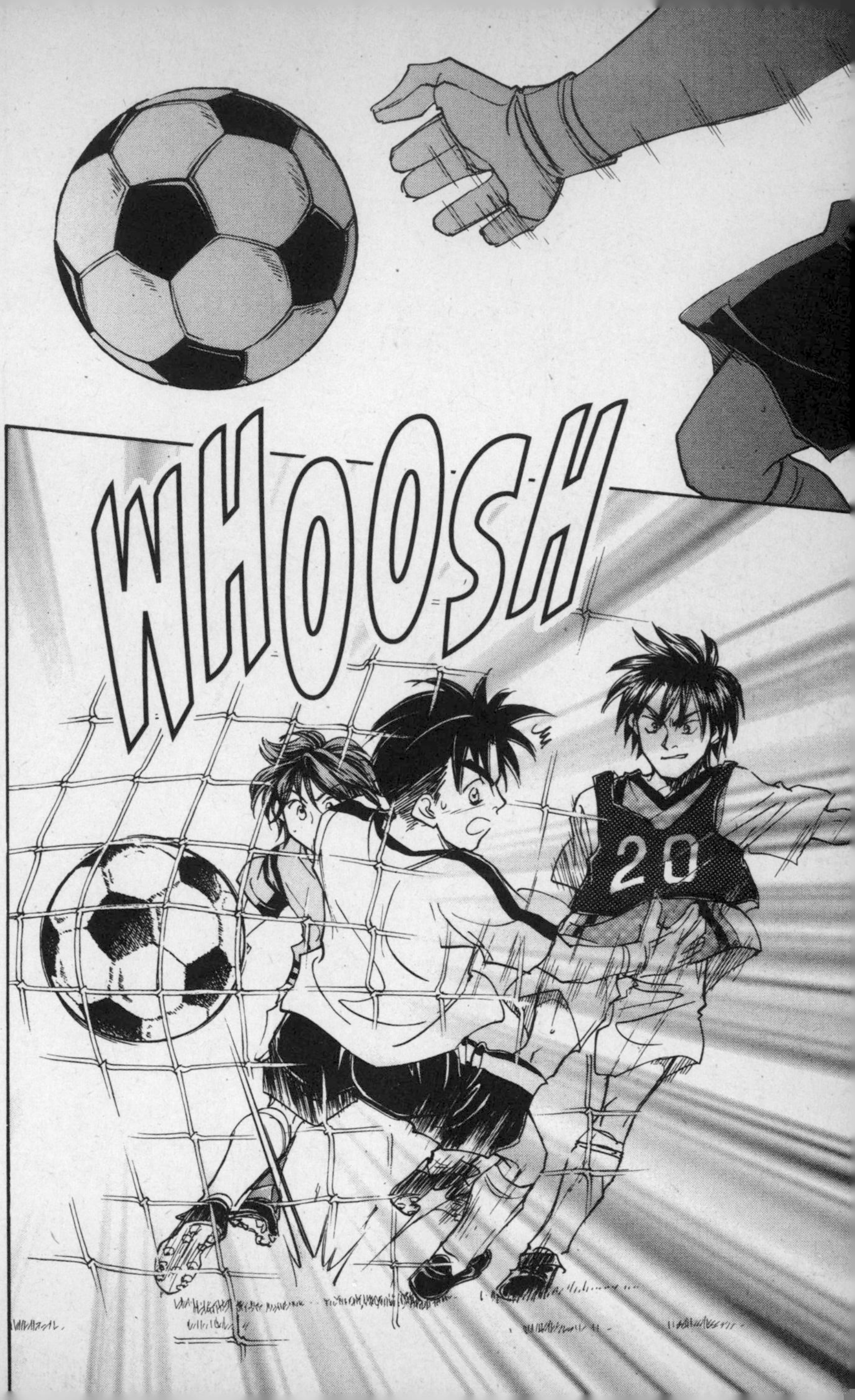
WHOOSH

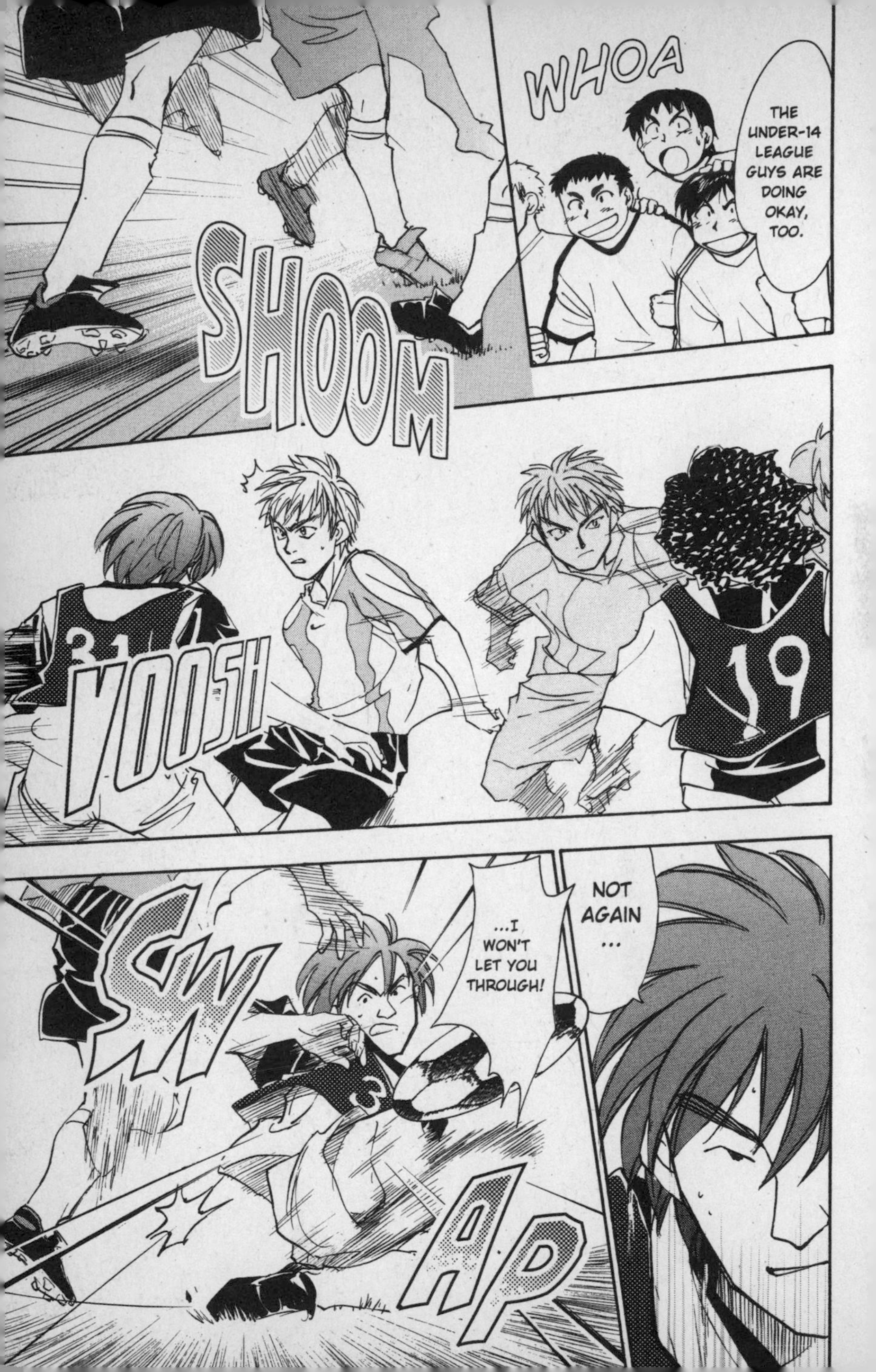
WHOA
THE UNDER-14 LEAGUE GUYS ARE DOING OKAY, TOO.
SHOOM
VOOSH
NOT AGAIN ...
...I WON'T LET YOU THROUGH!
SWAP

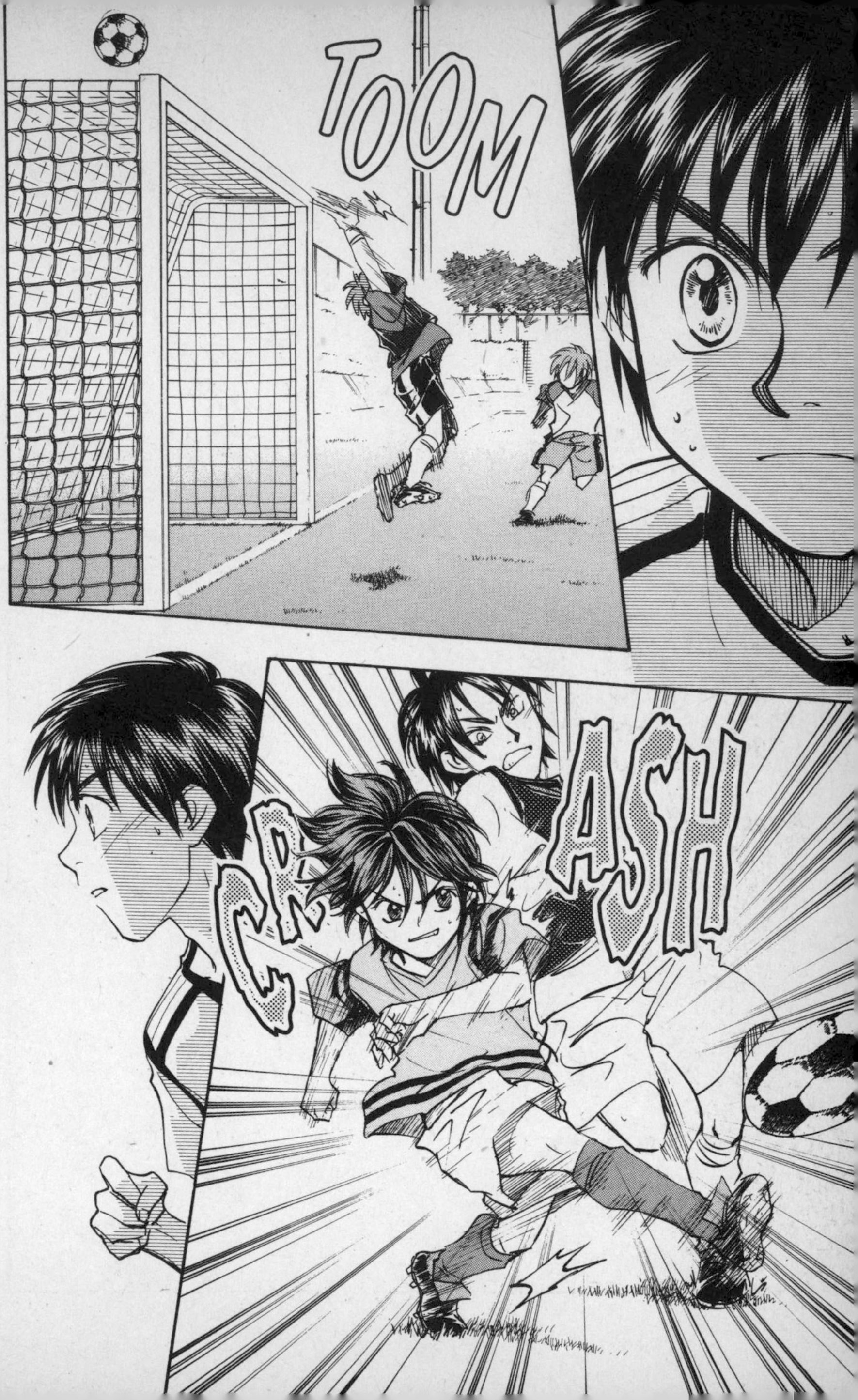
TOOM
CRASH

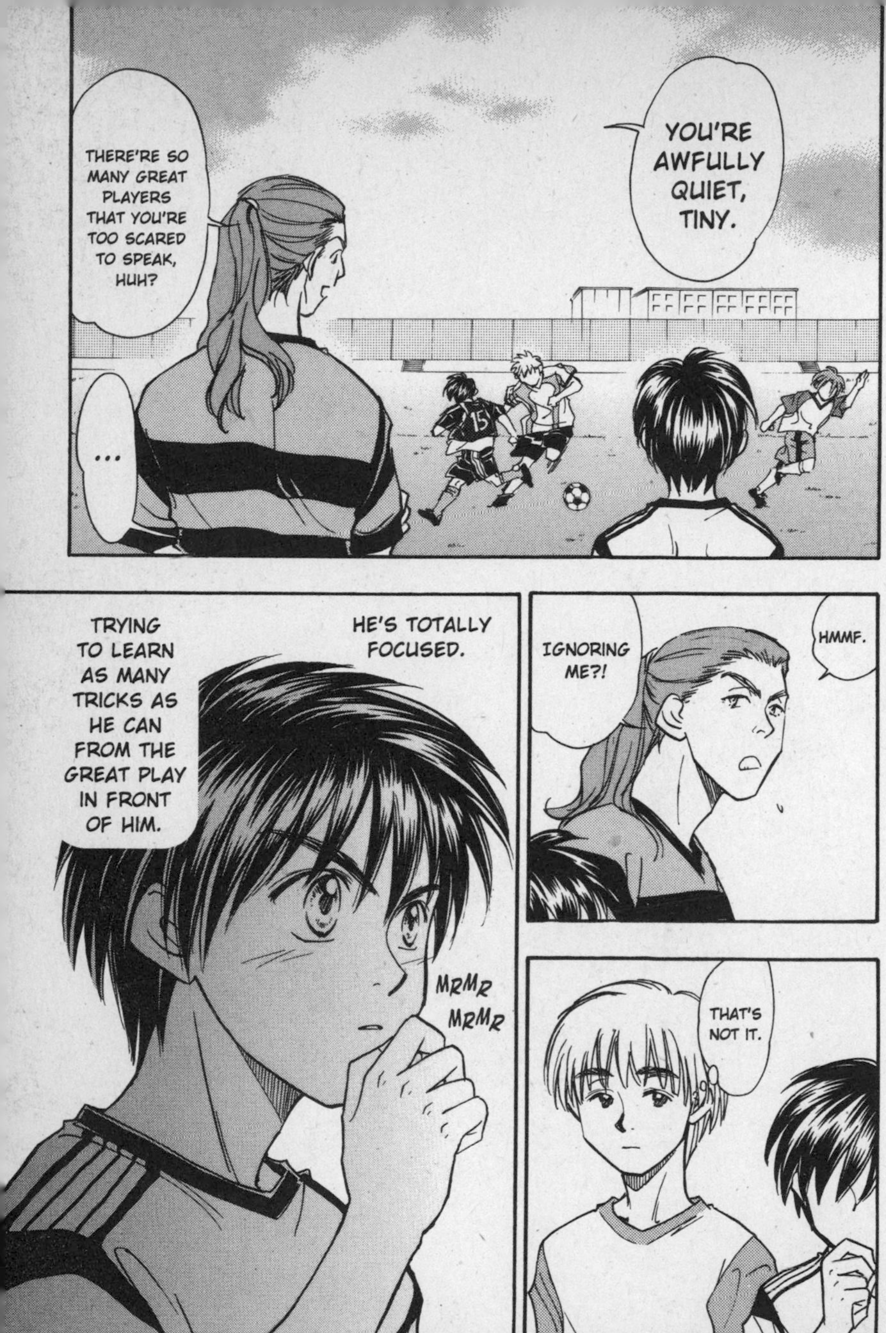
YOU'RE AWFULLY QUIET, TINY.
THERE'RE SO MANY GREAT PLAYERS THAT YOU'RE TOO SCARED TO SPEAK, HUH?
...
HMMF.
IGNORING ME?!
THAT'S NOT IT.
HE'S TOTALLY FOCUSED.
TRYING TO LEARN AS MANY TRICKS AS HE CAN FROM THE GREAT PLAY IN FRONT OF HIM.
MRMR MRMR

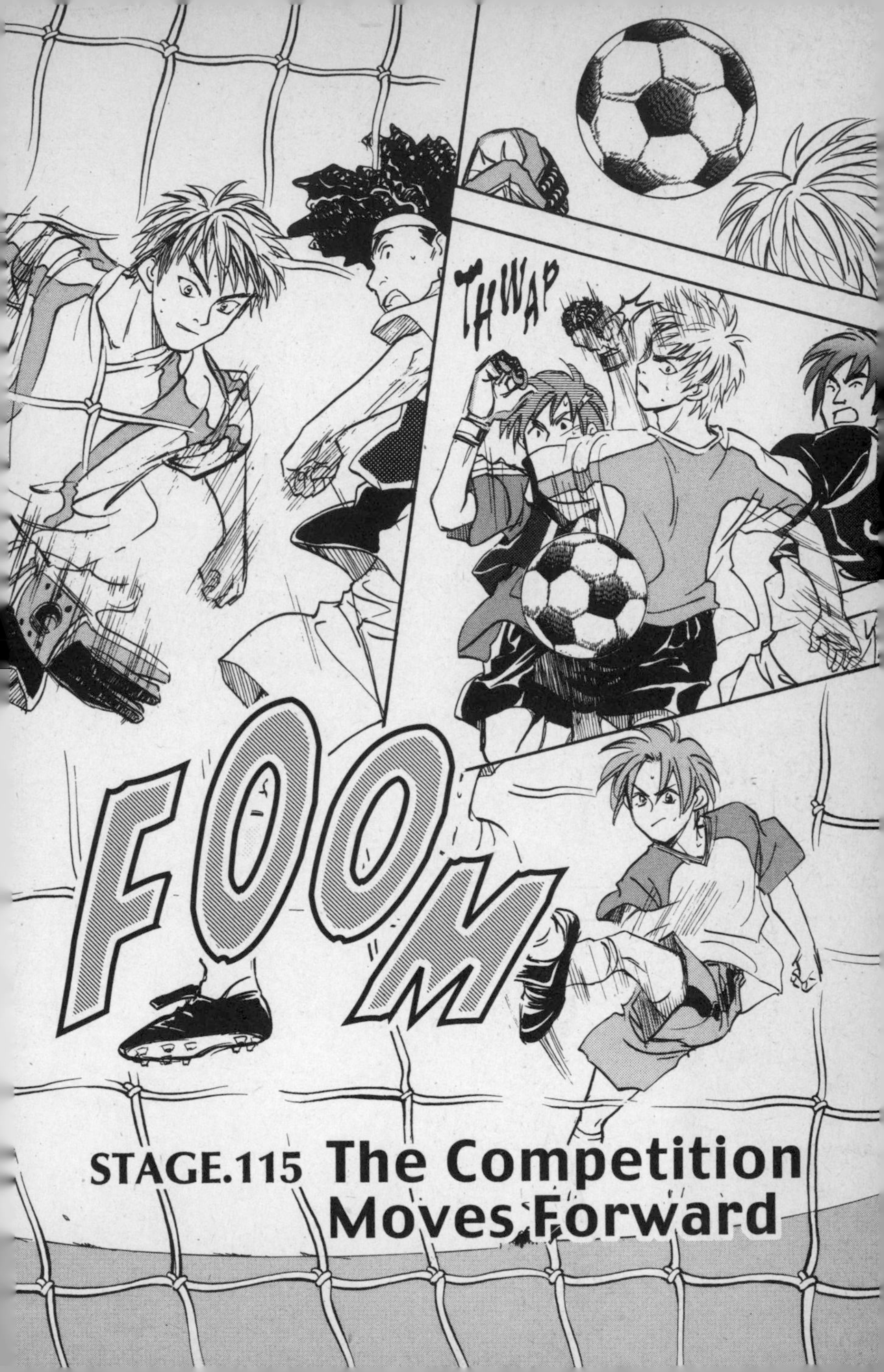
THWAP
FOOM

STAGE.115 The Competition Moves Forward

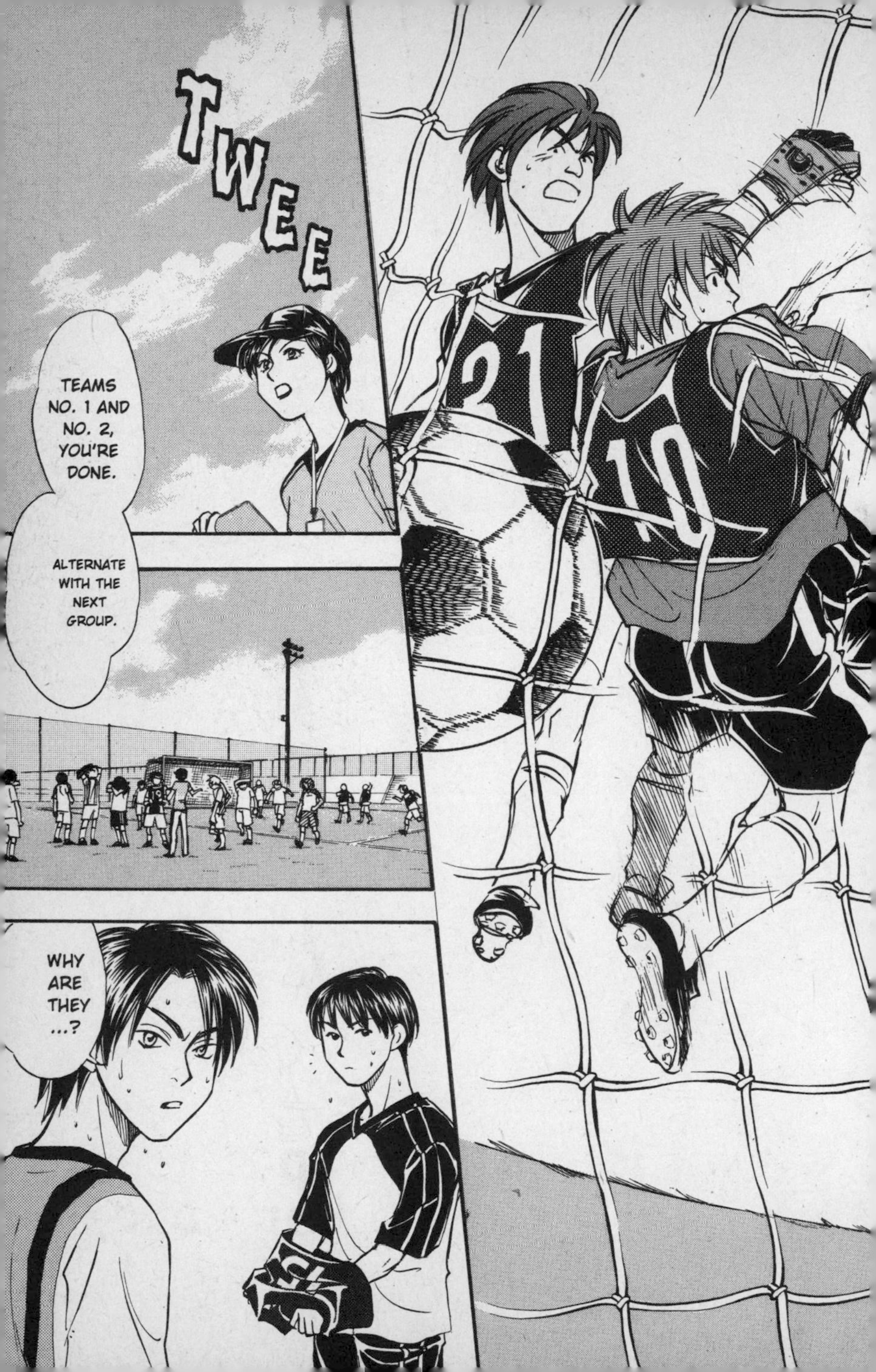
TWEEE
TEAMS NO. 1 AND NO. 2, YOU'RE DONE.
ALTERNATE WITH THE NEXT GROUP.
WHY ARE THEY ...?

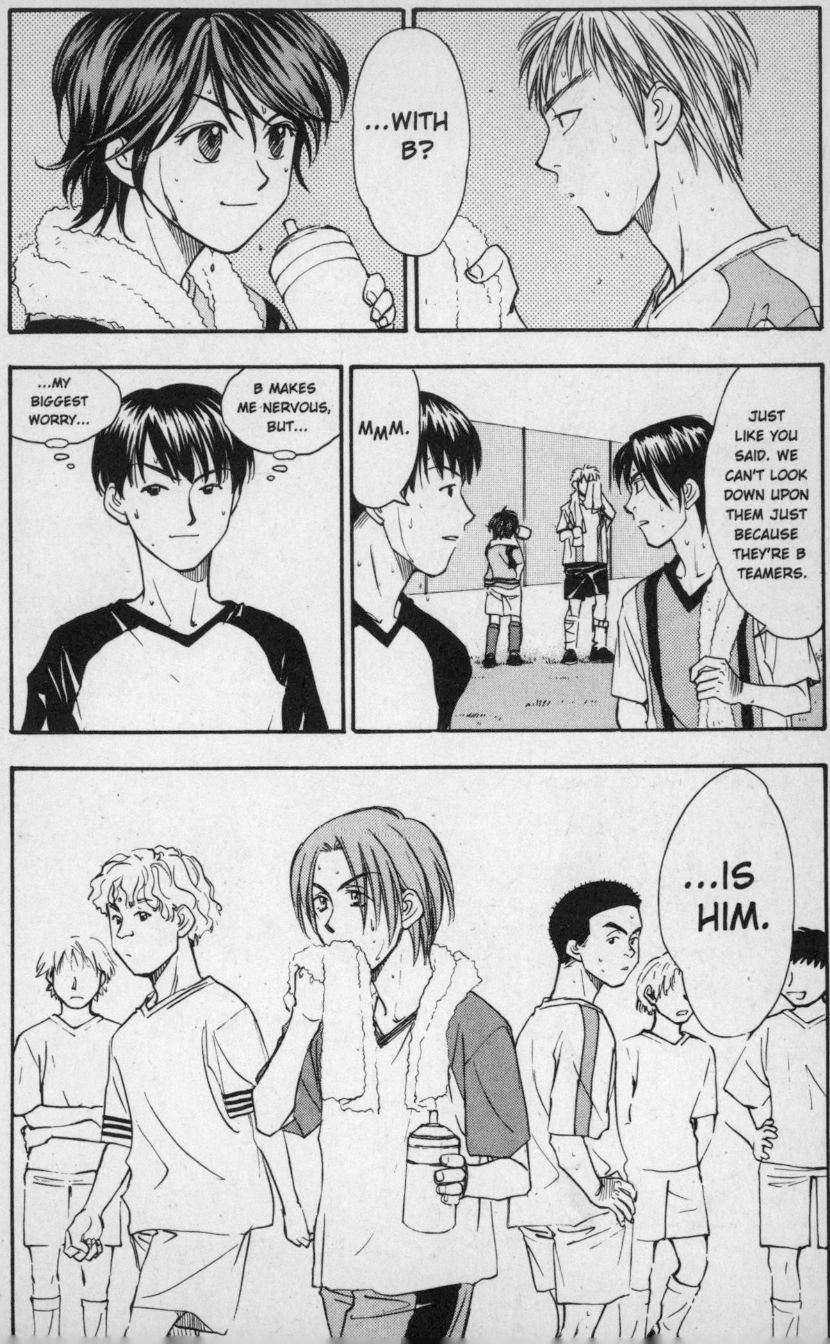
...WITH B?
JUST LIKE YOU SAID. WE CAN'T LOOK DOWN UPON THEM JUST BECAUSE THEY'RE B TEAMERS.
MMM.
B MAKES ME NERVOUS, BUT...
...MY BIGGEST WORRY...
...IS HIM.

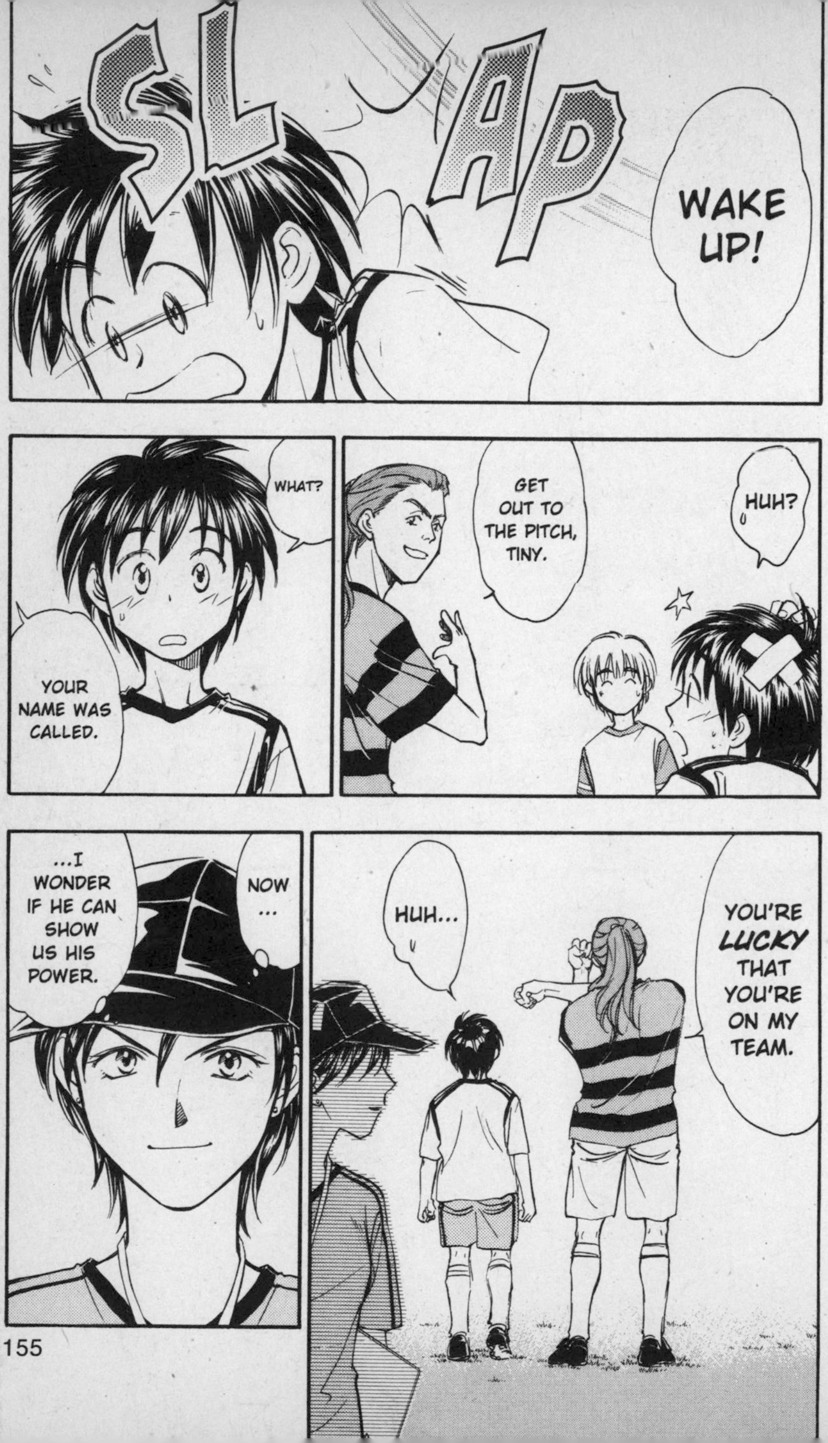
SLAP
WAKE UP!
HUH?
GET OUT TO THE PITCH, TINY.
WHAT?
YOUR NAME WAS CALLED.
YOU'RE *LUCKY* THAT YOU'RE ON MY TEAM.
HUH...
NOW...
...I WONDER IF HE CAN SHOW US HIS POWER.

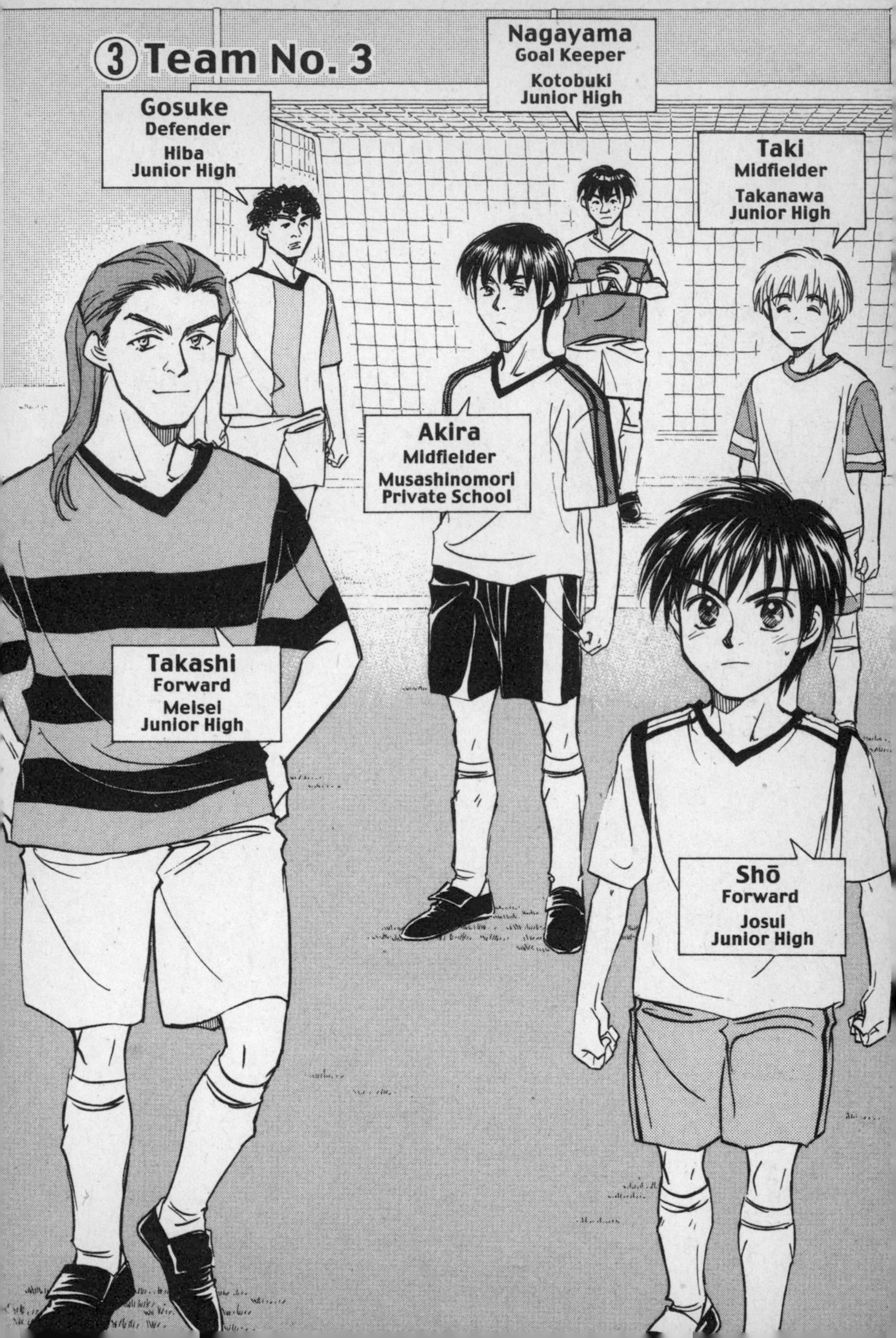
③ Team No. 3
Nagayama Goal Keeper Kotobuki Junior High
Taki Midfielder Takanawa Junior High
Gosuke Defender Hiba Junior High
Akira Midfielder Musashinomori Private School
Takashi Forward Meisei Junior High
Shō Forward Josui Junior High

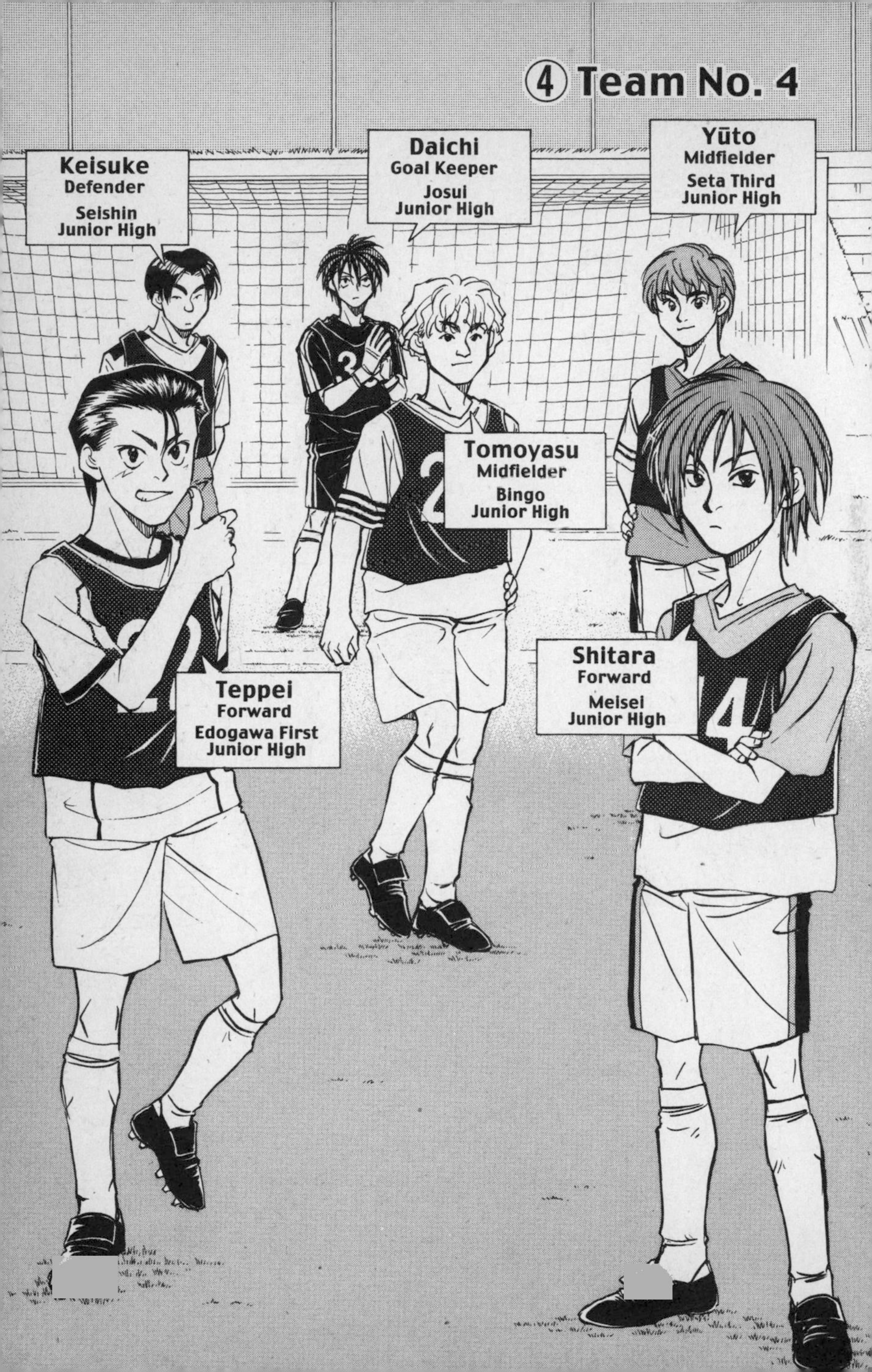
④ Team No. 4
Yūto Midfielder Seta Third Junior High
Daichi Goal Keeper Josui Junior High
Keisuke Defender Seishin Junior High
Tomoyasu Midfielder Bingo Junior High
Shitara Forward Meisei Junior High
Teppei Forward Edogawa First Junior High

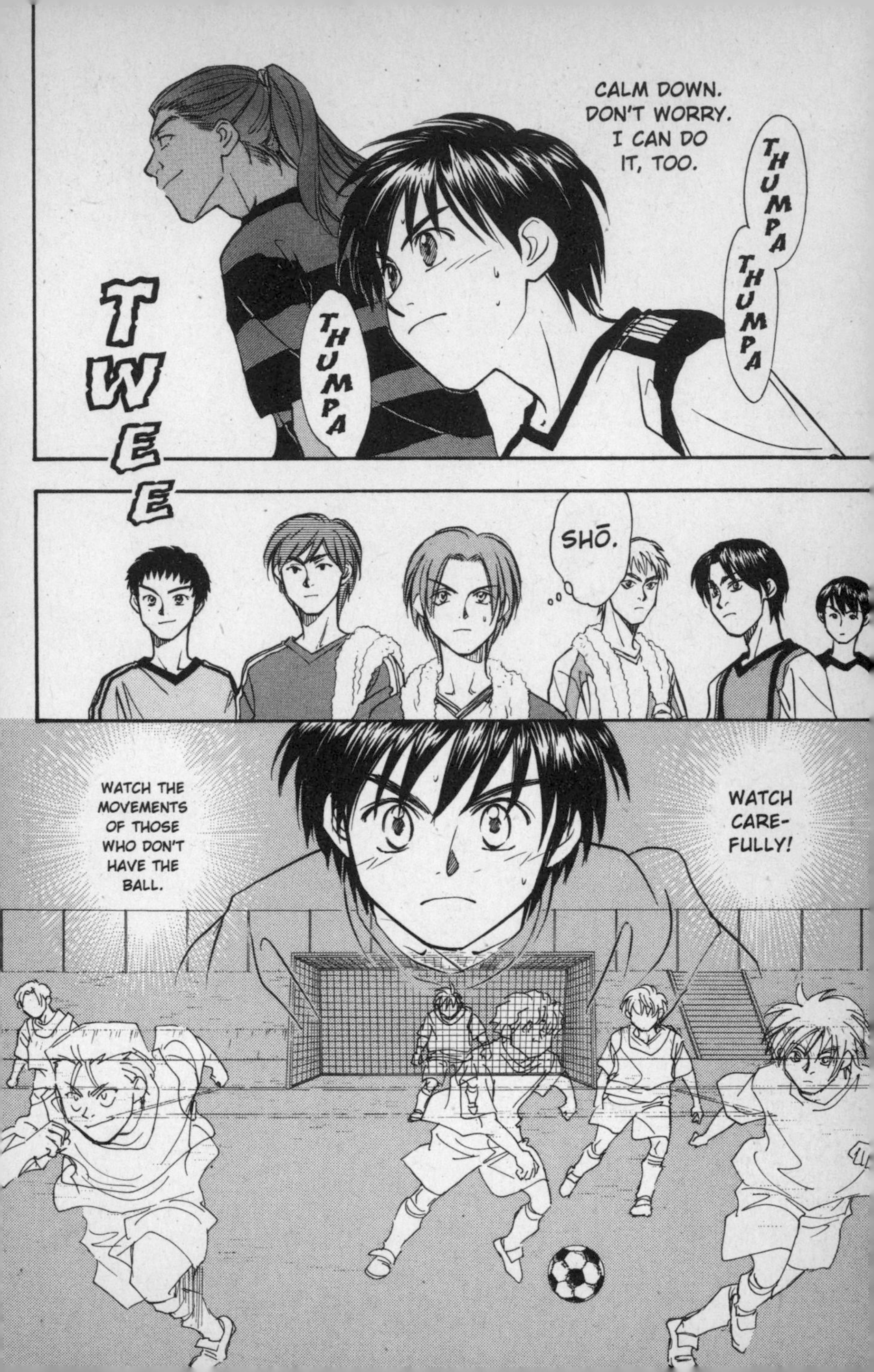
THUMPA THUMPA
CALM DOWN. DON'T WORRY. I CAN DO IT, TOO.
THUMPA
TWEE
SHŌ.
WATCH CARE-FULLY!
WATCH THE MOVEMENTS OF THOSE WHO DON'T HAVE THE BALL.

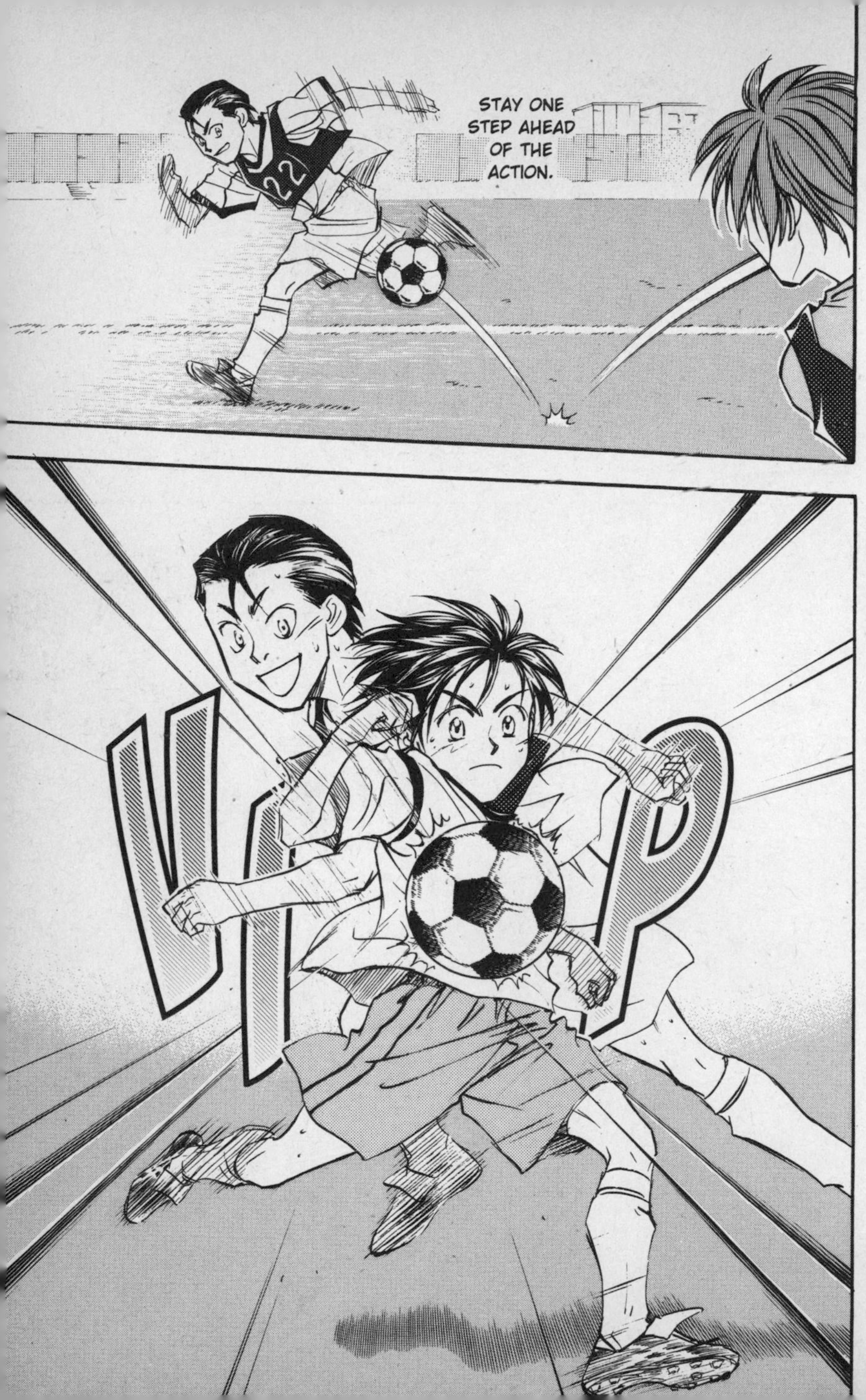
STAY ONE STEP AHEAD OF THE ACTION.
VIP

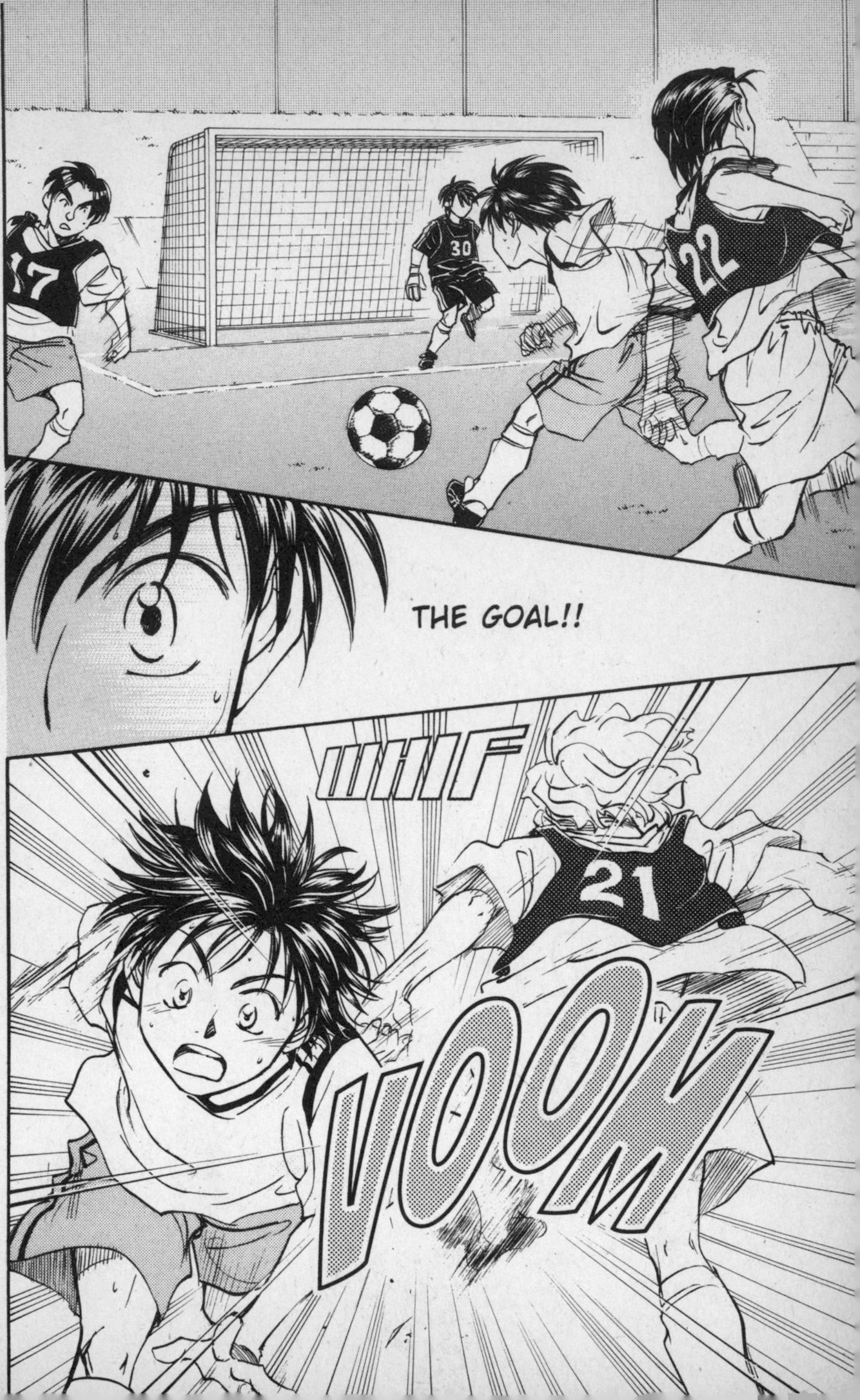
THE GOAL!!
WHIF
VOOM

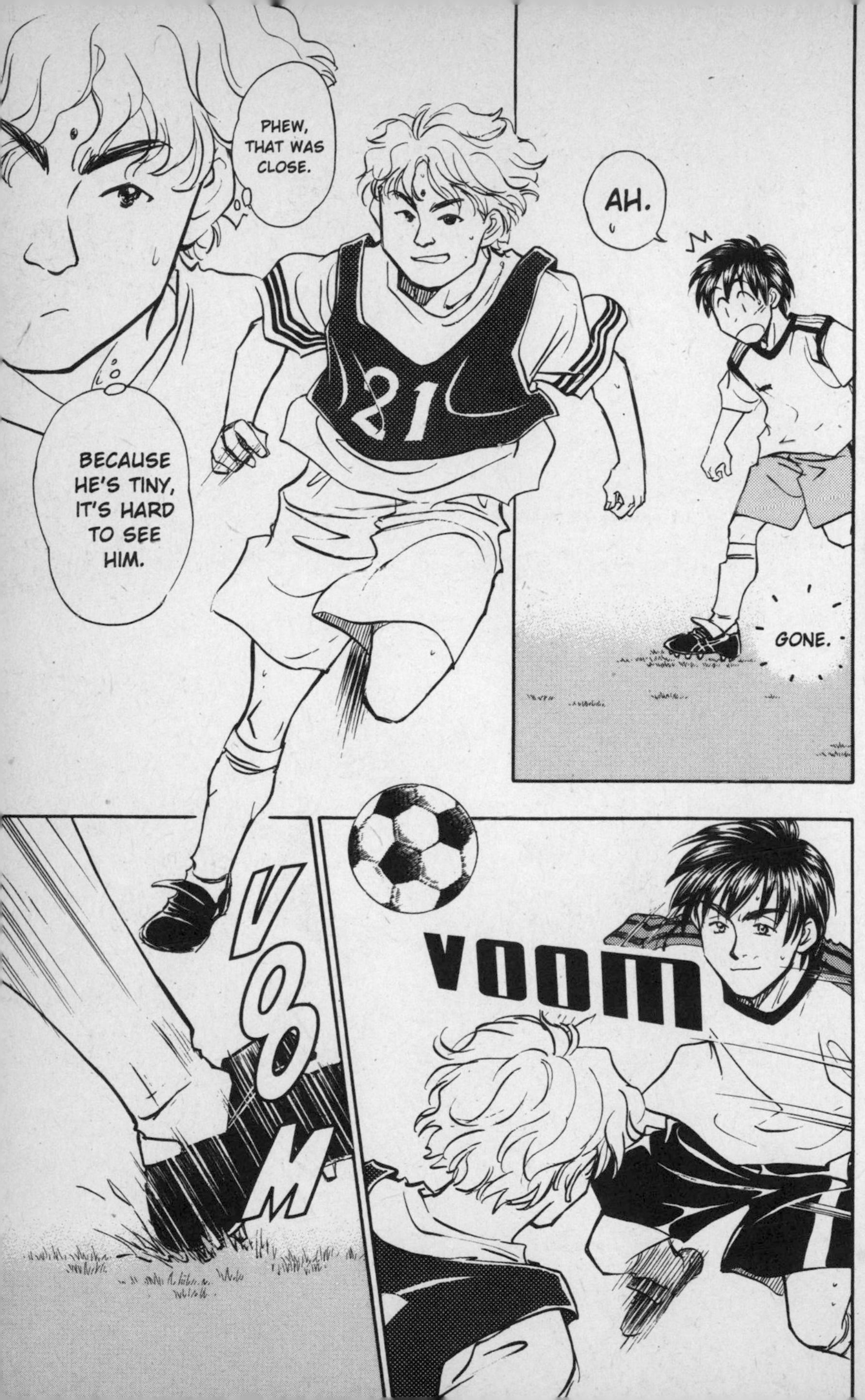
AH.
GONE.
PHEW, THAT WAS CLOSE.
BECAUSE HE'S TINY, IT'S HARD TO SEE HIM.
VOOM
VOOM

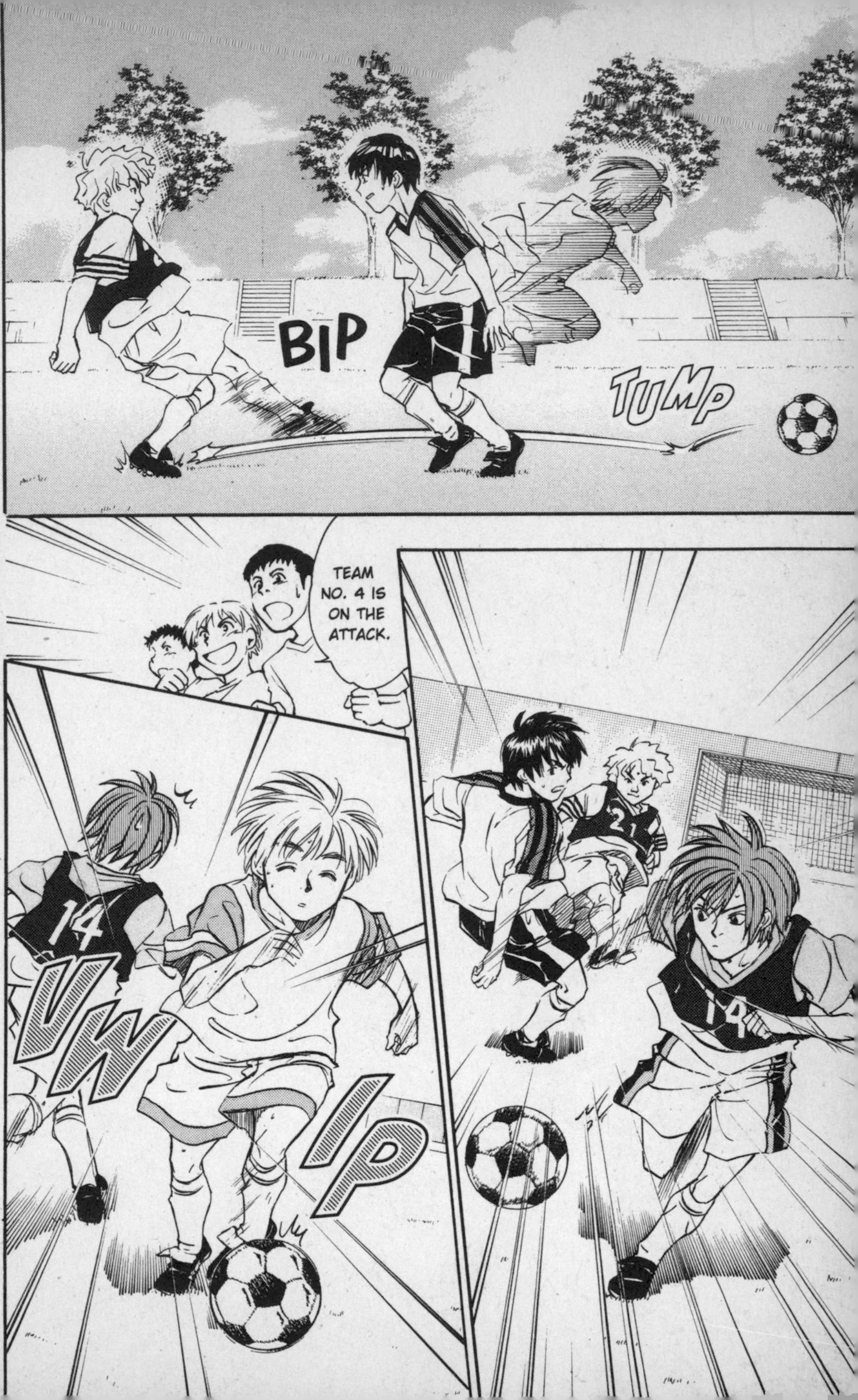
TUMP
BIP
TEAM NO. 4 IS ON THE ATTACK.
VWIP

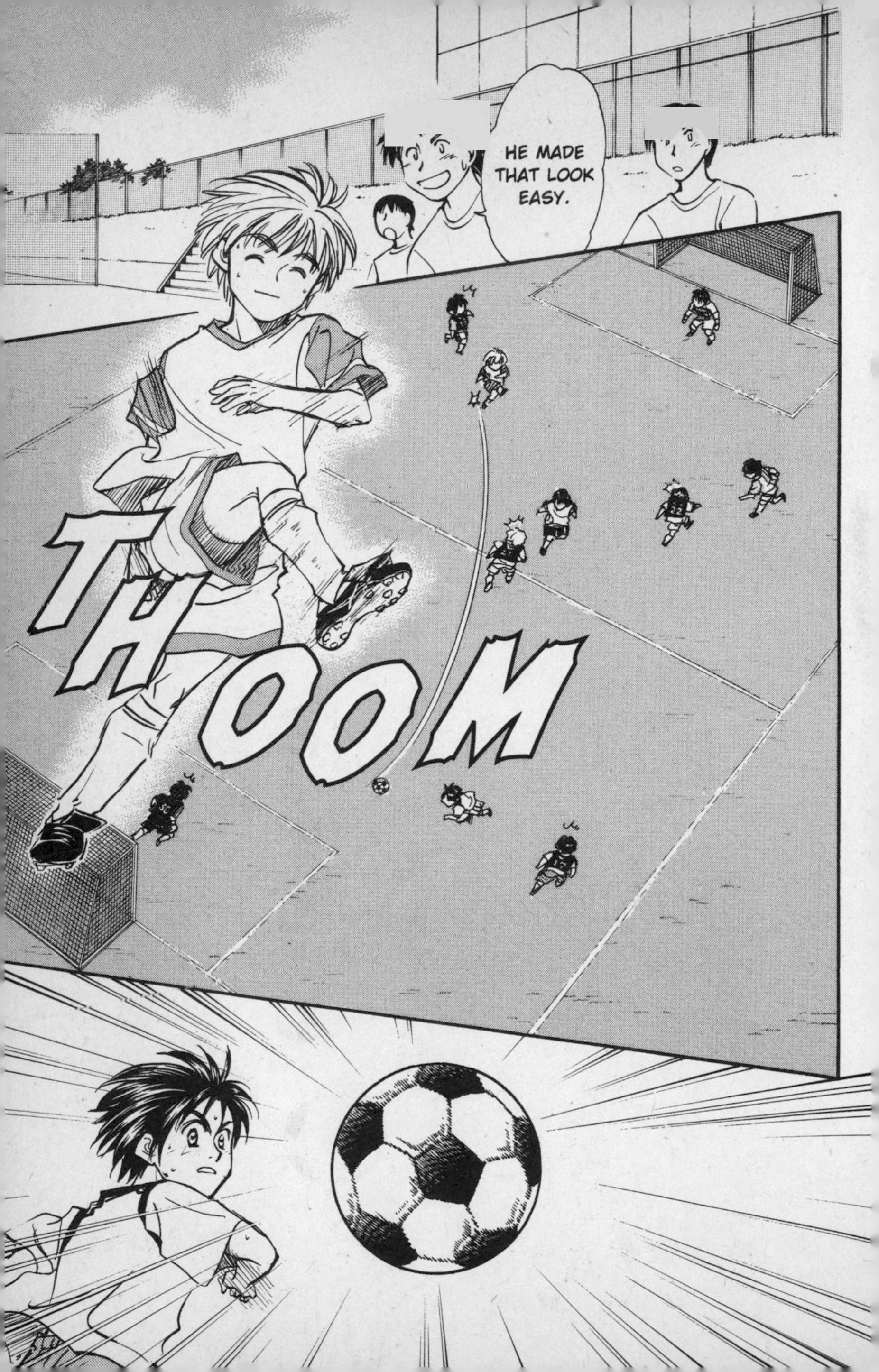
HE MADE THAT LOOK EASY.
THOOM

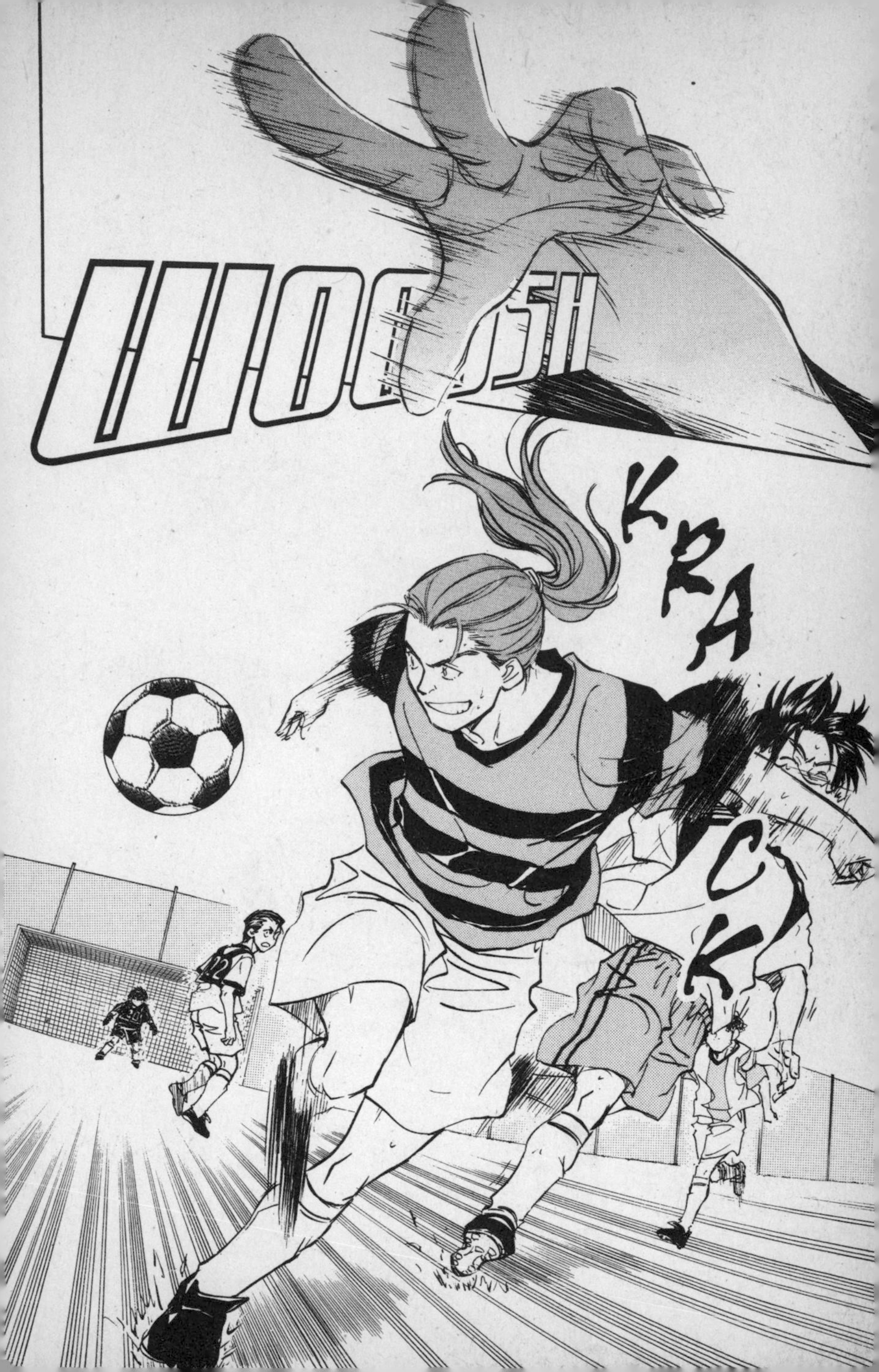
WHOOSH
KRACK

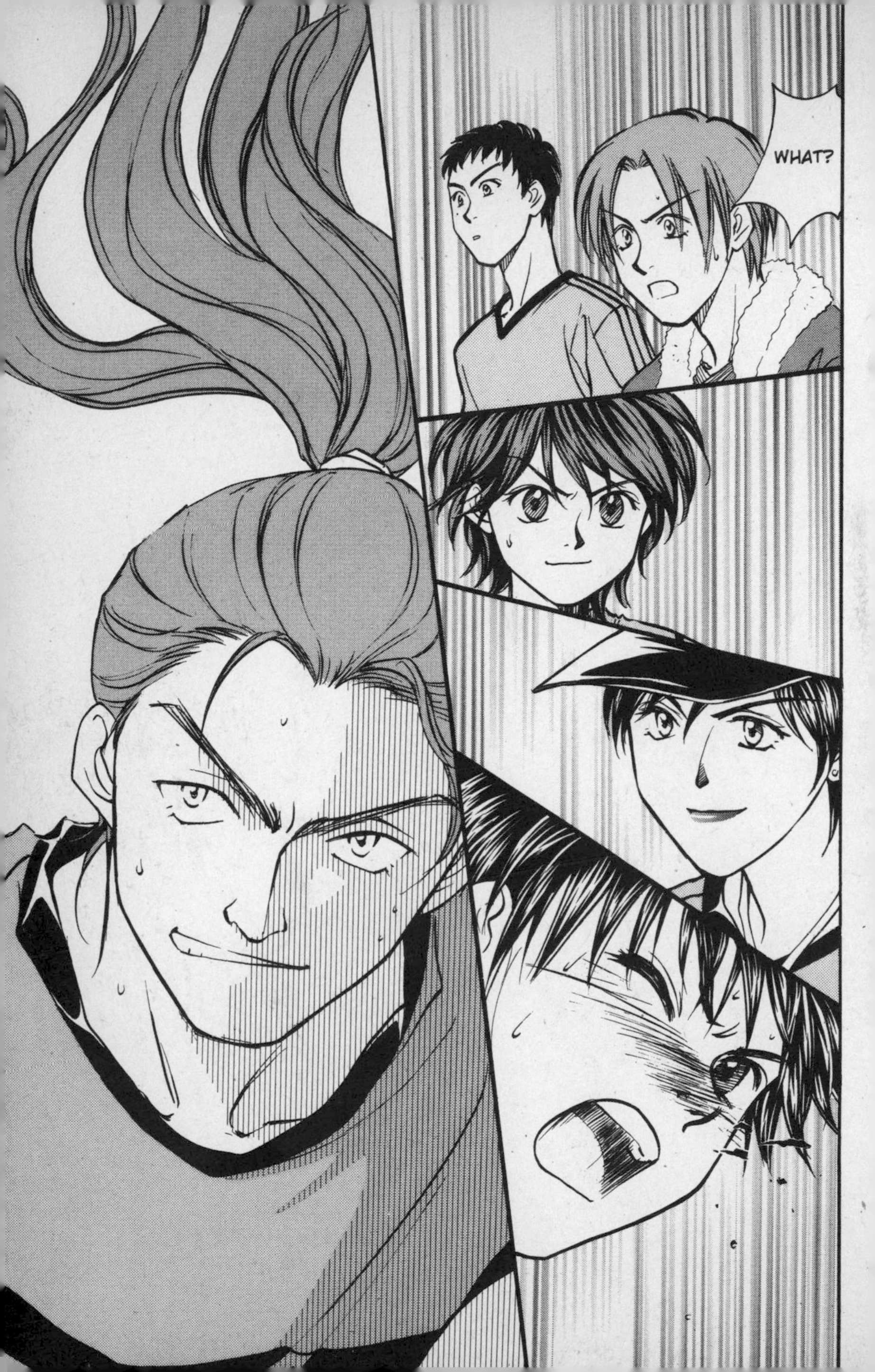
WHAT?

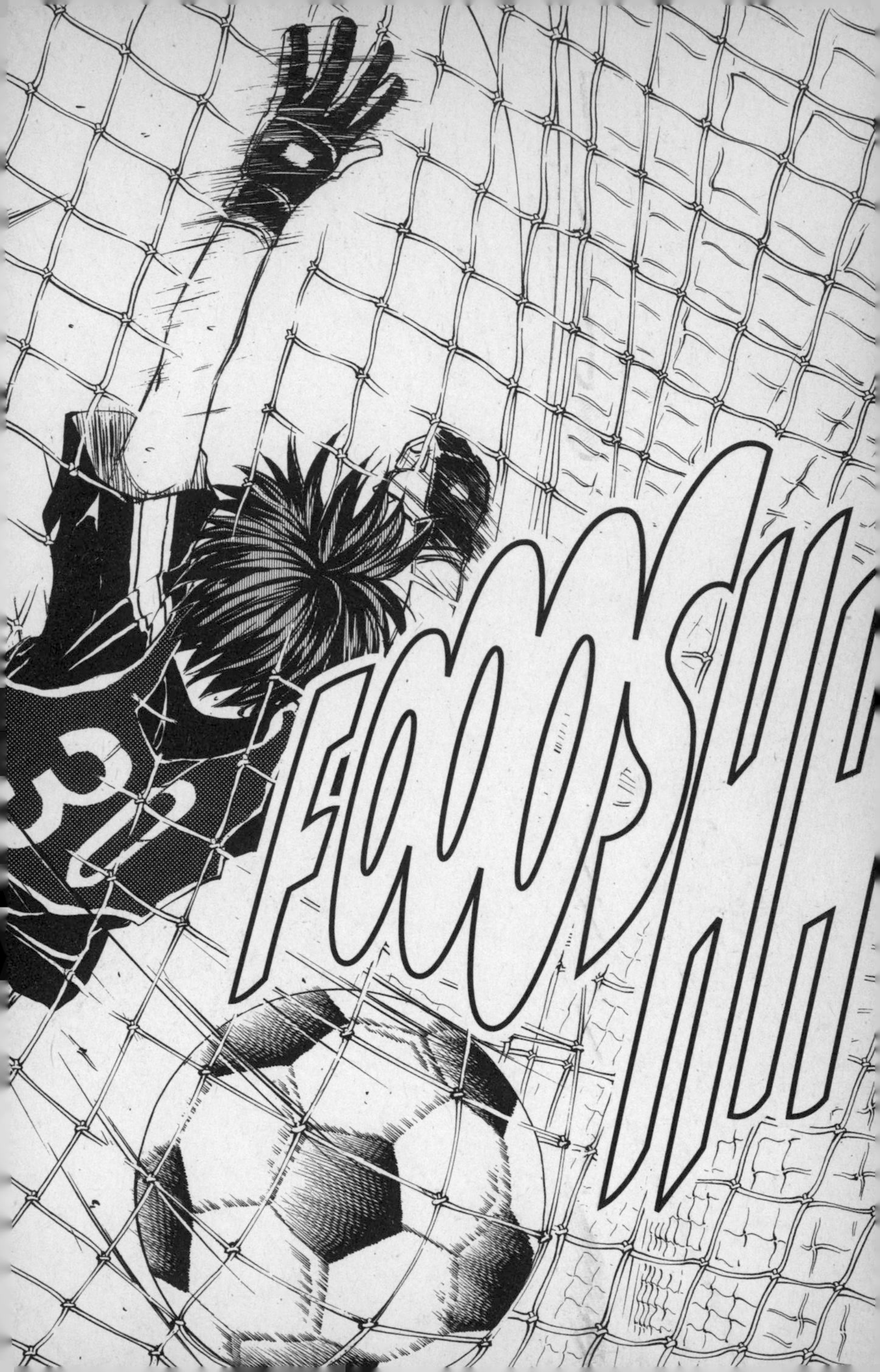
FOOOSHH

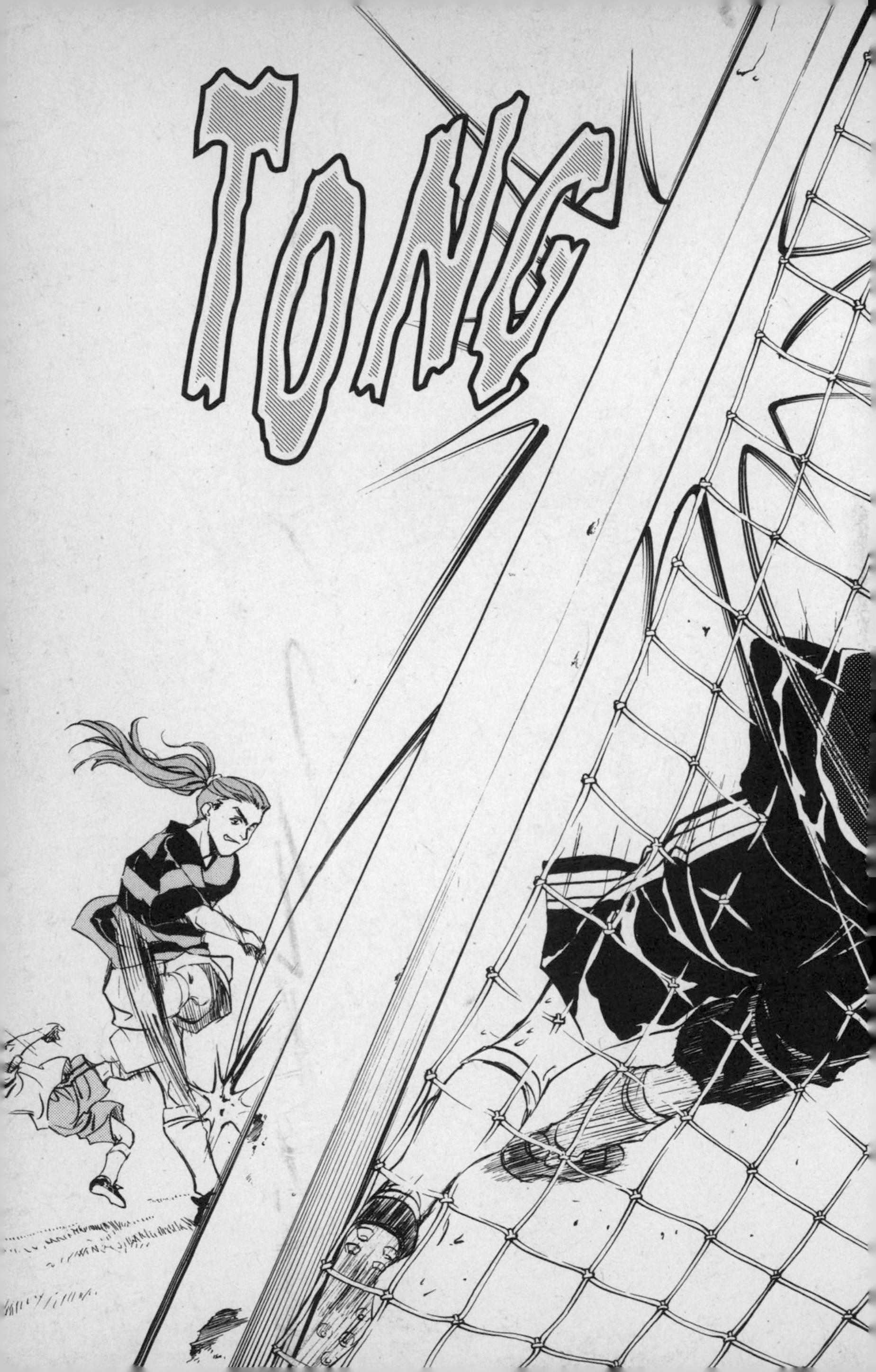
TONG

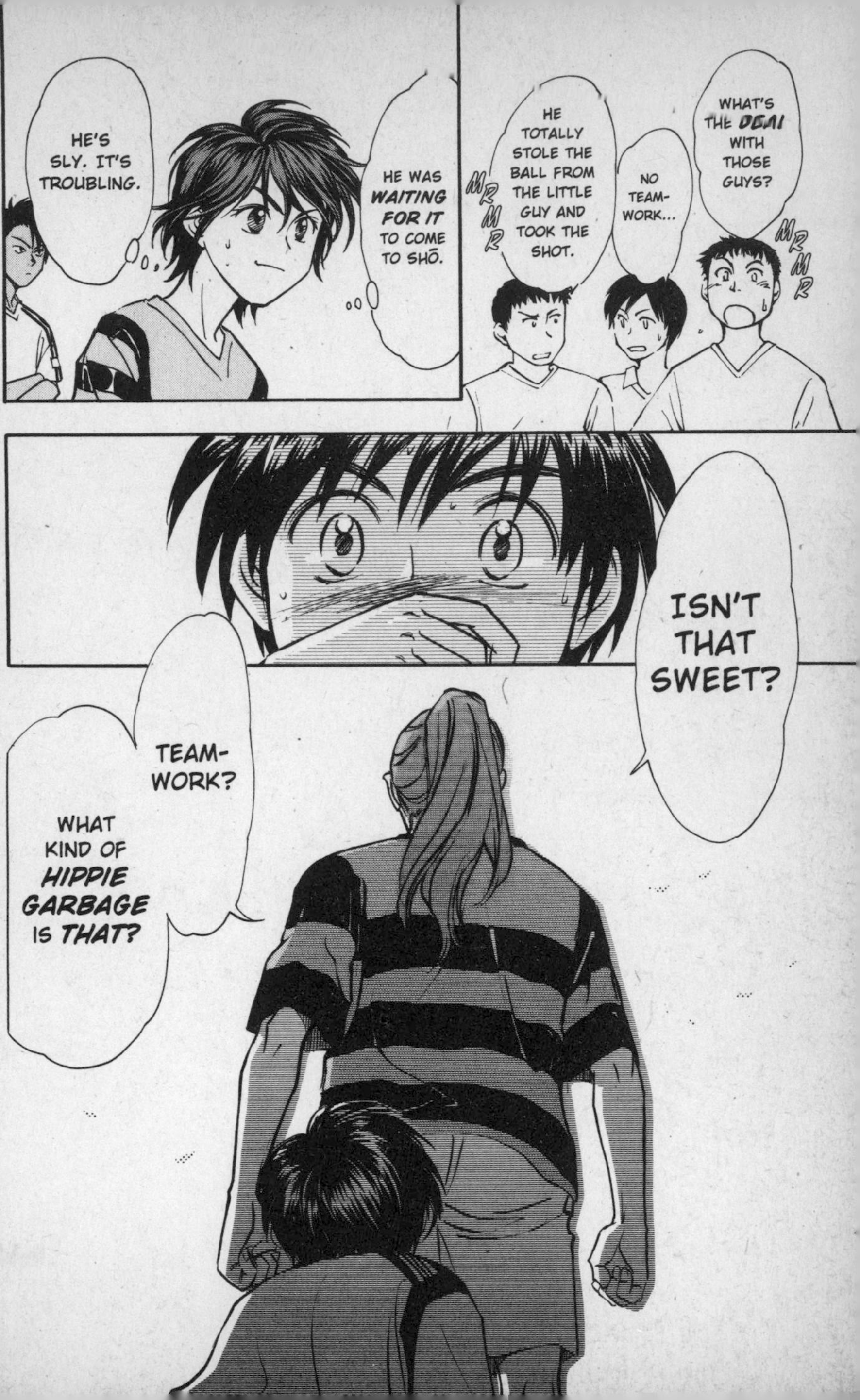

WHAT'S THE DEAL WITH THOSE GUYS?
MRMR
NO TEAM-WORK...
HE TOTALLY STOLE THE BALL FROM THE LITTLE GUY AND TOOK THE SHOT.
MRMR
HE WAS WAITING FOR IT TO COME TO SHŌ.
HE'S SLY. IT'S TROUBLING.
ISN'T THAT SWEET?
TEAM-WORK?
WHAT KIND OF HIPPIE GARBAGE IS THAT?

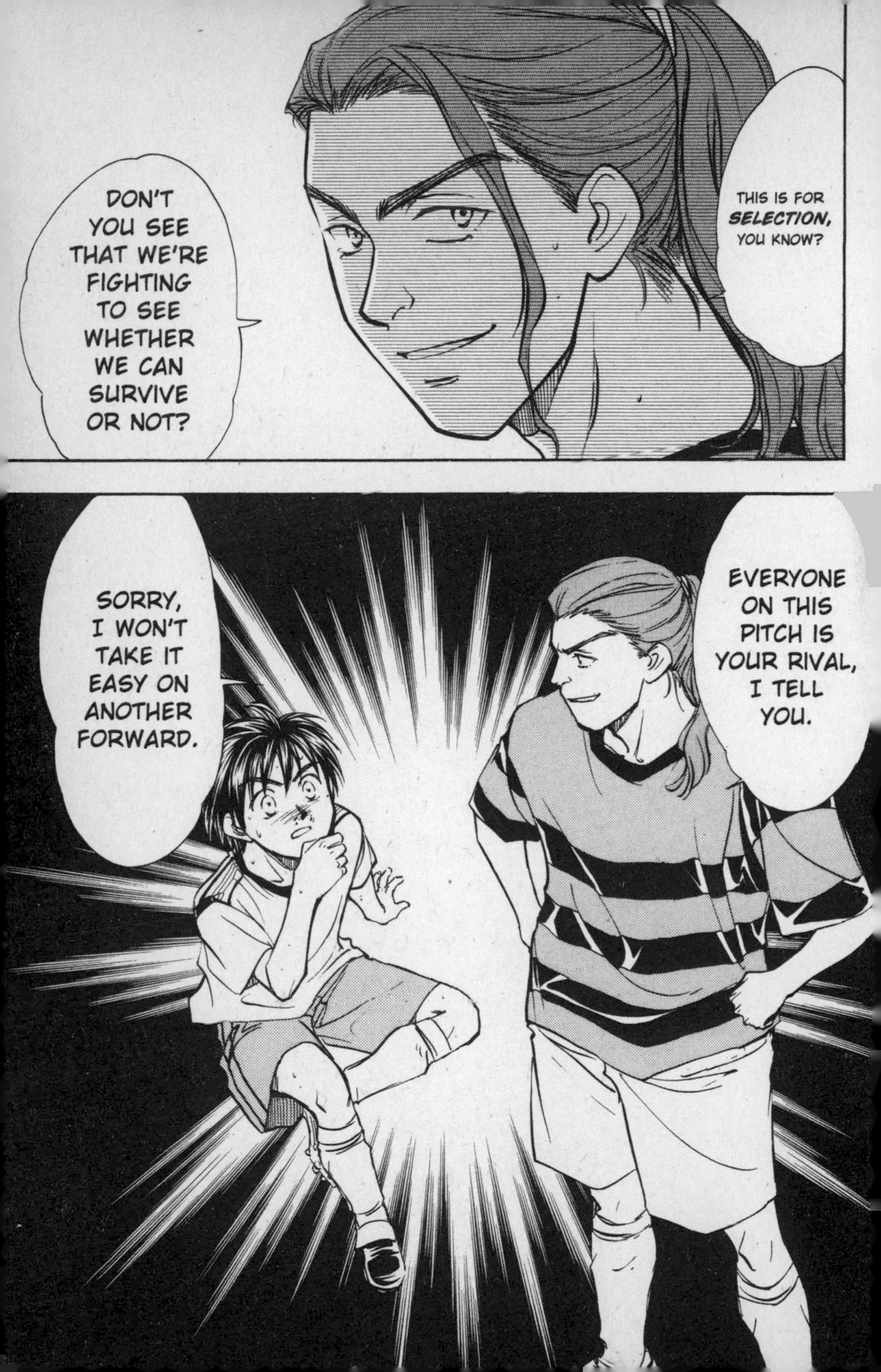
THIS IS FOR SELECTION, YOU KNOW?
DON'T YOU SEE THAT WE'RE FIGHTING TO SEE WHETHER WE CAN SURVIVE OR NOT?
EVERYONE ON THIS PITCH IS YOUR RIVAL, I TELL YOU.
SORRY, I WON'T TAKE IT EASY ON ANOTHER FORWARD.

WHISTLE!™

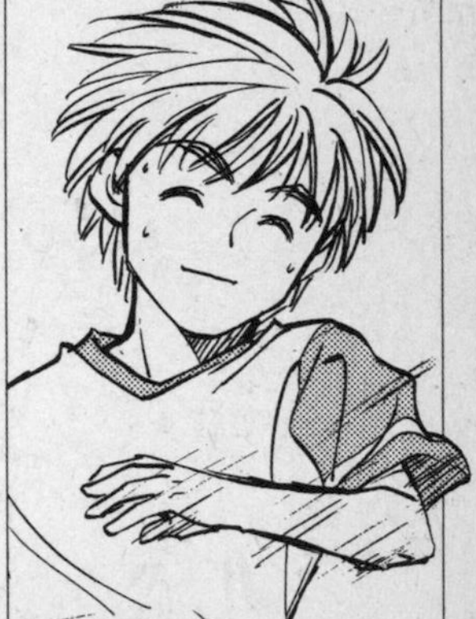

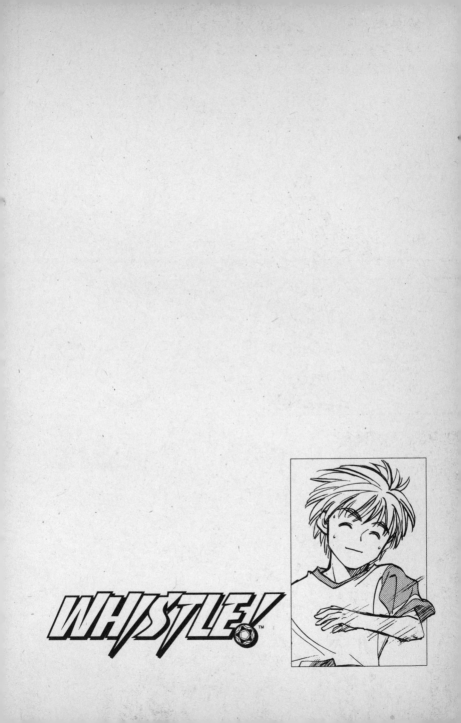

STAGE.116

My Value as a Forward

(DANCE WITH THE FEAR)

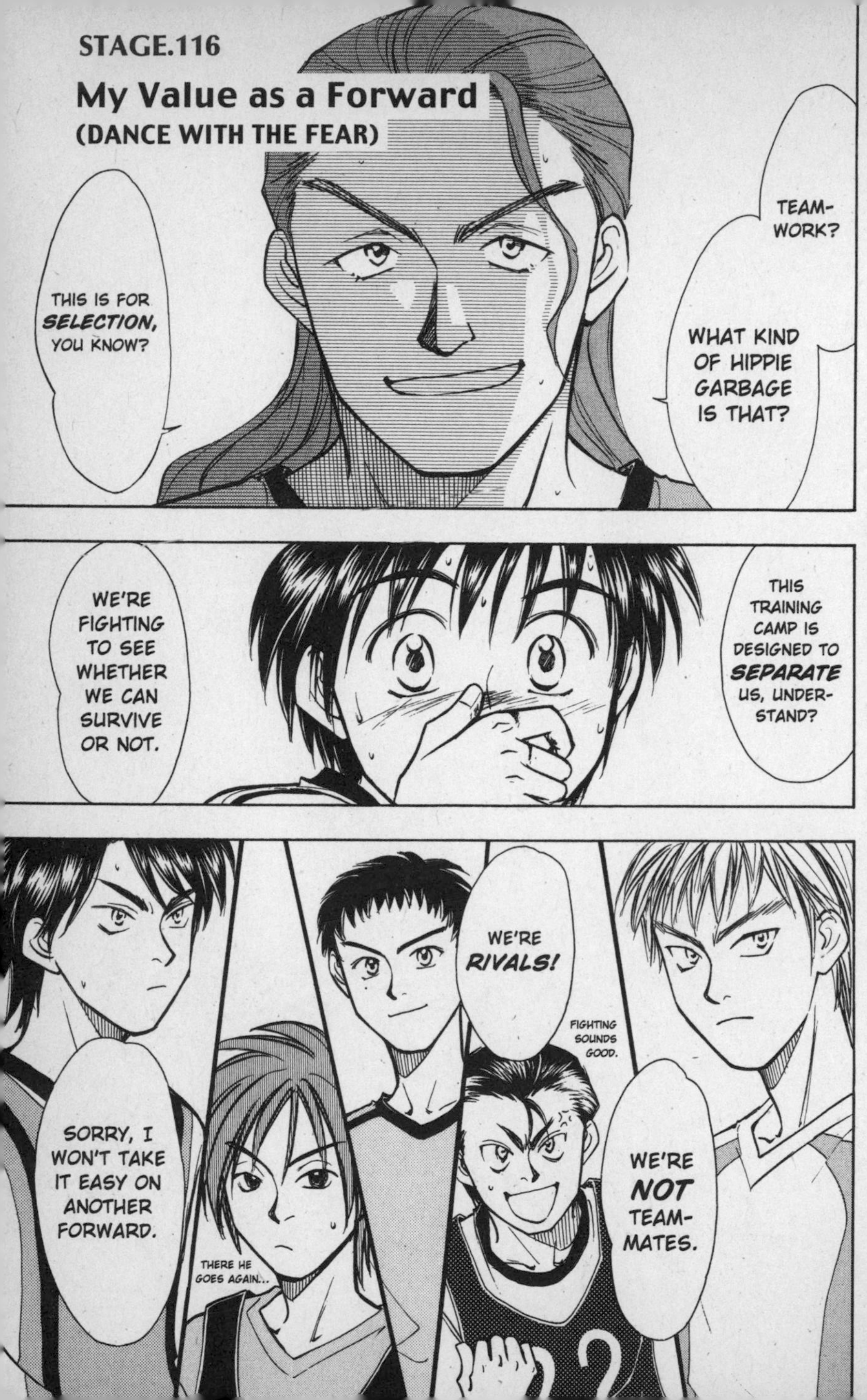
TEAM-WORK?
WHAT KIND OF HIPPIE GARBAGE IS THAT?
THIS IS FOR *SELECTION*, YOU KNOW?
THIS TRAINING CAMP IS DESIGNED TO *SEPARATE* US, UNDER-STAND?
WE'RE FIGHTING TO SEE WHETHER WE CAN SURVIVE OR NOT.
WE'RE *NOT* TEAM-MATES.
FIGHTING SOUNDS GOOD.
WE'RE *RIVALS!*
SORRY, I WON'T TAKE IT EASY ON ANOTHER FORWARD.
THERE HE GOES AGAIN...

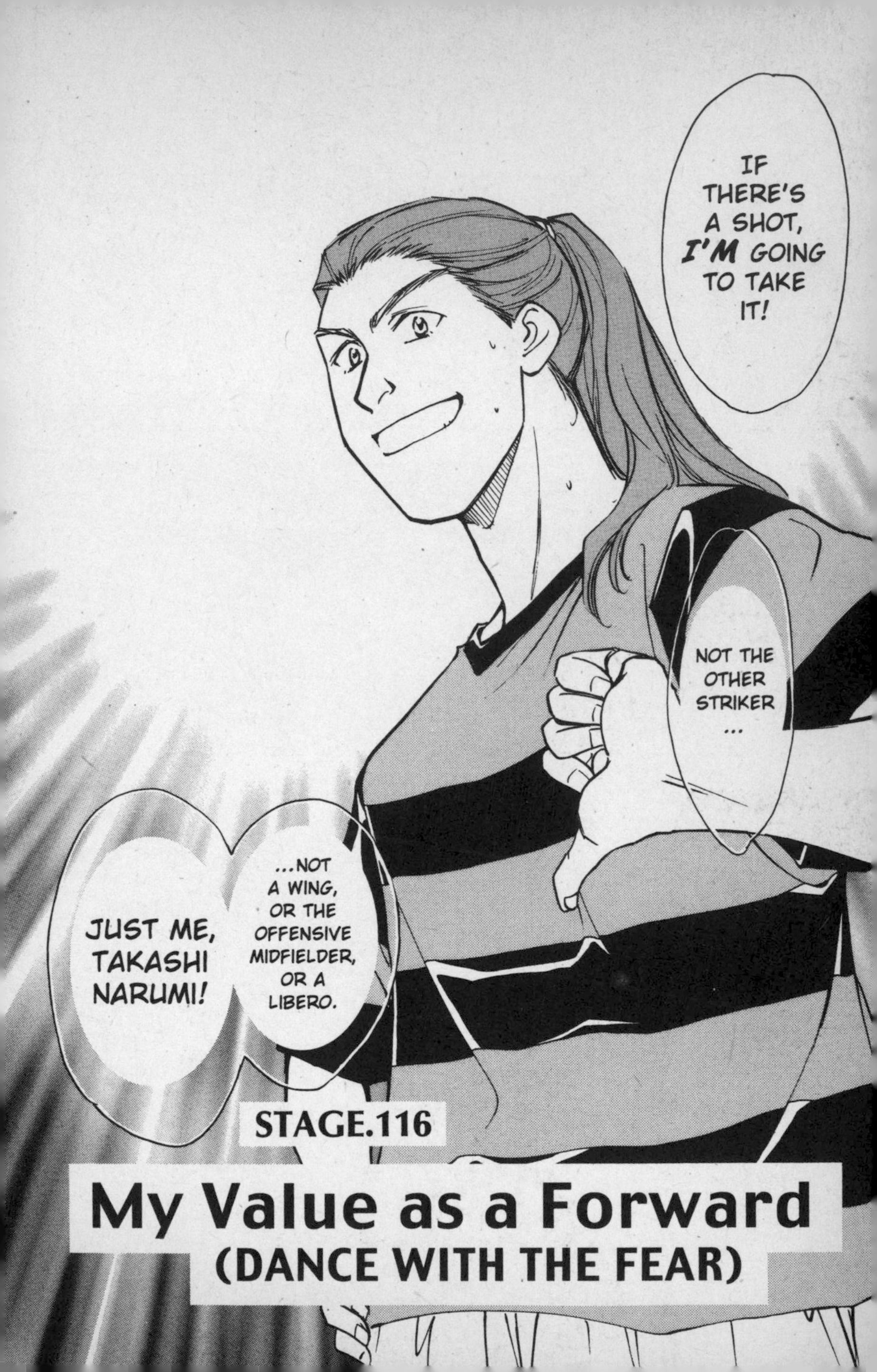
IF THERE'S A SHOT, *I'M* GOING TO TAKE IT!
NOT THE OTHER STRIKER...
...NOT A WING, OR THE OFFENSIVE MIDFIELDER, OR A LIBERO.
JUST ME, TAKASHI NARUMI!
STAGE.116
My Value as a Forward
(DANCE WITH THE FEAR)

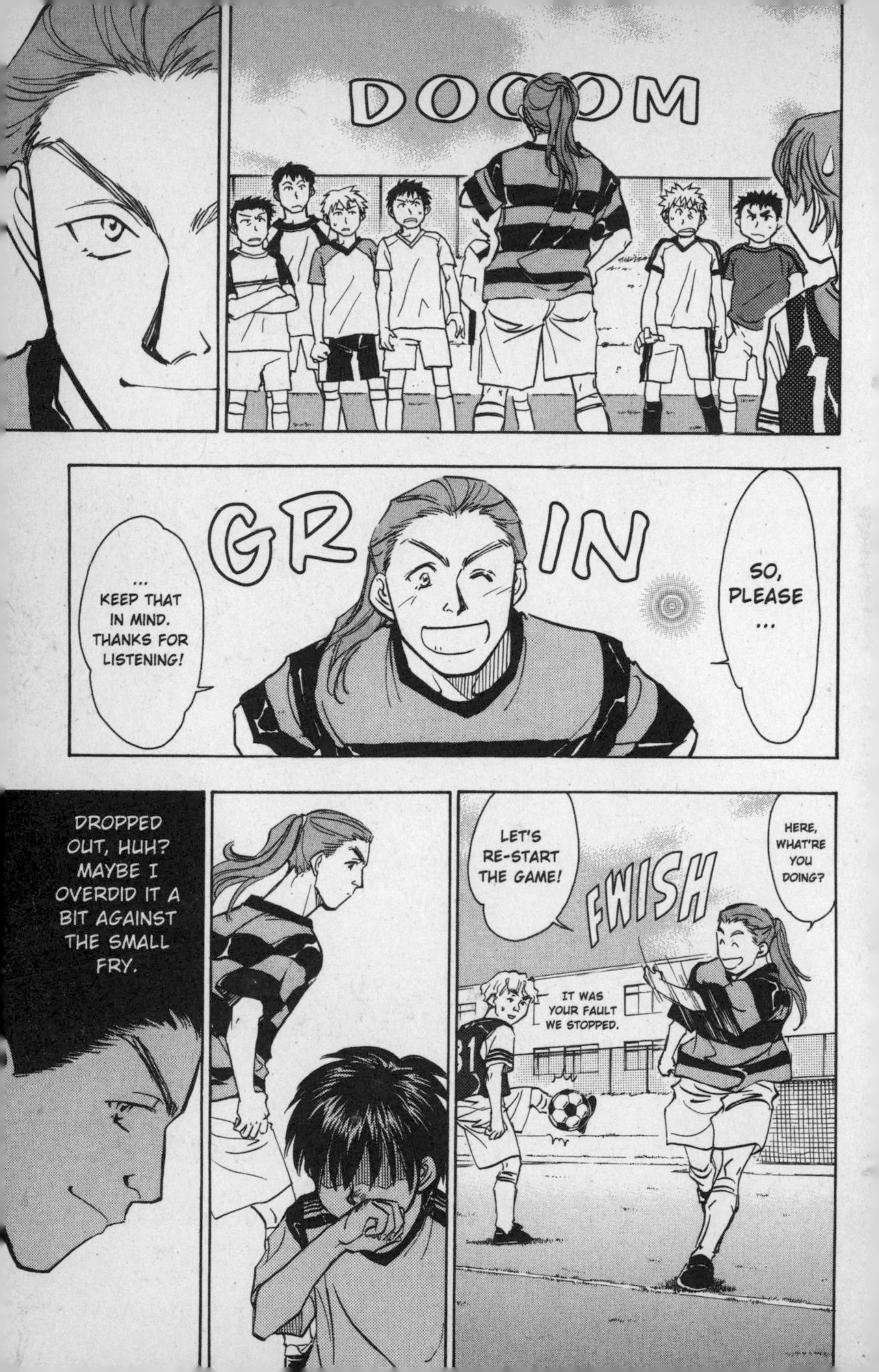
DOCOOM
SO, PLEASE ...
GRIN
... KEEP THAT IN MIND. THANKS FOR LISTENING!
HERE, WHAT'RE YOU DOING?
LET'S RE-START THE GAME!
FWISH
IT WAS YOUR FAULT WE STOPPED.
DROPPED OUT, HUH? MAYBE I OVERDID IT A BIT AGAINST THE SMALL FRY.

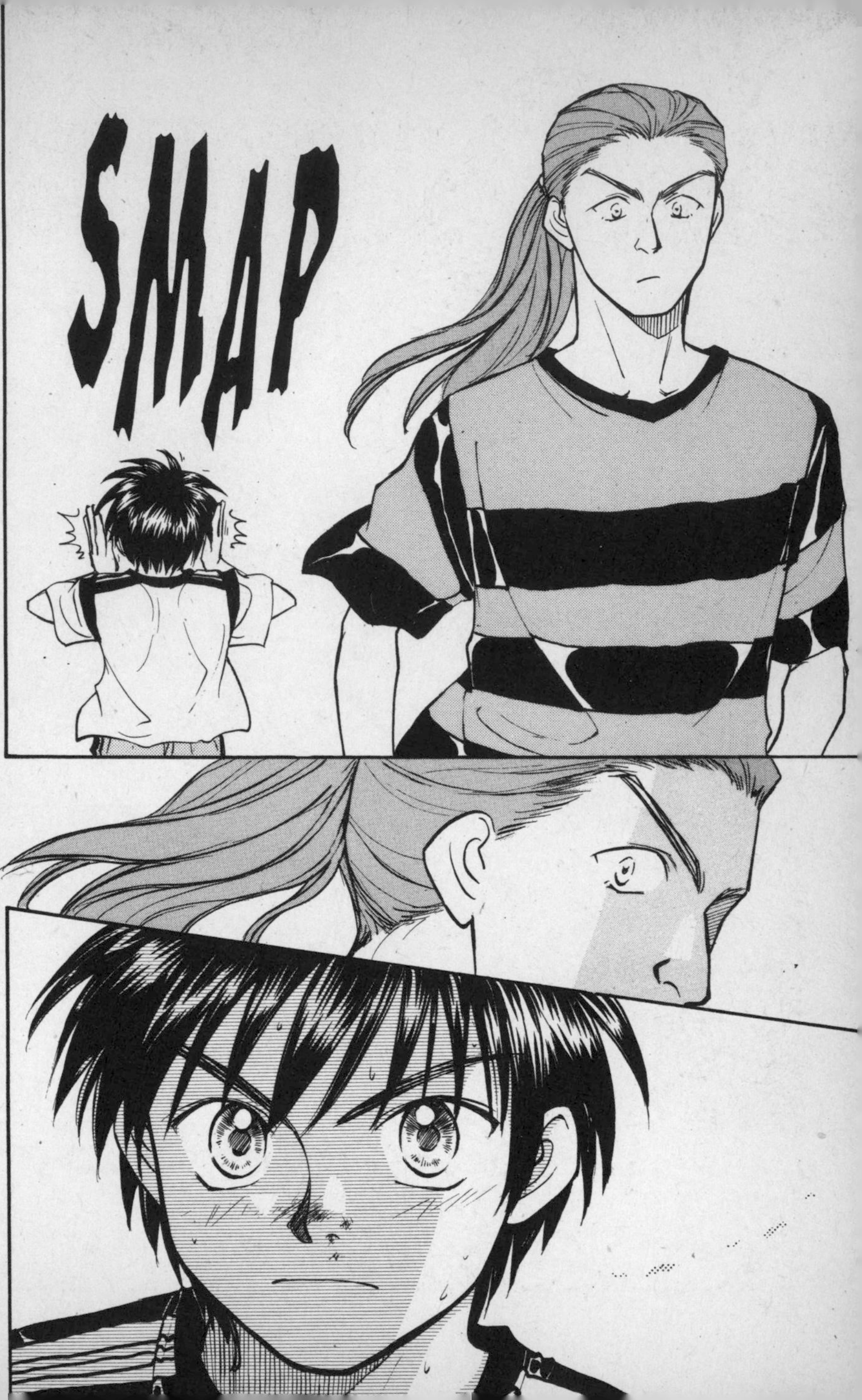
SNAP

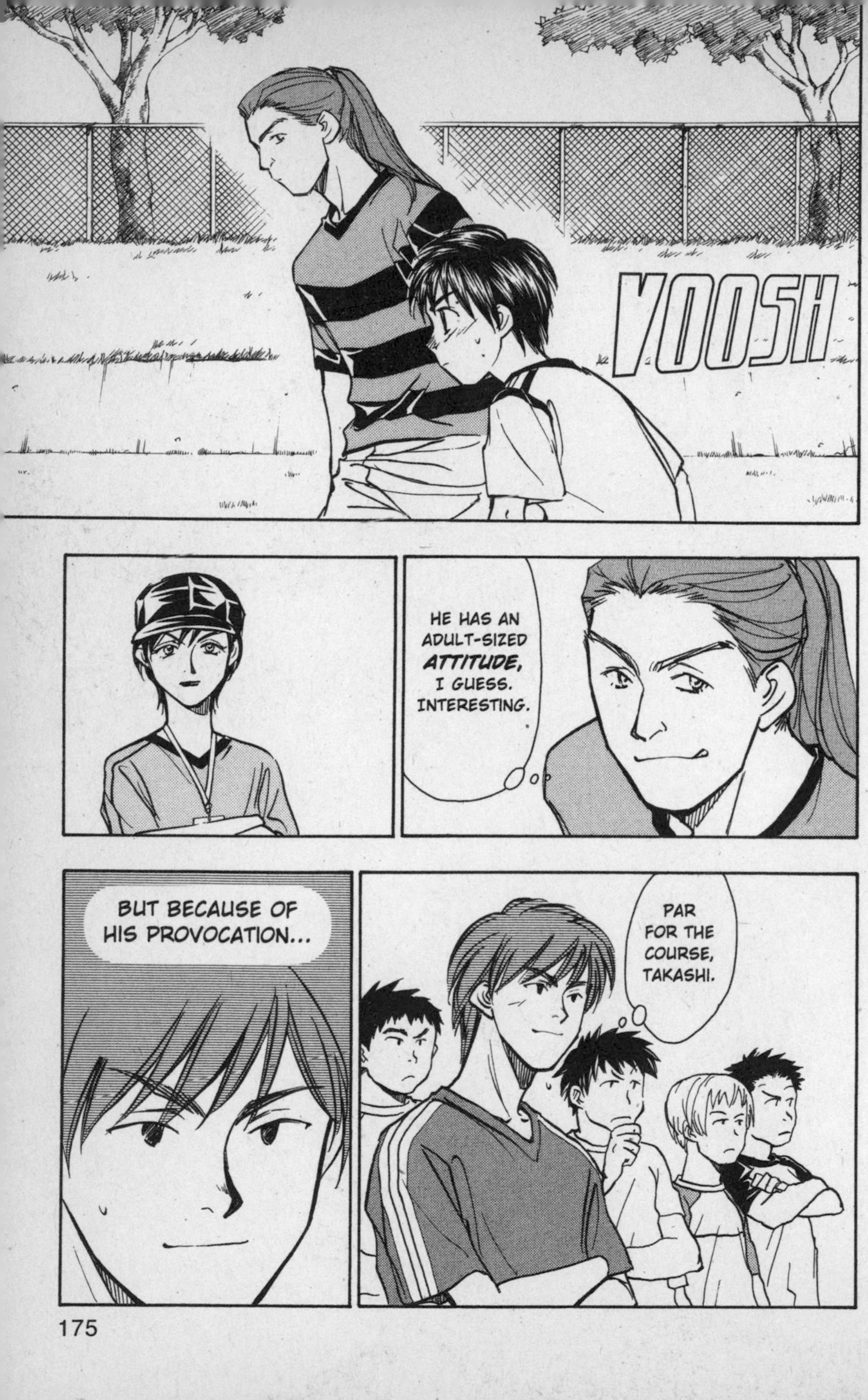
VOOSH
HE HAS AN ADULT-SIZED ATTITUDE, I GUESS. INTERESTING.
PAR FOR THE COURSE, TAKASHI.
BUT BECAUSE OF HIS PROVOCATION...

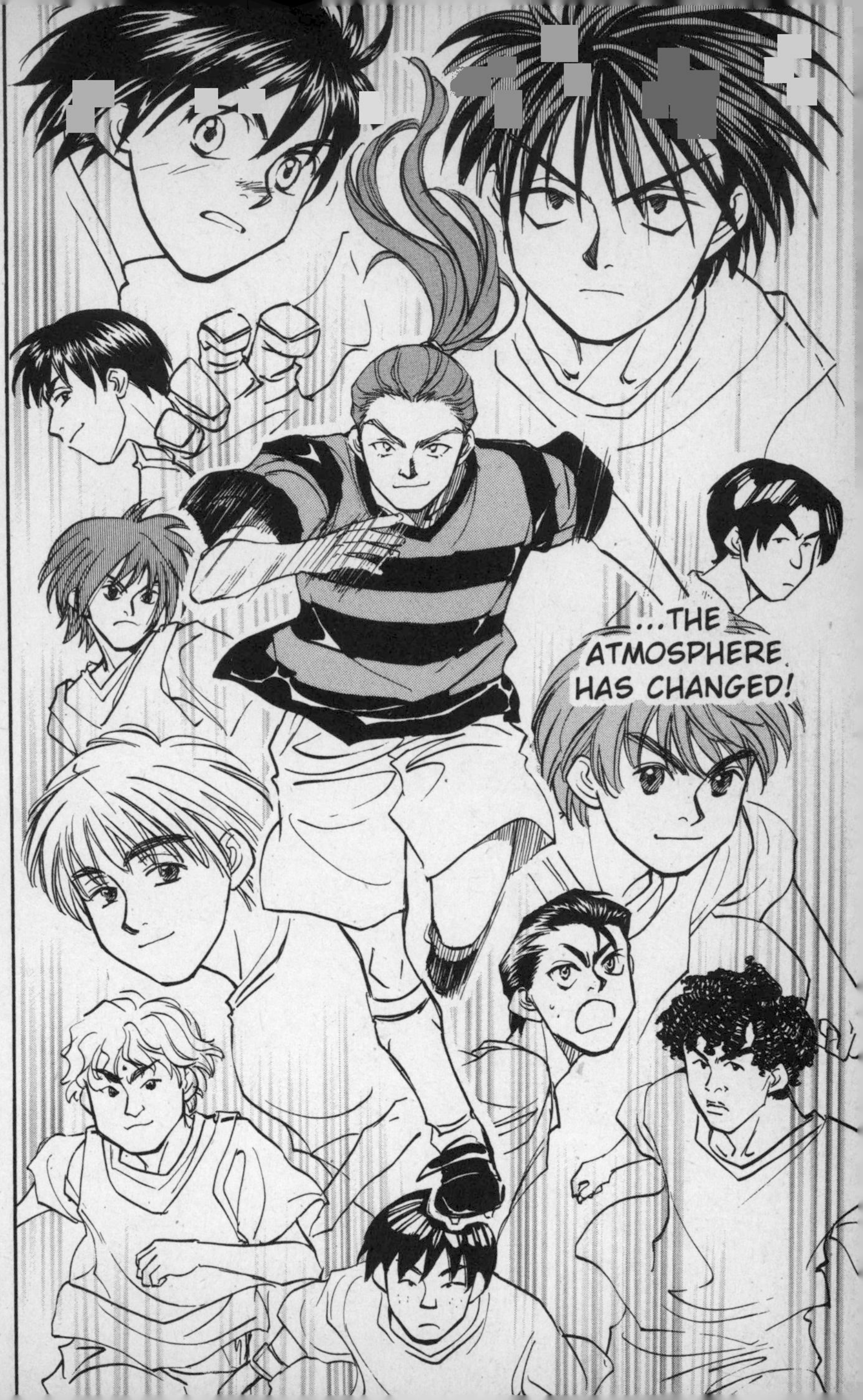
...THE ATMOSPHERE HAS CHANGED!

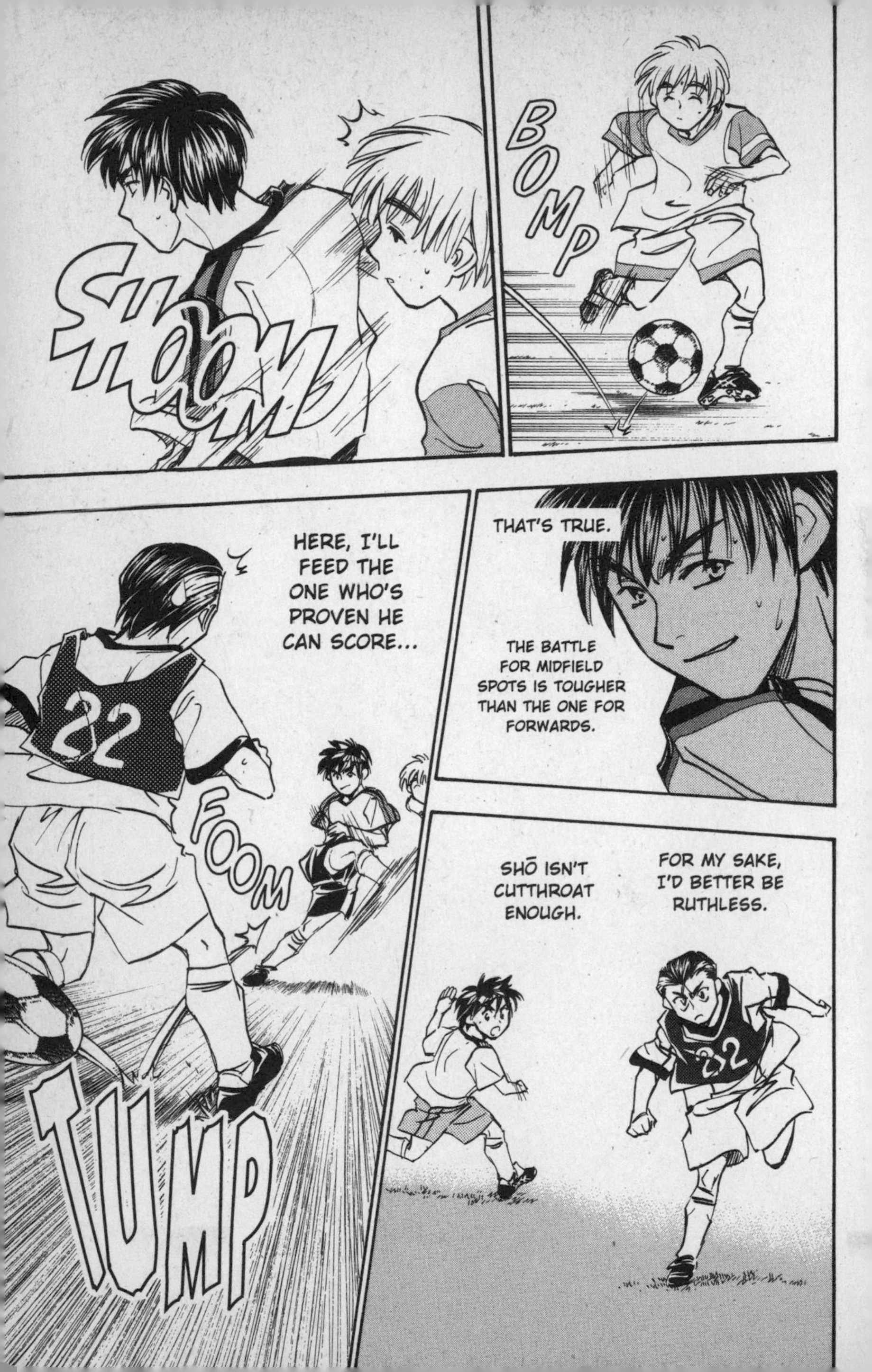
BOMP
SHOOM
THAT'S TRUE.
THE BATTLE FOR MIDFIELD SPOTS IS TOUGHER THAN THE ONE FOR FORWARDS.
FOR MY SAKE, I'D BETTER BE RUTHLESS.
SHŌ ISN'T CUTTHROAT ENOUGH.
HERE, I'LL FEED THE ONE WHO'S PROVEN HE CAN SCORE...
FOOM
22
TUMP

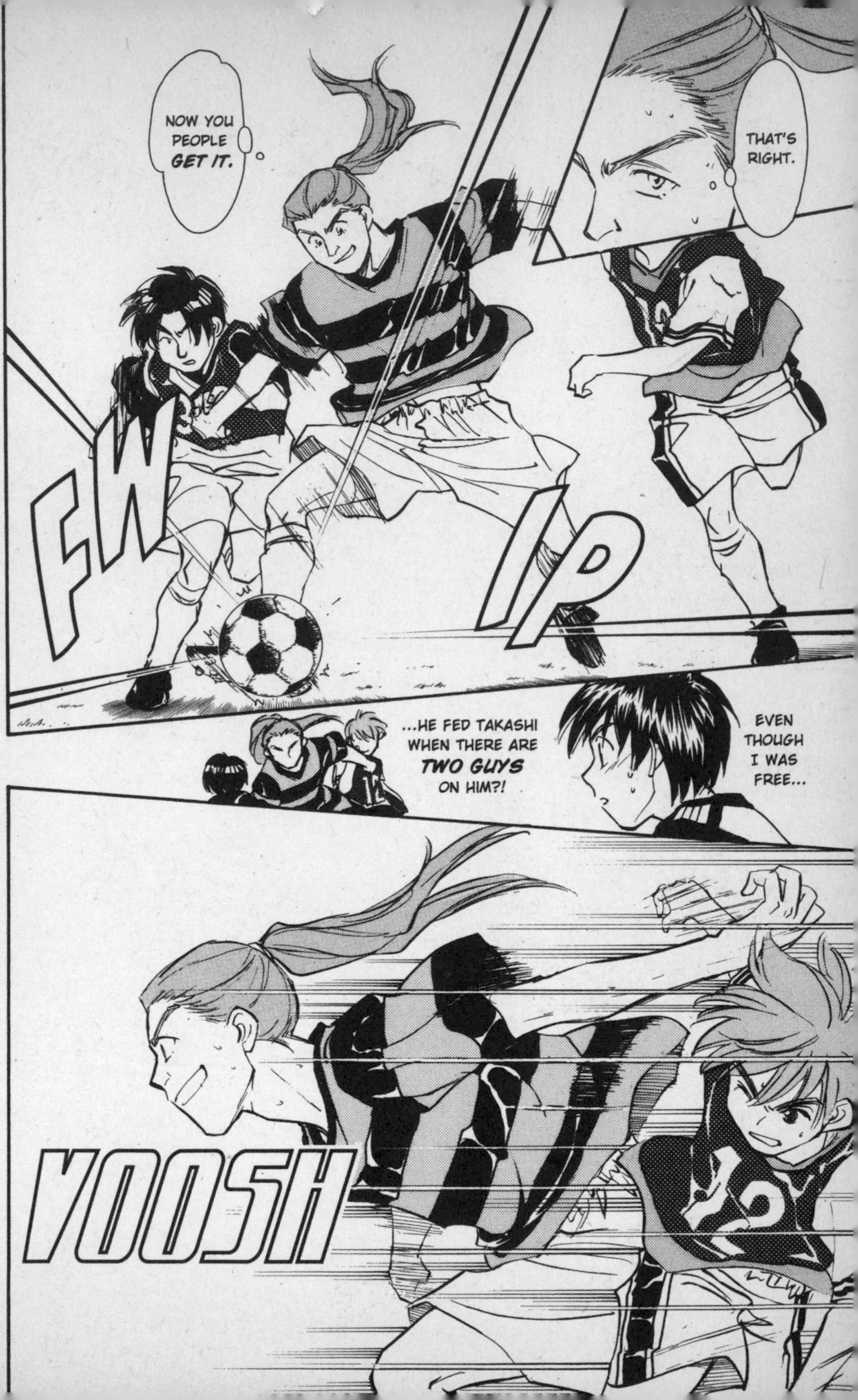
THAT'S RIGHT.
NOW YOU PEOPLE GET IT.
FWIP
EVEN THOUGH I WAS FREE...
...HE FED TAKASHI WHEN THERE ARE TWO GUYS ON HIM?!
VOOSH

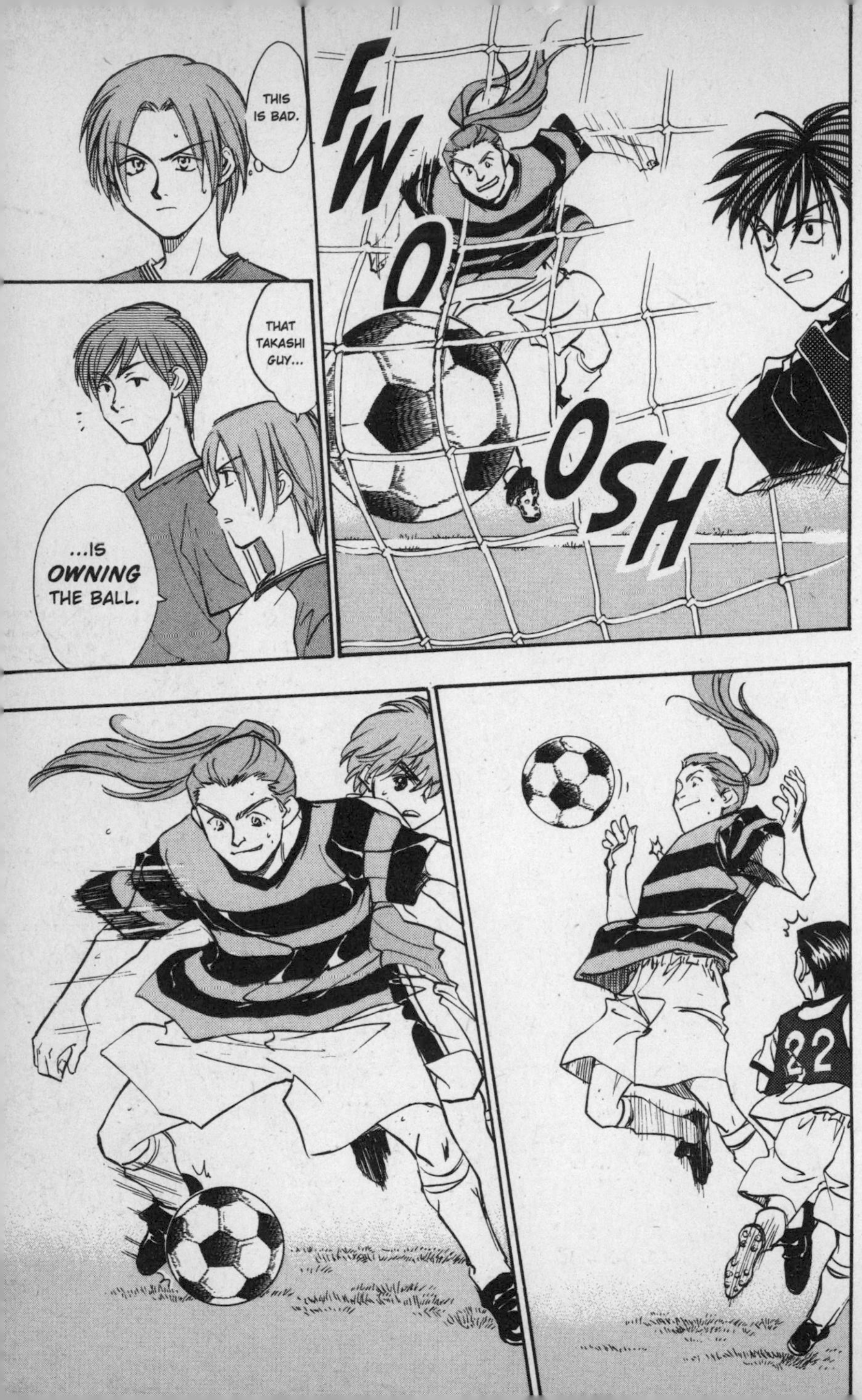
FWOOSH
THIS IS BAD.
THAT TAKASHI GUY...
...IS **OWNING** THE BALL.

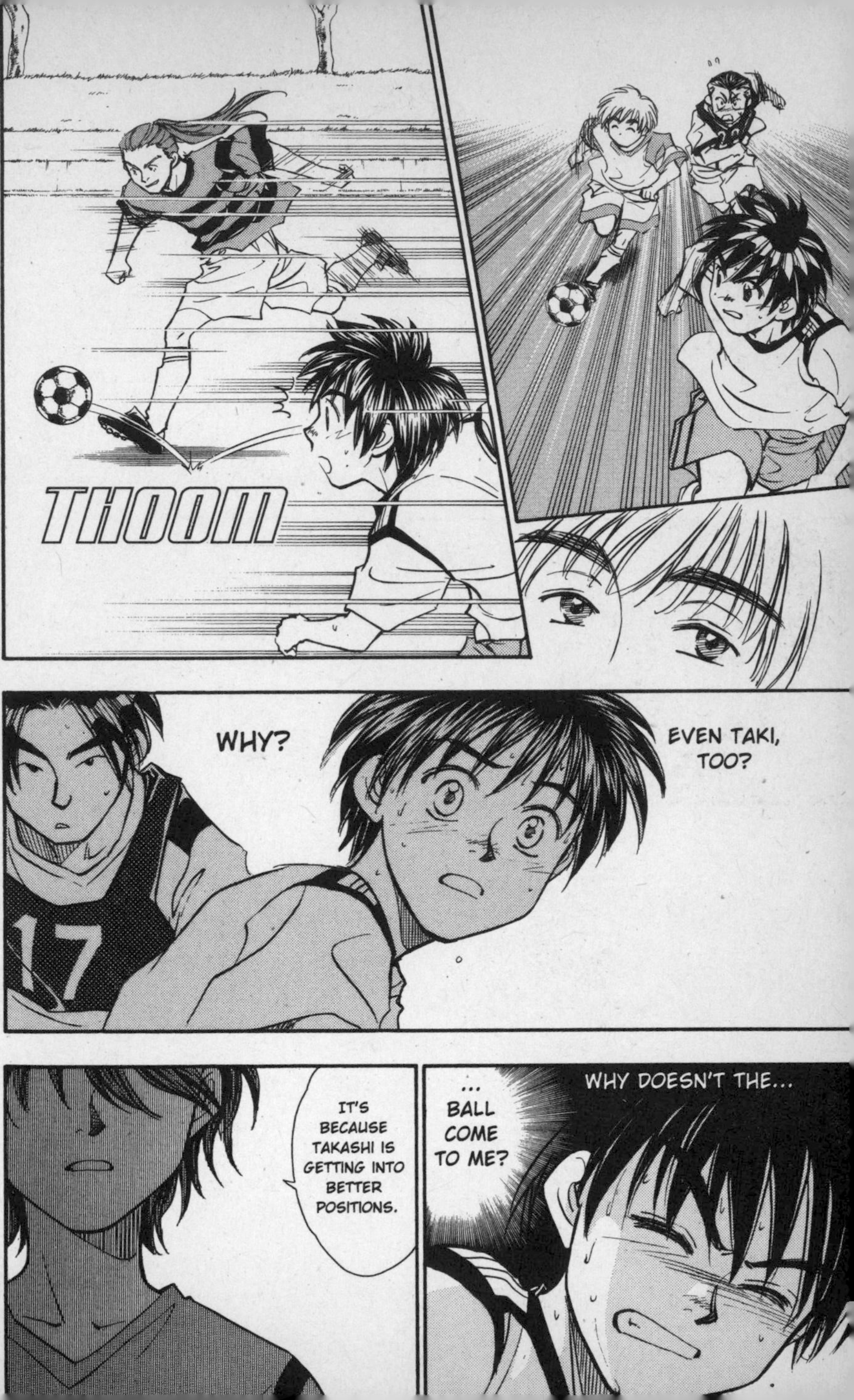
THOOM
EVEN TAKI, TOO?
WHY?
WHY DOESN'T THE...
... BALL COME TO ME?
IT'S BECAUSE TAKASHI IS GETTING INTO BETTER POSITIONS.

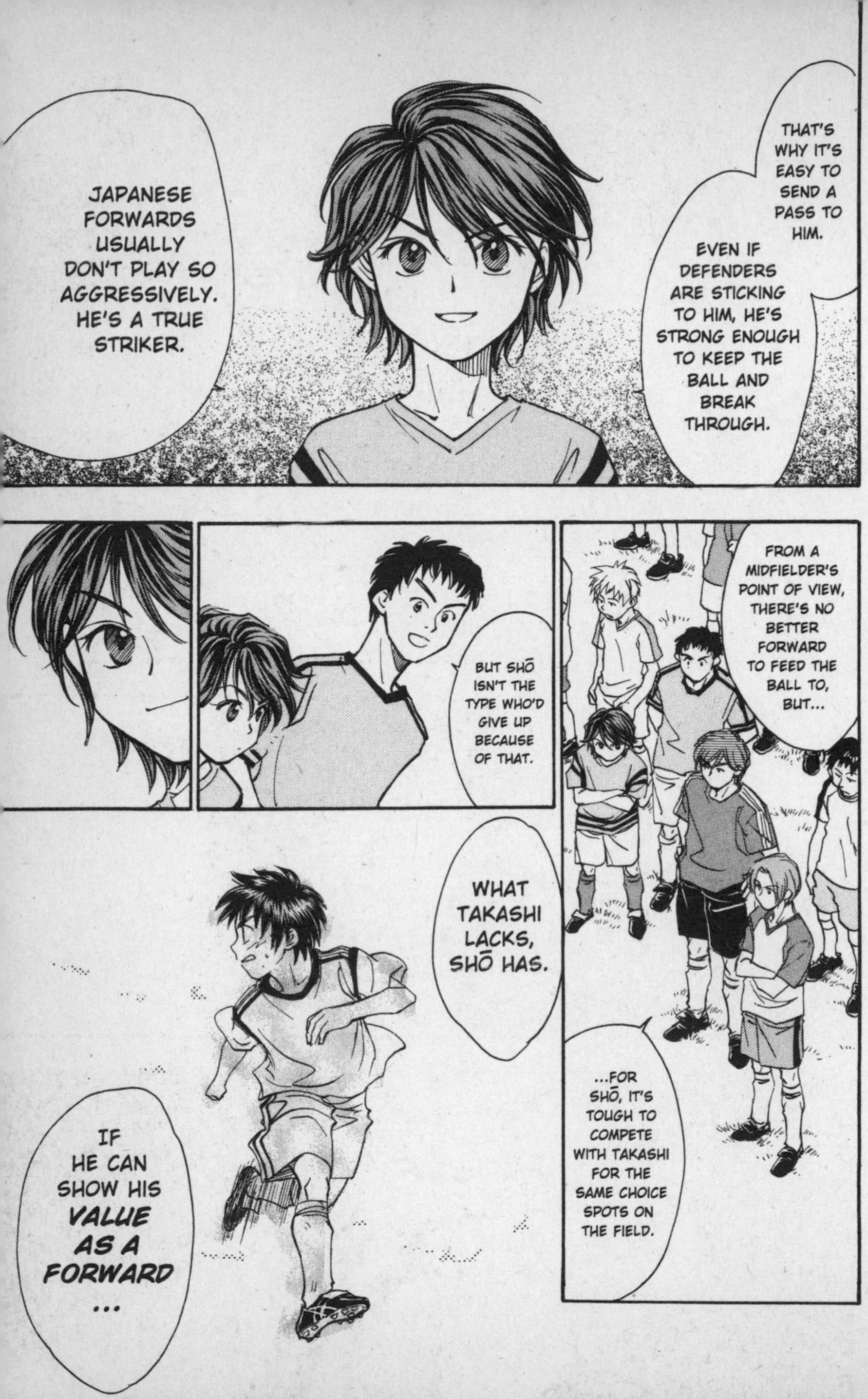
THAT'S WHY IT'S EASY TO SEND A PASS TO HIM.
EVEN IF DEFENDERS ARE STICKING TO HIM, HE'S STRONG ENOUGH TO KEEP THE BALL AND BREAK THROUGH.
JAPANESE FORWARDS USUALLY DON'T PLAY SO AGGRESSIVELY. HE'S A TRUE STRIKER.
FROM A MIDFIELDER'S POINT OF VIEW, THERE'S NO BETTER FORWARD TO FEED THE BALL TO, BUT...
...FOR SHŌ, IT'S TOUGH TO COMPETE WITH TAKASHI FOR THE SAME CHOICE SPOTS ON THE FIELD.
BUT SHŌ ISN'T THE TYPE WHO'D GIVE UP BECAUSE OF THAT.
WHAT TAKASHI LACKS, SHŌ HAS.
IF HE CAN SHOW HIS ***VALUE AS A FORWARD***...

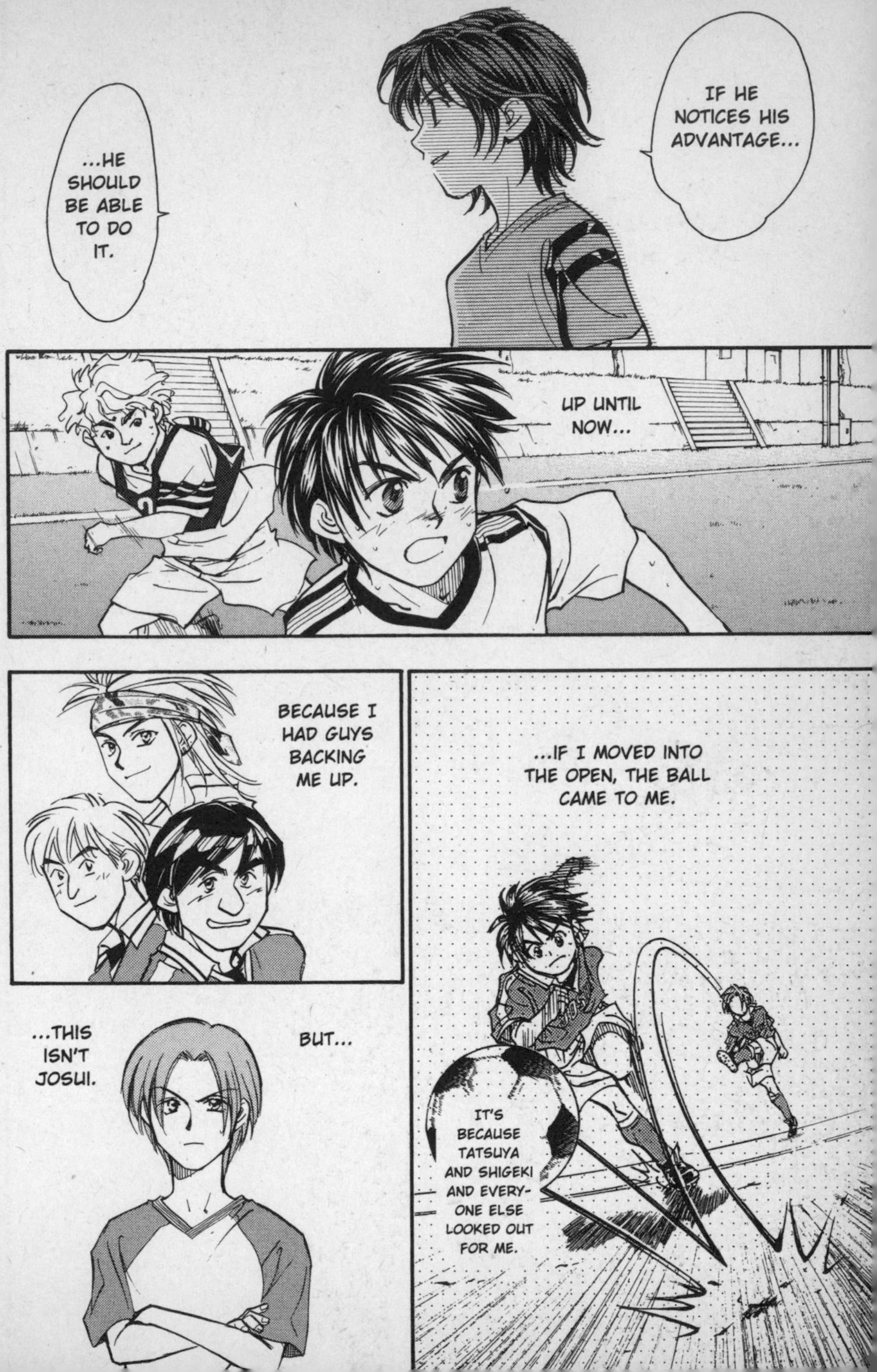
IF HE NOTICES HIS ADVANTAGE...
...HE SHOULD BE ABLE TO DO IT.
UP UNTIL NOW...
...IF I MOVED INTO THE OPEN, THE BALL CAME TO ME.
IT'S BECAUSE TATSUYA AND SHIGEKI AND EVERY-ONE ELSE LOOKED OUT FOR ME.
BECAUSE I HAD GUYS BACKING ME UP.
BUT...
...THIS ISN'T JOSUI.

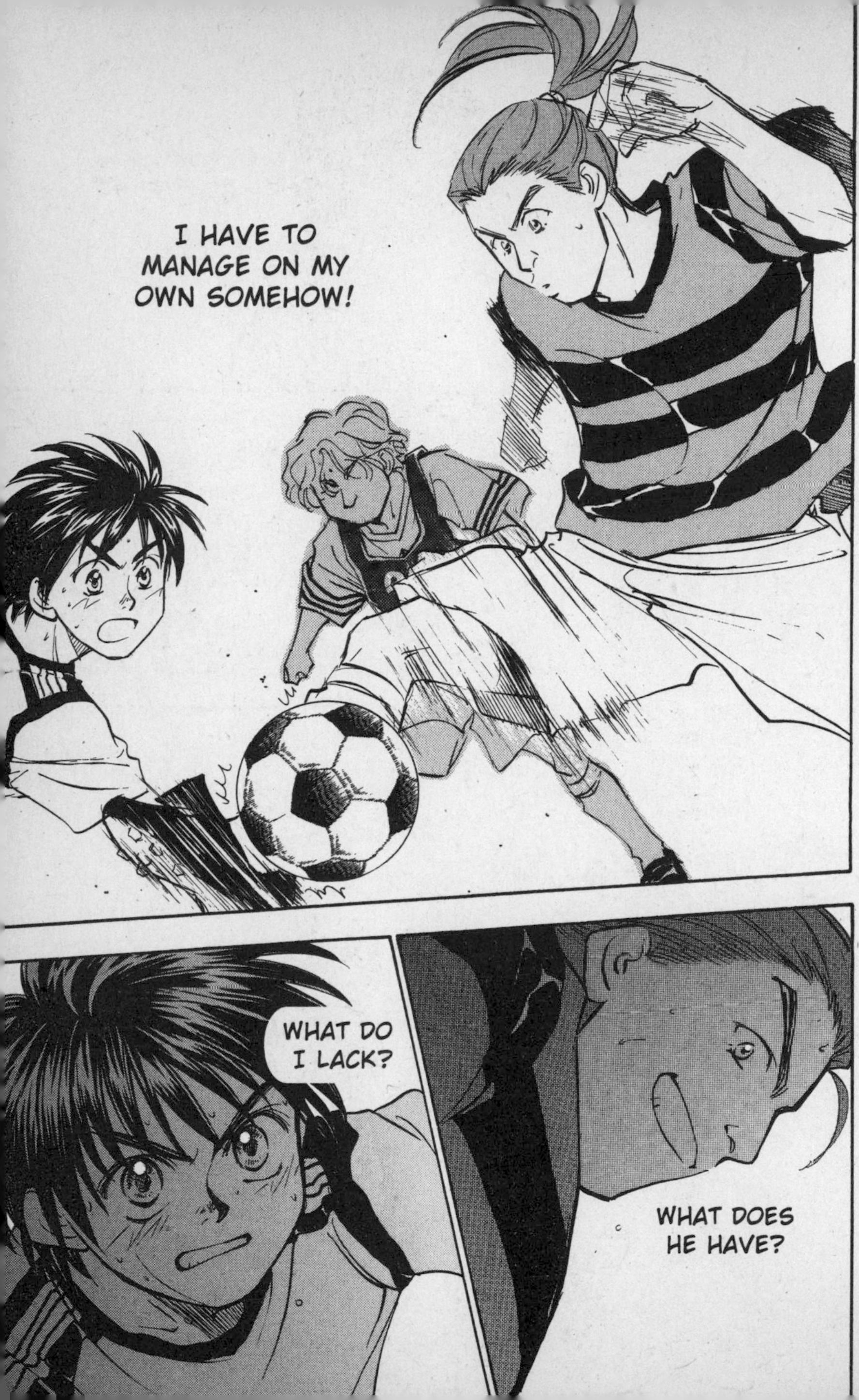
I HAVE TO MANAGE ON MY OWN SOMEHOW!
WHAT DOES HE HAVE?
WHAT DO I LACK?

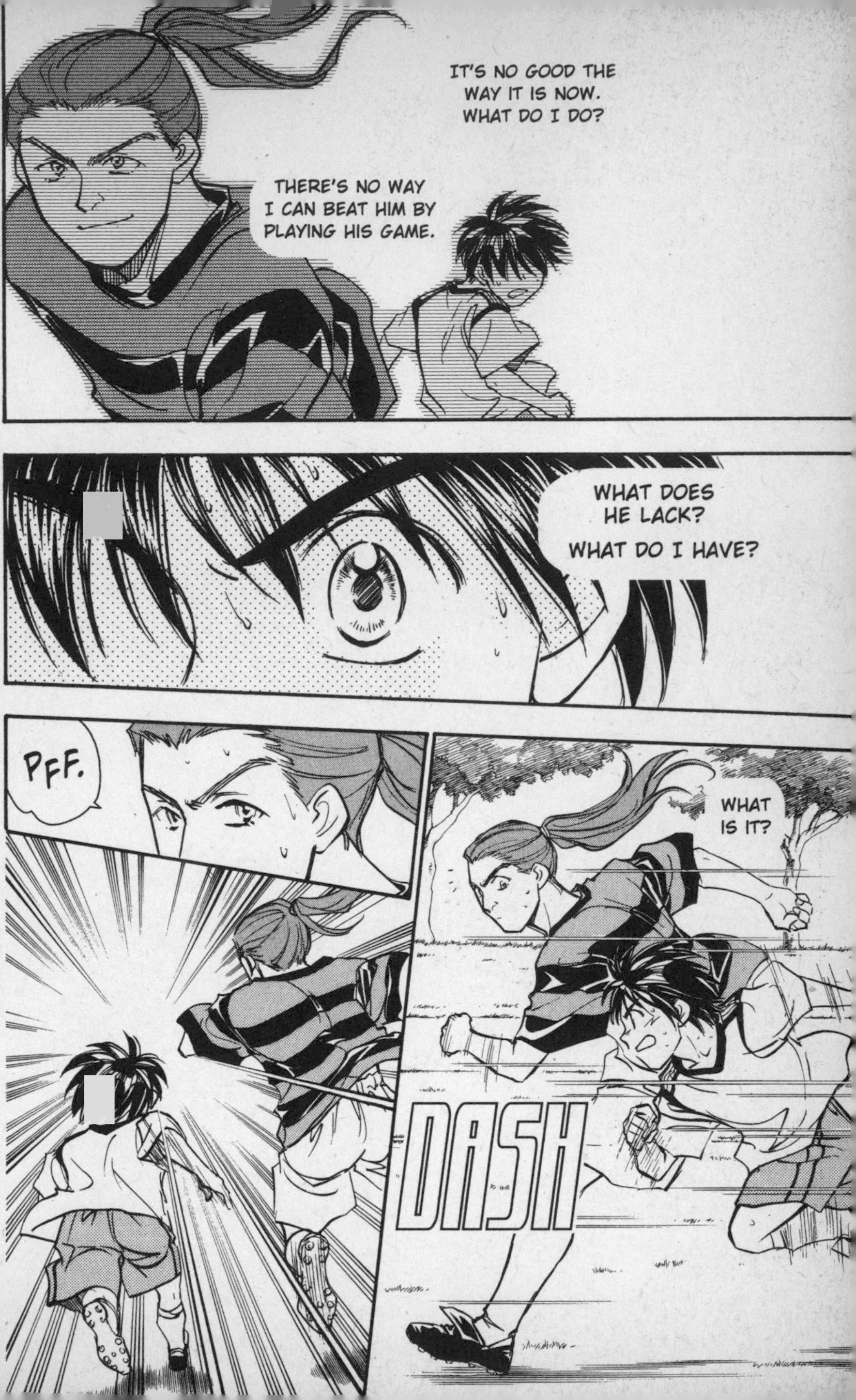
IT'S NO GOOD THE WAY IT IS NOW. WHAT DO I DO?
THERE'S NO WAY I CAN BEAT HIM BY PLAYING HIS GAME.
WHAT DOES HE LACK?
WHAT DO I HAVE?
WHAT IS IT?
DASH
PFF.

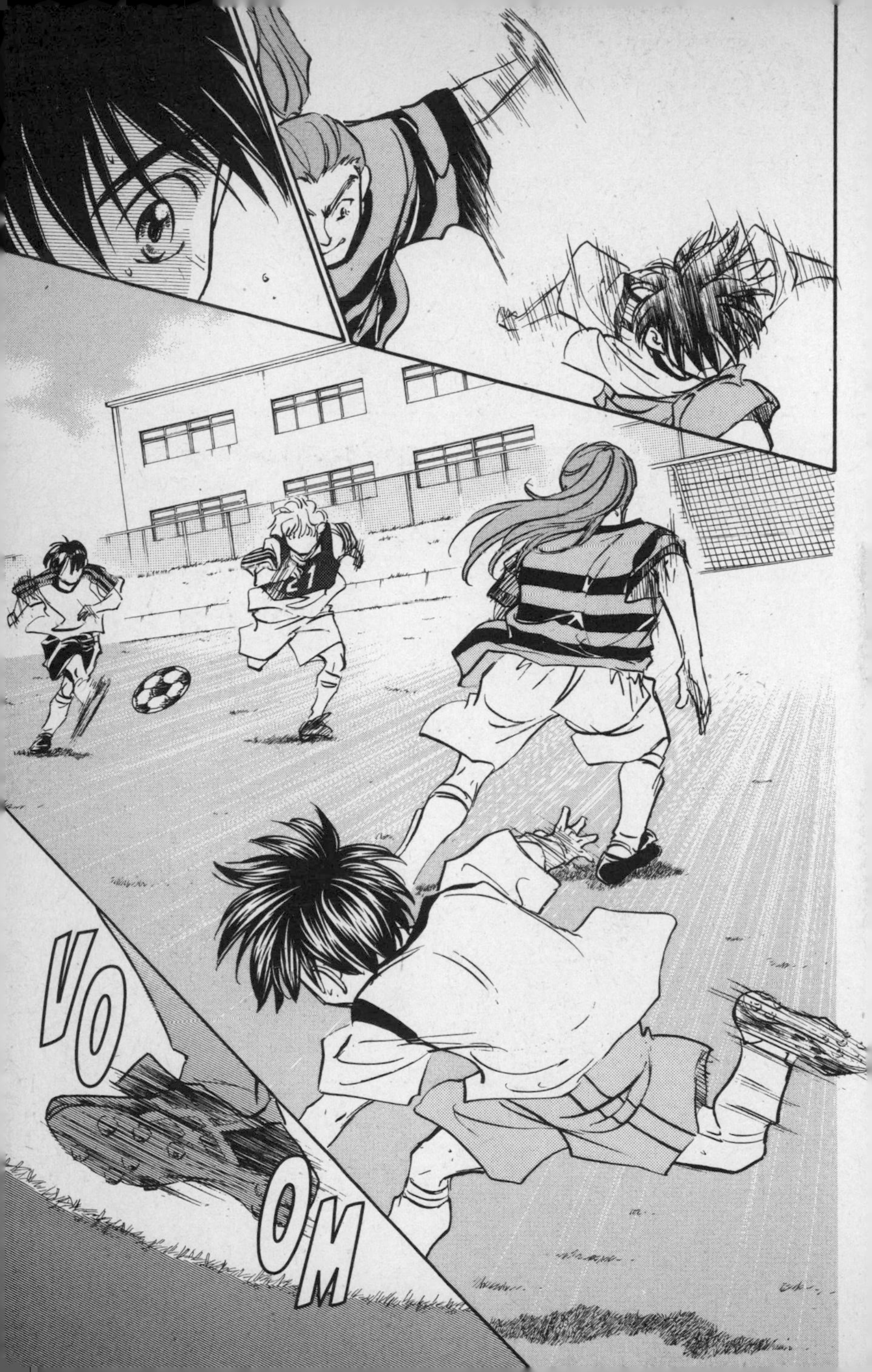
VOOM

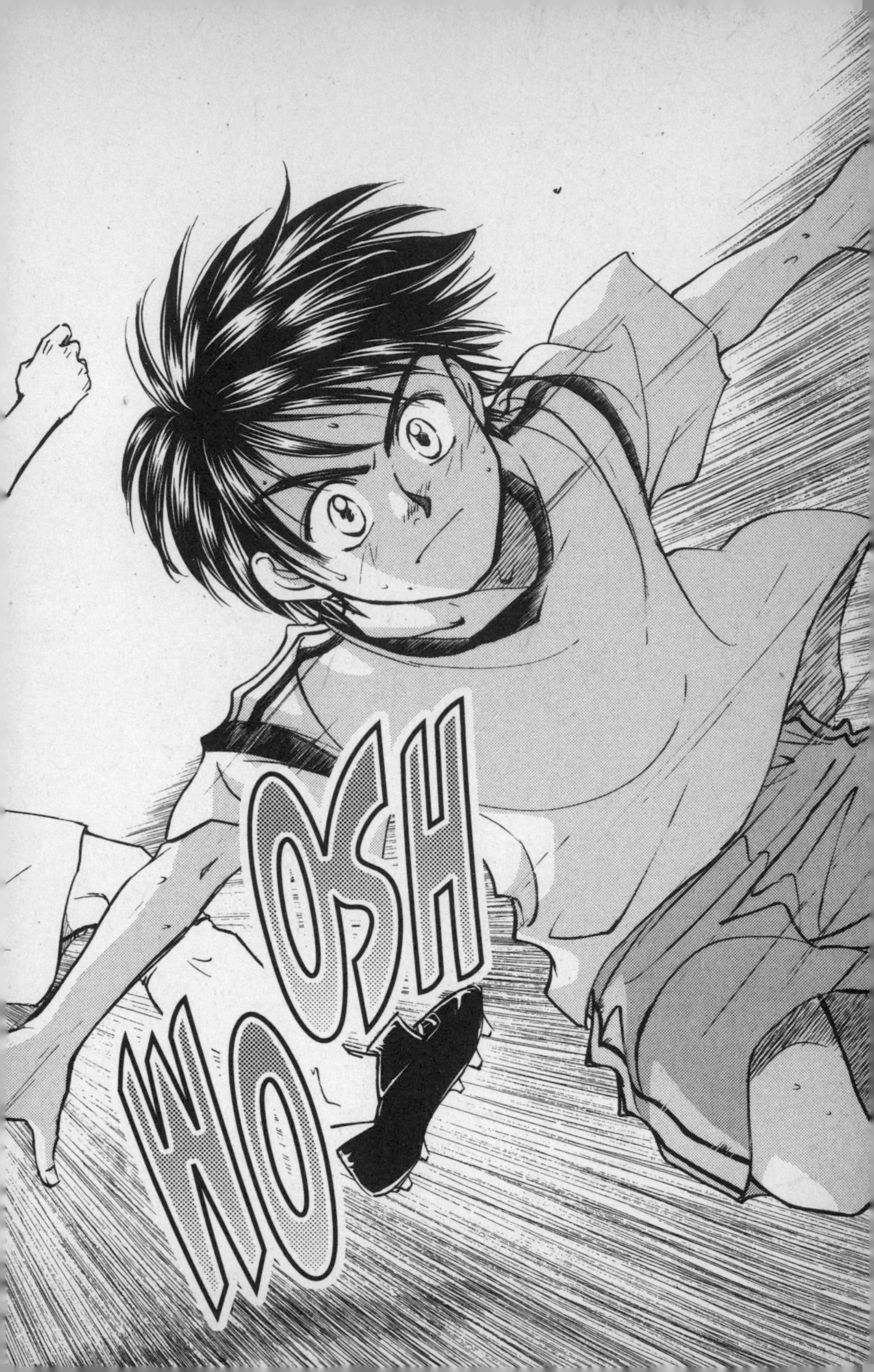
WHOOSH

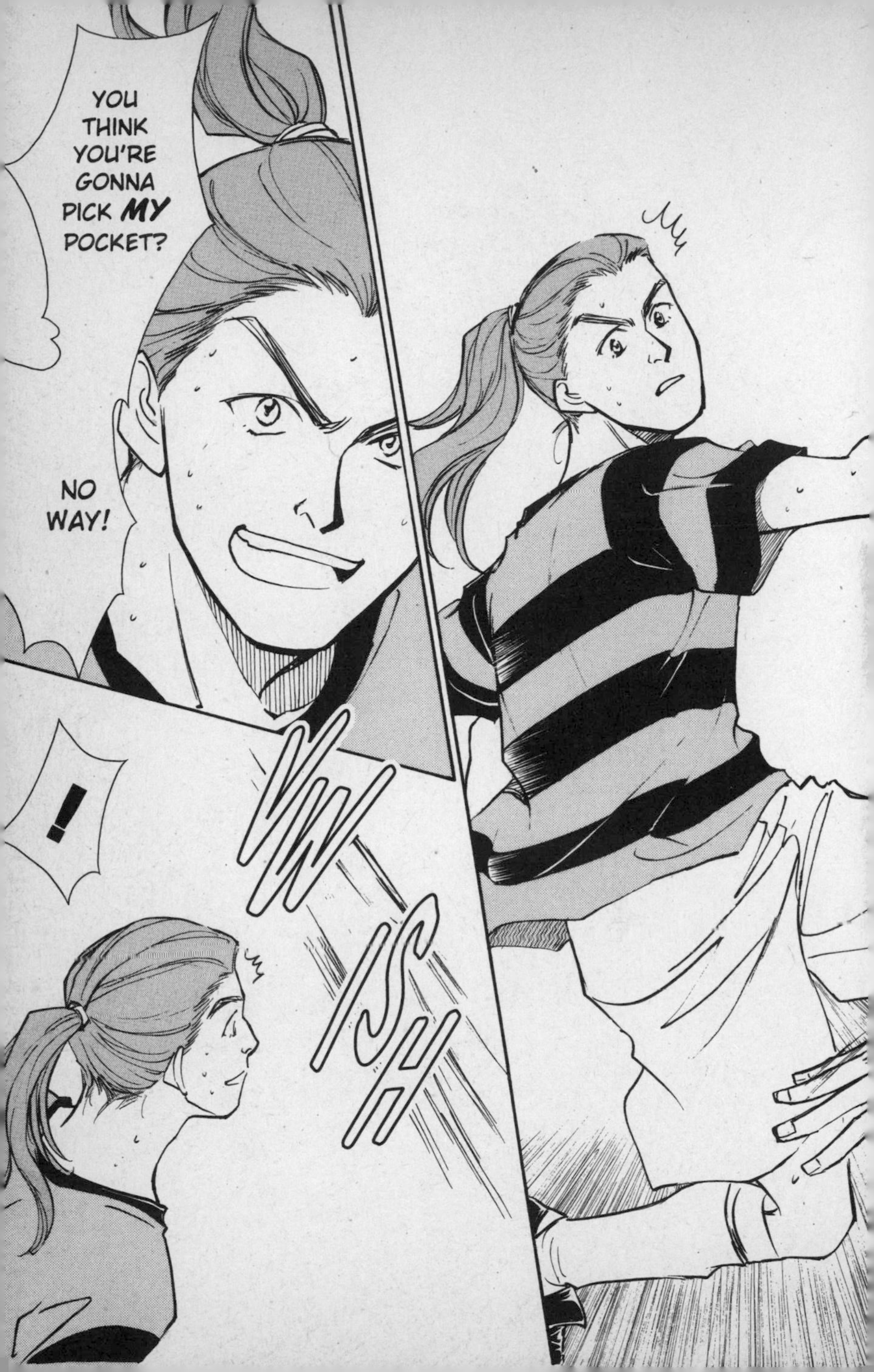
YOU THINK YOU'RE GONNA PICK MY POCKET?
NO WAY!
!
VWISH

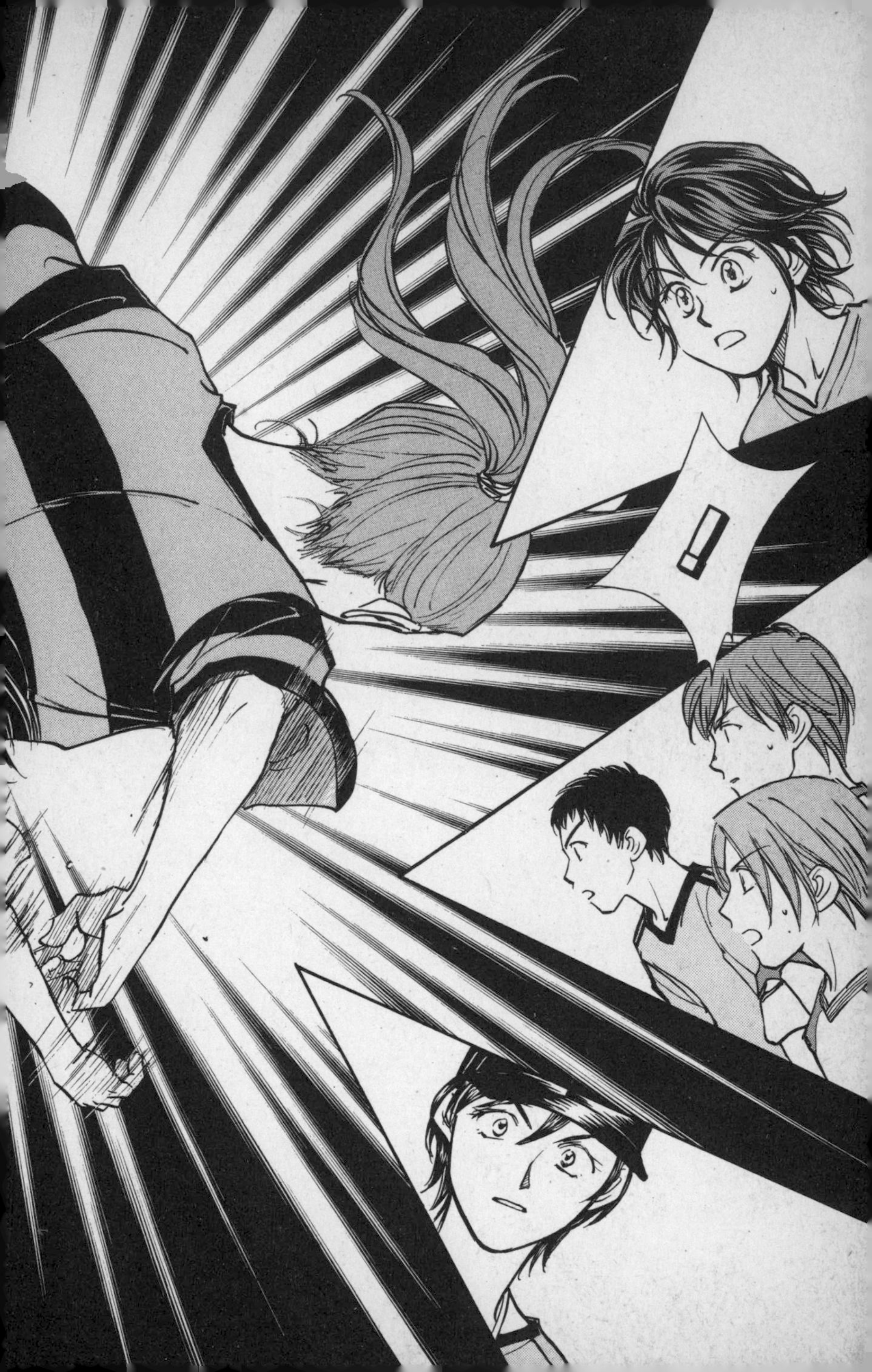
!

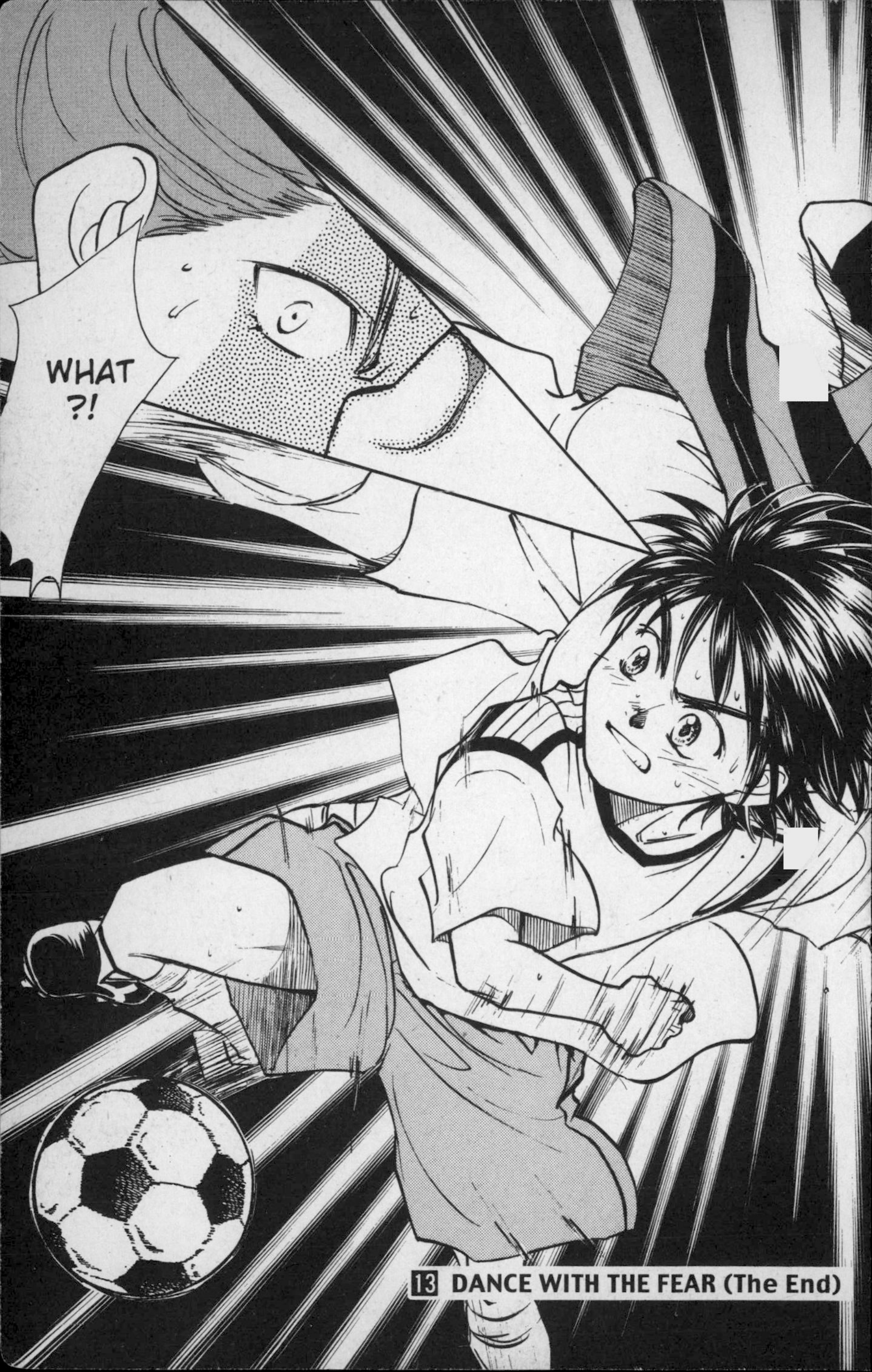
WHAT ?!
13 DANCE WITH THE FEAR (The End)

DAISUKE NOTE

	PERSONAL DATA		
BIRTHDAY:	JUNE 5, 1984	AUG. 20, 1984	JAN. 25, 1985
SIZE:	5'5" 123 lbs	5'6" 119 lbs	5'6" 117 lbs
BLOOD TYPE:	O	A	AB
FAVORITE FOOD:	CHICHIYASU YOGURT	EGG SANDWICH APPLE JUICE	KIMCHEE VEGETABLE SALAD
WHAT HE DISLIKES:	TOMATO	TYING A BUTTERFLY KNOT	FROG'S EGGS
HOBBY AND SPECIAL SKILLS:	CYCLING VIDEO GAMES (RPG) HAIR WEAVING	PUTTING THINGS AWAY NEATLY (APPLIES ONLY TO HIS BEDROOM) CALLIGRAPHY (NOT GOOD AT USING PEN)	FISHING GAME OF GO WEATHER FORECASTING (USING HIS INTUITION)
	YŪTO WAKANA	KAZUMA SANADA	EISHI KAKU

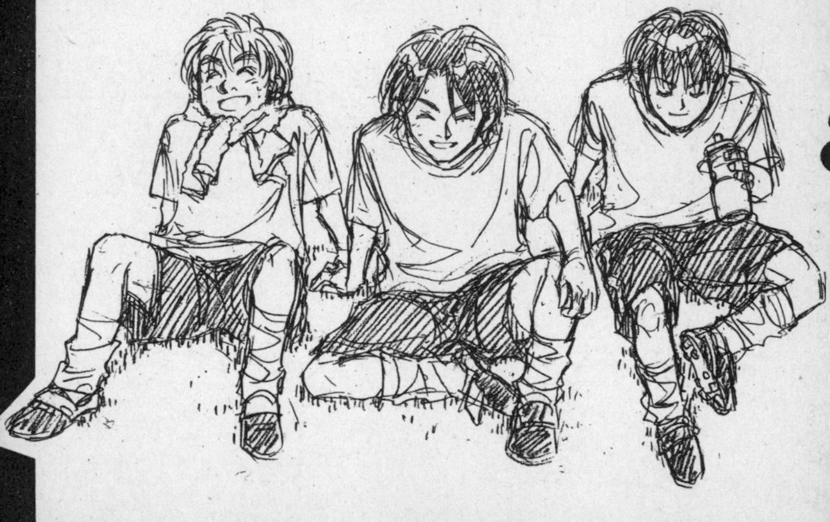

PERSONAL DATA	
BIRTHDAY:	MAY 9, 1984
SIZE:	5'4" 117 lbs
BLOOD TYPE:	B
FAVORITE FOOD:	YAKINIKU
WHAT HE DISLIKES:	GREEN ONION
HOBBY AND SPECIAL SKILLS:	MARTIAL ARTS IMPERSONATIONS

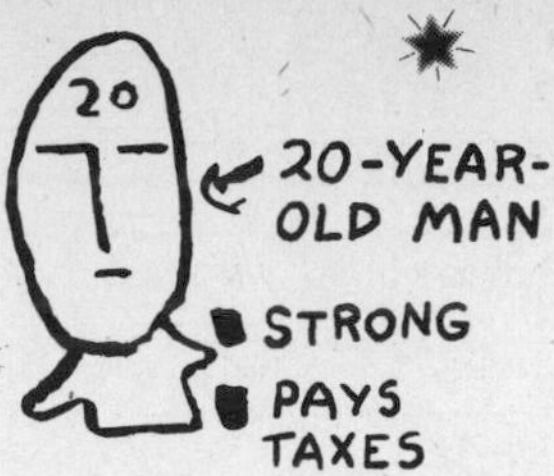
20
20-YEAR-OLD MAN
STRONG
PAYS TAXES

TAKI SUGIHARA

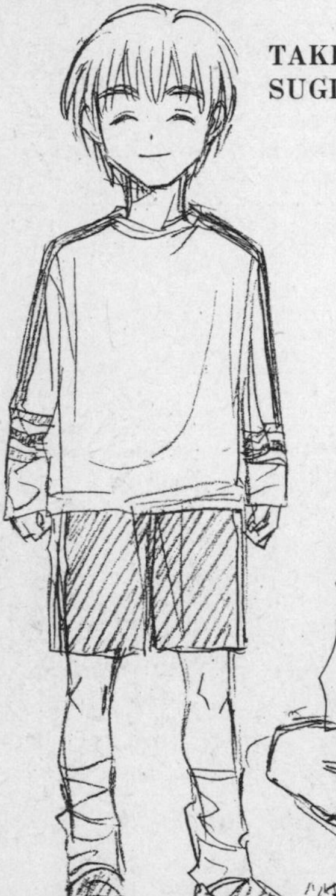

PERSONAL DATA	
BIRTHDAY:	OCT 1, 1984
SIZE:	5'24" 108 lbs
BLOOD TYPE:	O
FAVORITE FOOD:	MELON BREAD
WHAT HE DISLIKES:	BEEF
HOBBY AND SPECIAL SKILLS:	COLLECTING TRADING CARDS SPEAKING FAST

TEPPEI KOIWA

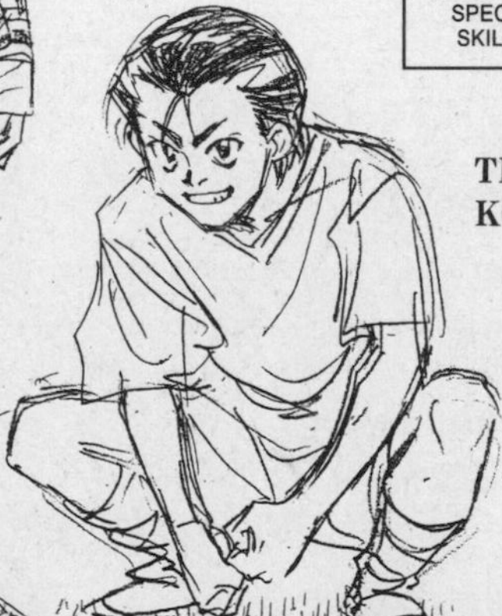

Next in Whistle!

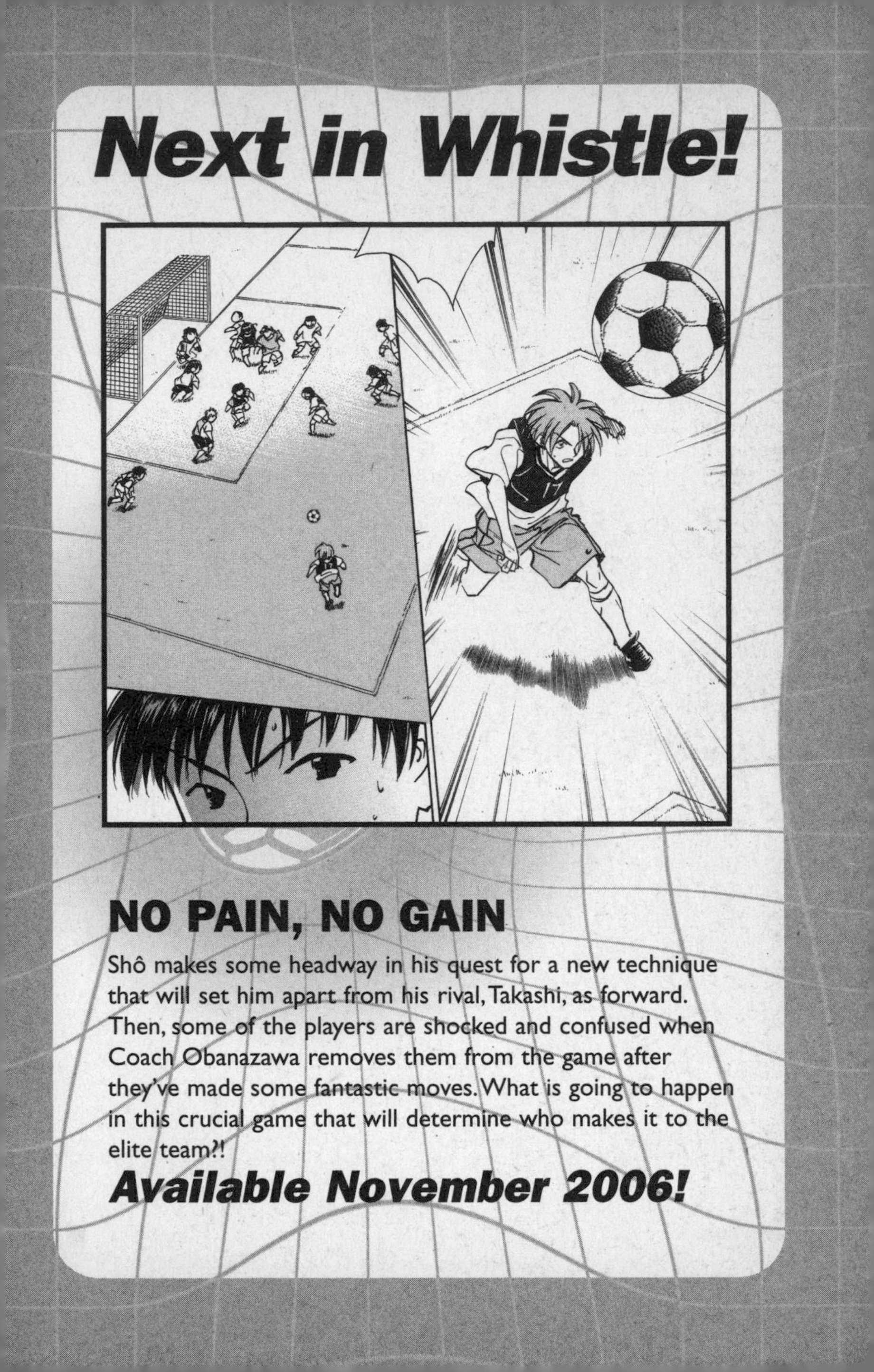

NO PAIN, NO GAIN

Shô makes some headway in his quest for a new technique that will set him apart from his rival, Takashi, as forward. Then, some of the players are shocked and confused when Coach Obanazawa removes them from the game after they've made some fantastic moves. What is going to happen in this crucial game that will determine who makes it to the elite team?!

Available November 2006!

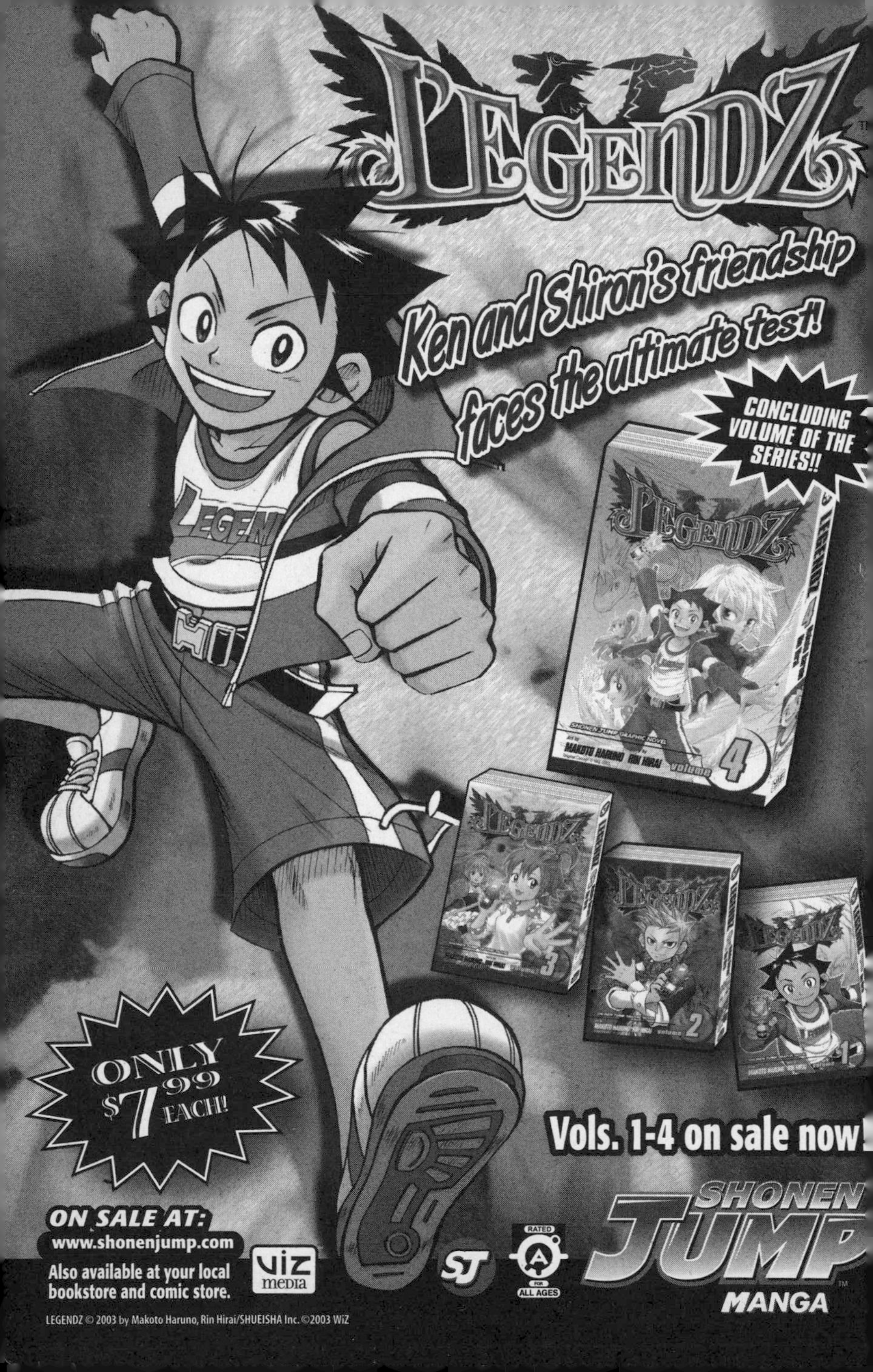
LEGENDZ
Ken and Shiron's friendship faces the ultimate test!
CONCLUDING VOLUME OF THE SERIES!!
ONLY $7.99 EACH!
Vols. 1-4 on sale now!
SHONEN JUMP MANGA
ON SALE AT:
www.shonenjump.com
Also available at your local bookstore and comic store.
LEGENDZ © 2003 by Makoto Haruno, Rin Hirai/SHUEISHA Inc. ©2003 WiZ

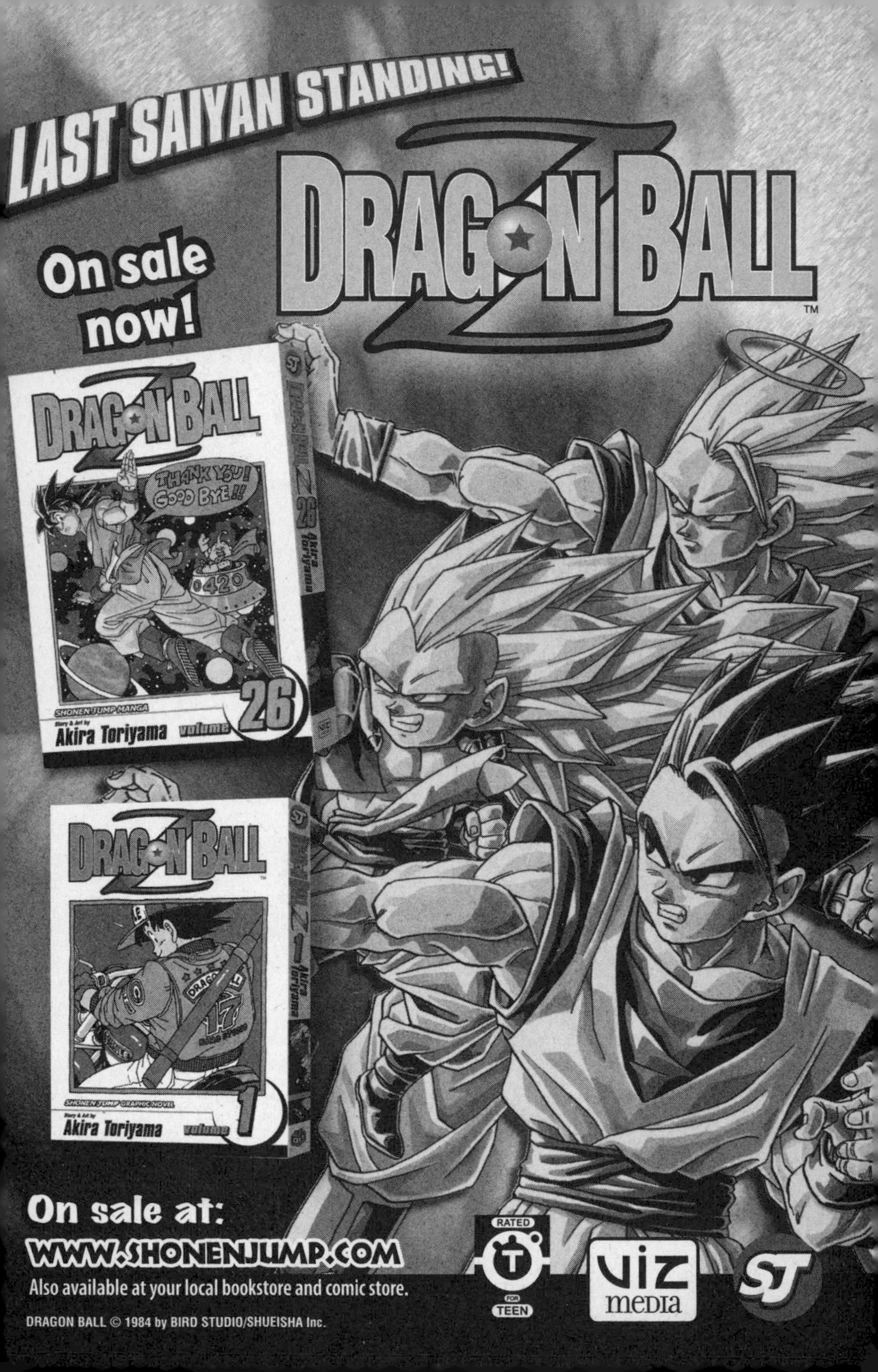
LAST SAIYAN STANDING!
DRAGON BALL Z™
On sale now!
DRAGON BALL Z
THANK YOU! GOOD BYE!!
0420
SHONEN JUMP MANGA
Story & Art by
Akira Toriyama
volume 26
DRAGON BALL Z
SHONEN JUMP GRAPHIC NOVEL
Story & Art by
Akira Toriyama
volume 1
On sale at:
WWW.SHONENJUMP.COM
Also available at your local bookstore and comic store.
DRAGON BALL © 1984 by BIRD STUDIO/SHUEISHA Inc.
RATED T FOR TEEN
viz media
SJ

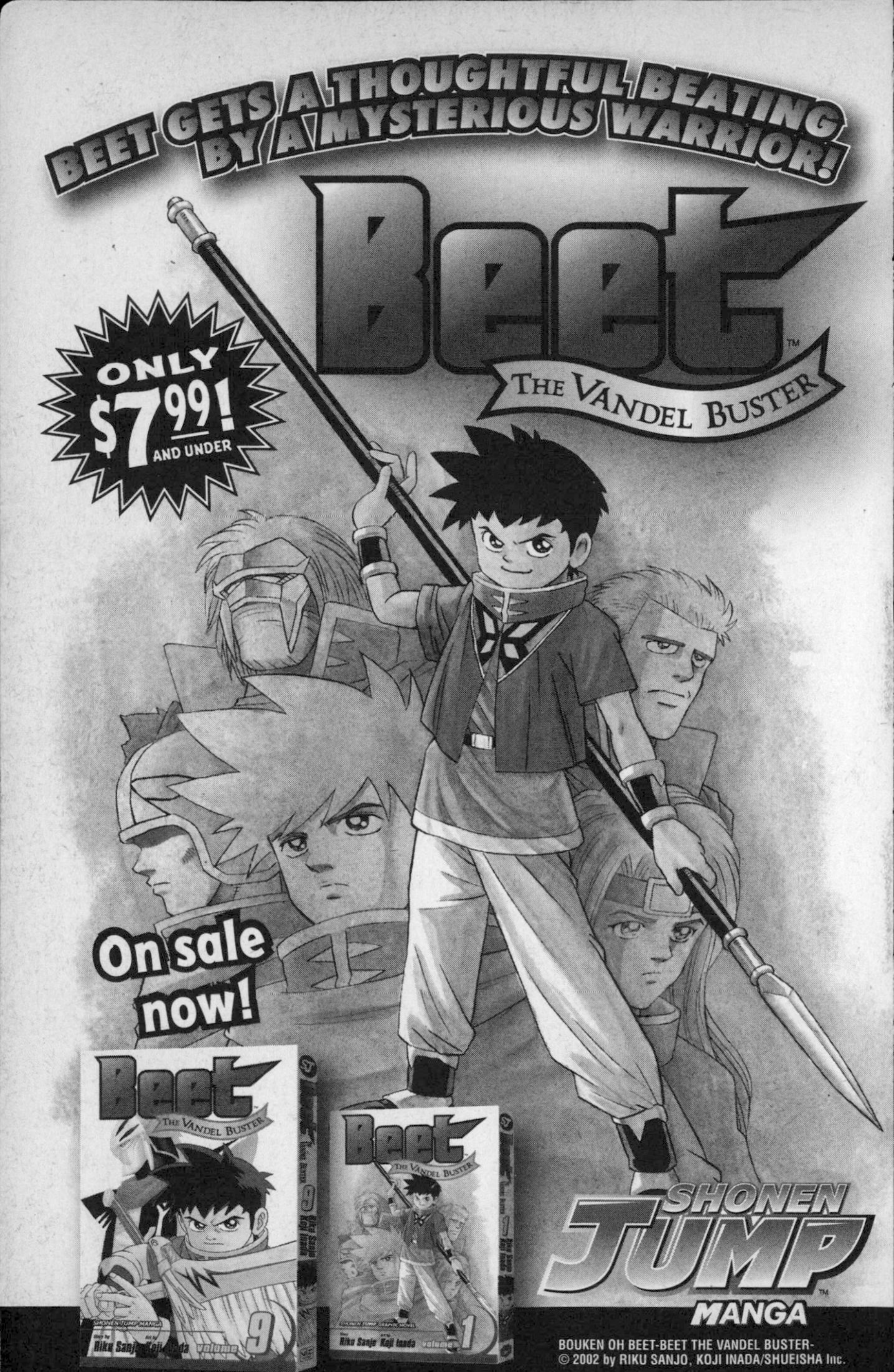
BEET GETS A THOUGHTFUL BEATING BY A MYSTERIOUS WARRIOR!
Beet
THE VANDEL BUSTER
ONLY $7.99! AND UNDER
On sale now!
SHONEN JUMP MANGA
BOUKEN OH BEET-BEET THE VANDEL BUSTER-
© 2002 by RIKU SANJO, KOJI INADA/SHUEISHA Inc.

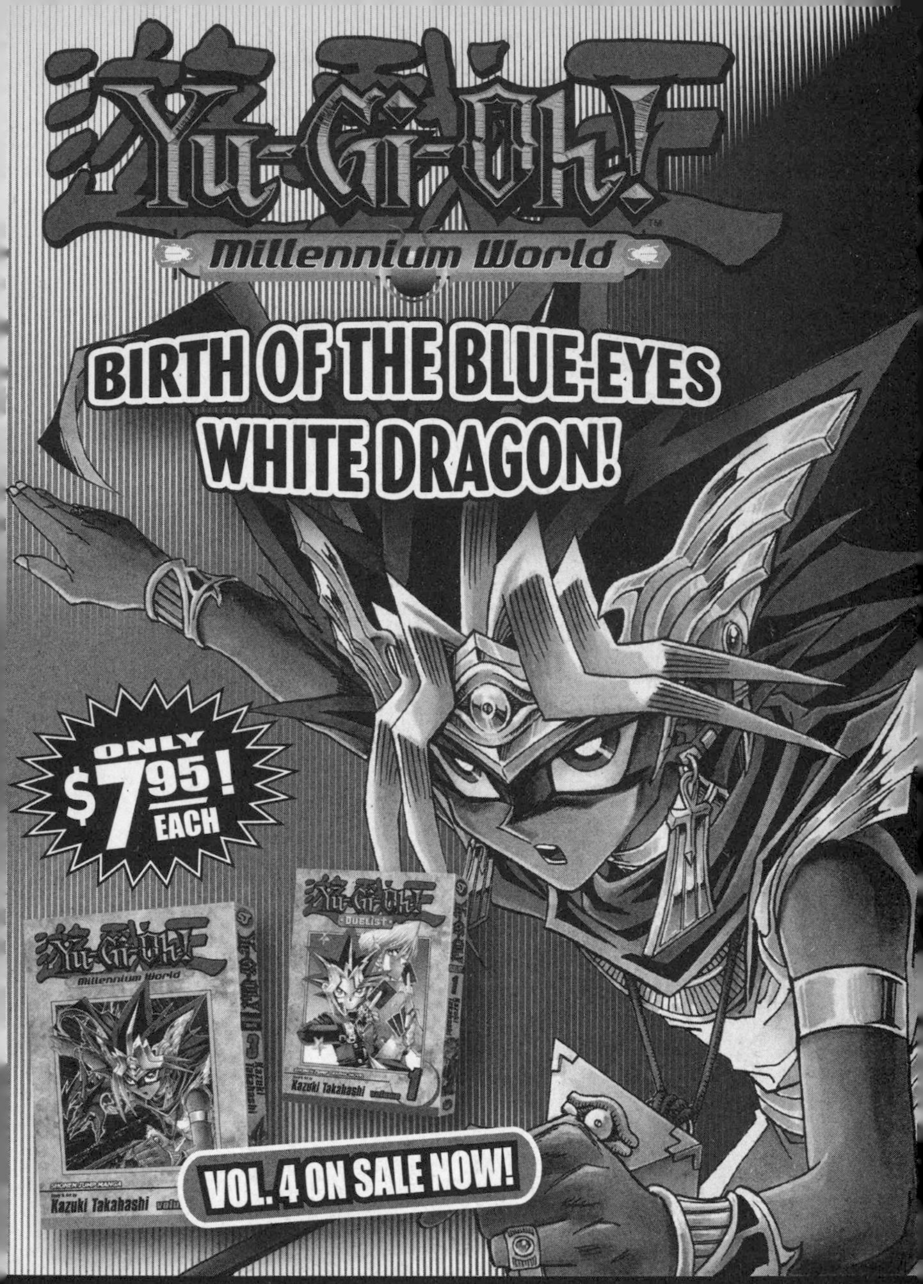
Yu-Gi-Oh!™
Millennium World
BIRTH OF THE BLUE-EYES WHITE DRAGON!
ONLY $7.95! EACH
Yu-Gi-Oh! Millennium World
Kazuki Takahashi
SHONEN JUMP MANGA
Yu-Gi-Oh! DUELIST
Kazuki Takahashi
VOL. 4 ON SALE NOW!

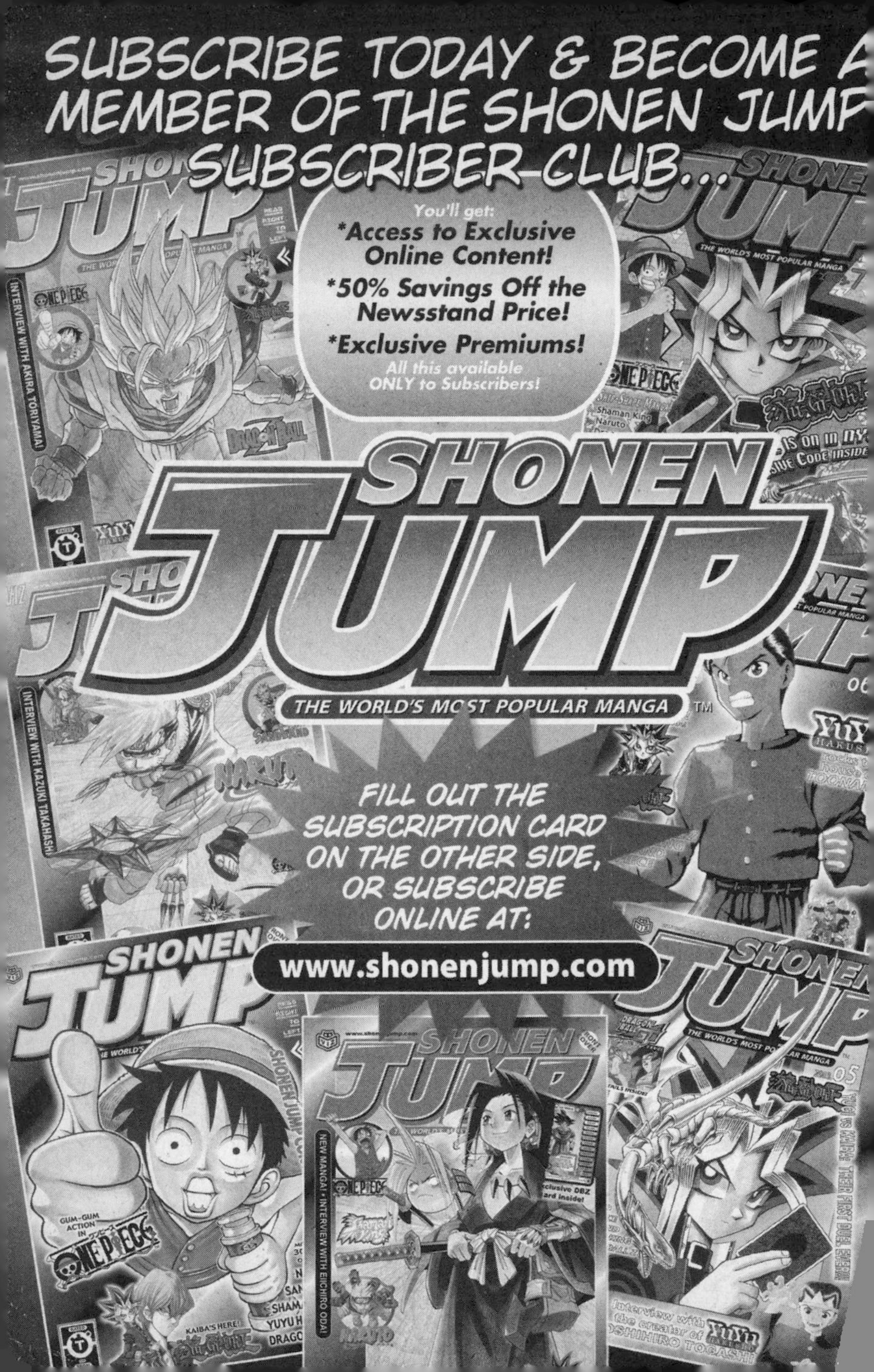
SUBSCRIBE TODAY & BECOME A MEMBER OF THE SHONEN JUMP SUBSCRIBER CLUB...
You'll get:
*Access to Exclusive Online Content!
*50% Savings Off the Newsstand Price!
*Exclusive Premiums!
All this available ONLY to Subscribers!
SHONEN JUMP
THE WORLD'S MOST POPULAR MANGA
FILL OUT THE SUBSCRIPTION CARD ON THE OTHER SIDE, OR SUBSCRIBE ONLINE AT:
www.shonenjump.com